The Phenomenology of Prayer

John D. Caputo, *series editor*

PERSPECTIVES IN
CONTINENTAL
PHILOSOPHY

Edited by BRUCE ELLIS BENSON
AND NORMAN WIRZBA

The Phenomenology of Prayer

FORDHAM UNIVERSITY PRESS
New York ■ 2005

Perspectives in Continental Philosophy Series, No. 46
ISSN 1089-3938

Library of Congress Cataloging-in-Publication Data

The phenomenology of prayer / edited by Bruce Ellis Benson and Norman Wirzba.
    p.   cm. — (Perspectives in continental philosophy,
ISSN 1089-3938 ; no. 46)
    Includes bibliographical references and index.
    ISBN 0-8232-2495-3 (hardcover) — ISBN 0-8232-2496-1 (pbk.)
    1. Prayer. 2. Phenomenology. I. Benson, Bruce Ellis, 1960– II. Wirzba, Norman. III. Series.
BL560.P48   2005
204'.3—dc22   2005017145

Printed in the United States of America
07 06 05   5 4 3 2 1
First edition

Contents

The Phenomenology of Prayer

Introduction

How could there be a vibrant religious life without the practice of prayer? In both theistic and nontheistic traditions, religious followers are generally counseled to steadfast prayer—to pray "without ceasing." Without prayer, religious sensibility would likely atrophy and perhaps die. Yet what makes prayer so essential to a life of faith?

Perhaps the most important answer is that prayer connects us to the divine, to something beyond ourselves and beyond immediate reality. Hence we find the following prayer in Brihad-Aranyaka Upanishad: "From the unreal lead me to the real! From Darkness lead me to light! From death lead me to immortality!" Similarly, the Bodhisattva prays: "Living beings are without number: I vow to row them to the other shore. Defilements are without number: I vow to remove them from myself. The teachings are immeasurable: I vow to study and practice them. The way is very long: I vow to arrive at the end."[1] Prayer is the moral and spiritual discipline that introduces and directs us to the sacred dimension that infuses and undergirds all that is. To know God and appreciate God's greatness leads to praise and adoration of God. "Bless the Lord, O my soul," the Psalmist writes, "and all that is within me, bless his holy Name" (Ps. 103:1).

Prayer, though, is not simply about a connection to the divine but also about *us*. That aspect is particularly evident in petitionary prayer, in which we make requests to God, and prayers for forgiveness, as when the Psalmist cries: "Have mercy upon me, O God, according to your steadfast love; blot out my transgressions" (Ps. 51:1). Less apparent are the many ways in which we are *changed* by prayer. In praying, we learn who we are and how we relate to God. Muhammad prays: "O God, give me light in my heart and light in my tongue and light in my hearing and light in my sight and light in my feeling and light in all my body and light before me and light behind me." Prayer also has the effect of changing our passions, so that we learn to live and love differently. From a religious point of view, it cannot be taken for granted that we always live appropriately or that we have attuned our aspirations and habits to divine ways. St. Paul prays: "May the God of peace himself sanctify you entirely; and may your spirit and soul and body be kept sound and blameless at the coming of our Lord Jesus Christ" (I Thess. 5:23). Prayer inspires and structures human life so that it becomes faithful and true.

What is it about prayer that gives it such a formative role in religious life, a role that informs, transforms, and conforms believers? One answer is that prayer is an "experience at the limit." Prayer effectively strips the soul of its pretense and makes it available before an inscrutable God. At its extreme, prayer leads to a breakdown of language as the believer enters a "dark night" or "blinding light" like those described by the great mystics. Prayer is reduced to mute, amorous praise, for the believer is now bathed in a transcendence that both exceeds and also sustains one's being. Prayer can also be described as the "intensification of experience," such that we have revealed to us the depth and breadth of what we otherwise overlook or take for granted—life's gratuity, fragility, terror, blessing, and interdependence. Such a revelation calls us to a more honest and authentic accounting of our lives.

To understand—however imperfectly—that divine grace permeates our being should give rise to dispositions of gratitude and sharing, our sharing being the fitting response to gifts lavishly given and appropriately received. Rather than simply being an instrument or tool in the service of mundane experience (as when we ask for more things or for comfort in self-chosen paths), prayer aims to elevate and deepen our experience so that it can be properly seen and evaluated in terms of its divine and eternal goals. All of our capacities— reason, speech, volition, affection, and action—must be molded by the activity of prayer. Moreover, as prayer becomes central in our lives, all that we do becomes part of prayer. As the Benedictine motto has it, *laborare est orare*—to work is to pray.

Given the complexities of prayer, one might ask: Can it become the subject of a phenomenology? If prayer is a "limit experience," then is it not beyond the limits of any schema of "intending consciousness" and "intended object," beyond the limits of language and thought, and (therefore) beyond the limits of phenomenology? Moreover, if prayer is a quintessentially religious act, could it even be a *proper* concern of phenomenology or philosophy in general? Perhaps prayer cannot be understood by way of conceptual analysis, either because analysis lacks the requisite tools or because it requires the kind of "scientific detachment" that would miss what prayer is all about.

It is not hard to imagine such a response to a phenomenology of prayer. On the one hand, prayer is often personal and private. As such, it would seem to be an act of an *inner I* that cannot be fully disclosed. Moreover, *should* anyone have access to something that takes place between God and me? Perhaps prayer is simply too intimate for disclosure. Perhaps it is even too intimate for a phenomenological investigation undertaken simply by and for me. Of course, such an understanding of prayer operates with the assumption that praying is primarily—or even exclusively—a private act. In contrast, most religious traditions take prayer to be at least as much a corporate activity and go so far as to build "houses of prayer."

A further problem is that if prayer at least sometimes takes the form of "groanings too deep for words" (Rom. 8:26), then it would seem that certain prayers are unclear even to the one praying. Precisely such a prayer would seem to be—as Aristotle claims (in *On Interpretation* 17 A 4–5) regarding prayer in general—beyond the realm of predication. One can even ask whether such a prayer is "mine." For St. Paul claims it is at the moment of our weakness that the Holy Spirit steps in to assist us with these "groanings," to pray on our behalf. And this aspect of not being simply "on our own" in the midst of praying is hardly unique to Christian accounts of prayer. It is likewise found, for instance, in Eastern prayer practices.

On the other hand, to whom do I pray? *Should* that question be answered, particularly by way of a phenomenology that seeks to lay bare the object of one's intention? For if God is truly beyond me, then it might appear that phenomenology is even inappropriate, even an act of analytical injustice. After all, the goal (albeit an infinite task) of phenomenology as articulated by Edmund Husserl is to achieve a one-to-one correspondence between my consciousness and the object under investigation. But is it appropriate even to try for such an "adequation" between knower and object known if that "object" is *God?* Such a phenomenology might be acceptable from a scientific point of view, but it seems almost sacrilegious from a religious believer's point of view. Yet even if we sanction such an investigation religiously or ethically, how far can it go in practice? If God is truly God, then the project of determining the one to whom we pray seems doomed from the start. At best one should have very modest expectations, realizing that prayer is never simply an individual's solitary effort but requires the help of others, even help from God.

Such aspects of prayer and concerns about phenomenological methodology are hardly lost on the writers represented in this collection. Indeed, each contribution can be read as a response to these questions and concerns. At least three important and complementary themes emerge in these essays.

The first theme is that we do not really know how to pray and so are constantly in the state of learning. While that aspect can be found in each of these essays, it is a central theme for some.

While fully admitting his own lack of understanding of prayer, Merold Westphal suggests that the proper *posture* of prayer must be a "kenotic" one in which we empty ourselves before God. To pray is to experience a profound "decentering" in which the self loses its preoccupation with itself and focuses instead on God. The result is that one is constantly learning to pray. Westphal considers the asymmetry found in Samuel's *me voici* (I Sam. 3) and Mary's "let it be unto me" in the Magnificat, contrasting these sharply with the "prayer" of Elvis—"I want you, I need you, I love you with all my heart." To pray is to give up the centrality of the self and instead allow oneself to be "gifted."

After charting the trace of the religious in the midst of Levinas's philosophical work by considering the speaking relation between self and other, Jill Robbins helps us see that the "I" who prays is always already "put into question by the other that inhabits it." Subjectivity is the site of transcendence, the "place" through which the divine presence in the world is intensified. Prayer is the activity through which the I, now understood in terms of its availability for the other, can become responsible for the universe. Robbins continues her discussion of prayer through a careful analysis of Levinas's Talmudic and confessional writings to show why Judaism, even in a time of secularism, understands religious life as a three-term, ethical relationship between self, other, and God. Hence prayer is intimately tied to the work of social justice.

Edward Mooney suggests that prayer is properly understood as arising out of our passionate life. Western philosophical traditions, of course, have tended to devalue the passions, viewing them with suspicion and fear. Mooney therefore sets out to give a description of the range of passions that circulate through human life and then shows how prayer connects us deeply with the world of others. As we attend to the complexity of the human passions and the drama of prayer at work within them, we may come to see the practice of prayer as moving us toward a more compassionate, merciful, faithful, and responsible life.

Arguing that prayer, particularly when understood as a form of petition, all too often implicates us in an economy of what René Girard calls "mimetic violence," James Mensch suggests that we think of prayer as the attempt to "make room" for the sacred. In order for such room to be cleared, the one praying must practice self-emptying, so that the sacred can incarnate itself in our bodily being and behavior. For this work of kenosis, Jesus Christ serves as a paradigm, since we see in him the full adoption of humanity's responsibility for the other person. By assuming responsibility, mimetic violence is undone.

While Friedrich Nietzsche hardly seems an advocate of prayer in the traditional sense, Bruce Ellis Benson shows how Nietzsche's early prayers as a youth prove structurally paradigmatic for his later thought. Interpreting Nietzsche's development as learning a new way to "pray," Benson argues that Nietzsche begins as and remains a deeply religious person throughout his life. The logic and even much of the content of Nietzsche's early pietism can be found in what Nietzsche comes to call his Dionysian "faith," a faith in which the trust he once had in God is now placed in "Life." The result is that Nietzsche's new sort of prayer bears striking resemblances to the sort he attempts to leave behind.

Finally, Norman Wirzba considers how transformations in daily, practical life inaugurated by modernity make prayer more difficult. If prayer is the life of attention and responsibility (Simone Weil), then we need to reform our understanding of subjectivity and the practical patterns through which we engage the world around us. Prayer inspires and animates a moral response to others, a response that is worked out through our hands, feet, and mouth as we promote the experience of kinship with the creation and the Creator. Prayer, in other words, is the daily work through which fidelity, care, humility, and responsibility are learned and the integrity, mystery, and sanctity of others are experienced.

A second theme is that our prayers always go "beyond." We always pray more than we can intend and, in so doing, become more than we are.

Cleo McNelly Kearns develops this theme by considering Luce Irigaray's encounter with Eastern yogic practice. In this tradition, we find a strong interweaving between breath, silence, and speech. Kearns notes how prayer in Western traditions is often linked with a verbal performance and hence is connected to the problems of logocentrism. Paying attention to breathing and noting its connection to the (maternal) divine breath that animates all that is makes possible a more profound and intimate experience of the divine. By considering how women and men experience breathing differently, Kearns opens the possibility for a fresh analysis of gender differences and their significance for religious understanding.

Through an analysis of Dilthey's and Heidegger's early work, Benjamin Crowe shows how a hermeneutical approach to prayer might proceed. Heidegger is particularly useful, since his early phenomenological analyses clearly had religious life, especially the life of early Christian communities, in mind. Crowe demonstrates that prayer is best understood when it is not disembedded from its home in factical religious life. Prayer gives expression and definition to habits formed in serving, expecting, and waiting for God. Its meaning cannot be determined in the abstract. If prayer is not to be reduced to a magical formula, it must always be understood in terms of a total life animated by the coming Kingdom of God.

Terrence Wright considers the role of prayer in the thought of Edith Stein, who focuses more on personal than corporate prayer. Using Teresa of Avila's imagery of the interior castle, Stein sees prayer as both helping us come to a knowledge of ourselves and developing ourselves. For Stein, prayer is the response to a call to us from God that enables us both to be who we truly are and to be in touch with God.

St. Paul's cryptic remark regarding the Holy Spirit's intercession on our behalf is the focus of B. Keith Putt's paper. Putt links Derrida's conception of the messianic prayer of the *oui, oui* to the coming of the "Impossible" with the impossibility of praying in Romans 8:26 by pointing out that the context of Romans 8 is itself the messianic. We live in a time in which we hope for what we have not seen and groan for that which we cannot name. Since we must pray but cannot (adequately) pray, the Spirit prays on our behalf in a divine "soliloquy" in which God addresses Godself. Such a prayer turns out to be remarkably like Derrida's messianic prayer.

Brian Treanor takes up the tension between private and public prayer. How are we to understand biblical mandates that clearly portray prayer as a corporate practice when other passages express misgivings about public piety? Treanor interprets the tension through a careful analysis of Levinas and Derrida and argues that love, because of its intersubjective character, overcomes it. Since prayer is understood as an ethical act, both its public and private forms lead to the same result; namely, the call to love the other. Love of God and love of neighbor are inextricably connected. Indeed, we cannot authentically perform the one without the other. Prayer calls us to perpetual self- and other-examination, so that the excesses of public and private piety can be seen and addressed.

Finally, Christina M. Gschwandtner focuses on the relation of personal and corporate prayer in Marion. Gschwandtner argues that the very structure of Marion's phenomenological project leads him to overemphasize personal prayer to the virtual exclusion of corporate prayer. Since Marion is chiefly concerned to "protect" God from idolatry, his emphasis is on purity and excess. Prayer becomes primarily the exchanging of two gazes, leaving little or no room for corporate prayer. Hence Marion's attempt to "save" God's name leads him to a view of prayer in which the social and ethical aspects of prayer are excluded.

The third theme is that prayer leaves us with a tricky balance. On the one hand, to pray is to pray to *someone* or *something*. Prayer cannot simply be without direction at all. On the other hand, to spell out that direction fully proves ultimately impossible and even undesirable. Prayer requires that we constantly negotiate this tension.

Mark Gedney considers the move made by both Jacques Derrida and John D. Caputo of reconfiguring prayer as "*sans*," in which prayer would be to "pray without [*sans*] knowing where to direct its prayers." Gedney asks not only whether such prayer is possible but also whether it reinscribes the exclusivist logic that it seeks to avoid. The problem is that such prayer seems to be presented as "superior" to that of traditions with a determinate messianism. But if such is the case, then Derrida and Caputo do not escape religious violence. Moreover, Gedney argues that prayer cannot be unmediated or "pure." It always has a kind of directionality and so cannot be *simply* a "*oui, oui*" and "amen."

Michael Andrews explores how prayer leads us outside ourselves, making us into something other than we were. Through a reading of Levinas, Derrida, and St. Ignatius of Loyola, he shows how prayer is not simply a self-indulgent exercise but rather is essentially dialogical in nature, moving the self to an infinite horizon of nonthematic givenness. Speaking of prayer in this way, however, takes phenomenology to the limit, since praying bespeaks an impossible intention. Following Meister Eckhart, we pray to God to rid us of God. Prayer calls us into the desert, introduces us to a life of wandering and wondering, as we encounter an infinite alterity that exceeds every phenomenological horizon.

That theme of going "beyond" is likewise found in Lissa McCullough's account of prayer as a hope that enables even the redemption of this world. Through an analysis of Kierkegaard and Simone Weil, she challenges accounts of prayer and the religious life that would reduce them to the temporal "waiting it out" until the end of time. Prayer delivers us into (rather than out of) our flesh so that we can bring the infinite to bear within time. It is thus an incarnational activity that enables us to embrace and love the world as divine creation. The world is given to us as a gift. Our task, maintained in the life of prayer, is not to despise it but to redeem and love it.

Mark Cauchi argues that prayer is "precarious," for it requires that we—in some sense—are both like and unlike God. Instead of focusing on how the other calls us into question, Cauchi considers how the one praying calls the *other* into question. He begins by explicating the prayers of Abraham and Moses in which they in effect go beyond themselves by making demands upon God. The seeming aporia of prayer is that in order to pray, we must already be beyond our limit, though prayer simultaneously requires the crossing of that limit. Yet Cauchi argues that this aporia is only apparent, for the "finite" subject—like God—is both limited and unlimited. Thus the supplicant is not "properly" finite and instead must already be infinite in order to pray to a God who is infinite.

Finally, Philip Goodchild provides us with an "Anselmian" meditation on Augustine's question: "What do I love, when I love thee, O my God?" His answer is: "I love that than which nothing that matters more will be conceived." But what exactly *is* this that one loves? Goodchild's meditation is a series of answers to this question, in which angelic and demonic voices attempt to persuade or dissuade the questioner of varying answers. The goal of the meditation is to move to a "purified" or apophatic conception of God. Goodchild concludes that prayer is a thinking about that which truly matters, a paradoxical thinking that goes beyond itself, and a thinking that is concerned with others.

No doubt these essays should prove to be of interest to anyone who prays or cares about prayer. For one will find much on the life of prayer and how prayer affects one's life. But even those who are less interested in prayer should find this collection of value. One reason, of course, is that phenomenology has—with such figures as Levinas, Derrida, and Marion—recently taken a "theological turn," as Dominique Janicaud memorably puts it. These essays arise out of that turn and themselves are important contributions to it. Yet there is a further reason why these essays should prove of value, even to those not particularly interested in prayer. In probing the dynamics at work in prayer, these essays have much to teach us about phenomenology itself. For prayer is a phenomenon that complicates the neat boundaries of phenomenology and thus requires that we think more carefully about phenomenology itself. The result is that the phenomenology of prayer ends up being as much about phenomenology as it is about prayer.

PART I

Learning How to Pray

Prayer as the Posture of the Decentered Self

MEROLD WESTPHAL

Our neighbors were visiting a cathedral in Italy with their three-year-old son. He saw a woman kneeling in one of the pews and asked what she was doing. "She's praying," he was told. "She's asking God for things." A few minutes later his parents found him kneeling in one of the pews. In response to their query, he replied that he was asking God for—gelato!

There is something right about that prayer. After all, Jesus teaches us to pray for our daily bread, if not exactly gelato. But it is the prayer of a three-year-old, a beginner in the school of prayer who is not yet ready even for kindergarten. I remember as a teenager seeing a book on my father's shelf entitled *Prayer: Asking and Receiving* and thinking that was not quite right, a bit oversimplified, even crass.

I remember much more recently reading a list of the five elements of prayer: praise, thanksgiving, confession, petition (for self), and intercession (for others). It triggered a shocking recognition: I do not know the first thing about prayer. I feel reasonably at home with the last four items on the list. I am comfortable asking for God's help for myself and for others I care about; I am comfortable asking for forgiveness, especially as I learn from Augustine and Kierkegaard that sins as seemingly isolated acts are but symptoms of sin as my fundamental project; and I am comfortable thanking God for the many gifts of divine mercy that have come my way. I am so much more fortunate than so many.

But praise? I have a friend who, when he says grace at mealtime, begins with praise: "Dear Lord, you are great. Your majesty fills the earth." And so forth. I have to confess to feeling distinctly uncomfortable at such times. It is not that I think there is any insincerity in his prayer or have the least suspicion that he is praying "so that [he] may be seen by others" (Matt. 6:5). It is just that I do not feel that I could pray that way. It would sound phony to me. So why the relative comfort with items two through five and the dis-ease with the first item, praise.

If we look closely, I think we can notice a difference between praise and the other phenomena under our gaze that will suggest an answer. We can distinguish praise from thanksgiving as follows: to give thanks is to praise God for the good things I have received from God, while to praise is to thank God for who God is, for what Luther calls God's "bare goodness," considered without reference to how I may benefit from it.[1] *Gratias agimus tibi propter magnam gloriam tuam.*[2] Such praise was expressed by a penitent of St. John of the Cross, who told him that her prayer consisted in "considering the Beauty of God, and in rejoicing that He has such beauty." To which Evelyn Underhill adds that such "disinterested delight is the perfection of worship"[3]—understanding her to mean precisely that praise is the perfection of worship and, we might add, of prayer. The other modes of prayer are not characterized by disinterested delight. I petition God for things *I* want or think *I* need, and I intercede for those for whom *I* care. I ask God to forgive *my* sins and to grant *me* the benefits of forgiveness; and I thank God for what God has given *me*. If, in the context of corporate prayer, the I is replaced by the We, it is only the size of the self that has changed, not its preoccupation with itself, its interests, and its agenda.

But with praise as disinterested delight in the bare goodness of God, I am preoccupied only with God. Gabriel Marcel helps us here, presenting the same essential structure in a lower register, so that it is about admiring other humans rather than adoring God, and in a kind of photographic negative where light and dark are reversed. A friend once told him that "admiration was for him a humiliating state which he resisted with all his force." Referring to the "suspicion [of] any mark of superiority" expressed in this attitude, Marcel suggests that "there is a burning preoccupation with self at the bottom of this suspicion, a 'but what about me, what becomes of me in that case?'" He concludes, "To affirm: admiration is a humiliating state, is the same as to treat the subject as a power existing for itself and taking itself as a center. To proclaim on the other hand, that [admiration] is an exalted state is to start from the inverse notion that the proper function of the subject is to emerge from itself and realize itself primarily in the gift of oneself and in the various forms of creativity."[4]

Now we can form an hypothesis about why I had to confess that I did not know the first thing about prayer. I was beyond the gelato stage, but not very far beyond. Perhaps there was a burning preoccupation with myself that could coexist with thanksgiving, confession, petition, and even intercession, even as it contaminated and domesticated them. Perhaps I sensed how deep was the chasm to be crossed before words of disinterested delight in God could flow with even a modicum of integrity from my lips or heart. While I would not have said that adoration and praise were humiliating to me, I could only recognize myself in Marcel's description of the self that takes itself as center. Which brings me to my thesis: prayer is a deep, quite possibly the deepest decentering of the self, deep enough to begin dismantling or, if you like, deconstructing that burning preoccupation with myself.

That is why praise is fittingly first in the list of the elements of prayer. But perhaps it is first in the Hegelian sense in which what we find at the end of the journey is that which is presupposed by all the earlier stages and without which the prior stages are "abstract," estranged from their proper home and to that degree distorted. No doubt prayer begins in the immaturity of mere gelato prayers, "Lord, give me. Lord, help me." Perhaps we are taught from the outset to include intercession with petition: "Lord, bless Mommy and Daddy and even sister Sue." Nor is it too difficult to teach even young children to ask God for forgiveness and to thank God for blessings, just as one sends thank you notes to Grandma and Grandpa for Christmas and birthday presents (all too often out of compulsion and calculation). So it remains an open question whether one's youthful heart is as fully into thanks and confession and intercession as into petition.

My focus, however, will not be on praise as I seek to explore the essence of prayer as a deep decentering of the self. Incidentally, we need not be skittish about essences as long as (1) we remember that as good phenomenologists we are merely trying to get to the thing itself, to let it show itself from itself; (2) we retain a measure of Socratic irony or Kierkegaardian humor about the finality of our *Wesensschauen*; and (3) we keep in mind Merleau-Ponty's reminder that the move "from the *fact* of our existence to its *nature*, from the *Dasein* to the *Wesen*" is not made because we want to achieve apodictic certainty or absolute knowledge but because "our existence is too tightly held in the world to be able to know itself as such at the moment of its involvement, and . . . it requires the field of ideality in order to become acquainted with *and to prevail over its facticity*."[5]

My focus will rather be on a kenotic gesture that can be seen as prior even to praise and as the condition for the possibility not only of praise but of all five elements of prayer, insofar as they can be united in a complex whole in which each knows its proper place and plays its proper role. We need not be skittish about this whole as a totality in which the other is reduced to the same. For praise as the context of the other four moments stands guard against the temptation of merely invoking God in them as a means to my ends, and intercession is a constant reminder of my responsibility to and for my neighbor in a circle of friends that knows no closure, since it even includes the enemy. As Carlo Carretto puts it:

> It is impossible to pray to a personal God—that is, love a personal God—and remain indifferent to your suffering brethren.
> It is impossible.
> Anyone who prays without suffering for his suffering brothers is praying to a pole, a shadow, not to the living God.
> Because if you pray to the living God, you who are living, He, the Living One, sends you to your living brothers.[6]

In this totality, the circle is always broken by the intrusion of both the divine and the human other.

To speak, as I have just done, in a nonnaturalistic way about the conditions of the possibility of various mental acts is to speak the language of transcendental phenomenology. But I do so with two important qualifications. First, as has already been hinted at and will become increasingly clear, the praying subject (individual or corporate) does not play the role of First *Sinngeber*, the origin and overseer of meaning and thus of truth. The transcendental is subordinate to transcendence, which means it is more a matter of response than of origination and of freedom than of either necessity or sheer facticity. Second, because I shall turn immediately to texts, this will be a hermeneutical phenomenology with all the contingency and concreteness that entails. The phenomenologist is as embedded in existence as the phenomenon (the praying soul) under investigation. Given the hermeneutical circle I inhabit, some of the texts will be biblical and thus saturated with Jewish and/or Christian context. Two points about that in passing and by way of bare assertion: (1) I believe the essential structures can find a home, mutatis mutandis, in other contexts; but (2) I am not sure they can flourish in just any soil or, to take the extreme case, in the soilless condition sometimes called pure reason, free of Scripture, tradition, and communal institution (synagogue, church, mosque, etc.). If they seem to, I suspect it is with the help of borrowed capital from one or more of the concrete, particular religions.[7]

I begin with the prayer of Samuel as we find it in 1 Samuel 3.[8] The LORD[9] called Samuel, who thought it was the priest, Eli, calling. Three times he runs to Eli, saying, "Here am I, for you called me." Finally, Eli realizes what is happening and tells Samuel next time to respond, "Speak, LORD, for your servant is listening." We can combine the two responses to make up Samuel's prayer, for the first response is more appropriate when addressed to God, who was actually doing the calling, than to Eli. So here is our first prayer: "Here am I, for you called me. Speak, LORD, for your servant is listening."

It takes little imagination to hear the resonances of Levinas's *me voici*, whose origins in any case are biblical, in Samuel's "Here am I." While this speech act is an expression of Samuel's freedom, there is more heteronomy than autonomy in it. He does not originate the conversation but is called, called forth, even called into being by a voice not his own. The meaning of the situation in which he finds himself is not determined by his horizons of expectation, which are simultaneously surprised and shattered. Nor is it just his situation that is changed; his very identity is changed, as he becomes no longer merely Hannah's son or Eli's helper, but the one who stands *coram deo*, in God's presence, by a call that is at once invitation and command. Everything begins with the "you called me." Prayer is the beginning of responsibility because it begins as response.

Samuel, who doubtless has been reading Levinas, acknowledges not only the alterity of the other's voice but also its asymmetrical authority. He identifies himself as the servant before his Lord. Actually, when he responds in accord with Eli's instruction, he does not name the speaker, but simply says, "Speak, for your servant is listening." But the omission of "LORD" is immaterial here. For the Tetragrammaton is more nearly a personal name than a generic name for a lord, like Adonai; and, in any case, the heavy lifting is done by Samuel's self-identification as the servant of the speaker, whose divinity he now recognizes. He calls himself *ebbed*, a bond-servant.

Heteronomy. Asymmetry. The relation between a lord and a servant. Is this the master-slave relation we know from Hegel, in which for the sake of freedom asymmetrical authority must be replaced by reciprocal recognition? Such a move is the essence of political modernity, whether we seek it in Locke or in Rousseau. But if, following Hegel, we extend this move from politics to religion, which is always a possibility, two consequences follow. First, God is either reduced to a president or prime minister, removable and replaceable at the will, even the whim, of the people. Or, more likely, God is reduced to something like the British monarchy, a powerless symbol of our own sovereignty. Second, our phenomenon begins to evaporate. Prayer, at least anything like Samuel's prayer, is quite meaningless in relation such a God.

Fortunately, at least for our exploration, there is another possibility, eloquently expressed by the same Levinas who borrows his *me voici* from Samuel and a host of other biblical characters. Seeking to preserve the asymmetrical authority of the voice of the other and not allergic to the alterity that can be expressed as heteronomy and as trauma, he insists that this is not slavery, since "no one is enslaved to the Good" and the Good "redeems the violence of its alterity," which is without alienation.[10] If God is the Good, as biblical faith believes, Samuel's posture as servant is not the sacrifice but rather the preservation of his humanity; for there is something demonic rather than human about the autonomy that is purchased at the price of estrangement from the Good, as the Genesis story of the Fall suggests. Perhaps that is why so many New Testament epistles begin with the author identifying himself as a slave (*doulos*) of God and of Jesus Christ,[11] and why Paul identifies the self-emptying (*kenosis*) of Christ as "taking the form of a slave" (Phil. 2:7).

There is a third dimension to Samuel's *me voici*. It begins with the identification of "you" as the One who by calling brings the world of this prayer into being. It continues with the identification of the "me" as the servant of the One who calls. But by themselves these two identifications do not take us beyond what Kierkegaard's Climacus would call objectivity to the subjectivity of faith. As Kierkegaard himself wrote in that famous Gilleleie journal entry of 1835:

> what good would it do me if truth stood before me, cold and naked, not caring whether I recognized her or not, and producing in me a shudder of fear rather than a trusting devotion? I certainly do not deny that I still recognize an *imperative of under-*

standing and that through it one can work upon men, *but it must be taken up into my life*, and *that is* what I now recognize as the most important thing. . . . It is the divine side of man, his inward action which means everything, not a mass of information.[12]

It is this inward action that is the third dimension of Samuel's prayer. Using a different vocabulary, we can say that Samuel's "Here am I" is only the beginning of a performative that completes itself in his "Speak, for your servant is listening." We learn four things about prayer from seeing Samuel's prayer in this light.

First, the priority of divine speech is here redoubled. First God calls. Then Samuel responds, but not by launching into praise, thanks, confession, petition, and intercession. His brief response is simply to indicate that he is ready for God to speak again. For Levinas, "The face speaks"[13] — and by speaking decenters me as the one addressed, removes me from the center of a universe governed my *conatus essendi* and my acts of *Sinngebung*. In prayer, it is the voice of the One whose face we do not see that "shatters" my cogito,[14] and thereby my I doubt, I understand, I affirm, I deny, I will, I refuse, I imagine, and I feel.[15] These are no longer the origin of either me or my world; and, since they are not its Alpha, they have no right to be its Omega either. We are "beyond intentionality"[16] or perhaps dealing with "an intentionality of a wholly different type"[17] — a reverse intentionality in which I am the intended one rather than the intending one. My transcendental ego, if I have or am one, is no longer the condition of the possibility of my experience. Relative to that possibility, what I may encounter is rather the Impossible.

Second, we learn how prayer is the task of a lifetime, so that even those who have been praying all their lives may not have gotten much farther than kindergarten. For the illocutionary act implicit in Samuel's prayerful speech act is the presentation of himself to God as a listener; and that is easier said than done. It is a performative, to be sure, but one that can scarcely be said to be performed more than to a certain degree. We know from merely human conversations how enormously difficult it is really to listen, to be fully present to our interlocutors. A fortiori, we only kid ourselves, like the tyro who reports that he learned to play golf yesterday, if we think we have finished learning how to listen to God as God deserves to be listened to. So we need not be skittish about a metaphysics of presence here, for although the praying soul seeks to be fully present to God, that is the always unfulfilled task of a lifetime; nor, from the other side, need we "worry" that God will become fully present to us, for as long as God is the speaker whom we do not see, God's presence will be inseparable from God's absence.

Third, we learn why silence is such an important part of prayer. It is those who seem to know the most about prayer who emphasize this most strongly, and now we can see why. We cannot listen very well to the voice of God if we are chattering ourselves or even if we merely keep ourselves surrounded by noise, almost as a barrier to protect us from hearing the voice of any other. As Johannes Tauler puts it, "And therefore you should observe silence! In that manner the Word can be uttered and heard within. For surely, if you choose to speak, God must fall silent. There is no better way of serving the Word than by silence and by listening."[18] Prayer needs silence, not only external but also internal silence; for our minds and hearts can be and usually are very noisy places even when we emit no audible sound. God speaks in and as the silence. On this "as" we might substitute "God" for Heidegger's "language" or "being" and say that *God* speaks "*as the peal of stillness*" (*das Geläut der Stille*).[19]

Finally, we learn why Scripture and prayer are so integrally intertwined, why prayer can never be separated from some form of *lectio divina*. God speaks as silence, to be sure, but prayer cannot grow in a purely apophatic soil if for no other reason than that in such a context no God personal enough to get prayer started by speaking to us is to be found. If we are engaged in prayer rather than yogic meditation, it is the God who speaks in Scripture for whom we listen in the silence and to whom we listen as the silence. By beginning *The Mystical Theology* with a prayer to the Trinity (which is one of the ways Derrida distinguishes negative theology from deconstruction),[20] Pseudo-Dionysius points us back to *The Divine Names*, in which he devotes far more space to telling us how to speak about God than he devotes in *The Mystical Theology* to telling us how not to speak about God.[21] And the names we are to use are those given to us in Scripture. The very call to which we may respond "Here am I" can come as a mysterious voice in the night, but it typically comes through the words of Scripture, directly or indirectly in preaching, hymnody, liturgy, and so forth. Before prayer is a fivefold speech act on our part, it is listening to the word of God as found in Scripture.

Very closely related to Samuel's prayer is Mary's prayer at the annunciation. This is the prayer that precedes the canticle we know as the Magnificat (Luke 1:46–55), and we can hear this earlier prayer as the prior condition of the possibility of that overflowing outburst of praise and thanksgiving. We might say that in the earlier prayer Mary assumes the posture from which her praise proceeds. The Magnificat is so heavily dependent on the song of Samuel's mother, Hannah (1 Sam. 2:1–10), that we can only assume that Mary also knows the story of Samuel and of his prayer, which is echoed in her own. In response to the angel Gabriel's stunning and scary news about what is soon to happen, she replies, simply, "Here am I, the servant of the Lord; let it be with me according to your word." (Luke 1:38). She speaks these words immediately to Gabriel, but she understands him to be an angel, that is, a messenger from God. Ultimately she is responding to God; her words are a prayer.

In this prayer, we find Mary's theology and ethics in a nutshell. The theology revolves around the notion of God as one who speaks or, better, as the One who speaks; for Mary is no ontotheologian, and God is not so much First Cause as First Speaker, the One whose word is always the beginning. Here "beginning" signifies not a Self-Explanatory Explainer in terms of which everything can be made transparent and intelligible but rather the fact that before I speak, or act, or even am, God has always already spoken. There is an echo, however faint, of this notion in the claim made in different ways by Heidegger, by structuralism, and by Derrida that language always precedes my own speech acts. Only here it is not an impersonal structural and possibly historical system that precedes me, but a very specific speaker.

Mary's ethics is one of holy *Gelassenheit*—let it be. It would be a parody to suggest that Mary means "let Being be" or "let language be," though once again we may hear faint echoes in Heidegger's *Gelassenheit*. Mary is the servant of the Lord, not the shepherd of Being. Still, this is an originary ethics, or, as I would prefer to say, and an adverbial ethics. It is about Mary's basic posture or fundamental project. It signifies the "how" rather than the "what" of her life, though it is not without a "what," as we shall see.

In looking at Samuel's "Here am I," the focus was on its secondary nature, and the emphasis fell on the "for you called." Its repetition by Mary gives us the opportunity to look more closely at the act itself. It is an act of self-presentation to the God who is already present. There is no attempt, because there is no need to find God. Having spoken, God is already present. Mary would easily understand Augustine's notion that God is nearer to us that we are to ourselves (*interior intimo meo*)[22] and his bittersweet confession, "Late it was that I loved you, beauty so ancient and so new, late I loved you! And, look, you were within me and I was outside. . . . You were with me, and I was not with you. Those outer beauties kept me far from you."[23] And perhaps she knew enough of the captivating, intoxicating, even addicting power of those outer beauties, physical and social, to be able to understand Augustine's, "Nowhere do you depart from us, and hard it is for us to return to you."[24] She understands that God is here, unusually so in the present instance, and the only question is whether I am willing and able to be here too. No doubt part of the problem is that while the messenger may be quite visible (we do not know the form of her visitation), God is not. As Chrétien puts it, prayer "is the speech act by which the man praying stands in the presence of a being in which he believes but does not see and manifests himself to it. . . . The first function speech performs in prayer is therefore a self-manifestation before the invisible other."[25]

She also understands that to be present to God, she must turn away from the world in which she has been immersed. Not that there is something evil about the world, into which, in fact, God will send her back with a task. It is rather that apart from that turning, the world is defined by her agenda, however innocent, and not God's. As Thomas Merton puts it so beautifully: "Detachment from things does not mean setting up a contradiction between 'things' and 'God' . . . as if [God's] creatures were His rivals. We do not detach ourselves from things in order to attach ourselves to God, but rather we become detached *from ourselves* in order to see and use all things in and for God."[26]

Here self-presentation is self-transcendence in the mode of kenosis, voluntary decentering of oneself. This is doubly confirmed by Mary's self-identification as the servant of the Lord and by her "let it be with me according to your word." Marcel's beautiful essay "Belonging and Disposability" is not a commentary on Mary's prayer or even in the first instance a reflection on the believing soul in relation to God. But we can read it that way, especially if we read it as a commentary on the theme of another essay, "I must somehow make room for the other in myself."[27] Marcel suggests that when I say, "*I belong to you,*" I am saying, "I am opening an unlimited credit account in your name, you can do what you want with me, I give myself to you."

Like Levinas, Marcel wants to deny that this involves alienation, so he immediately continues: "This does not mean . . . I am your slave; on the contrary, I freely put myself in your hands; the best use I can make of my freedom is to place it in your hands; it is as though

I freely substituted your freedom for my own; or paradoxically, it is by that very substitution that I realize my freedom."[28] If we pay sufficient attention to this paradox, we see that there is no substantive disagreement between Levinas and Marcel, on the one hand, and the biblical characters and writers, on the other, who are not skittish about using the language of servanthood and even slavery. Marcel accentuates the decentering nature of the "I belong to you" by contrasting it both with the "you belong to me," at least when it means *"you are my thing*; I will dispose of you as I want," and the ever so closely related "I belong to myself," which is "defiantly hurled at the conscience construed as traitor or as a spokesman of an abhorrent society" by an essentially anarchistic self in "a deification of self which is usually unavowed."[29]

The disposability that belongs to this belonging is, of course, not that of the disposable diaper or the disposable contact lenses. In contrast with the "you are at my disposal" that translates the "you belong to me," Marcel has in mind the "I am at your disposal" that renders the "I belong to you" more concretely. He immediately turns to the discussion of admiration cited above. One of the many ways of being at the disposal of another is to admire the other. Of course, one does not admire God, but one might adore God, and adoration is precisely what gets expressed in praise, the alpha or perhaps the omega of prayer.

The belonging and disposability expressed in Mary's "Let it be with me according to your word" are her adverbial holiness. The "how" of her prayer calls for enactment as the "how" of her life. But this ethics of prayer as life is not a form without a content, so the "how" as the "Let it be" will be as complex as the "what" that gives it content. Mary makes it clear that the "what" will be filled in by the word of God, whether that comes as the voice in the night, as a visit from an angel, or, more typically, in Scripture. So our question becomes: What kinds of speech act does God perform in calling us and evoking prayer? What is the nature of the word at whose disposal we place ourselves when our posture is that of prayer?

In biblical context, the primary divine speech acts are promises and commands. For prayer, life is a gift and a task, and God is both a god of grace and of law. Both types of speech act are decentering. The promise of grace signifies that we are not the origin of our life or of its meaning; these, rather, are a gift as we are from the outset caught up in a purpose beyond our own. The command of God's law signifies that neither our desires nor our insights are the highest norm for our life; just because the gift expresses a purpose not our own, it sets for us a task beyond our devising.

God's word to Mary through Gabriel is primarily a word of promise. Like the promise to Abraham, to which she will allude in her canticle (Luke 1:55; cf. 1:73), this promise marginalizes her own agenda. She merely wanted to be Joseph's wife and the mother of his children. Her self-chosen identity did not include being the mother of Messiah, much less the mother of God (θεοτόκος), as later generations would say in calling her blessed. But God is not promising her a rose garden, wonderful as the promise may be. She understands that she will have to bear the obloquy of being an unwed mother in a society that, unlike our own, does not celebrate shamelessness and does not portray all forms of shame as obstacles to be eliminated on the way to self-esteem. Moreover, she was about to be warned by Simeon that "a sword will pierce your own soul too" (Luke 2:35).

Mary's prayer is not without models. Perhaps when she says "let it be with me according to your word," she is thinking of the patience of Job, who, in the midst of unbearable suffering and loss, said, "Naked I came from my mother's womb, and naked shall I return there; the LORD gave and the LORD has taken away; blessed be the name of the LORD" (Job 1:21). His was a categorical not a hypothetical praise, not conditioned on God's word being in conformity with his desire and his agenda. The same can be said of David, of whom Mary might also have been thinking. When his son Absalom and rebelled against him and usurped the throne, David was forced to flee Jerusalem toward the wilderness. Loyal priests and Levites decided to bring the ark of the covenant of God with the royal party in flight. But David said, "Carry the ark of God back into the city. If I find favor in the eyes of the LORD, he will bring me back and let me see both it and the place where it stays. But if he says, 'I take no pleasure in you,' here I am, let him do to me what seems good to him" (2 Sam. 15:25–26). Job says, "I belong to you." David says, "I am at your disposal." And Mary says, "Let it be with me according to your word."

We are reminded in these stories that God allows bad things to happen to good people. In addition to words of promise and words of command, there are what we might call words of permission. For, as the story of Job makes especially clear, in biblical context the pain and suffering that comes our way may have its origin in the fallen freedom of created beings and need not be interpreted as divine judgment or punishment. Neither does it signify impotence or indifference; for without the permissive word of God, Satan would not have been able to torture Job, and the same understanding is implicit in the story of David and Absalom. Of course, Mary may not have had either of these stories in mind. But the condition for the possibility of her *Gelassenheit* is not some sort of Stoic resignation before blind fate but the faith she shares with Job and David that "in all things, as we know, [God] co-operates for good with those who love God and are *called* according to *his purpose*."[30]

While Mary may or may not have realized how her prayer echoed the prayers of Job and David, she surely could not have known how it would in turn be echoed in two prayers of her son. The first is the prayer he taught his disciples to pray. To get a feeling for its force, let us listen to the way it can all too easily be intended:

> Our Father in heaven,
> hallowed be my name,
> my kingdom come,
> my will be done on earth as yours is in heaven.

Even to the most cynical secularist, this is bound to sound like sacrilege. The crassness of this formulation is barely mitigated if we substitute *our* name, kingdom, and will for *mine*. We hear the decentering force of the prayer in its actual wording: *your* name, *your* kingdom, *your* will (Matt. 6:9–10). Here is a triple threat against all aspiration to autonomy, a triple abandonment of my preoccupation with myself. After, but only after I have made this move, I am in a position to pray rightly for material and spiritual blessings, daily bread, and forgiveness, for myself and for "us." And no sooner have I done so than the doxology, which is sometimes included in the prayer and sometimes serves as its liturgical trailer, reminds me of what I can so quickly forget: "for the kingdom, the power, and the glory are yours, now and forever." The Amen (so be it) that concludes this prayer, echoes the "let it be" of Mary's prayer, just as the "*your* name," "*your* kingdom," and "*your* will" echo her "*your* word." To feel the full force of the self-transformation called for by this self-transcendence is to understand how learning to pray is the task of a lifetime.

The second prayer in which Mary's is echoed in that of her son comes to us from Gethsemane. Anticipating the violent death that is about to strike, Jesus offers perhaps the most basic prayer of petition, which we might call the foxhole prayer: Lord, spare my life. "My Father, if it is possible, let this cup pass from me." But he prays this prayer from the posture that is its precondition in the sense that in a different posture it would be a different prayer altogether. The posture is that of belonging and disposability: "yet not what I want but what you want" (Matt. 26:39). Here Jesus remembers the "your name . . . your kingdom . . . your will" that he taught his disciples to pray; here he echoes his mother's "let it be with me according to your word," of which he may or may not have known anything; and here he enacts the kenosis celebrated in the early Christian hymn in praise of him who:

> emptied himself,
> taking the form of a slave . . .
> he humbled himself
> and became obedient to the point of death
> —even death on a cross. (Phil. 2:7–8)

Before a final point about Mary's prayer, a brief digression. The kenotic posture I have been describing plays a transcendental function. In place of the horizons of the decentered and no longer very transcendental ego, this scene is the horizon, the condition for the possibility of the five dimensions of prayer mentioned above. A full treatment would show not only how it makes praise possible but also how it conditions and thereby changes thanksgiving, confession, petition, and intercession. In lieu of such a treatment, I offer a couple of examples. The first is from the confession of the decentered self. The still-centered self might consider confession advisable in terms of a cost-benefit analysis. This act of humility, even if it has to be more than an act, is worth the indignity in exchange for the benefits derived, which may well include an assuaged conscience and, instead of divine punishment here and hereafter, divine blessings here and heavenly reward hereafter. The decentered self need not deny these considerations in order to confess differently, but only to do so in a different posture. This is beautifully expressed in a prayer of confession to be found in *The Book of Common Prayer* and the *Lutheran Book of Worship*.[31] A confession of sins is followed by a request for forgiveness. To what end?

> that we may delight in *your will*,
> and walk in *your ways*,
> to the glory of *your holy name*. Amen. (emphasis added)

The self that has begun the kenotic journey prays for forgiveness in order, above all, to be more deeply decentered.

The other example is from a prayer of thanksgiving found in *The Book of Common Prayer*. At about the midpoint, thanksgiving turns into petition, asking that God will:

> give us such an awareness of your mercies,
> that with truly thankful hearts we may show forth your praise,
> not only with our lips, but in our lives,
> by giving up our selves to your service,
> and by walking before you
> in holiness and righteousness all our days

This is not writing a thank you note to Aunt Susie after Christmas so she will be well disposed toward me when my birthday comes around in February. The telos of thanksgiving is that through an awareness of "your mercies" our lives may be more completely given over to "your praise" and "your service."

Finally, with respect to Mary's prayer, we can note that as in Samuel's prayer, there is a human silence before the divine word. In Samuel's case, it is the silence of listening that awaits God's word. In Mary's case, it is the silence of meditation that comes after God's word. When the promised son is born, she receives another message from God, this one doubly mediated by angels and shepherds, telling her that the boy is "a Savior, who is the Messiah, the Lord" (Luke 2:11). We read that "Mary treasured all these words and pondered them in her heart" (Luke 2:19). In the silence of this pondering, she once again places herself at the disposal of God's word and echoes in the stillness her earlier "let it be with me according to your word."

I have an icon of the Virgin Mary. It was originally a Christmas card that struck me so much that I kept it. It probably did not originate as an icon in the traditional sense. Mary's face is green and, to that degree, suggests a German expressionist portrait more than a Byzantine or Russian icon, though it totally lacks the bitter, biting edge of expressionist "iconography." There is, however, a yellow and gold halo that betrays more traditional iconic heritage. Mary's head is slightly bowed; her eyes are shut; her lips are closed, slightly turned down in an expression more sober than sad. She is not interacting with her outer environment; she is inside. Sometimes I think she is inwardly repeating those words long after the angel and the shepherds have departed, "Here am I, the servant of the Lord; let it be with me according to your word." But at other times I wonder if the silence is not more total, if her heart is not as silent as her lips as she simply ponders the word she has heard.[32]

The third prayer for our consideration is the prayer of Elvis: "I want you, I need you, I love you with all my heart." I know that it was not a prayer as sung by Elvis. It is addressed to the latest hormonal heartthrob, and the reference to the heart seems to be a euphemism for another seat of desire. But phenomenology is about possibilities, and imaginative variation is a time-honored strategy; so let us imagine the possibility of these words addressed by the believing soul to God. They exhibit the fundamental trope of Hebrew poetry, parallelism, in which the same thing is said a second and even a third time in a slightly different way. In Elvis' version, "I love you" adds nothing new to "I want you" and "I need you." And therein lies the problem. Even when we convert the earthly eros into the heavenly by addressing these words to God, it is all about what I want, what I need, and what I, in those senses, love. The prospects for deepening our understanding prayer as a deeply decentering posture do not seem very great.

If it is always darkest just before the dawn, we might find our way forward by seeing the problem in its starkest form. When I want to introduce my students to the difference between eros and agape, need love and gift love, where sexual desire is only a single instance of a more general structure, I say, "I love cheese omelet. Would you like me to love you too?" "I love cheese omelet" is a perfectly legitimate use of the word "love" in English. And its meaning here is clear. What I love is what I devour, what I assimilate to myself, what I make into a means to my ends. I give to it a double career: in part it becomes what satisfies and strengthens me and in part it becomes what I flush away as worse than useless. It is no wonder that Levinas speaks of the reduction of the other to the same as a stomach without ears.[33]

Now comes our first glimmer of hope. Even before we convert these words to a prayer, this alimentary attitude begins to unravel as I am deconstructed by my own desire. I want *you*, I need *you*, I love *you*. I can say these words in such a way as to make a sex *object* of the addressee. They can mean "I want you to belong to me so that *you are my thing*; I will dispose of you as I want." This project can be astonishingly and frighteningly successful. All too often it is possible to dominate another, who, in such a setting, becomes codependent on my addiction to myself. But my own word, "you," undermines and rebukes such a speech act. There is a performative contradiction in addressing someone as you in order to reduce her to some it. As Chrétien puts it, "For it is only in saying 'you' that objectivization runs up against an uncrossable limit. . . . It is only in saying *You* that the I can be completely exposed, beyond all that it can master."[34] It is still about what I want, but, as Buber reminds us, the I that is linked to you is a different I from the one that is linked to it. I am still the one speaking, not the one spoken to, but a certain decentering has begun, whether I like it or even notice it. It cannot address me, but you can. To desire *you* is to desire vulnerability to alterity.

Now let us return to the supposition that the you to whom I address these words is God. I could hardly mean—or at least could hardly admit to myself that I mean—"I want you to belong to me so that *you are my thing*; I will dispose of you as I want." That is as hopelessly crass as the "my name, my kingdom, my will" version of the Lord's Prayer we considered earlier. But I might mean by "I love you" simply that I want and I need your help, your blessings, the benefits of having you on my side. Here, once again, decentering seems to get derailed by my preoccupation with myself.

But now suppose that what I mean is really "I want *you*," you yourself, not your gifts:

> As a deer longs for flowing streams,
> so my soul longs for you, O God.
> My soul thirsts for God,
> for the living God. (Ps. 42:102)

> O God, you are my God, I seek you,
> my soul thirsts for you;
> my flesh faints for you,
> as in a dry and weary land where there is no water. (Ps. 63:1)

What has changed here is more fundamental than the replacement of a hunger metaphor with a thirst metaphor, and even more fundamental than the replacement of an "it" for a "you." This is not just any old "you," though what is true in this case may well be true in a measure in relation to human yous as well. But if we ask how it might be possible to "have" or to "possess" God, to drink of the living water (John 4:7–14, 7:37–39), we will realize that the "you belong to me" path leads away from our goal, and only the "I belong to you—I am at your disposal" path leads to it. God cannot be "had" in any other way. God is always at our disposal, always giving Godself to those who are willing to take. But the only way to take this gift is to place ourselves at God's disposal, to give not this or that but our very selves to God. The hymn writer gets it right when describing the love between Christ and the believer:

His forever, only His; Who the Lord and me shall part?
Ah, with what a rest of bliss Christ can fill the loving heart!
Heav'n and earth may fade and flee, Firstborn light in gloom decline;
But while God and I shall be, I am His, and He is mine.[35]

Only *after* I am His can it be that He is mine. To address God as "you" would seem to be a necessary condition for prayer. To present oneself as "yours," in which that "you" is *aufgehoben*, would seem to be the necessary and sufficient condition for prayer.

Kierkegaard calls this taking by giving, this possessing by dispossession, a paradox; Derrida sees in it the Impossible; and Marion finds such an experience to be a saturated phenomenon. In each case they designate a relation that exceeds not only our capacity for conceptual comprehension but also our capacity to produce such a result. Knowledge may well be power, but this taking that is only possible as giving bursts through the horizons of our knowledge and our power. It is a gift.

Just to the degree that we are enabled to experience such a miracle, a certain transubstantiation takes place, and water is changed into wine. What I mean is simply this: eros is not merely reconciled with agape; it becomes agape. Need love and gift love, desire and disposability, become two sides of the same coin. Or, if this metaphor still leaves them too distinct, we can speak of moving beyond the experiential space in which the difference between them makes any sense. Tauler expresses this nicely when he says that true prayer is a "loving ascent to God, in profound longing and humble surrender."[36] But perhaps we should not get too carried away, as if we occupy such a space very fully or for very long. The two-sides-of-one-coin metaphor reminds us that proximally and for the most part we experience them as distinct and all too easily fall back into such a space even after partial glimpses of their proper identity. Prayer is the task of a lifetime.

Prayer has many postures. People pray standing, sitting, kneeling, and prostrate. They pray with bowed head and folded hands. They pray with hands and face uplifted to heaven. They pray with eyes open and with eyes shut. Prayer engages the body in many different ways. But in speaking of prayer as the posture of the decentered self, I am speaking of a posture of the soul, of an inner attitude of the self that can appropriately express itself in a variety of outer stances. That is why I also described it as the fundamental project of the self. By reflecting on these three prayers, I hope to have indicated in a measure how this posture is possible only to a deeply decentered self.

Such a self constitutes one answer to the question: Who comes after the subject?[37] This self is not its own origin. It does not make itself but rather receives itself in receiving what is given to it by putting itself at the disposal of the gift. It is the gift that makes the response possible, which is why, following Marion, one can call such a self neither subject nor ego but "the gifted."[38] What Henri Nouwen says about prayer can be said with equal validity of becoming a self, which may be only the other side of the same coin: "So, the paradox of prayer is that it asks for a serious effort while it can only be received as a gift."[39] No doubt it is a privilege to be gifted; but there is a price. One must abandon the project of being the center in terms of which meaning, and truth, and goodness are defined. To dare to pray is to consider the price worth paying. To mature in prayer is to discover that the price itself is a gift.

But this is the task of a lifetime.

Who Prays?
Levinas on Irremissible Responsibility

JILL ROBBINS

The Trace of the Religious in the Philosophical

I begin by remarking the way in which the word *prayer* comes up in Levinas's philosophical writings, especially its insistent connection with ethical language.

Recall *Totality and Infinity*'s description that language, along with generosity, is the sole exception to the habitual economy that returns all alterity to the Self-Same. The relation to the other in language is said to maintain radical separation and distance. It preserves metaphysical asymmetry (the impossibility of viewing my relation to the other from the outside); it respects and affirms alterity. In *Totality and Infinity*, ethics happens in and as language.

The language that accomplishes this nontotalizing relation to the other is primordial: it precedes and underlies all language as communication. It has neither a semantic function (it is neither denotative nor referential), nor can it be conceived as a semiosis (which, as a system of referrals within immanence, would destroy transcendence). Ethical language is interlocutionary and interpellative: it never speaks about the other but only to him or her. Always addressed to the other, ethical language would be "pure invocation."[1] Like the conative mode Roman Jakobson analyzes in his functional description of the communication situation, such a language foregrounds the relationship to the addressee. Its closest grammatical equivalents would be the vocative and the imperative (cases of which, Jakobson says, one cannot ask, is it true or not?).[2] In the terms of the operative model of language in Levinas's later work, ethical language is a Saying (*un Dire*), a mobile orientation toward the addressee, before the phrase congeals into the thematization of the Said (*le Dit*).

In the ethical relation to the other in language, the fact of speaking is more important than any word or content. Ultimately the primordial "conversation" is contentless or prior to content. The very few examples of ethical language that Levinas provides are all empty bits of everyday language. They include: "*Après vous, Monsieur,*" the little courtesy that Levinas interprets as ontological courtesy, ceding one's place to the other, a being *for* the other (OB 117; IR 47, 106, 191); "Here I am" or *me voici*, the biblical *hineni*, an answer to God's call and a quasi-contractual announcement of readiness for service (OB 114); and "*Bonjour*" (elsewhere, *Shalom* [IR 113]). In a 1986 interview Levinas states: "Is not the first word *bonjour*? As simple as *bonjour*! *Bonjour* as benediction and my being available for the other. It doesn't mean: what a beautiful day. Rather: I wish you peace. I wish you a good day. Expression of one who worries about the other" (IR 47). This *bonjour* is "already presupposed by every cogito and by all self-reflection" (IR 211–212). The greeting (exemplified by *bonjour* and perhaps also by *adieu*) is not of the order of knowledge; it is blessing and benediction (IR 49).

With these phrases—"*Après vous, Monsieur,*" *hineni*, and *bonjour*— what Levinas calls "the extraordinary and everyday event of my responsibility" comes into view (OB 10). Extraordinary because it hardly ever happens. It is an exception to the habitual economy, or what in the later work Levinas calls the *conatus essendi*, the essential tendency for a being to persevere in its being—a concern for its own being which is the "source" of all egoism (IR 191). Responsibility to the other is an everyday event, however, insofar as it is ubiquitous in factical speech. Hence in the speaking relationship with the other, Levinas glimpses transcendence. Even in the late 1940s, Levinas had associated the facticity of the speaking relation with the other with prayer. In an essay on Michel Leiris, in a contrast between speech and visual experience, he writes, "by the word that is uttered [*par la parole proférée*], the subject who poses himself is exposed, and, in a sense [*en quelque manière*] prays" (LR 149).

There is nothing mystical about this sense of prayer. The ethical experience cuts against all experience that one could term mystical.

In *Totality and Infinity*, Levinas opposes the speaking relation to the other (that is already a prayer) from rite and liturgy. (The word *liturgy* does not yet have the positive sense it will acquire in the 1963 essay "The Trace of the Other," where it denotes a work without recompense and where it exemplifies the aneconomic relation to the other.) Note that in all these cases, Levinas's use of the word *prayer* is attenuated, at a distance from its commonly accepted meaning of the speech man addresses to God.

In this context, the question broached in this paper's title—Who prays?—would be very similar to the question: Who speaks? or Who responds? The question goes to the problem of the "who," the subject of this prayer or quasi-prayer. The answer to this question would be: a subject put into question by the strangeness of the absolutely other. Here the (ethical) putting into question of the subject is radical: not a consciousness *of* being put into question, but consciousness—put into question. (This latter is the condition of the former, Levinas specifies in "Meaning and Sense"). The I who prays would be an I dispossessed of its sovereignty and self-coincidence, "an I in which the active ego reverts to the passivity of an accusative form" (CPP 147), a uniqueness without identity or inwardness, an I which says "*me voici.*" This is a self that is not originally "for-itself," but "for-the-other." Not *le Moi* (uppercase), the Ego, but *moi* (lowercase), "me." Maurice Blanchot calls this "*un moi sans moi,*" an ego without ego.[3] In these formulations, in which the distinctive style and claims of Levinas's later work are in play, no longer is it a matter of the self in enjoyment put into question by the exteriority of the other. The self here is always already put into question by the other that inhabits it. Subjectivity—or, more precisely, disordered subjectivity—is now the site of transcendence.[4]

I want to mention one last reference to prayer in the philosophical works occurring in the first chapter of *Otherwise than Being*. This reference seems to get closer to the common meaning of prayer, although the diction in which it is inscribed is utterly uncommon. Prayer is an example of what Levinas calls "an other intrigue of time than that of the simple succession of presents." He writes: "In a prayer in which the worshipper asks that his prayer be heard, the prayer as it were precedes or follows itself" (OB 10). This reading of prayer has to do with Levinas's privileging of diachrony in the later work, of a diachrony refractory to the synchronization and simultaneity that invariably ruin transcendence. He privileges a temporality that is diachronously distended—out of phase with itself (*un dépha-*

age). Transcendence signifies by the reference to an (absolutely dia-chronous) preoriginal that cannot be captured by memory or history. This other temporality is the time *of* the other. It is by this trace structure, reference to an immemorial past, that transcendence can signify in a way that is not convertible into immanence. It is by this trace structure that transcendence can withdraw from being while still being signaled within it (OB 10), within a philosophy and a philosophical language in which "immanence always triumphs over transcendence" (CPP 173).

Religions, Levinas states in "Enigma and Phenomenon," come from a past more past than any past, a past that was never a pure now (CPP 68). It is in this way that, for Levinas, religion (not the same thing as philosophical theology, which, as a thematization, would be a destruction of transcendence) represents a challenge to the hegemony of presence in philosophy. The trace of the religious in Levinas's philosophical work has precisely to do with the way in which religion, as philosophy's nonphilosophical other, is able to challenge philosophy and to put it (ethically) into question.

The Confessional Works

While in the philosophical works the reference to prayer was attenuated and implicit, we find a much more extensive and explicit reference to prayer in the nonphilosophical or confessional works. Most of these discussions can be found in a cluster of essays Levinas wrote between 1978 and 1985, all part of his reception of and response to the work of Rabbi Hayyim of Volozin, whose work he sees as a "making explicit" of the implicit philosophy of rabbinic study" (LR 229). In the larger context of Levinas's confessional writings, this work of "making explicit" refers to the whole project of "translating" the Talmud into a Greek philosophical conceptuality. (As in Heidegger's existential analytic of *Dasein* in *Being and Time*, "making explicit" is everything.) Levinas talks about R. Hayyim's work in "'In the Image of God' According to Rabbi Hayyim of Volozin" (1978), "Judaism and Kenosis" (1985), and "Of Prayer without Demand" (1982). Another important confessional text in which the topic of prayer is introduced is "The Names of God after Some Talmudic Texts" (1969).[5]

R. Hayyim (1749–1821) was a student of the Vilna Gaon (1720–1797). Like his teacher, he is one of the *mithnagdim*, the opponents of Hasidic spirituality. He advocates an intellectualist approach to

Judaism over and against an emphasis on affectivity. He affirms the "spiritual primacy of Talmud study" (BTV 154). In his main work, *Nefesh Hahayyim* (The Soul of Life), Rabbi Hayyim even takes in Kabbalah and is more conciliatory toward it than his teacher was. Levinas observes that "much in [R. Hayyim's] book passes for mysticism, which our author rejects in its Hasidic excesses" (BTV 154). For the *mithnagdim*, the way to achieve proximity to God is through study, not through contemplation and fervent prayer. For R. Hayim of Volozin, as for Levinas, religion is ethics rather than mystical experience. Nonetheless, Levinas's discussions of R. Hayyim do give us a much more mystical Levinas than we are used to.

In a 1982 interview, Levinas formulates his own philosophical project as an effort "to imagine an anthropology different from that which starts from the *conatus essendi*" (IR 129). What he finds in R. Hayyim's work is precisely such an alternative anthropology, an anthropology of "limitless responsibility" (ITN 127).[6] Before persevering in being, the I responds to another.

R. Hayim's cosmology makes reference to God and the world*s* (plural), many or various worlds. According to Levinas, the term *worlds* designates being in its pluralism and the relations between different orders of real (BTV 155). In Levinas's less restricted usage, *worlds* designate other entities, spiritual collectivities, people, in relation to the I (BTV 161). There is, for R. Hayyim of Volozin, a hierarchy of worlds in which energy is spread from top to bottom (BTV 156). Levinas summarizes: "In the incatenation of worlds, man occupies an exceptional place. Man is simultaneously at the bottom of the ladder and above the throne. Everything depends on him" (BTV 158).

Hence all man's deeds are consequential. If he conforms to the Torah's commandments, he strengthens and reinforces God's association with the worlds. Man's bad acts, on the other hand, diminish God's association with the worlds; they destroy worlds and actually enfeeble the deity (BTV 159). In short, God's association with the worlds depends upon the conduct of the I—an I responsible for the universe (BTV 161). By being not "in-itself" or "for-itself" but "for-the-other," man supports the world. The world *is* because man is responsible for the other (ITN 126). The specific vocation of Israel, in this view, is to be the first one responsible.[7]

Rabbi Hayyim's discussions of prayer particularly interest Levinas. Because man is responsible for the maintenance of the worlds, God needs the prayer of men. At no time is prayer a demand for the self. Strictly speaking it is not a demand at all (hence Levinas's title: "Of Prayer without Demand," "Of Prayer without Petition"). Rather, prayer is an elevation of the soul that hopes to bring about the divine influx and intensify the divine presence in the world. To the extent that God is related to himself, he is unaffected by prayer, but to the extent he is related to the worlds, he needs man's prayer.

Prayer, in this view, is not a particular supplication: it is "pure invocation."[8] It seeks to ensure the salvation of others rather than of the self. (The preoccupation with personal salvation—part of the tension *over* the self—risks falling into an egoism, as Levinas has maintained since the 1950s and the 1960s in *Difficult Freedom* and in his readings of Søren Kierkegaard.) Is there no prayer, then, for one's *own* suffering? If real prayer is never for one's own needs, is not *for* the self, but *for* the others, the one who suffers prays not *to* God but *for* Him: "the One to whom [*à qui*] all prayer is addressed is also the One for whom [*pour qui*] all prayer is addressed" (ITN 130). One prays for God who suffers in one's suffering. Does not the psalmist say, in the words of Psalm 91:15, "I am with him in suffering"? This is kenosis—radical humility—of God, says Levinas, as Judaism announces it (IR 226–227; 281; ITN 130). This is kenosis "in its primordial meaning" (ITN 126), namely, "the proximity of God to human suffering" (ITN 115).

The purpose of prayer, which replaces the old sacrifice, is elevation of the soul. Like the smoke of sacrifice, this prayer is pure offering, what Levinas calls or "translates" as "a being disengaging itself from the unconditional attachment to being" (LR 233). This, then, is "dis-inter-estedness," a movement away from the interested business of being and away from the multiplicity of allergic egoisms characterized by a war of all against all. Prayer brings into view an I responsible for the universe.

God Prays

The other important place in the confessional writings where a discussion of prayer occurs is in a talk Levinas delivered in 1964 at a conference devoted to "The Situations of French Jewry," entitled "Education and Prayer," reprinted in *Difficult Freedom*.[9] While this text does not refer to R. Hayyim of Volozin explicitly, Levinas does in effect sign on to what R. Hayyim says about prayer, and a number of his insights seem "motivated" by R. Hayyim's work.

Levinas prefaces his comments with two reflections, rendered in terse and paradoxical fashion: he affirms that in Judaism pride of place goes to prayer, then grants it only second place. This curious double affirmation, in which prayer is first asserted to be primary, and is then made secondary, will be explained in the course of his reflections. Suffice it to remark here that Levinas again gives voice to a characteristic mithnagdic emphasis, the spiritual primacy of Talmud study. Following a classical rabbinic hierarchy, Torah and Talmud study are valued even over prayer.[10] Such a mithnagdic sensibility—intellectualist rather than emotional—is prominent throughout *Difficult Freedom*. In Part I of the book, entitled *"Au-dela du pathétique"* (Beyond Pathos), Levinas's interpretation of Judaism announces itself precisely as this going beyond pathos. Judaism can be understood, he suggests, as "a passion distrusting its pathos" (*une passion se méfiant de son pathos*) (DF 6). The very function of Jewish ritual life, he says, is to break up spontaneity, to break up the *élan* (naïve springs) of the heart: therein lies its ethical dimension. In Part I's second chapter, entitled "A Religion of Adults," he asserts: "The entire effort of Judaism consists in understanding the holiness [*sainteté*] of God in a sense that stands in sharp contrast with the numinous meaning of the term. . . . The sacred [*le sacré*] that envelops and transports me is a form of violence" (DF 14).

The distinction asserted here, in an essay first published in 1957, between the sacred and the holy runs through all of Levinas's subsequent discussions of religion. The title of his second collection of talmudic writings from 1977, *Du sacré au saint* (From the Sacred *to* the Holy), not only makes the passage from the one to the other explicit, it identifies this passage with extracting the ethical meaning from the Bible over and against any numinous sense. Similarly, the 1975 essay "God and Philosophy" opposes the fear and trembling before the sacred to the separation that characterizes holiness. Moreover, when Levinas asks, in the lead essay of *Difficult Freedom*, from 1952, "Can one still be Jewish without Kierkegaard?" and answers "It is a good thing we have Hasidism and the Kabbalah!", clearly his polemical target is not just the Christian experience of the numinous but the mystical joy and emotion associated with Hasidism. In other words, the division between the pathetic and the nonpathetic is also internal to Judaism.[11]

In "Education and Prayer" (1964), Levinas begins his comments on prayer by saying, "Whatever be the ultimate meaning of prayer . . . , it is collective prayer . . . which opens this ultimate meaning" (DF 270). That is (and here is a first sense of this assertion): In Judaism you do not primarily pray alone, you need a *minyan* (a quorum), a minimum of ten men. While one may pray privately, there is special merit in praying with others as part of a congregation; this is underscored by that fact the Jewish prayers are formulated in the plural rather than in the singular.[12] "Solitary prayer [*la prière d'isolés*] is a last resort. . . . The proximity of the divine is inconceivable for a Jew without the presence of all the people of Israel" (DF 270).

The distinction Levinas makes here between solitary and collective prayer is not an empirical one; it is phenomenological. Collectivity, as that which *opens* the ultimate meaning of prayer, is the condition of prayer, it is what makes prayer prayer. Collectivity is the essence of prayer, whether that prayer is performed privately or publicly. The imperative in Judaism that prayer be collective (in an empirical sense), arises because its ultimate meaning is or is opened by an essential collectivity. Solitary prayer does not have that opening function. The collectivity that opens the ultimate meaning of prayer is itself conceived as a keeping open or a holding open of the possibility of community. It is more of an interrogation than an assertion. According to the metaphorics of Levinas's text, not praying with others is to be walled in, is to be in "a windowless room" (*un pièce sans fenêtre*) (DF 270). Collective prayer is a room with windows. This figure of opening is prolonged when Levinas states "God is close to whomever invokes him (a virtual citation from Psalm 145), but the invocation presupposes an opening" (*une ouverture*) (DF 270). Collectivity qua opening is constitutive of prayer. I admit that I am drawing attention to the recursivity of these formulations, the consequences of which will be unpacked by Levinas later in his essay. Suffice it to say here with regard to the question Who prays? that it is not necessarily a singular subject that is at issue. (Ultimately, it is a plural subject that will in turn make possible what Levinas calls *uniqueness*, or individuation through responsibility.)[13]

For Levinas, the invocation of God presupposes a concrete opening unto community. Levinas continues: "A God lending himself to a tête-à-tête apart from all of Israel is a dangerous abstraction, a source of suspect drunkenness" (DF 270). This reference to intoxication should alert us that we are in the presence of a polemic that runs throughout *Difficult Freedom*. There, intoxication, enthusiasm, ecstatic behavior, the ludic—all of which are associated with sacred participation—are opposed to Jewish ritual life and ethical comportment. Levinas's Judaism is, as he puts it, not poetry but prose (DF 54).

This Judaism is sobriety itself. Tellingly, the epigraph to the section "Beyond Pathos" is Rashi's comment on Leviticus 10: "Let them not enter the sanctuary drunk."[14] Of course, the polemic against partici- pation also runs through Levinas's philosophical work. In *Totality and Infinity*, Section III.B.3, ethical experience is pointedly distinguished from mystical experience and is lined up with all the governing oppo- sitions in Levinas's work: frankness or sincerity versus intoxicating equivocation, discourse versus incantation, prayer versus liturgy, discontinuity versus fusion, false transcendence versus true transcen- dence. There, too, we find an opposition between ethical discourse as rupture and commencement and the poetry that enraptures and transports. We have already noted the importance of the contrast in "God and Philosophy" between the desire for union with the tran- scendent being that characterizes the sacred, and the holy, character- ized by separation.

By way of contrast to the abstract fusion of a tête-à-tête with God that leaves out the concrete relation to the third party, Levinas refers us to a Talmudic extract from *Berakoth* that asserts that the Lord him- self puts on tefillin—or phylacteries—each morning. Levinas does not give an exact reference, but the extract to which he refers is part of a constellation of statements in *Berakoth* 6a–7a, all of which turn on the anthropomorphic image of God praying. This anthropomor- phism, which is to be taken in an allegorical sense, is not necessarily surprising. Compare the epigraph to the final part of *Difficult Freedom* entitled "Hic Et Nunc," where Levinas cites the talmudic statement (from *Abodah Zarah*): "Since the time of the destruction of the Tem- ple, God spends a quarter of each day teaching." In *Berakoth* 7a, a playfully literal reading is the prooftext used to establish the fact that God prays:

> R. Johanan says in the name of R. Jose: How do we know that the Holy One, blessed be He, says prayers? Because it says [in the words of Isa. 56:7], "Even them will I bring to My holy mountain and make them joyful in the house of My prayer." It doesn't say, "their prayer," but "My prayer"; hence [you learn] that the Holy One, blessed be He, says prayers.[15]

The phylacteries or tefillin, one for the hand and one for the head, are worn by adult male Jews at weekday morning services. They consist of two small leather boxes to each of which is attached a long leather thong and each of which contains parchment on which are inscribed four passages from the Pentateuch. One of these passages is the prescription for the phylacteries, the first paragraph of which is the *Shema*: "Hear, O Israel, the Lord our God, the Lord is one. . . . And [these words which I command you this day] you shall bind them as a sign on your hand and they shall be as frontlets between thine eyes" (Deut. 6:4–9). The other inscribed scriptural passages refer to the promise of the covenant and the miraculous deliverance from Egypt respectively.[16] Other readings are in *Berakoth* 6a:

> R. Abin son of R. Ada in the name of R. Isaac says [further]: How do you know the Holy One, blessed be He, puts on tefil-lin?: Because [in the words of Isa. 62:8] "The Lord has sworn by His right hand, and by the arm of His strength" [or "by His mighty arm"]. "By His right hand": this is the Torah. . . . "And by the arm of His strength": this is the tefillin [namely, the (left) arm on which tefillin is placed].

Hence if God is obliged to put on tefillin every morning, God prays in the same manner as man prays. Man's prayer emulates God's (or the reverse). This is the *imitatio* and the correlation that are at stake in the image of God praying.

But one might wish to ask: Even if God prays in the same manner as does man, *to whom* does God pray? In *Berakoth* 7a, Rabbi Nahman ben Isaac poses the question in this way: "What is written in the te-fillin of the Lord of the Universe?" The extract Levinas summarizes is R. Hiyya b. Abin's answer to this rabbinic question: "To the 'Hear O Israel, the Lord our God, the Lord is One,' inscribed in our terres-trial tefillin, corresponds, in the celestial tefillin, "Who is like your people Israel, nation unique on this earth?'" (DF 270)

Written in man's tefillin is an assertion of the uniqueness and one-ness of God (the *Shema*), followed by the prescription for the tefillin. Written in God's tefillin, according to the above-cited midrash, is David's prayer before God in I Chronicles 17:21 (also found in II Sam. 7:23): "Who is like thy people Israel, unique on this earth ?" The form of the prayer is very similar to the Song of the Sea (in the Jewish prayer book, "The Blessing of Redemption," which follows the *Shema*: "Who is like Thee, O Lord, among the gods?" [Exod. 15:11]). The answer to all these (rhetorical) questions is: no one.

For Levinas the rabbinic answer to the question of what is written in God's tefillin suggests that, "to worship the eternal is not to evade the unique and eternal humanity over whom God bends [*se pend*] and towards whom the eternal thought overflows" (*s'epanche*) (DF 270).

Exploiting the homonym, Levinas says that God is bent over humanity (in a gesture of radical humility, and—another anthropomorphism—is bent over in prayer) and also that His Eternal thought overflows (one of Rabbi Hayyim's words for the divine influx that the prayer that is augmentation hopes to bring about). In other words, for Levinas, the significance of what is written in God's tefillin has to do with the irreducible relay in Judaism between God, man, and the neighbor. That the relationship with God never accomplishes itself in the absence of a relation to the human is a familiar enough emphasis within Levinas's hermeneutic of Judaism in *Difficult Freedom*. In "A Religion of Adults," he asserts: "The way that leads to God therefore leads *ipso facto* and not in addition to man" (DF 18). This is consistent with what Emil Fackenheim describes in Judaism as not a two-term relation between God and man, but a necessary and internal relation between three terms: God, man, and the neighbor.[17]

It turns out that God's prayer is not so much a prayer *to* Israel; it is more like a prayer about Israel. Not a prayer *to* but a praise *of* Israel, a praise of Israel's uniqueness. The *Berakoth* 6a extract in full (which Levinas does not cite)—R. Nahman b. Isaac's response to R. Hiyya b. Abin—makes this clear:

> Does, then, the Holy One, blessed be He, sing the praises of Israel?—Yes, for it is written: "Thou has avouched the Lord this day . . . and the Lord hath avouched thee this day" [Deut. 26:17–18]. The Holy One, blessed be He, said to Israel: "You have made me a unique entity in the world, and I shall make you a unique entity in the world." "You have made me a unique entity in the world," as it is said [in Deut 6:4]: "Hear, O Israel, the Lord our God, the Lord is one." "And I shall make you a unique entity in the world," as it is said [in I Chron. 17:21], "Who is like Thy people Israel, a nation unique on this earth?"

The verse from Deuteronomy 26:17–18, "Thou has avouched the Lord this day . . . the Lord has avouched thee this day," is a reference to the covenant. At stake here is the reciprocity, albeit a reciprocity between two absolutely dissymmetrical singularities. The reciprocity is between two uniquenesses: God's and Israel's. (The word *uniqueness* here is important as it is also Levinas's technical term in the later work for the election of the I in responsibility.) And just as the tefillin are called a crown of glory for Israel, so too God becomes glorified by being mentioned in man's tefillin.[18]

Levinas offers another important gloss on these texts almost twenty years later in the discussion following the lecture "Transcendence and Intelligibility": God's putting on tefillin, as well as the correspondence between the celestial and the terrestrial tefillin, expresses the intimacy and the correlation between God and man. For does not God say, in the words of Psalm 91:15, "I am with him in suffering"? (IR 281). Kenosis of God, once again! Rabbi Hayyim's own comments, in *Nefesh Hahaim*, Second Portal, chapter 11, are an important intertext here:

> The Midrash says, in effect: "R. Meir says: How does the Shekinah express his own lamentation over the suffering of man? 'That my head be comforted, that my arm be comforted.' Our teachers declared in the same manner [in the words of Song of Sol. 5:2] 'I was sleeping . . . I heard my beloved knocking, "Open to me . . . , my perfect one [*tematy*].'" Read not *tematy* ["perfect one"], but *teumaty*, ["twin"]. Just as when one twin has a headache, the other feels it, so too God says [to Israel], "I am with him in suffering." [Ps. 91:15][19]

Levinas paraphrases and glosses R. Hayyim of Volozin's comment. For Levinas God's lament—"That my head be comforted, that my arm be comforted"—is the prayer of God whose head and arm are tied around by the cords of the tefillin, the prayer of God who carries all the weight of the suffering of Israel (IR 281–282). This would be the significance of the tefillin of the hand and the tefillin of the head.

Let me add some further comments about what may be at stake in the image of God praying in Levinas's philosophical works. In a footnote to "Enigma and Phenomenon" (1965), Levinas refers to but does not cite *Berakoth* 7b, which he also discusses in "Revelation in the Jewish Tradition." *Berakoth* 7b contains a rabbinic comment on God's saying to Moses, in Exodus 33:23: "And I will take away My hand and thou shall see My back": "Rabbi Ḥama b. Bizina said in the name of R. Simon the Pious: 'This teaches us that the Holy One, blessed be He, showed Moses the knot of the tefillin.'"

In other words, Moses did not see God's face, as he had requested. He saw God's back. But he did not see God's back either; he saw the knot of the tefillin on the back of the divine neck. Moses saw neither God's face (i.e., full presence) nor his back (a partial glimpse, limited and finite). He saw or found himself in relation to an absence. He saw an enigmatic mode of presentation, a proximity in retreat. And even if he did see God's back, as Scripture seems to suggest, what he saw was God—leaving. After all, when a trace leaves a trace, it leaves (T 357). "Anchoretism of the irrepresentable!" as Levinas characterizes it,[20] in which it is up to subjectivity—which Levinas calls, in "Enigma and Phenomenon," "enigma's partner" (CPP 70)—"to retain this insinuation" (CPP 67). Or, as he puts it in the same essay, "it is up to *me*" (CPP 66). There is, however, within this apparently negative theology a positive sense of God's retreat: its positive sense is responsibility to the other.[21]

The Religion of the Undoing of Religion

The next step of Levinas's paper is no longer a gloss on R. Hayyim. The relation between collectivity and prayer has been shown to be irreducible. It turns out that collectivity is not only constitutive of prayer in the religious sense; it is constitutive of prayer in the nonreligious sense. Levinas's argument proceeds as follows. Insofar as Judaism announces a three-term rather than two-term religious relationship, refusing any tête-à-tête with God that would take place without referral to the other and the other*s*, prayer can be seen as the very substance of Jewish life *qua* religious life. "Better still," he writes, and we must attend to this move, "in this (same) sense, prayer supports even in a Judaism that no longer wishes to be religious" (DF 271). But it is this very fact—namely the prolongation of prayer within a nonreligious as well as religious collectivity—that ought to, he says, "render us more circumspect with regard to this priority of prayer" (DF 271), and here his remarks explicitly take on what he calls a "pedagogical" character. Recall that Levinas is speaking at a conference on the "Situations of French Jewry." For a session entitled "The Philosophy of Prayer," he was asked how he would respond to a nonobservant young man (a rationalist and a materialist, no doubt) who expresses some interest in Judaism, and how he would explain prayer. He is speaking, then, to a Jewish organization in the professional capacity of cultural critic. (Many of the essays reprinted in *Difficult Freedom* reflect the similar pragmatic contexts in which Levinas's thoughts were originally formulated.)

"We live in an open world [*un monde ouvert*]. The Jewish collectivity is attracted (or tempted) by all the activities of the modern world, rational and political commitments *which are experienced religiously*. Religious salvation, on the other hand, is seen as no longer possible so long as reason and justice are left unsatisfied" (DF 271; emphasis mine). Such a (secular) Judaism has become a search for social justice. Judaism has become a humanism, in effect, a humanism of the other man. With these remarks, Levinas registers the fact of assimilation as decisive for Jewish modernity. One should take care to note that Levinas by no means regards assimilation as a bad thing. On the contrary (given his own haskalah background and given the encounter he himself stages between Judaism and modern philosophy), he would probably endorse the formulation of Gerson Cohen regarding "the blessing of assimilation" in Jewish history.[22] Levinas acknowledges that for the contemporary Jewish consciousness, prayer, which he has described as the very substance of Jewish religious life, no longer opens up (*ne s'ouvre plus*) in the direction of God and humanity. The Judaism of the house of prayer is, in fact, "no longer transmissible" (DF 271). Our collective prayer has become, paradoxically, a form of isolated, solitary prayer (*une prière d'isolés*). In Levinas's metaphorical terminology, a room with windows has become walled up.

One is reminded here of the equally unsparing diagnosis offered by Franz Rosenzweig, who says, in the lecture collected in *On Jewish Learning* entitled "*Zeit ist's*" ("It is Time," a citation from Ps. 119): "the institutions of Jewish worship have become both the sieve as well as the reservoir for everything good in the tradition."[23] Levinas's circumspection with regard to the primacy of prayer turns out to be an assertion of the primacy of study. "We must return to Jewish wisdom, to the texts themselves" (DF 271), he says (in what is a repeated exhortation in *Difficult Freedom*), "The Judaism of reason must take precedence over the Judaism of prayer. The Jew of the Talmud must take precedence over the Jew of the Psalms" (DF 271).

Here, then, would be yet another inflection of this paper's title and question (this time rendered with an impatient shrug): Who prays? Who prays when the visible world is yet to be redeemed and there is social justice still to be accomplished? Who prays when there is so much Talmud to study? Not to mention phenomenology.

"We must follow," Levinas says, "with more confidence, the generous actions of youth, even when this youth . . . expressly refuses Judaism" (DF 271), that is, when their relation to the Judaic source is one of supreme ingratitude. (Did not Levinas himself write, in a 1963 essay, one year before "Education and Prayer," that "the radical generosity of the same who in the work goes unto the other . . . requires an ingratitude of the other. Gratitude would in fact be the return of the movement to its origin"[T 353])? Within the terms of

Levinas's argument, "the generous actions of youth" refer to step-ping outside the synagogue toward the secular collectivity. This step, which amounts to a certain "ingratitude," nevertheless affirms the one-way movement of generosity. It could be said to maintain the opening function of prayer. Levinas continues, "We must learn to read the signs. But where are the signs?" Not in the synagogue on Yom Kippur filled with once a year Jews, but in "less consecrated places, and in less assured persons"(DF 272).

Here follows the essay's central assertion: "Our election, that is, our irremissible responsibility, marks us, not so much in the solem-nity of worship, but in the flash of Talmudic genius when we are still capable of perceiving it" (DF 272). This election, which we should take in the sense of election to responsibility, can be perceived, in other words, in the secular prolongations of talmudic study, a study ideal that, in overtaking prayer's first place, still essentially under-stands itself in terms of collectivity:

> Election is manifested each time also there is struggle for a just cause among men, each time that — under a vocabulary which threatens to render it unrecognizable [*sous un vocabulaire qui menace de le render méconnaissable*], up to the point where its typi-cal physiognomy takes on unrecognizable features [*ignorant jus-qu'aux traits de sa typique physionomie*], the ancient message that guides these just struggles, as if by a miracle, shines through" (DF 270).

In short, such an election or responsibility — even a situation in which one's "own" language is not one's own and in which the form (but not necessarily the face) of Judaism has been disfigured — is still reli-gion, as Levinas defines it in *Totality and Infinity*, the nontotalizing bond with the other. Religion in this sense is ethics. And within a Jewish provenance, responsibility is still caught up with prayer — otherwise.

The Trace of Judaism

"But," Levinas writes, and we have learned to pay attention to the adversative clause in Levinas, "we must be open to [*il faut s'ouvrir à*] yet other signs." There is a risk attendant upon stepping outside the synagogue that Levinas points to: "Behold the builders of a better world — who in the name of Reason, ignore the Judgment — are enclosing and walling up our sons like the living bricks of biblical Egypt spoken of by the Talmud" (DF 272).[24]

The risk in secular (haskalah) Judaism is of becoming enslaved (in the name of liberation) to enlightenment values. The risk of stepping outside the synagogue toward the secular collectivity is that one steps out too far. This risk is that in the name of Reason, "the rational and political commitments that are now experienced religiously," one elides the biblical notion of Judgment that stems from the same source. In the Preface to *Totality and Infinity*, Levinas proposes an opposition between prophetic eschatology and the ontology of war. To the eschatological judgment, which institutes a relation with beings beyond the totality, is opposed to the "cruel and virile" judgment of history, associated with Hegel's philosophy of history, in which the deployment of reason in history excludes singularities (reduces them to instances of a universal concept) and leaves nothing outside itself. The eschatological judgment is not the last judgment but the judgment of all the instants in time when the living are judged, whereas the judgment of history, set forth in the visible, excludes the invisible, the victims, and is written, Levinas says, by the survivors. Levinas reinscribes the eschatological as the beyond of history which draws beings out of the jurisdiction of history and challenges the political and ontological concepts of totality that coincide in the term "war."[25]

If we look at Levinas's sentence again, however, "The builders of a better world—who in the name of Reason, ignore the Judgment—are enclosing and walling up our sons like the living bricks of biblical Egypt" (*comme les briques vivantes de l'Egypte biblique*), we realize that the phrase "living bricks of Egypt" does not refer to the spiritual servitude of biblical Israel in Egypt, as one might expect. In the Talmud it is a truly horrible image: "Whenever any deficiency was discovered in the measure of their daily bricks, the taskmasters of Pharaoh would go to the women of the children of Israel and take their infants from them, as many as the number of bricks lacking in the measure, they put into the building instead of the missing bricks."[26]

Levinas's hypotactic and demanding syntax continues, "And in these uniform bricks, which were supposed to prefigure a humanity based on equality, a strange germination is manifested—strange within such homogeneous matter—Difference, under which stirs an obstinate and difficult freedom."[27]

This sentence's difficulty is conceptual as well as syntactic. The uniform *blocs* in question would seem to be not just material but also

mental. It is as if, in the necessity to step outside Judaism in its prolongation from religious to nonreligious collectivity, there is a risk
that the struggle for difference be absorbed in indifference. The interchangeable *blocs* in which a future justice is envisioned risk eliding
the demand of the singular other. When ethical alterity is thus absorbed in homogeneity, a new walling up occurs, not to mention the
violence that is murder. But the specifically Judaic difference —
flagged by the term "difficult freedom" — is still legible under its era-
sure.

Abbreviations

BTV *Beyond the Verse.* Translated by Gary D. Mole. Bloomington: In-
diana University Press, 1994. *Au-delà du verset.* Paris: Minuit, 1982.
Contains "'In the Image of God' According to Rabbi Hayyim of
Volozin" [1978] and "The Names of God After Some Talmudic
Texts" [1967].
DF *Difficult Freedom.* Translated by Seán Hand. Baltimore, Md.:
Johns Hopkins University Press, 1990. *Difficile liberté.* Paris: Albin
Michel, 1976 [1963].
CPP *Collected Philosophical Papers.* Translated by Alphonso Lingis.
Dordrecht: Martinus Nijhoff, 1987. Contains "Enigma and Phe-
nomenon" [1965] and "God and Philosophy"[1975].
IR *Is it Righteous to Be? Interviews.* Edited by Jill Robbins. Stanford,
Calif.: Stanford University Press, 2001.
ITN *In the Time of the Nations.* Translated by Michael B. Smith.
Bloomington: Indiana University Press, 1994. *A l'heure des nations.*
Paris: Minuit, 1988. Contains "Judaism and Kenosis" [1985].
LR *The Levinas Reader* Edited by Seán Hand. Oxford: Blackwell,
1989. Contains "The Transcendence of Words" [1949] and "Of
Prayer Without Demand" [1982]. "De la prière sans demande,"
Les études philosophiques, n. 2 (1984).
OB *Otherwise than Being or Beyond Essence.* Translated by Alphonso
Lingis. The Hague: Martinus Nijhoff, 1987. *Autrement qu'être ou
au-delà de l'essence.* The Hague: Martinus Nijhoff, 1987.
T "The Trace of the Other" [1963]. Translated by Alphonso Lingis.
In *Deconstruction in Context.* Edited by Mark C. Taylor. Chicago:
University of Chicago Press, 1996. "La trace de l'autre." Re-
printed in *En découvrant l'existence avec Husserl et Heidegger.* Paris:
Vrin, 1974 [1967].

TI *Totality and Infinity.* Translated by Alphonso Lingis. Pittsburgh, Pa.: Duquesne University Press, 1969. *Totalité et infini.* The Hague: Martinus Nijhoff, 1961.

Thanks to Cathy Caruth, whose critical response to this paper significantly influenced its final form.

Becoming What We Pray:
Passion's Gentler Resolutions

EDWARD F. MOONEY

> Beyond the question of knowledge
> are poetry, madness, love —
> but if these are not and cannot be knowledge
> they may yet be best of all[1]

Toward the end of his reflective philosophical journal *The Inward Morning*, Henry Bugbee recalls a searing moment in the mid-Pacific during World War II when he served as captain of a minesweeper.[2] He recalls bringing down kamikaze pilots close enough that he and the crew of his small vessel could see the incoming pilots face-to-face. As that memory floods his present consciousness, he asks, pen in hand and eight years later, if it is not true that "*we were not enemies,*" though by all accounts they would have been. And he follows by asking how, if "we were not enemies," he could "be answer for those men, *living* men, perishing in flames"? He could be answer, he writes "only as I could articulate a true prayer."[3]

Could it be that "true prayer" might temper the pathos of that moment to yield a life lived as unqualified compassion? Is there a spot we might triangulate where passion, prayer, and life commingle?

Thanks to a member of Friends Meeting, Cambridge, for the words "we become what we pray."

I.

Prayer belongs to the life of the heart, to the life of the passions and the sufferings and joys of mood and emotion. Perhaps it is close to the divine madness of love and poetic inspiration as Plato described these in the *Phaedrus*. This would link prayer not just to passion but to poetic imagination.[4] And prayer works in less poetic contexts; it can clear the way for action or be a reflection on deeds past. Some pray before contests, and others pray for forgiveness. But even here there may be imagination, madness, and love. Insofar as prayer is akin to contemplation or meditation, it can align itself with intellect. In any event, even as it reaches out to poetry, deeds, or intellect, prayer seems firmly centered in the heart, in those passions that infuse the center of the person, the center of the soul.

If I am right in this, bringing prayer to view—the sort of "true prayer" Bugbee seeks—means placing it in passion's territory.[5] But in the main, at least since Plato, philosophers have been suspicious of passion, taking its clearest exemplars to be the irrational disruptions of violent fear, anger, or grief. The gentler passions—wonder, sympathy, or attachment—unfortunately get buried when attention gets fixed on the more violent passions that surely *can* subvert a worthy life. The disparagement of passion goes hand in hand with the elevation of knowledge and pure intellect, which are seen as models of *dispassion*. In a measured account, legitimacy would remain for a love of wisdom or attachments to friends or a quickness to be outraged at injustice. But the central story has passion signal a loss of composure, a wild abandon, or a mindless zealotry. So bringing prayer to view requires bringing passion back from disrepute. I here portray prayer as a refinement of passion and, correlatively, as a refinement of identity, a tempering and realignment of the soul.[6]

In his moment of crisis, Henry Bugbee finds himself called to articulate—live out—a true prayer. This places prayer partly in inwardness. Yet the refinement of a personal identity prepared by prayer gets played out publicly as well. Articulating "true prayer," in his case, will amount to meeting others with compassion. So however private prayer may seem, it often gets realized in community and can take its cue from there. When prayer is linked to vocation, its sense is negotiated in communities whose identities are themselves consolidated through ceremonial prayers and public pledges. Apart from prayers, personal callings, too, can be responsive to public attestations. Derrida's "I have lived in prayer" and his invocation of St. Augustine is a call to Jack Caputo, who responds, inwardly but also publicly, with *The Prayers and Tears of Jacques Derrida*.[7] And this then sets us all rethinking prayer, sometimes in solitude, sometimes in open forums. These public attestations lay out a space for prayer.[8]

The world or space of prayer that Derrida or Caputo circumscribes is quite other than the world of Teresa of Avila, say, whose prayerful tears watered the garden of her Lord. Kierkegaard, in still another vein, confides that prayer, like possibility, is the breath of spirit—and thus prayer makes space for life's necessary passions.[9] Another point of orientation for placing a prayer that could clarify the passion of our calling might be Wittgenstein's remark that "faith is a passion, while wisdom is cool gray ash."[10] This underlines the tension already noted between the loves and faiths that set out and support our course or calling and the more dispassionate pull of cool reason or the subtle beckoning of wisdom.

II. The Happy Inevitability of Passion

Lacking time and resource for anything like a survey, let me offer an impressionistic sketch of the fate of the passions, starting with the deathbed scene where Socrates sends the mourners packing. In keeping with disdain for passion's excess, he makes an offering in his final words to Asclepius, a god of healing. It is as if he is thankful that death will bring relief from passion's tumults.[11] Tears and grief are false, misplaced, perhaps always, but certainly in the event of death.[12] It is the better part of wisdom to nip unruly passion in the bud. Yet surely there is a place not just for tears at the demise of those we love but also for warm delight in the welcome of the living. Furthermore, a strictly Stoic view cannot credit Socrates with the passions to which he already accords great honor. I think of the Socratic passions of wonder, of love of knowledge, of hatred of pretense and fraud, and the passion to preserve one's civic hearth. Despite Wittgenstein's pronouncement, wisdom has its warmer side.

Plato's view is more nuanced than commonly assumed. He scorns lowly passions but prizes passion's outrage at indignity, a gut reaction essential to an effective military temperament.[13] And love of learning and of beauty and the good are undeniably essential. In Christian traditions, although lustful passions and many vices of the passions are appropriately viewed as demonic, an intense love of God can hardly be disparaged. Ascetic practices rein in passions, but only, so it seems, to make room for *proper* passion. David Hume, a pillar of the Enlightenment, declares reason to be a slave of passion. Without a motivating passion, he sees no way for reason to gain traction. Kierkegaard links faith to passionate inwardness, and Sartre sees freedom as a passion—albeit a "useless" one. Tillich speaks of the primitivity of "ultimate concern,"[14] which sounds quite like a passion. Being gripped by a "passion for the impossible" is a familiar theme in Derrida, a thought that echoes Kierkegaard's passionate interest in "the paradox." In quite another vein, Bertrand Russell confides that "Three passions, simple but overwhelmingly strong, have governed my life: the longing for love, the search for knowledge, and unbearable pity for the suffering of mankind."[15] From these glancing allusions it is clear that passion can at times receive a positive philosophical review.

Let us look more closely at the *welcome inescapability* of passion in human affairs. Socrates prizes rational critique, but passion fuels its movements. Darwin notes our capacity for laughing and crying, which express the passions of grief, delight, and melancholy. Setting philosophical worries aside, it is hard *not* to take us as creatures of consuming joy and anguish, anger and fear, hope and despair, wonder, ambition, and envy. We are surely capable of great love and great hate. There is something deeply human about Achilles and Ahab *despite* the fact that they model rage. And it is clear that not all passion is dangerous or unruly. "Passion" covers a wide and varied field. We are subject to grand passions and lowly ones (envy, malice, and hoarding) and to a slew of unimposing ones. The *Oxford English Dictionary* takes passion as "an eager, out-reaching interest toward things,"[16] which allows love of reading, gathering stamps, or interest in the news to count as passion. Whether banal or grand or lowly, passion can be aptly characterized as primitive. Without it, no capacity definitive of our nature could get in gear.

Without passions, there would be no urge to speak or know or do. We would have no language, knowledge, or action. There would be no urge to care or to commit, to till land or measure stars, to make cities, art, or bridges. Yet the standard anglophone approach to understanding human beings takes language, knowledge, and practical agency as the essential "primitives" from which to build.[17] The view that passion is a primitive controverts this standard view. Passion is what *animates* our language use, our pursuit of knowledge, our interest in free action, not to mention our concern for art or ethics, God or justice. Without that animating energy, we would have neither cultural structures nor interest in them, neither recognizably human lives nor accounts of them, neither language, nor knowledge, nor action.

We might picture passion metaphorically as an energy that is wide and unsettled like the sea.[18] Bertrand Russell pictures the passions governing his life as "great winds, [that] have blown me hither and thither, over a deep ocean of anguish."[19] This is preferable to some standard mechanistic views that figure passion as a set of "drives" and it also improves on the common assimilation of passion to "Eros" or desire. Awe and grief are modes of passion but neither has the immediate look of a desire. Kierkegaard's Climacus speaks of grief's passion not as a sea but as a river. He describes an old man bent in sorrow uttering a choked sigh. "Feeling," he observes, "is like the river Niger in Africa; no one knows its origin, no one knows its mouth, only its course is known."[20] The same might be said of passion: we know neither its source nor its terminus, but only its course at a particular time and place, even as its flow congeals as grief or perhaps as awe or compassion. The several phases of the variable sea of passion can be mapped more systematically. States of emotion (say, rage) can be helpfully distinguished from pervasive moods (for example, melancholy), which in turn contrast with irruptions of feelings (excitement) or long-term interests, concerns, or desires.[21] The capacious and informal view that I offer here takes moods, emotions, feelings, and concerns as so many forms that passion can assume.

III. Passion and Prayer

Say we become what we pray as we live out "true prayer." That will be true because our course or calling, all that we become, is a matter of the incoming and outgoing of phases of passion. The detail of these eager outreachings and retreats makes up the story of our identity or character. The prayerlike plea "Why has Thou forsaken me!" might well up from fear, anger, or despair—in any case, a cry wells up as passion. Person, cry, and prayer are linked in passion's primitivity. Fear fuels flight but also flows toward the anger of attack or toward beseeching, prayerlike cries for help. Tears fuel grief or mourning and their adjunct prayers. Passion phased as grief can migrate toward an aching need for consolation and for such understanding as might lift the burden of this need. Such modulated grief can culminate in petitionary prayer: "Help my affliction!"—which is a cry of passion that sustains grief and pleads for recognition of a need. As a vector in the field of passion, prayer can gather grief and mourning to venture out beyond themselves; prayer can move the afflicted self from despair toward passionate reinvestment in the world. A similar fluid transformation can be traced from primitive elation to delight and celebration, culminating in prayers of gratitude or praise. Prayer then becomes an extension of delight-in-the-world.

The drama of a king in Shakespeare's *Winter's Tale* displays passion's fluid moves from jealousy to rage, from rage to remorse, from remorse to mourning, from mourning to wonder, from wonder to serenity.[22] A Christian drama might depict passion's moves from rage to fear to stark despair and then, perhaps, to humility, joy, or a still serenity—an ongoing tempering of passion ministered by prayer. Prayer can move those passions that place us beside ourselves and out of sorts (in grief or anger, say) toward less rending or disruptive ones. It can challenge the arrogance of anger, remind a giddy joy that perishing, too, exists, rescue grief from despair, and open doors on hope. We might imagine Christian prayer as a fluid "energy exchange" within a field of love, with love's eager reaching-out-toward-another-love being met by a returning loving reach. If love, through such mutual reinforcement, has a capacity for increase within the ecology of passion, this might explain its power to move more violent passions (anger, fear, or grief) toward gentler, less self-assertive ones (compassion, wonder, or mercy). Achilles directs his prayer toward a god who will intensify his wrath or gird up his courage. A Christian prayer would call on love to palliate a violent passion. Love flows reciprocally from above to below and from below, above. It is worth remembering that passions, as I take them, are not agitations within a self-enclosed Cartesian consciousness. They are channels or conduits of connection, of attachment, that carry animating two-way impulses and in fact *are* those impulses, both incoming and outgoing.

Prayer is passion that is quiet but inwardly intense—a lively immobility. Physical immobility calms violent expressions, making space for a gentler passion's alert mobility. Prayer can start only as the vehemence of an agitating passion subsides, permitting change to quieter keys. A devotee of gentle, petitionary prayer allows its ameliorating presence to work among the passions. In the event of grief or fear, it recognizes an urgent need for rescue. It embodies humility in the recognition that human artifice is unequal to the task of answering that need. And it willingly, patiently awaits whatever deliverance may be offered from a more-than-human source.

Reason might suppress wrath, taking on the role of a tribunal with authoritative jurisdiction. But prayer would counter wrath differently, through a caring, pleading empathy—passion to passion, mercy to anger. From this angle, the question is not "Shall reason prevail?" but "Which passion shall prevail?" Anger interrupted by prayer confirms the ministrations of a quieter, tender passion that, however hidden or unnoticed, is already presently engaged. Prayer takes up with fear or anger as like to like. It does not suppress a passion from the presumed superior vantage of reason but instead cajoles and pleads and waits, one passion to another. Prayer awaits a gentler ecology of passion where love presides.

Not only petitionary prayers but prayers of praise or gratitude can also work as passion, as ameliorating passion. Say we are struck in astonishment at the grandeur of a scene, unsure if we are large or small before it, as in the onset of a wondrous sublime, itself a kind of passion. Prayers of gratitude might ease the tension between this passion and its competitors—say, an inflated sense of self or an abased humiliation. In clarifying gratitude, it might release one to a less anxious or intoxicated access to the world.

Granting this rough placement of prayer amidst passion in the unfolding of the moods and attachments and disappointments of a life, it is natural to step back at this point to consider two questions. First, if we set reason to one side, what will regulate the passions? Second, what about recipients of prayer? To speak of prayer, do we not need assurance that someone (or something) is really there to listen?

IV. Is Passion Self-Correcting?

The telos of gentle, purifying prayer is openness to otherness, the otherness of all that elicits wonder or love, gratitude or generosity. In the ecology of passion, this telos encourages an equilibrium slanted toward the tender Christian virtues. (Of course, these virtues are not Christianity's alone.) When it is activated in prayer, this pull among passions toward the openness and receptivity of love is like the pull among opinions toward consistency and correctness. There is no guarantee we will be correct in belief or that we will let a pull toward correctness have its way. Likewise, there is no guarantee that our dispositions will be correctly aligned or that we will let the pull toward love have its way. But a kind of regulative ideal may nevertheless be at work. Why not propose that cognitions and passions each incline toward propriety or truth?[23]

Of course, truth is not single here, for if truth is a measure of worth, the worth of cognitions is assessed on a different scale than the worth of passions. We have true friends, true grief, and true prayer, as well as true opinion. In matters of truth, of whatever sort, we seek the rather abstract desiderata of coherence, appropriateness of fit, and proper causal and cultural antecedents. A person's grief should cohere with what we know of a wider narrative of her history; it should have fittingness to the situation of its expression; and it should not be induced by drugs or threats or brainwashing. Otherwise we would face false grief. The daunting problem is to fill in what would concretely satisfy these desiderata in contested instances where it is urgent to know of friends if they are true, or of grief or opinion if it is true or false.[24]

Hume held that sentiments can be self-correcting, a more worthy sympathy reversing a less worthy indifference or aversion.[25] Just as better cognitions keep worse ones in check, so better passions might ride herd on unruly ones. Achilles prays to Apollo, mobilizing courage to correct melancholy, complacency, or an anxious dispersal of interest. He pleads for the better passion to prevail. Similarly, a prayer that one be enabled to forgive corrects a passion for vengeance, and seeking a life of true prayer corrects a passion for violent confrontation. One shuns false passion. (At least we hope one's better self does.)

We might picture the deep primitivity of passion fanning out as mood, feeling, concern, or emotion, and developing a sort of open-ended ecology of passion characteristic of identity or calling. Within this loose ecology, the pressures of more "mature" or "reality-sensitive" or "worthy" passions, through the alembic of their extension into prayer, work to constrain those that are darker or lowly. They aim to purify or refine the tainted heart in the way critique aims to purify or refine a rough and tangled mind.

V. To Whom Is Prayer Addressed?

Even if we take prayer to be a moderating phase of faithful passion, to its devout practitioners it is more than gentle contemplation. The faithful address their prayers to the divine and then await an answer. So far we have said nothing about the destination of a prayer. Perhaps Henry Bugbee's plea for strength to live out true prayer puts the stress where it belongs: on the living-out rather than on whoever (or whatever) might receive the plea. Nevertheless, there clearly is a plea here, which raises the issue: To whom is it addressed? The uncertainty of our response — the uncertainty of what we might name by "God" or "the divine" — marks a feature of the playing field. It reminds us that prayers are by their nature conducted in a surround of inexpugnable uncertainty. In detached, dispassionate objectivity, we know next to nothing about how mortals and gods communicate, if they do. Nevertheless, those who pray have hunches and convictions that go with a cultivated, invested interest.

There is nothing unusual or irregular about this tension between objective uncertainty and a living, engaged conviction born of care and cultivated sensibility. We "know" where the stress belongs in this line of poetry, in this line of music, in this response to a child's effort. Such instilled sensitivity is won through practice in the terrain. There might be little of an objective nature that we could cash in in support of our hunches here. By analogy, we might address our prayers to an unknown and indeterminate recipient, and sense (or "know") in our bones that we are on track with this. We have "been there," as we might think, and know the feel of the place. Yet we would quickly own up, if we were asked for a less engaged, more detached appraisal of the matter, to being beset by a troubling objective uncertainty.

Take a painter who sees her work as clarifying a passion and whose activity is, in that respect, like prayer. As she paints, she may have an audience or addressee in mind — but then again, she may not. If she does, she nevertheless has no obligation to divulge the identity of her addressee. One might say that the form of her activity presupposes an intended audience. But she still might not know or reveal her "real-life" audience, the person or persons to whom she presumably addresses her work. She might feel her work was addressed toward some vague and unnamed intended recipient whose reality is yet to be established. "I paint for the eyes of another age," she says, when asked. She insists that her primary attention as an artist and our primary focus as art lovers should be on the painting itself, on what it does or will do, on what it says or will say, on how it says it, on what it shows and how. To inquire of the addressee is not only to ask (in this case) a question without a helpful answer; it is also to distract from the painting itself.

Or consider a love sonnet — an intimate expression of the heart that is only haltingly made public. We might have no clue as to the "real-life identity" of the intended recipient. A Shakespeare sonnet might be addressed to a man or woman, old or young, real or fancied.

We just do not know. But we are none the worse for this. And perhaps our not knowing keeps our attention where it belongs: on love and the work of love, not on relatively extraneous historical concerns. The passion of the poetry shines through no less for all our ignorance.[26] The passion of our prayers shines through no less for all our ignorance.

Prayers of the form "Grant us peace!" or "Forgive my impatience!" imply an intended addressee, but to understand their thrust we need not fill in the addressee's whereabouts, powers, name, or status. The epistemological challenge is defused as we grant an objective uncertainty while sustaining the certitude that accompanies trust in a venture like composing a sonnet or a portrait intended for an indefinite or unidentified other, a trust that animates a sense of "knowing one's way about." A minimalist communicative frame specifies only an open place for an intended recipient, present or absent, attentive or distracted, namable or beyond names, all-powerful or less than all-powerful. Different prayers, different devotees, will articulate a trust in an intended recipient in ways implying different theologies. But these more theoretical elaborations rest on this narrower, minimalist assurance that to ground the communicative thrust of prayer, it is enough to have the open-ended, incomplete idea of an intended recipient. This does nothing to unsettle but instead sustains the guiding insight that the fundamental context in which prayer comes alive is caught in a passion-based account.

Yet we can still ask why the intended recipient of prayer should be more than human. A brief answer would suggest that prayer sets out to temper overweening passion, and thus it makes sense that prayer calls on non-Promethean powers to moderate or curb the urge toward total mastery. Calling on divinity is the other half of enacting humility.[27] Calling on "human powers only" in ultimate torment or distress *reaffirms* claims to human self-sufficiency, thus disowning finitude, disavowing deep limits to our effectuality. A more-than-human status for intended recipients of prayer keeps intact a humbling, tempering effect. This means that some thin content clings to prayer's intended recipients. But despite this thin content, skeptical worries about purported inhabitants of a transcendental realm will have no purchase if we concede a fundamental ignorance of that realm and its inhabitants. We pray not in knowledge but in ignorance. Our deepest convictions and passion exceed objective warrant, for they provide the context within which warrants play their part. A passion for truth and the conviction that its pursuit is worthwhile necessarily predate the business of rounding up warrants for holding on to more local convictions. Conversely, to have full knowledge and warrant at our disposal would reduce the play of conviction and passion.[28] Prayer abides this tension between passionate conviction and objective uncertainty.[29]

VI. Prayer in the Cadence of Life

We now take up a philosopher's evocation of prayer in the course of his reflections on an eventful life. Henry Bugbee wrote his philosophical journal at the end of his stay as a Harvard professor in the mid-1950s. Here is life with a full measure of delight and deep calling, of wonder and even terror. His reflections in *The Inward Morning* do not center on prayer, but this makes the few spots when it does rise to the surface all the more striking.[30] Such moments of prayer arrive unheralded, without fanfare. Prayer is linked to vocation, and Bugbee offers several angles on his calling, including one that frames it surprisingly as *a meditation of the place*.[31] Perhaps the place that calls for meditation is the place of moving waters or of teaching; it might be the place of still mountains or of violent battles. We could say his passions are enacted as a mobile meditative prayer. And the prayers, the philosophical meditations, are worked out, as William James put it, *ambulando*. Their sense is worked out in walking them out, living them out, in what Bugbee calls a *walking* meditation of the place.[32]

Midway through *The Inward Morning*, Bugbee places us knee-deep in a rushing stream following a day of disciplined casting on the waters.[33] In that quiet moment beneath vaulting redwoods in the whisper of the river's flow, he offers prayerful thanks, *just for being there*. This thankful offering is continuous with the passionate attention, the reaching out, of the fisher's task. Thanksgiving is a phase of passion. The passions of work and gratitude become one as his identity gathers in a prayerful offering: "It is a glorious thing to know the pool is alive with these glancing, diving, finning fish. But at such moments it is well to make an offering in one's heart to the still hour in the redwoods ascending into the sky. . . . On such mornings, too, one may even catch nothing at all."[34]

Later still, we join him as he meets a beckoning hour of teaching. A familiar bell declares the time across the campus green. It bespeaks, he says, "the namelessness of that which we must serve."[35] And he finds himself again in a prayerful mood, placed patiently, humbly, before demands he can hardly name. When teaching lifts above banal routine, we must all be struck by "the namelessness of that which we must serve." Mission statements hardly say it. "The good and true" are just other names for nameless mystery. And prayerfulness seems right as we absorb the yawning gaps between the gravity of what *must* be said and our stumbling efforts. That which we must serve addresses us, even as we are at a loss to specify by whom or what we are addressed. And we pray for wit and strength to meet these demands, even as we are at a loss to specify the recipient of this prayer. Awaiting class, he waits on openness and energy to meet his calling gracefully, responsibly. He waits not in knowledge but in ignorance and yet in trust upon a sea of faith that he may be equal to the hour. At that moment, prayer might refine and clarify the passion of one's calling, the passion of one's being.

Prayer is also invoked dramatically on the occasion we have visited, an occasion more ominous than casting for trout or casting for words to meet the hour. We remember that moment at sea in the Pacific when kamikazes descended on the ship in his command. Gunners open fire, ship and plane slide unwaveringly toward mutual doom. On the bridge he waits, then returns fire, then finds the pilot so close that they are face-to-face. *What is it to be known* by another in such circumstance? Something unspeakable:

> I think of the suicide planes that I *witnessed*. They still call out to me, lives perishing in flames. What, what indeed, can I make of them? Oh, I must be answer for these men. Men I never knew. Living men. How can I find answer except as I can articulate a true prayer? Is it not true that we were not enemies? And who will believe this, how can it be believed?[36]

There were no prayers at the time, only desperate action. Five years after, Bugbee can relive that crisis, working through the desperate horror. He is called to compassion, regard, even reverence, for all things of creation, under siege of war or no. He is called to honor his communal ties to others, expressed through his wartime service. Responding to this call to military service necessarily rips the fragile remnants of would-be encompassing compassion. The heat of these colliding passions is by no means abstract. His guns bring down a man in flames—not a faceless "enemy" but a pilot he has known face-to-face.

In this impossible strait, he asks how his life can be answer for those lives, perishing in flames. He can address the "unfinished business" delivered on that fateful day, be answer for those lives, only as his life articulates true prayer. To articulate true prayer he first asks "Is it not true that we were not enemies?" True prayer does not continue violence by continuing to name enemies. Yet this refusal of violence is conjoined with another stark realization: "And who will believe this, how can it be believed?" The clash of these dark passions—that there are enemies, that there are no enemies—is answered not intellectually, not dogmatically, not blindly but by taking simple steps, steps that will enact the passional truth, "we were not enemies."

That this was not a confrontation of enemies bent on mutual destruction seems unbelievable. From the standpoint of ordinary possibilities, how could Bugbee hold the view, "we were not enemies"? Yet in the grip of compassion and his deepest humanity, the writer holds to that impossibility, "we were not enemies."[37] Prayer tips the passional balance toward compassion and works out its resolution by taking steps.[38] One is answer for those men not as one speaks or thinks on this or that occasion but as one *makes the truth of compassion true* — by walking through remaining life in compassion that is unstinting. As one *makes* something true in the gentle composure of steps, one is answer for those men. "True prayer" tempers passional conflict through being true to gentler passions; its mercy and compassion consolidate identity in gentleness.

There are prayers of gratitude for the world and prayers that one may be equal to the day. Like these, prayers in dark times require maximal openness to otherness. The wholly other, in this instance, is the terrifying collision between Bugbee as captain of a minesweeper engaged in deadly combat and Bugbee as fellow creature embracing the preciousness of life. Prayer opens the soul to intractable passional collision, gathering those passions it must register truthfully. It opens the soul to the "impossible possibility" that a faithful passion can emerge from this cruel crucible. And it unfolds as a life in answer to those perishing in flames. It unfolds as steps taken to make the unbelievable now believable. This walk makes it true that writer and pilot known face-to-face are at last not enemies.

As gentle passions ease from violently conflicting ones, prayer becomes a faithful encounter with the other, under whatever guise.

4

Prayer as Kenosis

JAMES R. MENSCH

Prayer, both private and public, is one of the most common of human activities. All human history records it; its roots probably go back to before recorded history. Yet when we attempt to submit its most common form, that of petition, to philosophical analysis, we run into difficulties. All too often we pray for things, such as victory or gaining a desired position, and forget that there are losers in such competitions. Prayer, here, seems caught in the "mimetic violence" that René Girard describes. According to Girard, our socialization involves our imitating others. It thus leads us to desire what they desire and hence to compete with them, often in violent ways, for possession of a desired object.[1]

Our focus on objects in petitionary prayer also seems to trap us within what may be called an "earthly economy." We pray to God for some object and often promise something to God, some sacrifice on our part, in return. As Plato long ago noted, the piety evinced by such prayer "would then be a sort of trading skill between gods and men"—one involving a mutual exchange of benefits (*Euthyphro*, 14e). The difficulty is that the gods neither need nor depend on our sacrifices (13c). What benefit could the gods receive from us? How can we enter into a process of exchange with them? (15a) Plato's critique, which Derrida repeats, makes us ask: How can prayer relate us to the sacred? How can we ask for things and not be trapped in an "earthly economy?"[2]

To answer these questions, I propose to examine prayer phenomenologically—that is, in terms of the appearing of the sacred. My thesis is that the above difficulties can be resolved if we can see prayer as the attempt to provide a space where the sacred can appear. The key concepts here are those of kenosis and incarnation. Providing a space for the sacred, I shall argue, involves a form of kenosis or self-emptying, one that permits the sacred in petitionary prayer to incarnate itself in our bodily being and behavior.

Two Concepts of the Sacred

The first and perhaps most basic concept of the sacred seems to stand opposed to any attempt to analyze it phenomenologically. Phenomenology is the study of appearing, but the sacred seems to signify what cannot appear. The Israelites believed that no one can see God face-to-face and live (Exod. 33:20). The Greeks, too, had a sense of the killing splendor of God. When Zeus fulfills his promise to Semele to show himself as he is, he does so in a bolt of lightening, reducing her to ashes.[3] Behind such examples stands the notion of the otherness of the god, of its not fitting into the contexts in and through which things are normally given.

Such contexts are those of the "earthly economy"—that system of exchange through which things come to us. Our bodily metabolism with its organic needs is an example of this economy; so are our normal, everyday commercial transactions. They point to our dependence on the world, that is, to the fact that we live only through a constant process of exchange with it. The otherness of the sacred manifests itself in its not being part of this economy. Thus, the Greek root of the Latin, *sacer*, means "safe," in the sense of being kept apart or reserved for the divinity.[4] As consecrated to the god, the sacred cannot be used by us. One cannot, for example, cut down and use the timber of a sacred grove. The trees forming the grove are inviolate. One should not, in fact, even enter the grove. As Sophocles has the stranger say to Oedipus, who has strayed into a sacred place, "It is forbidden to walk on that ground. . . . It is not to be touched."[5] A similar sense of the sacred is present in God's first encounter with Moses.[6]

Fortunately for our purposes, there is a second notion of the sacred, one that has an equal place with the first. This is the sense of the sacred as coming into the world by incarnating itself. Zeus, for example, can appear on earth as a wanderer, one to whom we owe the obligation of hospitality. For the Israelites, God becomes present in the law he gives to Moses. The law is their "life." It is that which makes them into God's people.[7] The most striking example of incarnation is, of course, that of Christ. In its specifically Christian sense, incarnation involves the notion of *kenosis*, that is, of God in Christ emptying himself and taking on the form of a slave (Phil. 2:7).

This self-emptying can be seen as a response to the problem raised by the biblical concept of the alterity of God. God is the absolute creator of the world. As such, he exists prior to the world and hence independently of it. His creative action, as responsible for the world, cannot have worldly constraints or conditions. It thus cannot be made manifest by a worldly process. Accepting this, we face the problem of the presence of God. If God's being is *before* the world, how can he appear *within* the world? How does this being manifest itself *as it is*? Closely related to this is the problem of what may be called the "killing splendor" of God. The prohibitions against seeing God face-to-face imply that were God to appear as he is, he would burst the bounds of the world. His appearance would be deadly in its overwhelming splendor. Given this, how are we to conceive the Incarnation? Kierkegaard puts this problem in terms of the love that the Incarnation is supposed to make manifest. Referring to God's telling Moses, "man may not see Me and live," (Exod. 33:20), he writes: "there was a people who had a good understanding of the divine, this people believed that to see the god was death."[8] Given this, how can his love appear? In Kierkegaard's words, "Who grasps the contradiction of this sorrow: not to disclose itself is the death of love; to disclose itself is the death of the beloved."[9]

The Christian answer to these difficulties involves the divine kenosis that Paul mentions in Philippians 2:7. The verb Paul uses means "to empty out" or "make void." The New International Version of the Bible translates it as "made himself nothing." To take this literally is to see the Incarnation as the progressive emptying out of God, one that culminates in the Cross. This is because such self-emptying is the only way that God can manifest his *nonworldly* being. He shows himself *as he is* by exhibiting a lack of such being—that is, by being outside the earthly "economy." Such exhibition is his manifestation *in* the world of his being *outside* the world. It is, phenomenologically, his giving himself as not-being-able-to-be-given in the terms of this economy—that is, in terms of its power and might. To accomplish this, he must empty himself. He must, in Paul's words, take on "the form of a slave" and identify himself with the powerless and oppressed. This self-emptying, or becoming nothing, comes to completion with his death on the Cross.

The Gospels use a number of examples to illustrate the connection between incarnation and kenosis. I shall mention only two of the most striking. In the Last Judgment, according to Matthew, Christ will admit into his kingdom those who fed him when he was hungry, who gave him drink when he was thirsty, who clothed him when he was naked, who made him welcome when he was a stranger, and visited him when he was in prison. When asked by the elect, "When did we do this?" he replies that it was when they did it "to one of the very least"—that is, to the hungry, the naked, the rejected of society (Matt. 25:33–40). The completion of this self-emptying is, I said, Christ's appearance on the Cross. At the end of his earthly life, he appears as the wretched creature who, like Job, cries out, "My God, my God, why have you deserted me?" (Matt. 27:46). In Christ's very nakedness and exposure, Christians are supposed to see God.[10]

How does this vision of God on the Cross accord with the above mentioned "killing splendor of God"? Phenomenologically speaking, we have to say that the two concepts of the sacred, rather than contradicting each other, designate alternative ways of relating to the sacred. Thus the Crucifixion does not deny such splendor; it does, however, exhibit it by its absence. To see the divine splendor and *live* is to grasp this splendor in its absence from the worldly context. This does not mean that this splendor does not, in a certain sense, appear. It must, if we are to see the Crucifixion as the culmination of the Incarnation and see the Incarnation as manifesting God's love (1 John 4:9). In Kierkegaard's terms, what we have here is a disclosure of the divine love that does not result in the death of the beloved. Manifesting a complete lack of worldly power and might, Christ on the Cross exhibits the splendor of the love for the beloved that proceeds to the point of death. What is disclosed here is the splendor of the divine kenosis that exhibits this love.

The alternate way of relating to the sacred involves bypassing the Incarnation in favor of an unmediated vision of God. This is generally attempted in two opposing ways. The perishing that results has, correspondingly, two different senses. In the first way, which is that of mystical vision, we separate ourselves totally from the worldly context whose economy sustains our worldly life. Here, the vision of the divine draws us out of the world, out of all our human possibilities and resources, including those of aiding the poor and afflicted. The perishing that results is that of mystical rapture. As long as we are in its grasp, we are dead to the world. In the second way, instead of our leaving the world, we attempt to draw God into the earthly economy. Here, we treat the sacred as a good we can consume. We try to use God to gain a political, social, or economic advantage. The perishing that results from this attempt consists in all the political, social, and economic disasters that have so marred the history of our relation to the divine. To speak in this context of the killing splendor of God is to remind ourselves of them. It is to draw the moral lesson of the sense of the sacred as that which is "set apart" and "not to be touched."

Kenosis as Receptivity

The above implies that if we wish to encounter God within the world, it must be on an appropriate level. Given that this level is one of "absence" and "lack," how is this possible? God is in the world by virtue of having emptied himself. To encounter him, we must also empty ourselves. Through such kenosis, we provide a space in which he can appear. Self-emptying is, in other words, a form of receptivity.

The Bible provides us with two figures or types to understand this relation. The first is the "empty waste" that existed before creation. The second is the creative breath, the *ruah* or "spirit of God," that hovers over it. In the Bible, creation is accomplished through this breath. Hence when God creates Adam, it is by exhaling. Having fashioned Adam from the "dust of the soil," Genesis relates that "he breathed into his nostrils a breath of life, and thus man became a living soul"—in Hebrew, he becomes a *nefesh*, a living breath (Gen. 2:7). This action of creating by breathing out is repeated each time God expends breath to say "let there be." It is the general action of creation. As God says to Moses, in explaining why the Sabbath or seventh day should be set apart, "Between myself and the sons of Israel the Sabbath is a sign forever, since in six days Yahweh made the heavens and the earth, but on the seventh day he rested and drew [back in] breath" (Exod. 31:17, JB 118).[11]

In John's Gospel, Christ's claim to incarnate God is shown by his possession of this breath. John the Baptist recognizes Christ because he sees the spirit (the *hagios pneuma* or divine breath) descending and remaining with him (John 1:32–33).[12] As permanently possessing this Holy Spirit, Jesus must be the one who incarnates the very presence of God, the creator. He is also, however, according to Paul, the one who has emptied himself, becoming nothing. As such, he is equally in the position of the "empty waste" before creation. Emptying himself, he thus becomes the perfect figure of a pure receptivity to God's creative action. The receptivity is such that he receives and embodies this action. He takes it on as his own.[13]

If we make Christ our paradigm of this relation to the sacred, then the relation involves both self-emptying and receptivity. Thus, to engage in the prayer that brings one into such a relation with the sacred is to empty oneself so as to provide a space for the divine in the form of the Holy Spirit to appear. It is to imitate Christ as the self-emptying of God, as the one in whom the Holy Spirit or creative breath acts. Receptive to the Holy Spirit, one takes upon oneself its creative action. How are we to understand this? How can we imitate God's creative action *within the already created world*? As existing prior to all that is, God creates from nothing. Creative action thus occurs prior to its object. How can we engage in this?

There is a traditional Christian answer to this question. It frames the more general, phenomenological response I give below. Christians see creation in terms of the love that is prior to its object—the love that brings about what it desires. Such love is not a making. It is not a fashioning of something from something else. We imitate this creative love whenever we provide the space, the environment that allows the coming to be of the object. All forms of nurturing are examples of this creative, human love. A parent who engages in it creates the adult by providing the environment in which the child can grow and develop. The farmer does the same thing with regard to the seed. The seed without the proper receptivity of the soil cannot grow. The seed is as little the plant as the child is the adult. Both need the proper space in order for the "let-there-be" of creative action to occur. The frequent references to love in the Gospels point to the action of providing this space—that is, of allowing what will be to incarnate itself and hence come to be.

Empathy and Incarnation

A strictly phenomenological account of the relation of kenosis and incarnation can be made in terms of empathy. The word comes from the Greek *pathein*, "to suffer or undergo," and *en*, signifying "in." According to its etymological sense, the sense I shall employ, empathy is a *feeling* (a suffering or undergoing) of the world *in* and through another person. At its most basic level, empathy is bodily. Another person hurts his hand, and we reach for our own. We see someone cut himself, and we wince. In each case, we take on the other's flesh. We allow the other, at least as long as empathy lasts, to incarnate himself in us. This letting ourselves be shaped by the other's circumstances can extend to taking account of the other's bodily condition: sex, health, and so on. The same holds for the other's memories and anticipations. Insofar as these are known to us, they too can become components of our empathy.

In each case, empathy involves both a self-emptying and an assumption of the other—a letting him or her come to be in our person. Its moral aspect is shown by the impulse it gives to our following the "golden rule." If, through empathy, we have the capacity of experiencing the distress of others, then we refrain from harming them. Positively, we treat them as we would like to be treated. Both actions occur as a function of our taking on the selfhood of the other. The fact that variations of the golden rule are found in all the world's major religions is testimony to the universality of this capacity to assume another's selfhood.[14]

When empathy takes on its radical, religious form, it exhibits a striking combination of passivity and activity. Insofar as empathy involves kenosis, it can lead to a passivity to the other that is reminiscent of the passivity of the "empty waste" before the creative action of God. In its ultimate form, what we have is a passivity similar to that which Levinas speaks of in describing substitution. Experiencing it, we experience "the impossibility of evading the neighbor's call." We find that "we are not free to distance ourselves from him or her."[15] What we undergo is a "passivity without the *arche* of identity," one where our selfhood, our "ipseity is a hostage." In such a situation, Levinas writes, "The word 'I' means to be answerable for everything and for everyone."[16] In this radical substitution, self-responsibility becomes responsibility for the other. Incarnating the other becomes a "passion" involving "the assumption of the suffering and failings of the other."[17]

What we have here is a responsibility for the other's responsibility. Taking on the other's failings, we assume responsibility for the wrongs done by the other.[18] In the religious language that characterizes Isaiah's description of the suffering servant—a language mirrored by the Gospel's account of Christ—we take the other's sins upon ourselves. For both Levinas and the biblical accounts, this does not mean that we engage in the other's sins. Substituting ourselves for the other does not signify our assuming the other's lies, self-deceptions, and vices. It points to our assuming responsibility for the results of another's actions. The activity this implies is the other side of empathy. It is that of taking up the task of *undoing the harm* done by the other. This is the harm done to the others of this other, those others who can include ourselves. It is also the action that makes good the harm that the other does to himself. The result, then, of incarnating the other's needs and failings in our bodily being and behavior is a certain type of action. Ideally, this is the action of the "good works" that identify those who have assumed a relation to the sacred. For Christians, it is the action of the Holy Spirit.

Escaping Mimetic Violence and the Earthly Economy

When we imitate the other to the point of desiring what the other desires, we tend to enter into competition with the other. The result, in Girard's phase, is "mimetic violence." Such violence and the aggressive feelings that accompany it can be highly destructive of society. According to Girard, societies purge themselves of this aggression by directing it toward a sacrificial victim. The guilt its members feel for their actions is taken to be the guilt of the victim or "scapegoat." The scapegoat takes responsibility for the wrongs they have engaged in. Redirecting their mutual aggression toward the sacrificial victim, they do away with him or her. Murder relieves them of their sense of guilt. It quells, for a while, the violence that threatened to undermine social relations.[19] Such, according to Girard, is the pattern of "natural religion."

The uniqueness of Christ is that of reversing this natural religion. Christ is the *innocent* victim. He suffers not for his own but for our sins. His very innocence gives the lie to the victim's guilt. It thus gives the lie to the violence associated with the sacred. Meditating on his innocence, we are forced to recognize our own responsibility.[20] The incarnate empathy that I described has an equivalent effect. Understood as our imitation of Christ, it prevents us from projecting our sins onto the other. Imitating Christ, we *take on* the sins of the other. We assume them as part of our responsibility. In other words, in assuming responsibility for the other, the individual becomes himself the scapegoat. He or she takes up the task of undoing the harm done by mimetic violence.

There is a parallel reversal with regard to our involvement in the earthly economy. Christ's appearance as the victim is also his appearance as "one of the very least." It is his presence in the person of the poor, the dispossessed, and the afflicted. Insofar as the divine appears as need, our relation to it is not to some good that can be consumed. It is not a function of our appetites. As a call to relieve the distress of the other, the relation to the divine is a call *to be good* rather than to receive goods.

Levinas writes, in describing this relation to the sacred, "in order that the Desire beyond being, or [the desire for] transcendence, might not be an absorption . . . the Desirable or God must remain separated in the Desire; as desirable—near yet different, Holy." "This," he adds, "can only be if the Desirable commands me to what is the nondesirable, to the undesirable *par excellance;* to another."[21] This "undesirable" is the person in distress, the other who, in his poverty and privation, lacks everything I might desire. To direct me toward this other is to command me to see the goodness of God in this person's need. As Levinas puts the moral aspect of this, the Desirable or God, "is Good in this very precise, eminent sense: He does not fill me with goods, but compels me to goodness, which is better than to receive goods."[22] It is this focus on doing good rather than receiving goods that ultimately moves me beyond the earthly economy.

What Should We Pray For?

Given the above sense of the divine, the prayer that opens us up to the sacred is not a function of the earthly economy. Still less is it an expression of mimetic violence. It is, rather, an imitation of the divine in its action of kenosis. Engaging in it, we empty ourselves and open ourselves to the other. In this very action, we open a space for the divine in its creative action. The sense of this self-opening can be put in terms of our praying for another and for ourselves. In praying for the other, I do not compete with him but, rather, give way. I pray that good come to the other. Concretely, this means that I both pray that his need be met and take on this need. Taking it on, I attempt to relieve it. In other words, I assume, as much as I can, the action I pray for. Can I pray that my own needs be met? To deny that I can would seem to assume that I am of less worth than the other, that my own sufferings are somehow of less account. This cannot be taken for granted.

Accepting this, however, one must also admit that to receive goods is not necessarily to become good. Still less is a loss of goods to be considered as a decline in a person's moral worth. Insofar as prayer is a relation to the Goodness that makes one good, one can, therefore, pray for goods only as a *means* to do good. This implies that every petitionary prayer is also a promise. It is a promise to receive the object as a means, as a gift that one will pass on to the other. The same holds for one's prayers for the other. All goods, all fulfillments of needs, should be prayed for as a means to become good. Only by becoming good, rather than simply possessing goods, can we escape from the violence that characterizes the earthly economy. Only by doing so can we enter into a living relation with the sacred. To do so is to share in the unfathomable generosity of God's kenosis. It is to participate in his creative love. Doing so, we become the nurturing space that is receptive to the "let there be" of the action of this love.

The Prayers and Tears of Friedrich Nietzsche

BRUCE ELLIS BENSON

> I have firmly resolved within me to dedicate myself for-
> ever to His service. May the dear Lord give me strength
> and power to carry out my intention. . . . Yes, dear Lord,
> let thy face shine upon us forever! Amen!
>
> —*Aus meinem Leben*

> When I have looked into my *Zarathustra*, I walk up and
> down in my room, unable to master an unbearable fit of
> sobbing.
>
> —*Ecce homo*

From Nietzsche's first work to his last, one finds the intonation of
prayer and the stain of tears.[1] The child who weeps over the deaths
of father and brother becomes the man who sobs peering into the
abyss of the tragic or encountering a horse being abused. The child
who instinctively knew how to pray becomes the adult who struggles
to find a new way to pray, one that follows other instincts.

That transition from one sort of prayer to another is neither easy
nor simply instinctual for Nietzsche. Both Augustine's *Confessions*

Resonance here with John D. Caputo, *The Prayers and Tears of Jacques Derrida: Religion without Religion* (Bloomington: Indiana University Press, 1997) goes beyond
merely the title.

and Nietzsche's *Ecce homo* can justly be called "books of tears," as Derrida claims. Yet to what degree is *Ecce homo* truly, as Derrida says, a "Dionysian counter-confession"?[2] Does Nietzsche *reach* the Dionysian? Or does he merely tearfully long for it? One might be tempted to characterize Nietzsche's "confessions" in *Ecce homo* as the inverse of Augustine's—not the tortured move to faith but the tortured move away from faith. But my argument is that Nietzsche moves—and not all that successfully—from one faith to another. *Ecce homo* is thus a "confession" in both senses of that term: of things done and left undone and a statement of belief that is characterized by both a measure of belief and an aspiration to further belief. One might say that Nietzsche's mature faith still seems "all too Christian" rather than "purely Dionysian," so that *Ecce homo* bears a surprising connection to *Aus meinem Leben*. In opposition to those who interpret the adult Nietzsche as someone who has simply abandoned his childhood faith, I argue that his childhood faith proves decisive for his later philosophy.[3] What I hope to show is not merely the deeply religious quality of Nietzsche's thought but also the role that prayer plays in shaping that thought.

There are two aspects to the following analysis. First, I argue that Nietzsche remains a person of faith and prayer, though he attempts to shift both the logic and the content of that faith and prayer. Of course, I am using the terms "faith" and "prayer" in a broad sense. Nietzsche's "Dionysian faith" (as he calls it) is not a "faith" in the sense of "belief in God." Yet even though the mature Nietzsche no longer professes a faith in God, he professes something like a faith in Life. Further, whereas Nietzsche's early prayers are addressed to someone, it is not clear to whom or what his later "prayers" are addressed. Second, I argue that Nietzsche retains not only the basic logic that emerges in his early prayers but much of its content. So that shift is at best only partially successful.

To see how Nietzsche arrives at *Ecce homo*, we need to follow the path that leads from *Aus meinem Leben*. In so doing, we shall see the evolution of Nietzsche's God and thus the evolution of his relation to that God. We shall also see just how "faithful" Nietzsche turns out to be.

From the God of Pietism to the *Unbekannter*

What was the faith of the young Fritz, known for his "ability to recite scriptural passages and religious songs with great pathos" and hence called the "little pastor"?[4] We get a vivid picture of that faith in the following prayer, which closes *Aus meinem Leben* (1858):

> I have firmly resolved within me to dedicate myself forever to His service. May the dear Lord give me strength and power to carry out my intention and protect me on life's way. Like a child I trust in His grace: He will preserve us all, that no misfortune may befall us. But His holy will be done! All He gives I will joyfully accept: happiness and unhappiness, poverty and wealth, and boldly look even death in the face, which shall one day unite us all in eternal joy and bliss. Yes, dear Lord, let Thy face shine upon us forever! Amen![5]

Although the depth of religious zeal in this prayer may seem strange when juxtaposed with Nietzsche's later writings, it should not surprise us. None of the elements of this prayer are unusual. They are typical of the German pietism of Nietzsche's upbringing.[6] Further, given Nietzsche's later vehemence against Christianity, one would almost expect that level of criticism to be matched by a previous level of devotion.[7]

What we find in this prayer is, first, an outpouring of the heart, one more interested in Christian practice than any set of beliefs. Second, it is a prayer of bold resolution: there is no room for inconstancy here. Third, that resolve is — nonetheless — tempered by an admission of inability. Only by way of the strength of another can that resolution be carried out. Fourth, with an openly proclaimed and even celebrated childlike trust, Nietzsche is convinced that God will provide. Fifth, even if God brings what seems like misfortune, Nietzsche still affirms it as God's will. Whatever happens, Nietzsche is content to "joyfully accept" it, to say "yes" and "amen" to all that comes. Sixth, although God is not specifically identified, Nietzsche clearly has no questions regarding who he is.

Yet these elements are put into question in a poem written only three years later (1860), *"Entflohn die holden Träume"* (Fled are the Lovely Dreams).[8] It, too, is an outpouring of the heart. But this heart is disillusioned, uncertain, and full of tears. What exactly has fled becomes clear when Nietzsche says:

> I do not know what I love
> I have neither peace nor rest.
> I do not know what I believe
> Or why I'm still living. For what?

Finally, the poem ends with three incomplete stanzas. One senses Nietzsche struggling for words, unable even to follow the basic form of the poem:

> Man is not a worthy image
> Of God
>
> From day to day more distorted
> . . . .   [the line is simply left blank]
> I form God
> According to my rudimentary character.
>
> I awoke from heavy dreams
> Through a dull ringing.[9]

Nietzsche no longer affirms his earlier promise to serve God, his unwavering childlike trust that God is good, his willingness to accept whatever God gives, and his certainty of who God is. These have become part of a lovely dream from which he has — quite sadly — awakened. Having realized that God — as earlier configured — does not exist, Nietzsche is now uncertain what to put in its place. One should read Nietzsche's claim that *"Der Mensch is nicht der Gottheit / Würdiges Ebenbild"* (Man is not a worthy image / Of God) in light of the claim *"Nach meinem Urcharakter / Gestalt ich mir auch Gott"* (I form God / According to my rudimentary character).[10] Nietzsche's picture of God has changed because he himself has changed, and thus he sees God differently. But this new picture of God is one that he is reluctant to accept. It is all too human and so "unworthy."

That Nietzsche was struggling with how to conceive of God is evident from two slightly later poems. The first, *"Du hast gerufen — Herr ich komme"* (You Have Called — Lord, I Come), was written in 1861 and seems to revert to Nietzsche's earlier conception of God:

> You are so gentle,
> Faithful and sincere,
> Genuinely earnest,
> Dear savior image for sinners!

It is hard to imagine a more "pietistic" image of God. And it is to this God that Nietzsche says:

> You have called
> Lord, I rush
> With circumspection
> To the steps of your throne.

Glowing with love,
Your glance shines into
My heart so dearly,
So painfully: Lord, I come.[11]

Still, it would be too simple to assume that Nietzsche has here simply reverted to pietism. For his prayer is clearly tempered by hesitation, fear, and growing uncertainty. Nietzsche presents us with a pietistic conception of God and promises to heed his call. But then he says *"Herr: ich eile / Und weile."* It is the religious double gesture: he hurries but he also holds back (*weile*). Nietzsche seems to be unsure even in the midst of rushing back to God. Why is he so reluctant? While he first says he feels "a shudder" (*ein Grauen*) "from the sin" (*vor der Sünde*), he expands on this by describing it as the *"Nachtgründe"* (the abyss of night). Is Nietzsche's problem simply remorse for sin? It is hard to think of sin as the abyss for Nietzsche now. Much more likely is that his "sin" is that of having peered into the abyss — the nothingness — of unbelief. But can he really return to his earlier conception of God? Given both the earlier poem and the ambivalence expressed here, he seems to be well aware that this attempt may fail. So the prayer is a move of desperation, a desperation that will characterize all of Nietzsche's further attempts to deal with God, Christianity, and religion in general.

As it turns out, Nietzsche's attempt does not succeed. By 1864, although Nietzsche has not completely given up on God's existence, he certainly sounds as if he has finally given up on his pietistic conception of God. The second poem, *"Dem unbekannten Gott"* (To the Unknown God), was written on day of his graduation from Pforta at the age of nineteen:

> . . . I lift up my hands to you in loneliness —
> you, to whom I flee,
> to whom in the deepest depths of my heart
> I have solemnly consecrated altars
> so that your voice
> might summon me again.
>
> On them glows, deeply inscribed,
> the word: To the unknown God
> I am his . . .
>
> I want to know you, Unknown One,
> you who have reached deep into my soul,

into my life like the gust of a storm,
you incomprehensible yet related one!
I want to know you, even serve you.[12]

Nietzsche desperately wants to know this *Unbekannter* (Unknown One). Moreover, this is not the first time he has cried out to this *Unbekannter*. He says: *"Noch einmal"* (once again). His "consecration" of altars suggests an ongoing willingness to know God, for the inscription on them is *"tief eingeschrieben"* (deeply inscribed). Further, Nietzsche says *"sein bin ich"* (I am his) and (once again) expresses his desire to serve God: *"Ich will dich kennen, selbst dir dienen"* (I want to know you, even serve you). But he is no longer sure who this "God" is. It is, to be sure, the God who *"tief in meine Selle Greifender"* (has reached deep into my soul). But Nietzsche now identifies this God as the *"Unbekannter,"* the *"Unfaßbarer"* (Incomprehensible One) — in short, the "Other" whose identity has not been revealed and cannot be known. So he has not exactly left God behind, even if he has left a particular sort of God behind.

Dionysus and Life

But then who — or what — takes over the role of "God" for Nietzsche? And to whom — or what — does Nietzsche now "pray"? Nietzsche's contemporary Lou Salomé points out that Nietzsche remains obsessed with God throughout his life:

> Only when we enter Nietzsche's last phase of philosophy will it become completely clear to what extent the religious drive always dominated his being and his knowledge. His various philosophies are for him just so many surrogates for God, which were intended to help him compensate for a mystical God-ideal outside of himself. His last years, then, are a confession that he was not able to do without this ideal. And precisely because of that, time and again we come upon his impassioned battle against religion, belief in God, and the need for salvation because he came precariously close to them.[13]

But it is not just that Nietzsche's "philosophies" function as "surrogates for God." Nietzsche actually gives us at least two "gods" who are surrogates for the God to whom the young Fritz once prayed: Dionysus and Life. Both are variations on the *Unbekannter*, and Nietzsche comes to use them almost interchangeably. Moreover, Nietzsche contrasts what he terms "Dionysus" and the "Crucified" as two different religious types. Whereas the follower of the Cruci-fied (the Christian) denies life, the follower of Dionysus affirms life.[14]

Early on in *The Birth of Tragedy*, Nietzsche speaks of "the mysteri-ous primordial One" (*das geheimnissvolle Ur-Eine*).[15] Given the influ-ence of Schopenhauer on Nietzsche at this point (1871–1872), it is natural to equate the *Ur-Eine* with Schopenhauer's *Wille* (remarkably like the *Unbekannter*—unknown, unpredictable, and incomprehensi-ble).[16] But in his "Attempt at Self-Criticism" (1886) Nietzsche im-plies that Dionysus is this One.[17] Note that Dionysus is a particularly good replacement for the *Unbekannter*. As the god of becoming, he is described as *polumorphos* (polymorphous) and *polueidēs* (appearing in many ways).[18] Yet not only is Dionysus himself able to take on multi-ple appearances, those whom he inspires are likewise enabled to be-come "other" in two ways. First, the actor in Greek tragedy—the *hupocritēs*—puts on masks, allowing him to take on a different per-sona. Second, the *Rausch*—frenzy or rapture—that one experiences when under the spell of Dionysus brings about an "ecstasy"—an *eks-tasis* that removes one (even if only temporarily) beyond normal exis-tence. The substitution, then, of Dionysus for the God of Christianity not only changes the identity of God for Nietzsche but also enables Nietzsche to change his own identity. Increasingly, Nietzsche comes to speak of himself as Dionysus. Thus *Ecce homo* concludes with the famous line "Dionysus versus the Crucified."[19]

The *ekstasis* that Nietzsche seeks is precisely what would allow him to become what he terms a "free spirit" (*freie Geist*). Of course, Nietzsche does not claim to be a free spirit. Not only does he say that "'free spirits' of this kind do not exist," he also makes it clear that one *becomes* a free spirit: "One may conjecture that a spirit in whom the type 'free spirit' will one day become ripe and sweet to the point of perfection has had its decisive experience in a *great liberation* and that previously it was all the more a fettered spirit and seemed to be chained for ever to its pillar and corner."[20]

Even the arrival of free spirits does not signal that they have truly arrived. Nietzsche characterizes free spirits as "those who attempt" (*Versucher*), not those who necessarily succeed.[21] Indeed, he admits "*we, too, are still pious,*" for even "we godless anti-metaphysicians, still take *our* fire, too, from the flame lit by the thousand-year old faith, the Christian faith."[22] So Nietzsche is still a *Versucher*, an experi-menter in the project of self-overcoming.

Just how far, though, does Nietzsche get in his *Versuch*, particu-larly in terms of becoming a "godless anti-metaphysician"? Heidegger has famously questioned whether Nietzsche is truly an "anti-metaphysician," accusing him of elevating "'will to power,' 'becoming,' 'life,' and 'Being' in the broadest sense" to metaphysical principles.[23] But my charge here is that Nietzsche is not truly godless. For Nietzsche, "Life" is the *Unbekannter* who replaces God. Of course, even this move of replacing God with Life proves difficult for Nietzsche. So one can level at least three charges against Nietzsche: (1) he has not left metaphysics behind; (2) his move from the God of Christianity to the *Unbekannter* known as "Life" means that he has not left religion behind; and (3) his attempt to replace "God" with "Life" is itself only partially successful. We shall take up the second and third of these charges. Although they are different charges, if Nietzsche is guilty of either, then he is not truly "godless." And, as we shall see, Nietzsche still "prays."

Assuming Zarathustra is one of the masks Nietzsche wears—not exactly Nietzsche per se but *a* Nietzsche or a perspective on Nietzsche—then Zarathustra provides us with some idea of Nietzsche's own *Versuch* to leave the God of his youth behind and become a truly free spirit. *Thus Spoke Zarathustra* opens with Zarathustra praying to the sun, after which he immediately encounters a saint who says, "With singing, weeping, laughing, and humming I praise the God who is my God."[24] Zarathustra has nothing to say to the saint, but the saint's formula of "singing, weeping, laughing, and humming" will become his own, in praise to the God who is *his* God. But we turn to that shortly. In contrast to the saint, though, Zarathustra's "message" can be summed up as *remain faithful to the earth,"* rather than be swayed by otherworldly hopes and values.[25] In *Zarathustra,* Dionysus is in effect replaced by Life. Of course, Zarathustra realizes that—in order for "Life" to take the place of "God," along with an accompanying "revaluation of all values"—one must undergo a series of "metamorphoses of the spirit." One must move from being the carrier of burdens (the camel, who can be said to represent the religious person) to the destroyer of values (the lion), to the child who is "innocence and forgetfulness, a new beginning, a game, a self-propelled wheel, a first movement, a sacred 'Yes.'"[26] As opposed to the morality of Christianity, which Nietzsche sees as reactionary and fueled by *ressentiment,* Nietzsche desperately seeks a new logic, one that is true to Life. What Nietzsche wants is first, *"to learn to think differently"* and second, *"to feel differently."*[27]

Yet "starting over" is easier prescribed than accomplished. That practical inability becomes evident in, for instance, the section "Of the Tarantula" (*Zarathustra* II) in which Zarathustra admits that he too has been "bitten" by the desire for revenge that characterizes Christianity. The problem is that he has not yet learned to *"think differently,"* even if that is what he preaches. Zarathustra is forced to confront his inadequacies in "The Stillest Hour" (end of Part II). There he is told "voicelessly": "O Zarathustra, your fruit is ripe but you are not ripe for your fruit." At this, Zarathustra "wept loudly."[28] For he admits that he is still not a lion and so cannot become a child. This inability to believe and live out his own doctrines — of not yet being "ripe" — recurs not merely in *Zarathustra* but in Nietzsche's later works as well. Nietzsche copes with this inability by emulating the saint: "singing, weeping, laughing, and humming" — in effect, praying.[29]

In "The Other Dancing Song" (*Zarathustra* III), Zarathustra attempts to dance with Life, who says to him: "You are not faithful enough to me! You do not love me nearly as much as you say; I know that you are thinking of leaving me soon." To leave Life would be to be take refuge in wisdom as a kind of defense against Life (which Nietzsche sees both philosophy and religion as doing). As a response to Life's charge of infidelity, Zarathustra sings "The Yes and Amen Song" (the subtitle of "The Seven Seals"),[30] which has the repeated refrain *"For I love you, O Eternity."*[31] It seems this is not the song of "Zarathustra the faithful" but of Zarathustra who longs for faithfulness, who sings a song of affirmation of faith but still lacks faith.[32]

Like many hymns, this hymn is clearly a prayer — addressed to Life. But what kind of prayer is this? One would suppose that is not the prayer of which Nietzsche speaks when he says, "you will never pray again, never adore again, never again rest in endless trust; you refuse to let yourself stop to unharness your thoughts before any ultimate wisdom, goodness, or power."[33] Nietzsche exhorts us not pray in such a way that we trust in any "wisdom, goodness, or power." In contrast, Nietzsche calls for *"faith in oneself."*[34] Yet even Nietzsche questions whether this project of renunciation of reliance on another is truly possible, for he asks: "Who will give you the strength to do so? No one has yet had the strength!"[35] Does Zarathustra/Nietzsche really give up such prayer? I think he does not, in at least two ways. On the one hand, his dance with Life ends by him saying that now "Life was dearer to me than all my wisdom ever was."[36] So we have transference of adoration — and trust — from the Christian God to Life.

Further, the important elements of Nietzsche's prayer of 1858 can be found in Nietzsche's later thought. First, there is an outpouring of the heart in "The Other Dancing Song" that sounds remarkably like pietistic devotion. Although Nietzsche remains inconstant, he at least wants to be faithful to Life. Second, even though Nietzsche wants to give up prayer, the question "who will give you the strength to do so?" implies that Nietzsche cannot give up prayer and reliance on his own. But then, on whom or what is Nietzsche relying? Is it not Life herself? Third, what Nietzsche had earlier said to the God of Christianity ("I have firmly resolved within me to dedicate myself for ever to His service") and then to the *Unbekannter* ("I want to know you, even serve you") he now pledges to Life.[37] Finally, Nietzsche's earlier affirmation of God's will—"His holy will be done! All He gives I will joyfully accept"—now becomes the prayer of "Yes and Amen." So while Nietzsche is no longer a pietist, he retains the basic framework of pietism.

Of course, Nietzsche tries to renounce any dependence upon "ultimate" wisdom or power. In terms of wisdom, Nietzsche wishes to give up the attempt to provide anything like a "final" answer. This is one reason that Nietzsche says, "I distrust all systematizers and stay out of their way. The will to system is a lack of integrity."[38] But even if Nietzsche does leaves wisdom and its systems behind (and it is not at all sure that he does), Life certainly seems to be Nietzsche's ultimate "power."[39] So Nietzsche himself does precisely what he warns against.

Although *Thus Spoke Zarathustra* ends with Zarathustra proclaiming "the lion came, my children are near, Zarathustra has ripened, my hour has come,"[40] it is difficult to be convinced. Even if we were to accept that the lion has truly come, just how near are the children? We get a glimpse at Zarathustra's continuing vulnerability in "The Magician" (Part IV), who represents both Wagner and Nietzsche himself. This magician prays to the *Unbekannter*, saying "you unknown—*god*" and even "you malicious, unknown god." He asks: "What do you want?" and "Would you climb *into* my heart, climb into my most secret thoughts?" and "*Me*—you? want me? / me—all of me?" The pietistic overtones of this prayer are unmistakable, as are the similarities with Nietzsche's earlier poetry/prayers. The speaker is clearly torn. On the one hand, he proclaims:

He is gone!
He has fled,

my sole companion,
my great enemy,
my unknown,
my hangman-god! . . .

On the other hand, he goes on to say:

No!
come back!
with all your torments!
All the streams of my tears
run their course to you!
and the last flame of my heart —
it burns up to you!
Oh come back,
my unknown God! my *pain!* my last happiness! . . .[41]

Only if the God departs can the one who prays become truly an individual (characterized by *"faith in oneself"*).[42] But then there is the desire for the God's return.

Although Zarathustra accuses the magician of dissembling and the magician admits that he has said these words to put Zarathustra to the test, there is an undeniable tension in these last two stanzas. One possible interpretation is that the magician demands both that God leave and that God return precisely because each departure serves to make one harder. Yet I think there is something more here. The magician admits that he is acting out "the ascetic of the spirit" and that "it took a long time" for Zarathustra to realize that it was an act.[43] Why is Zarathustra so slow to see through the ruse? His explanation is that he has to be "without caution: thus my lot wants it." But even if Zarathustra as an overman figure must throw caution to the winds, why does he so quickly take pity upon the magician and reach out to comfort him? Clearly the magician touches Zarathustra's heart. And he touches Zarathustra's heart because Zarathustra sees himself in the magician. The magician's double gesture — of desiring God to depart and yet return, of being free from God yet afraid of the abyss — closely mirrors Nietzsche's early poetry. So Zarathustra/Nietzsche has not simply left that ambiguity behind.

Decadent Nietzsche and the Evangel

In his later works, Nietzsche's continued faithfulness to his reworked pietism likewise proves problematic. That dissonance can be worked out in at least two respects. First, Nietzsche admits that he himself is guilty of *"décadence"* — the negation of Life.[44] Although he desperately attempts to combat decadence, he is well aware that he does not succeed. Second, Nietzsche depicts the Evangel (as opposed to the Crucified) as the free spirit he hopes to be. In comparison to Nietzsche, the Evangel seems to have achieved something to which Nietzsche can only aspire. Both of these aspects end up being ones that for Nietzsche result in prayers and tears.

Despite the late appearance of the term *"décadence"* in Nietzsche's corpus,[45] it is as if he has finally discovered the perfect term to describe what he has been fighting all along, the term that in effect supplants and sublates *Entartung* (degeneration),[46] *ressentiment,* and *nihilimus.* Nietzsche even goes so far as to say, "Nothing has preoccupied me more profoundly than the problem of *décadence.*"[47] And Nietzsche's interest in decadence is profoundly personal. While there are various ways to describe decadence, they come down to the same thing — a devaluation of Life, both practically and theoretically. Practically, Nietzsche says, "to choose instinctively what is harmful to *oneself,* to be *enticed* by 'disinterested' motives, is virtually the formula for *décadence.*" So one acts decadently by choosing against Life. Theoretically, decadence is manifested by considering Life to be of no value: "Instead of naively saying, *'I'm* not worth anything anymore,' the lie of morality says in the mouth of the *décadent*: 'Nothing is worth anything — *life* isn't worth anything.'"[48]

How is one to be "saved" from decadence? In Nietzsche's reading, Socrates employs dialectic. Yet Nietzsche thinks that such a strategy is not only ineffective but also self-deceptive: "It is a self-deception on the part of philosophers and moralists to think that they can escape from *décadence* merely by making war against it. Escape is beyond their strength: for what they choose as a means, as salvation, is itself just another expression of *décadence* — they *alter* its expression, they don't do away with it itself."[49]

In contrast, Nietzsche tries a different sort of salvation. Admitting his own decadence, Nietzsche claims: "I comprehended this, I resisted it." Strangely enough, though, Nietzsche goes on to say, "The philosopher in me resisted."[50] Yet how can Nietzsche really resist "philosophically" when Socrates was unable to do so? Clearly the answer is not a different sort of dialectic. Instead, Nietzsche claims he follows an ascetic strategy of "special self-discipline" that includes "self-overcoming" and "self-denial."[51] Here we can ask (1) what self it is that Nietzsche wishes to overcome; and (2) what such "self-over-coming" would look like.

The self that Nietzsche wishes to overcome is, as I have been ar-guing all along, that of the pious young Fritz. But does Nietzsche really overcome this self? We have already seen that Nietzsche re-mains remarkably true to his pietistic roots in important ways. True, he moves from his old faith in the God of Christianity to faith in Life, resulting in both a desire to serve Life and a willingness to say "Yes and Amen" to Life rather than God. But he has not left what Salomé terms the "mystical God-ideal" behind. And he seems quite unable to leave it behind. Moreover, even in his desire to serve Life he turns out to be a decadent. He attempts to resist that decadence, but it is a resistance that seems (on Nietzsche's own account) to grow more and more futile the more he becomes convinced that the ideas of "free will" and "human agency" are merely fictions.[52] Nietzsche real-izes that he is not true to Life and he feels deep remorse for his infi-delity.

But there is a far greater problem that Nietzsche faces. Not only does he wish to be free from the God of Christianity, he also wishes to be free from the very hope of redemption. He speaks of "redemp-tion *from* the redeemer" (*Erlösung dem Erlöser*)—a salvation from the very desire for salvation.[53] But can Nietzsche make such a move? It would seem that to be saved from salvation—or redeemed from redemption—is once again to repeat the very logic from which one wishes to escape. Nietzsche does realize that one cannot escape deca-dence merely by making war against it, as is clear from his quote about Socrates above. But how, then, can Nietzsche truly escape from escaping, overcome overcoming, redeem himself from redemp-tion, or save himself from salvation?

At this juncture, Nietzsche makes (not surprisingly) what is clearly a religious move. He claims that redemption from redemption can be accomplished only by faith, a faith that is "the highest of all faiths," one he has "baptized" with the name of "Dionysus." Only with this faith—"a glad and trusting fatalism in the midst of the uni-verse"—can one become a free spirit.[54] Of course, one can move to this faith only by becoming a child. Nietzsche has hopes for making this move, for he claims that he is "at the same time a *decadent* and a *beginning*."[55] But we are back to the same problem we noted in *Zara-thustra*. Has Nietzsche truly become a child? Or does Nietzsche merely "pray" to become one—a prayer that in effect takes the form "Life, make me a child" or even "Life, may I be born again."

While Nietzsche can only hope and pray to become a child, he portrays the Evangel—at least in one crucial respect—as someone like the person he himself wishes to be.[56] To be sure, Nietzsche tempers his praise of the Evangel by calling him both a "decadent" and "sickly." But Nietzsche also considers him to be truly "childlike." Thus the Evangel *is* a free spirit, not merely an aspiring one like Nietzsche. He is *already* the perfect child, not one who has to undergo the difficult metamorphoses that lead to the child. Moreover, he exhibits childlike behavior precisely because "to negate is the very thing that is impossible for him."[57] He is instead only able to say "yes." Thus the Evangel does not operate according to the logic of *ressentiment*, a reactive logic. "He does not resist, he does not defend his right." Instead, the Evangel simply acts. As Nietzsche puts it, "The life of the Redeemer was nothing other than *this* practice." What the Evangel knows is that "it is only in the *practice* of life that one feels 'divine,' 'blessed,' 'evangelical,' at all times a 'child of God.'" Thus he "resists any kind of word, formula, law, faith, dogma."[58]

Even though Nietzsche goes on to speak of "we spirits who have *become free*,"[59] the kind of freedom manifested by the Evangel is something Nietzsche aspires to but has not yet reached. While Nietzsche wishes to escape from the sort of reactive logic that characterizes *ressentiment*, his strident protests against Christianity and the Crucified are actually indicators that he is not free. He hopes and prays to be free. He hopes and prays to be a true follower of Dionysus. But he knows he is unfaithful. So Nietzsche's last of nine autobiographies, *Ecce homo*, is an attempt to reinterpret his life as a faithful follower of Dionysus. It is a confession of faith and a confession of unfaithfulness. When Nietzsche claims that *Ecce homo* is designed to tell us "*who I am*," that claim is only partly right.[60] For it is also designed to tell us whom Nietzsche wishes to be. "I am a disciple of the philosopher Dionysus," writes Nietzsche.[61] Such is both what Nietzsche is and what he also wants to be. In effect, Nietzsche says: "I believe; help my unbelief."

Nietzsche is rightly interpreted as giving us an aesthetic creation of himself in *Ecce homo*, a self that is constructed by masks and the *Rausch* that takes one out of oneself. But *Ecce homo* also fits with Nietzsche's long history of prayer—not the prayer of the weak but the prayer of the strong, the ones who use songs and rituals to reinforce that strength. For example, one can only interpret the following as Nietzsche wanting and praying for this to be true: "Really *religious* difficulties, for example, I don't know from experience. . . . 'God,' 'immortality of the soul,' 'redemption,' 'beyond'—without exception, concepts to which I never devoted any attention, or time; not even as a child. Perhaps I have never been childlike enough for them?"[62] None of this describes Nietzsche, neither the old Nietzsche nor the young. He has in fact been obsessed with these concepts and continues to be. His problem is that he is not childlike enough, though in exactly the opposite sense from what he means here.

Yet, despite his attempt to be strong, Nietzsche is not so strong after all. He is all too well aware of his failings to live up to his own teachings. He tells us, "When I have looked into my *Zarathustra*, I walk up and down in my room for half an hour, unable to master an unbearable fit of sobbing."[63] Why does he sob? Right before this passage, he says that the great writer (Shakespeare being the comparison here) writes "*only* from his own reality—up to the point where afterward he cannot endure his work any longer." So it is in looking into himself that Nietzsche begins sobbing. And he goes on to describe himself as "an abyss." Thus Nietzsche's tears are at once for the nothingness within him and the nothingness without. It is the abyss of which he had written in "*Du hast gerufen—Herr ich komme*," the abyss that he had earlier said gives him *ein Grauen*.

Yet his very sobbing is "unbearable." For, as the supposedly free spirit with "Dionysian faith"[64] enabling him to say "Yes and Amen" to all that comes, he ought not to be sobbing. Instead, he should have the resolution of the young Fritz to say: "All *Life* gives I will joyfully accept: happiness and unhappiness, poverty and wealth, and boldly look even death in the face." That would be the expression of the childlike trust after which Nietzsche so desperately seeks. What Nietzsche calls "the *free spirit* par excellence" is able to dance "even beside abysses."[65] But, lacking that faith, Nietzsche prays to be rescued from himself, to become a child. His tears are for his inability to make that a reality.

"Nothing like (*Zarathustra*) has ever been written, felt, or *suffered*," writes Nietzsche. But, when he goes on to say "thus suffers a god, a Dionysus," it is merely a hopeful—and tearful—prayer.[66]

6

Attention and Responsibility
The Work of Prayer

NORMAN WIRZBA

> Absolutely unmixed attention is prayer.
>> —Simone Weil, *Gravity and Grace*

> *Laborare est orare* — To work is to pray.
>> —A motto of the Benedictine Order

According to Aristotle (in *On Interpretation*, 17 A 4–5), prayer is a logos or speech that is not susceptible to truth or falsity. Unlike declarative propositions that assume a possible correspondence between our words and the affairs of the world — a correspondence that can be checked or verified by the methods of scientific observation — prayers do not illuminate or clarify the world in the way that more or less scientific statements do. They cannot be tested according to the rigors of scientific procedure because they follow a different grammar, obey rules of use in which considerations other than truth or falsity come into play.

It would go too far, however, to suggest that with prayer all considerations of truth fall by the wayside. After all, it is well known that one can pray in a false spirit or with a deceptive heart. Similarly, we should not think that prayer is irrelevant as regards our perception, understanding, and handling of the world, particularly if we understand the praying act as a faithful and loving attention to others. Indeed, prayer is appropriately understood as the most intimate and honest means through which an understanding of our place in the world can be achieved; in prayer we see more truly and clearly because the ego that would otherwise come between us and others has, through the discipline of attention, been properly humbled. In our praying, we potentially plumb the depths and breadth of experience so that we may honestly see and then reconfigure our identities and vocations as intimately bound up with all created life. As I argue below, prayer has the capacity to situate our life properly and justly among the lives of others. If this is so, we would do well to evaluate our praying intention more from the perspectives of social and economic life, since it is in terms of our practical, day-to-day handling of creation that we can more honestly discern the faithfulness and responsibility of our piety.

The connection between prayer and attention is crucial, because as a discipline attention clears my vision of vestiges of the ego so that a humble, compassionate, and just regard for others can occur. Simone Weil insists that without the discipline and the waiting of attention we close ourselves off from the truth and grace of the world, and consequently run the risk of embracing a counterfeit world, a world primarily of our own liking and making: "Attention alone—that attention which is so full that the 'I' disappears—is required of me. I have to deprive all that I call 'I' of the light of my attention and turn it on to that which cannot be conceived."[1] The discipline of attention, in other words, makes it possible for monological speech (and prayers of mere wish fulfillment) to be transformed into a true dialogue, a conversation in which our pleas, laments, questions, hopes, and desires can be intersected, penetrated, informed, and corrected by another.[2]

On this reading, though prayer does not claim to operate with the same grammar as scientific discourse, it does turn out to be the indispensable propaedeutic for truth claims of whatever kind because it has as its goal an attentive and faithful response to the world. The work of prayer is essential in the pursuit of truth because it prepares us for a compassionate embrace of reality. Prayers are hence true in the way that people can be "true" to each other, true in the sense that they express a nonevasive, just regard for others. Prayer, in other words, is the practice wherein epistemology and ethics meet, the site in terms of which the moral and spiritual meaning of others becomes clearer. Through the action of prayer, we come to know others differently.

To speak this way about prayer requires us to think more about the act of praying itself and less about a prayer's content. "What" we say (a prayer's propositional content) matters less than "how" we say it. More specifically, what matters most is how our praying has the practical effect of repositioning us within the world—making us more perceptive, more sympathetic, more charitable—so that we no longer perceive and engage it in the same way as before. Obviously, what we say is important because it reflects a self-understanding of our position in the world and what we take our mission in life to be. But the praying act itself, its posture and disposition, is primary not simply because it demonstrates our passion but because it practically situates us before God and within creation: prayer inspires and animates a moral response to the world.

In the Johannes Climacus authorship Søren Kierkegaard made a similar distinction between the "what" of objective certainty (philosophical reason) and the "how" of subjective uncertainty (faith). In matters of religion, he claimed, "truth is subjectivity," a demonstration of passionate inwardness and decision. Thus one can pray in truth even as one may "in fact" worship an idol, because what matters most is not what is said but how it is said.[3] Clearly, Kierkegaard is correct to emphasize the significance of passionate inwardness in the life of prayer, since we know that the same words uttered in the mouth of another can ring untrue or inauthentic. We each inhabit different stages on life's way and so approach and relate to the infinite in our own unique manner, that is, the assurance of uniform and universally applicable religious and philosophical doctrines in no way excuses us from the lifelong task of personal appropriation, of untying the knots of life for ourselves.

Where his analysis falls short, however, is in limiting the how of prayer to the believer's inwardness, the passionate relation (decision in the face of uncertainty and risk) the speaker maintains *to what is said*. A more complete account of the "how" of prayer must also include the believer's relation *to the world*, not simply through passionate decision but through faithful response and action, because the world, understood as God's creation, informs the practical bearing of prayer. Put another way, Kierkegaard's account of subjectivity, particularly in the Climacus texts, is too much confined to the life of the individual—the how of inwardness. It lacks sufficient appreciation of the subject as a created being enmeshed within a created world, a being that must learn to comport itself practically in ways that reflect its creaturely status—the how of outwardness.

In this respect, Thomas Merton's account of prayer is more helpful, because he appreciates how created life is always already in relation to the Creator. To be sure, this relation can be dissimulated or denied. But one of the primary aims of prayer is to rekindle and restore the relation between creation and Creator. Speaking of monastic life as above all a life steeped in prayer, Merton says "the monk abandons the world only in order to listen more intently to the deepest and most neglected voices that proceed from its inner depth." Prayer demands solitude (which is not to be confused with seclusion) and the purification of our hearts (attention) because listening to or welcoming the call of God is so very difficult for us. Rather than "finding ourselves in God's truth," more often than not we see reflected in our engagement with the world *our* desires, *our* fears—*our* tenacious drive to assert ourselves over and against all others. Our aim in prayer should be to "understand the meaning of our life as children of God," to "lose ourselves" in the divine love, and to find our rest in the divine life.[4] But how, short of becoming monks ourselves, are we to realize this life and rest in God?

We do not appreciate enough how difficult it has become for us to enter into a prayerful life. In part this is because we have, as Kierkegaard suggested, become speculative, having taken the risk and paradox out of religious life. A more systemic problem, however, has to do with the heritage of modernity itself. To be modern is to be fully aware of ourselves as historical beings, as self-conscious and autonomous agents who design and control the world according to our own liking (rather than the laws of Nature or God).[5] Practically speaking, this means we have increasingly come to inhabit and identify ourselves with built environments and symbolic universes that reflect entirely human goals and concerns. In this profane context, authentic prayer runs the risk of being forced or purely ornamental, an irrelevant display, because in most matters of daily and practical significance—in economics, politics, education, even religion—we are in firm control of the agendas in terms of which we live. If God appears in this practical context at all, it is more likely as the extension or imprimatur of self-chosen aims. We have, in short, reversed the sense of authentic prayer as one of the primary means through which we become properly situated in God's creation, with the result that our lives often (despite our prayers or in direct contradiction of them!) bespeak an improper orientation, a myopic, unjust, destructive engagement with the world of others.

In the effort to come to an understanding of God and our place in creation, there is ample room for distortion and dishonesty. We may, for instance, become idolaters who lay waste to the world in the rush to maximize our own control and comfort (indeed, we make idolaters of the whole creation as it is made to submit and bow down before our technological power and prowess). Our gaze and ambition can be arrogant and consequently cloud, if not entirely dissimulate, the costly grace that creation itself is. Or, more simply, we may become oblivious to the world *as creation* through careless and mindless consumptive patterns that naïvely assume the world is ours for the taking: the world is reduced to and now signifies primarily as a consumable "good." As self-assured historical beings, we forget ourselves *as creatures* enmeshed in a common life with others before God.[6] Given these temptations, how do we attain the purity of heart and mind that will bring us into the presence of an incomprehensible God, into the divine light that shows us our darkness, and hence also into right relations with each other?

We can find help if we remember that Scripture admonishes us to "pray without ceasing" (1 Thess. 5:17). We must pray constantly so that we do not—whether out of hubris, ignorance, neglect, or personal inertia—disfigure or dissimulate the relations that bind us to God, each other, and the creation. Here we see a call to steady attention and vigilance. Because our most fundamental dispositions and orientations are so out of alignment, we need to embark upon a new regime of practical, daily habits that will gradually wean us away from our self-absorbed ways.[7] We cannot simply add a few more moments of "prayer time" to an otherwise self-absorbed day and expect to find ourselves within God's truth or intention.

To speak of constant prayer, however, requires us to broaden prayer's scope to include all dimensions of practical life (where our relations are concretely worked out), including our work life, so that in the end our whole life can be offered to God. Clearly, spoken forms of prayer, whether liturgical or informal, communal or private, play an important part in religious life. But they do not exhaust it. In a certain sense we can say that practical or economic life is primary, since it gives a more authentic and honest expression of our devotion and desire and thus grounds our speech in the world as we intimately experience and engage it. We cannot pray honestly or truthfully if our lives reflect shoddy work, broken relationships, violent intent, or destroyed habitats.[8] Work done excellently, with attention and care, demonstrates more directly than our words the truth or falsity, the rectitude or evasiveness, of our praying intention.

If we are to speak of prayer in this more expansive way, we should consider more carefully who the praying subject is, and then articulate the practical conditions and habits that will best lead us into postures we might recognize as prayerful. In other words, we must understand how subjectivity and practical life together are transformed so that the "how" of authentic prayer can be realized. Here the problematic inheritance of modernity is revealed in its truncated portrayals of subjectivity and in the reduction of practical (work) life to a utilitarian calculus. Together, these transformations would have a determinative effect on the way we understand and practice various dimensions of religious life.

If we turn first to modern philosophy and its account of subjectivity, what needs to be overcome is not only what Nicholas Lash has called the "spectatorial" model of knowledge, the idea that the paradigm of learning is the disinterested, objective observation of a world entirely distinct from the knower,[9] but also the subject's self-enclosure that follows from such atomistic spatialization. As self-enclosed or turned back upon itself, a subject becomes disenchanted with and isolated from the world of which it is a part, cut off from the world in which it moves and from which it draws its breath, water, and food. Equally important, the subject, now left to its own devices, becomes the gatekeeper or judge that determine how all reality is to be perceived, understood, and handled. Kant gave what is perhaps the most succinct account of the reduction of a meaningful world to a transcendental (and thus inattentive) subject when he said: "For experience is itself a species of knowledge which involves understanding; and understanding has rules which I must presuppose as being in me prior to objects being given to me, and therefore as being *a priori.*"[10]

What is lacking in this account is the subject's participation in a world that is already meaningful and a reckoning of how our participation might call into question claims to knowledge. We are helped in our understanding of this participation and what its implications are for knowledge and self-understanding if we turn to the early phenomenological investigations of Martin Heidegger. In Heidegger's view, a human being as *Dasein* is not an object that simply exists alongside other objects in the world. It is a being (*Seiendes*) that intends a world, is always directed (theoretically, but also practically) to a world that appears and is meaningful in terms of a horizon of care (*Sorge*). Human life is not only constituted from out of itself but in and through its attachments with a world that is always already of concern. The sense of our participation in a world comes through clearly in the following: "What we are concerned about and attend to shows itself as that *wherefrom, out of which*, and *on the basis of which* factical life is lived." The world signifies and is meaningful in terms of our practical, day-to-day engagement with it (the myriad tasks of producing things, arranging things, protecting and securing things, etc.). In this engagement, Heidegger says, "life approaches itself and addresses itself in a worldly manner."[11] We understand ourselves not in terms of our self-reflexivity but as we meet ourselves in our dealings in the world. Moreover, we understand the world primarily not in terms of an objective, theoretical stance but from within our practical engagement with it. We might say that the sense of who we are and what the world is dawns on us in and through our participation and activity with others.

But what is the character of our day-to-day participation in the world, and how has modernity affected it? Is our engagement with others attentive or inattentive? These are vital questions because, as I have already noted, the effect of modern industrial economics was to reduce practical life to its utilitarian core. Does the horizon of care, which informs our practical dealings, reduce the world and the divine to things that exist primarily for our own use and benefit?[12] Or, more radically yet, can we continue to speak meaningfully or with any depth about a horizon of care at all, given that we live in a global consumer economy that is sustained and propelled by spontaneous, fluctuating, and media-manufactured desires?

The sociologist Zygmunt Bauman has usefully described our time as "liquid modernity." What he means by this characterization is that fluidity, risk, and unpredictability now dominate our economic and practical lives. The contexts of work and social and political relationships are saturated with uncertainty, giving life an overall precarious feel. Put another way, if modern industrialism weakened, postmodern globalization nearly severs the bonds that tie us to each other, our communities, and our world. The fast, fluid nature of economic transactions (often "decided" in anonymous conditions), and the instability and anxiety that are their inevitable result, train us to perceive and handle the world and its inhabitants as consumable, disposable items. Even "bonds and partnerships [between people] tend to be viewed and treated as things meant to be *consumed*, not produced; they are subject to the same criteria of evaluation as all other objects of consumption."[13]

What we see here is that the volatile context of daily life renders superficial our attachments to the world. Our engagements with and commitments to others become increasingly tentative and temporary, a reflection of the anonymous, transitory character of global markets. The self-possession that characterized modernity is here replaced by the sense that we are little more than the playthings of invisible forces. In this context of hyperreality, it is increasingly difficult to conceive, let alone instantiate, care-ful relationships conducive to fellowship or kinship with God, each other, or the created world. Rather than finding ourselves lost in the divine love and hence deeply immersed in the divine life, we are simply lost, cut off from the divine action in creation that would call forth a prayerful response. One might even suppose that dispositions like attention and fidelity, dispositions central to the life of prayer, are well nigh impossible, because the patient responsibility that is their prerequisite has all but evaporated.

In times of crisis, religious leaders are known to call us to prayer, believing as they do that prayer will somehow rescue us or at least return us to our proper support and guide. In our time, however, it appears that the practical conditions that would enable us to pray have been undercut. We cannot trust our calls or pleas to God because they may signify little more than the emotional outbursts of consumers (perpetually) dissatisfied with the latest religious product. And so we find ourselves in the unusual position of needing to pray for the ability to pray.

If we are to recover a sense of authentic prayer, it is important that we not treat this problem primarily as a theoretical difficulty, believing that we have not yet thought correctly about what prayer is. Clearly our thought is important, but what is even more important is the reordering of our practical lives and habits so that a recovery of the experience of sacred kinship might emerge. Does or can our participation with others bear witness to the sacred character of deep relationships? From the experience of sacred kinship, the dispositions of praise, thanksgiving, worship, lament, and so on—all dispositions central to the life of prayer—will naturally, even if surprisingly, follow.[14] We will not understand or realize authentic prayer in the abstract but only as we commit ourselves to an attentive, affectionate, and responsible engagement with the world. For this, we need patience and resilience to discover the forms and patterns evident in life. We need the instruction that follows from our practical commitments and care, that builds upon our availability to the world's dynamism and grace. Without this deep immersion, we will remain adrift, insulated from the very action of divine life that would inspire and correct our intentions and desires.

The significance of sacred kinship for the life of prayer should not be underestimated, particularly if we understand by prayer the faithful response to the mystery and grace of the world. For many, prayer seems hollow and merely formulaic because God, often understood in deistic ways, seems far away, cut off from the action of daily life. Viewed from a Trinitarian perspective, however, "God's utterance [in creating the world] lovingly gives life; gives all life, all unfading freshness; gives only life, and peace, and beauty, harmony and joy. And the life God gives is nothing other, nothing less, than God's own self. Life is God, given."[15] God's love is incarnate and is expressed in the divine delight that finds creation delectable and worthy of friendship and redemption. Divine friendship, in turn, is communicated in God's abiding care and commitment that continually sustains life[16] and in the invitation to us to participate, through our own work and care, in God's own delight. God, in other words, is intimately involved in the "hows" of life: the birth of babies, the decomposition and reconstitution of organic matter, bodily healing, photosynthesis, respiration, the growth of food, the power of energy, the grace of charitable acts. As we practically engage these "hows" in our work and play, our living and our dying, we respond in friendship to God's prior kinship with us.

Practical, daily work can serve as the primary entry or introduction to the experience of kinship we need. It can do so because it is through our work that we express ourselves and make manifest what we take to be good and valuable in life. In our work we make manifest the character of the world as we understand it (as sacred or profane). Perhaps more important, however, the character and sense of the world is impressed upon us as we engage it attentively and responsibly. We cannot have a deep connection with or understanding of reality if our experience of it (as mediated through alienating work patterns) is shallow.

When we are passive consumers, it is much more difficult for us to appreciate the signification or meaning that comes to us through productive engagement with the world. The traditional artisan, for instance, understood his or her art to be an immersion into reality so that the products made could be in better alignment with the beauty, goodness, and usefulness already there. Rather than trying to be innovative or express personal creative genius, the artisan aimed to reflect or bear witness to reality's mysterious, fecund depth in his or her work and design. Aristotle understood this well when he tied efficient causality firmly to the other three causes. We cannot know how to make things well if we do not at the same time have a good sense of a thing's material and formal nature or a sense for its overall fit within a larger cosmos. Equally significant, however, is the fact that deep understanding grows through our efforts to make things. In the activity of making itself we learn about good (useful, functional) design, the character (limits, possibilities) of the material world, and the overall fittedness (purpose) of things and our work in the larger whole.

As is well known, in an industrial and now globalized marketplace work has become the means of our alienation from ourselves, each other, and the world. It has, often due to the superficiality of our relationships, led to the thoughtless degradation of people, things, and habitats. But it need not be so, particularly if we understand work in its most expansive sense as the production of anything — breakfast, friendships, gardens, tables, solidarity, community institutions — and do not confine it to wage labor (what we do for our bosses). Meaningful work makes possible our most intimate engagement with a world of others. It serves as our most direct (though by no means linear) entry into the ways of grace and so calls forth our capacity to express gratitude and demonstrate care.

In a consumer culture, as we have already noted, such intimacy is difficult to come by. What we need are models that show us how care is possible and the conditions needed for the realization of attention and responsibility. For this purpose, the work of the Kentucky farmer and poet Wendell Berry proves invaluable. Berry begins his analysis by noting how evasive our culture has become. We cannot be attentive or responsible because, at a bare minimum, we have not committed ourselves to staying in one place long enough. The history of American "settlement" has, in varying ways, been one long imperial quest for El Dorado. We are all always on the move scanning for new and better (more profitable) opportunities.

This mobility stands in considerable contrast to indigenous and agrarian cultures that for centuries defined themselves in terms of particular places, communities, and traditions. Fidelity to place, community, and tradition was essential, because it was through these that one found one's proper identity and vocation. To bring ruin to one's place or community, whether that be through inattention or simple disregard, was also to bring ruin to oneself. But as consumers, we have little allegiance to place because we are always drawing our sustenance from some other, usually unknown, place. There is little that practically or directly ties us to the places we merely occupy or to the people we simply live with. The first step toward the recovery of a deep attachment to place and others will therefore be that we commit ourselves to a place, to a community, and to the traditions that have sustained it through time. The goal here is not provincialism or a myopic following of tradition but, rather, the growth of fidelity and the sense that we live necessarily and beneficially through the lives of others and hence, as mature individuals, must learn to accept responsibility for them.

Berry often uses the examples of marriage and farming life to show what this fidelity practically entails. The new spouse, just as the new farmer, usually approaches the significant other with great ideas about what the future holds, ideas that often turn into struggles and disappointments (since they were based on unrealistic or arrogant assumptions or a superficial estimation of who or what is there). Given sufficient staying power and communal support, however, these struggles can lead to the correction of one's initial ideas and hence the deepening of one's engagement with reality. Berry notes that:

> if one's sight is clear and if one stays on and works well, one's love gradually responds to the place as it really is, and one's visions gradually image possibilities that are really in it. Vision, possibility, work, and life—*all* have changed by mutual correction. Correct discipline, given enough time, gradually removes one's self from one's line of sight. One works to better purpose then and makes fewer mistakes, because at last one sees where one is.[17]

Work is crucial in this deepening of our engagement, because it is through work that we realize success and failure and, provided that we have the resolve to live with and correct rather than evade or dissimulate the harmful effects of what we have done, we will come to see more honestly. Our work becomes less an imposition on others and more a faithful response to and cooperation with others because, as Weil would put it, we have learned to deprive the ego of its distorting, suffocating, and finally destructive attachment to itself. In our fidelity to place and community, we come to see that we do not live from ourselves alone but are everywhere and at all times supported and benefited by the generosity of others—family, friends, chickens, cattle, plants, earthworms, sunlight, water, soil—who make our living not only possible but also potentially a joy. Work, in this sense, is a perpetual apprenticeship into reality, a constant training in the integrity, mystery, and sanctity of others.

It is in terms of this context of our commitment to places and communities, a commitment made practical and visible through our daily work of feeding, building, teaching, healing, celebrating, and so on, that the conditions for attention and affection can grow. We become genuine care-takers of creation because, now having sensed the divine kinship, we appreciate and respond to the grace and care that is always already there. Furthermore, the clear sense of our interdependence with others leads to the development of authentic humility, humility that is based not on self-hatred but rather on the honest sense that we live through the grace of others. Attention, as the realization of the noncentrality of the ego, now joins hands with affection, the care-ful embrace or, as Berry would say, dance with others that grants to them their unqualified right to be and to flourish.

With this brief description of the parameters of responsible work, we can now consider work's relation to the life of prayer and so flesh out the Benedictine maxim "To work is to pray." The first point to be made is that authentic, productive work leads us into a more sympathetic encounter and engagement with reality and thus overcomes the superficiality characteristic of consumer culture. Care-ful work introduces us to the sanctity of the world or, as Henry Bugbee would put it, the wilderness that everywhere surrounds us: "The more we experience things in depth, the more we participate in a mystery intelligible to us only as such; and the more we understand our world to be an unknown world. Our true home is wilderness, even the world of everyday."[18] Patience, care, and skill become the primary virtues that will lead us into the depth of creation so that we can be met there by God's friendly call.

It is this sense of the grace of the world that then compels us to reposition ourselves in the world, beginning with the commitment to do excellent work, work that honors creation and the Creator. The realization of sanctity everywhere around us invites (demands?) a moral response. It requires of us that we reverse existing patterns of shoddy, careless work, just as it calls us to promote convivial and just work environments. The taste of divine kinship invites daily self-examination, as we come to see the narrowness and the arrogance through which we have sought to understand and manipulate the world. We learn to appreciate what Marion calls the "poverty of givenness" that follows from the scientistic and utilitarian theories of knowledge that have governed philosophy in its key moments.

We also learn that the praying subject is not first and foremost a constituting subject, a subject that determines through the free exercise of its will the nature and destiny of the world. To experience sanctity, to experience the world *as creation*, is to experience oneself as caught up in the ways of grace and giftedness that overwhelm and comprehend us. We do not comprehend this world, even as it comprehends us. Marion observes: "The constituting subject is succeeded by the constituted witness. As a constituted witness, the subject remains the worker of truth, but no longer its producer."[19] We are constituted in and through the many lives and habitats that literally and figuratively feed us. Authentic human life and prayer must constantly bear witness to this irreducible fact.

Should not this realization of our constitution in and through others, a realization garnered in and through our practical living and work, spontaneously lead to praise and thanksgiving and thus rekindle two key moments in the life of prayer? As moderns or postmoderns, we do not take well to the idea that we are dependent on others. We fear oppression and violence wherever interdependence is invoked and thus cling to the dream of an autonomous, unencumbered life. This dream, however, is only a dream. Practically speaking, as Berry observes, there is "no such thing as autonomy . . . there is only a distinction between responsible and irresponsible dependence."[20] We do not, cannot live alone. The question, therefore, is whether we can turn our self-imposed isolation and division into the wholeness of friendship and health that would constitute our salvation. For this task, the work of prayer, which is the work of attention and responsibility, is essential.

PART II

Praying and the Limits of Phenomenology

7

Irigaray's *Between East and West*
Breath, Pranayama, and the Phenomenology of Prayer

CLEO   MCNELLY   KEARNS

> In the same way the Spirit also helps our weakness; for we
> do not know how to pray as we should, but the Spirit him-
> self intercedes for us with groanings too deep for words.
>
> — Romans 8:26

> I knew that the body is potentially divine, I knew it nota-
> bly through my Christian tradition, of which it is, in fact,
> the message, but I did not know how to develop this di-
> vinity.
>
> Luce Irigaray

In *Between East and West*, her recent reflections on the encounter between her yoga practice and her work in Western philosophy, Luce
Irigaray notes that breathing and speaking are, for most people, inverse operations, using the body, the diaphragm, and the lungs in
almost opposite ways.[1] The result is a split, an alienation, between
the verbal and the organic rather than a mutual enrichment of the
two. Irigaray goes on to warn that "a religion centered on speech,
without the insistence on breathing and the silence that makes it possible, risks supporting a non-respect for life" (51). As she develops
this theme, Irigaray notes in passing both the interweaving of breath,
speech, and silence in the New Testament Annunciation to Mary and
the oscillation between speaking, breathing, singing, and chanting in

the prayer life of many religious traditions. Her remarks help to open up a passage between philosophy of religion and the discourse of prayer, a passage that can perhaps help to articulate some of the issues at stake between them.

The topic of prayer is of great interest to phenomenologists in part because, as Aristotle noted long ago, the discourse of prayer seems to call into question or suspend the propositional language that so quickly reifies into logocentrism.[2] Prayer thus suggests a different way of deploying language and another modality of meaning, tantalizing in its proximity to and yet difference from that of philosophical discourse "proper." In most phenomenological reflections, with some exceptions, prayer is still presumed to be largely a verbal performance. On the role of breathing, for instance, or silence as ways of cultivating spiritual discipline (not to mention music, and even, as the monastic tradition would suggest, work), most philosophical and theological writing in the West have very little to say. Irigaray's recent work is an exception and it indicates, if only in a preliminary way, what may be gained by attending to breath and silence as modes of prayer, though it indicates as well the kinds of problems this attention may raise.

In *Between East and West,* Irigaray offers the seeds of an understanding of the practice of prayer not only at the verbal level but at the level of the body, and she does so with particular reference to the breath and to the rests, silences, and pauses that articulate speech. Irigaray correlates this understanding from time to time with the terms of Christian theology, but she elaborates it primarily with reference to Eastern philosophy and religion, more particularly to the various schools of yoga and to the practice of conscious breathing advocated by these traditions and known as pranayama. While Irigaray is by no means attempting to "erase from her mind" all the categories and distinctions common to European philosophy, as T. S. Eliot once put it of his own study of yoga, she is struck by the application of Eastern traditions to European or Western problems in religious discourse and she attempts to provide the beginnings, at least, of a point of entry into their pursuit.

There are three insights arising from her practice and study of yoga and pranayama that seem, to Irigaray, key to a revitalizing of breath and silence in Western philosophy and spiritual practice: (1) that speech should be organically related to but may in fact be relatively divorced from or counterproductive of breath and silence; (2) that a more flexible way of breathing—and hence of speaking and praying—may be cultivated, even to the point of spiritual transformation; and (3) that breath itself and the kinds of religious discipline related to it are situated in the body and may hence be, at least in some of its manifestations, gendered. Each of these insights has a bearing both on the mode of Western speculation on religious discourse and on its content, and though each raises a host of methodological, ideological, and philosophical problems, each also provides a new slant on a number of issues that arise in connection with the phenomenology of prayer.

Irigaray begins her exploration of these three points by noting the way in which practices of constricted talking at the expense of full breathing and the rhythmic silences that support it divorce speech from bodily experience. Informed by her own instruction in yogic breathing, she observes that people who breathe poorly are often extremely loquacious. "It is their way of breathing, and notably of exhaling in order to draw another breath," she comments (51). Irigaray does not speak here metaphorically but literally: she is pointing out, as her yoga instructors have no doubt pointed out to her, that those who do not fully exhale from a supple and relaxed diaphragm often subconsciously force speech in order to activate that diaphragm and clear the lungs for the next in-breath. Speech used in this way—used, that is, as a kind of substitute for organic breathing—is also associated, we may add, with a slight gasping or grabbing at the next breath as it comes along or, conversely, with an anxious pause at the end of the exhalation. It also goes along with either a constriction of the torso, a kind of hugging in or narrowing, and/or a laxness and looseness of posture, a weakness through the body's core.

Though Irigaray does not elaborate the point in this way, the resulting measurable deprivation of air—the material and somatic support for spirit in many traditions of spiritual practice both East and West—has not only health effects but effects on clarity of mind, on pertinence of thought, and on communication as well. It produces speech that is, as we say, "dry" or "vapid," but also dogmatic, alienated, and dull, lacking elemental qualities of authority, force, flow, inspiration, and spaciousness or organic relationship to context. At the other end of the breathing spectrum are those who underarticulate, or swallow their words. Stammering, muttering, and poor articulation are gross manifestations of this counterproductive relationship between speech and breath, but there are manifestations at the level of content and effect as well. Talking here becomes a substitute for or an impediment to flexible and responsive speech, a way of galvanizing and forcing a constricted bodily practice that has become narrowed by anxiety and chronic tension and forcing it into at least a semblance of oxygenation and life support.

Drawing on her long immersion in postmodern philosophy, Irigaray associates this divorce from organic life with discourses that attempt to be definitive or that take place almost exclusively in the imperative voice, discourses that become, in content as well as mode, dogmatic. As she puts it:

> the act of using breath to define more or less definitive words, of using nature and living bodies to develop a social worship becomes destructive because of a lack of recognition and regeneration of this contribution of [organic] life. Such spiritual and religious practices or theories quickly become authoritarian through the immobilization of breathing. They become dogmatic by forgetting the gift that comes from the living world—in particular the vegetal world—and from human bodies—in particular female bodies. (51)

It is this alienated speech that is often invested in the effort of what Irigaray calls "definition" for short but that we may understand to mean the effort to enunciate a position, a final logos, that will foreclose debate. This effort often involves the use of speech and breath simply to occupy unlimited space and time, to have, as we say, "the last word." It is an effect as exhausting to the mind as to the body, unless it is regulated by punctuation, pause, and a bracketing that allow the in-breath and hence the silence that opens to a response from the addressee.

Living, supple, and effective speech (and by extension living, supple, and effective prayer) may hence be defined by contrast as speech that rides upon the breath, speech that does not interrupt or choke off the rise and fall of the diaphragm but harmonizes with it and remains aware both of the symbolic or "content" level of what is said and of the semiotic-somatic rhythms entailed in the shaped flow of air both inside and outside the body. Such speech is not only relieving to the speaker but communicative to the spoken-to, for, again, there are verifiable effects of the breathing of speakers and the rhythms of their speech on the breath of those who listen—and by the same token, effects on their emotional responses. Furthermore, at the most practical level, speakers who give time and tempo to their own in-breath necessarily create the silence and the space necessary for others to respond.[3]

A second and very important aspect of the understanding of breath that informs *Between East and West*, but that may be lost on ears accustomed to a very different kind of religious and philosophical discourse, is that the alternative kinds of flexible, organically rooted, open-ended, and eventually transformative breathing and speaking practices for which this critique implicitly calls *can be cultivated*—even to the point of spiritual transformation. Indeed, the religious discourse on which Irigaray is drawing here, the manuals and teaching traditions of yoga, are almost entirely devoted to the techniques for this cultivation and transformation. This emphasis makes these classics of Eastern spirituality very different from the kinds of devotional and spiritual texts most privileged in the West, and it points to an axiomatic divergence so deeply rooted as to appear almost invisible from within each paradigm taken on its own terms. To undertake this deliberate cultivation, for instance, is, from a Western theological point of view, to blur the kinds of distinction between innate and infused grace, between given and constructed categories, and between "authentic" and contrived experience that have long been of great concern to Jewish and Christian seekers. It is also to raise the specter of deification.[4]

Prescinding from these issues for a moment, we may note that for Irigaray, at least, it is possible to envisage spiritual transformation through the bodily breath in Western as well as Eastern terms. As Irigaray puts it of her own Roman Catholic spiritual formation:

> I knew that the body is potentially divine, I knew it notably through my Christian tradition of which it is, in fact, the message, but I did not know how to develop this divinity. Through practicing breathing, through educating my perceptions, through concerning myself continually with cultivating the life of my body, through reading current and ancient texts of the yoga tradition and Tantric texts, I learned what I knew: the body is the site of the incarnation of the divine. (61–62)

"Music, colors, smells, tastes, singing, carnal love . . . can be of use in this transubstantiation," she goes on (62) to note, and it is the potential for the steady cultivation and spiritualization of sensory and sensible experience through bodily techniques rather than through some externally generated and quasi-metaphysical dynamic of fall and redemption that has come to her through her practice of yoga as a surprise and a delight. "Becoming spiritual," she concludes, "amounts to transforming our elemental vital breath little by little into a more subtle breath in the service of the heart, of thought, of speech" (70).

The theological implications of this potential for cultivation and spiritualization of bodily experience and the story of its simultaneous occultation and transmission in Western art and religious tradition would fill volumes. Of greater interest for the moment, however, are its implications for the phenomenology of prayer and perhaps for the phenomenological method itself, which, in spite of its critique of Cartesian principles, continues to postulate a relatively static realm of the experiential, including the religious experiential, upon which philosophical reflection operates as if from outside. Breath as a conscious discipline of transformation, however, tends to destabilize this assumption, for when sensory life is consciously breathed as a spiritual practice, it changes beneath the breather just as, to use a traditional analogy, a horse changes gait under a rider.

Irigaray's critique of reified and inflexible speaking as a factor of unschooled or uncultivated breathing is closely tied not only to her valorization but to her critique of Western religious discourse, including the discourse of prayer. In one of her more pregnant paragraphs, Irigaray remarks:

> In the passage from traditions that respect the breath to those that submit (themselves) to speech without concern for the breath, the mode of speaking has evolved from poetic saying, from the hymn of song, from the prayer of praise to already written discourses or texts, often in the imperative, addressing the individual in his relation to society more than to the cosmos, an individual whose paradigm is the adult man subject to the authority of the often-absent gods of his gender. (53–54)

However fraught with theological and ideological problems, this remark does draw attention in a fresh way to the close associations between prayer, breath, chant, and song in many religious traditions. It suggests that this relation is not simply ornamental but functional as well; chant and poetic discourse have to do deeply with attention to the breath, rest, and silence in the activity of prayer. They hence work, to speak for a moment theologically, directly, as it were, on spirit, and they help to imbricate or incarnate spirit with body, yoking or joining them together in the work of praise.

If nothing else, then, this observation of Irigaray's may help to re-situate if not to depose the emphasis on prayer in phenomenology as a verbal activity of the ratiocinative mind and place it in the context of a wider variety of practices and modalities. Gregorian chant, for instance, is from this perspective not simply prayer set to music; rather, the music and the words *together* form the prayer, the long lines helping to extend and deepen the breath and the sonorities opening and vibrating the nasal cavities and the cavities of the lungs. Thus it is also with religious poetry, poetry that is much about attention to rhythm, pulse, length of line, and sonority of sound. Here, too, may reside the roots of the frequency with which many religious traditions turn to an archaic or alternative special language for their prayers, whether it be the Latin of the Mass and Psalter or the ancient Sanskrit of mantra *dikṣha* (repetition of mantram as a spiritual practice) and *kirtan* (devotional chanting). The intoning of prayers in a language distinct from that of ordinary speech both decenters or displaces the discursive meaning and draws attention to sound, silence, and breath.

The work of Julia Kristeva on the semiotic helps to support this understanding, for one key to speech that moves with and in complement to—as opposed to against and in displacement of—the breath lies in semiotic manifestations, in rhythms, pulses of sound, and pauses, in the soft or percussive, labile or palatal movements of speech in the mouth, nasal cavities, lungs, and diaphragm. When Kristeva speaks of the thetic cut that brings the symbolic or rational and logos-bearing aspect of speech into and sometimes athwart the semiotic, or when she talks of the sacrifice of the murmuring, flowing subvocalizations of childhood and motherhood necessary to that level of precision, definition, and codified communication,[5] Irigaray might respond that we can, with the practice of breath, begin to locate that moment of cut in the body and learn to work with and perhaps mitigate its more violent manifestations. In the context of an understanding of breath and its role in sacred discourse, then, the rigidities and reifications associated with the symbolic can, as Kristeva would certainly affirm, be situated in bodily as well as in rhetorical and discursive practices but they can also be mitigated by a more flexible, conscious, and cultivated deployment of breath as a form of mediation.

The third—and perhaps most problematic—point Irigaray wishes to make comes with an extension of her critique of constricted breathing to some remarks on the gendered quality of breath and of its cultivation with respect to nature on the one hand and spiritual transformation on the other. For her, as several of the citations above make clear, organic breathing practices are closely associated with gender difference. "In fact," she opines, "what attracts man and woman to each other, beyond a simple, corporeal difference, is a difference of subjectivity, and notably a difference of relation to the breath" (84). Man, she argues, emphasizes the external movement of the breath; he situates the breath in the world. Woman, by contrast, keeps the breath inside her: "Her breath need not leave her in order to build, to fabricate, to create" (85). This construction of the breath leads Irigaray to posit a special guiding role for women not only in erotic life but in the unfolding life of the soul, a role based paradoxically on a kind of spiritual virginity, an achievement of autonomous personhood that no carnal experience can breach, one she does not hesitate to call Marian. In making love, she says, desire is used to fund this energy and "for the transformation of sexual attraction into love, into speech, into thought" (87).

Although she mentions the shared breath of maternity, the passage from individual to corporate breathing lies for Irigaray primarily, it seems, through the erotic.[6] In fact, she says, we fail to understand human sexual attraction when we divorce it from that to which it is tied: "to the invisible and to the imperceptible of the flesh: to the soul, to the breath" (82). Because women have, in her view, a greater fund, a greater reserve, of breath than men and keep the breath better funded and supported internally, they can communicate this deeper breathing to the male in sexual experience. The result is a synergy, a higher energy for both. This reservoir of sexual power is the preliminary step to an understanding that consciousness and culture "cannot be entrusted to one subject alone." Rather, they are "engendered in the interaction between two subjectivities irreducible to one another: that of man and that of woman." Irigaray goes on to argue that in such a double regime there no longer exists "one sole logos, defined always and forever in the horizon of only one absolute or only one God, and supposedly inscribed in the neurons of the human species" (99). Rather, "two linguistic chains enter into interaction . . . leaving open the totality of meaning" (100).

Without following Irigaray into the wilderness of ideological, theological, and philosophical problems that her remarks here raise (among other things, it is surely many years since we have heard the terms *man* and *woman* deployed in quite this naïve a way), we may consider both the matrix of these remarks in Irigaray's experience of yoga and their implications for the discourse of prayer. For Irigaray's remarks on these matters, however problematic, do not come out of thin air or even necessarily out of some feminist *parti prise*, but from her immersion in the theory and practice of pranayama and of tantric yoga techniques, in which issues of the organic and gendered bodily base of prayer and meditation have long been entertained in ways for the most part quite foreign to Western thought. The reader may, then, forgive a brief excursus into one aspect, at least, of this theory and practice, if only in order to clarify some of Irigaray's terms and contexts.

The locus classicus for the practice and theory of breath and meditation in yoga is the work of Patanjali (circa. 400 B.C.E.–400 C.E.), whose *Yoga Sutra* has been the core textbook for practitioners in many places and in many religious contexts.[7] The *Yoga Sutra* is notoriously hard to understand and translate, for it is a series of pithy aphorisms designed primarily as mnemonics for the practice of directed breathing and its modulation into refined states of meditation, together with indicators of the theoretical implications drawn from the experience of these states in several different schools of thought.

These aphorisms range from entirely practical reminders about posture, comfort, and ease to extraordinarily technical discriminations of various spiritual attainments, their phenomenological manifestations and accompaniments, and their philosophical freight. To supply a context that helps these sutras make sense is, then, no easy task, especially for those versed in Western philosophical and religious discourses. As T. S. Eliot once wrote:

> Two years spent in the study of Sanskrit under Charles Lanman and a year in the mazes of Patanjali's metaphysics under the guidance of James Woods, left me in a state of enlightened mystification. A good half of the effort of understanding what the Indian philosophers were after—and their subtleties make most of the great European philosophers look like schoolboys—lay in trying to erase from my mind all the categories and kinds of distinction common to European philosophy from the time of the Greeks.[8]

The term "pranayama," as deployed in texts such as these comes, from the Sanskrit *prana*, from the prefix *pra-*, "to bring forth," and the root *yama*, "rein, curb, bridle; a driver, charioteer." *Ayama* is often translated as "control," and yet, as Richard Rosen reminds us, the effort toward control in the sense of mastery is highly counterproductive in the practice of breathing. It is more a matter of "lengthening, directing and regulating" than of limiting or restraining the breath (19).[9]

The question of what, indeed, is natural or what is forced here arises, it must be noted, in a context that requires at once discretion and critique. Is the breath culturally constructed? Yes, the practitioner of yoga according to Patanjali's theory and method would answer, to some extent it is. As those who teach pranayama have often pointed out, it is demonstrable that different cultures and societies, and the men and women in them, breathe differently; the frequently constricted upper-chest breathing of the urbanite, the male, and those under chronic stress is quite visible. The limits of this cultural construction, however, both at the "lower" end, the end at which breathing is essential to and even definitive of organic and animal life, and the "higher" end, the end at which it is spirit, inspiration, *spiritus, pneuma, ruach,* are precisely what is at issue in pranayama and in the many schools of Eastern philosophy dedicated to its exposition, for the presupposition is that these limits can be expanded and contracted, perhaps to the point of qualitative change.

The second of Irigaray's points here comes into play again: the insistence that a more flexible, open, and hence transformative mode of breathing can be cultivated. The key to this approach to the cultivation of speech and prayer through techniques of breathing lies in one of the more remarkable phenomena of breath: its extreme responsiveness both to emotion and to directed awareness or consciousness.

The most obvious manifestation of this responsiveness is the hot, panting breath of anger, fear, or lust, but there is an infinity of subtler modalities as well, changes in the time, texture, space, and rest, or articulation of silence, sound, and movement that are constantly changing in relation to the external and the internal environments of the psyche and soma.[10] The relationship here is reciprocal; that is to say, calming the breath will dissipate the anger just as anger will excite the breath. Furthermore, when awareness comes into play—when the breath is observed both in its microscopic subtleties and its broader context of earth, air, and sky—the breath automatically lengthens, regulates, and becomes more efficient in terms of oxygen use and more capable of direction.

Paradoxically, the simple act of conscious attention to the breath inaugurates this change. One of the more distinct qualities of the breath is that it occurs on the cusp between the voluntary and involuntary bodily movements, between the sympathetic and parasympathetic nervous systems. Most importantly, this is a phenomenon, a form of power that can be cultivated, if only by the simple act of observation, which changes the data according to a kind of Heisenberg principle of its own. The breath is thus both automatic or self-generating and capable, under conscious direction, of receiving impetus and direction from the will. Most of the time, however, we are breathed as much as or even more than we breathe.

It is observations such as these, together with the accompanying exploration of different states of spiritual awareness and their metaphysical implications, that make such texts as Patanjali's important matrices for the sometimes controversial or apparently outré speculations Irigaray offers in *Between East and West*, including her speculations on gender. Indeed, in support of her interest in such texts and perspectives, we may note that the extensive critique of will, mastery, and sovereign individual consciousness in postmodern philosophy, a critique that, while important, has often led to a cul-de-sac, might well meet some useful supplementation here. For Patanjali's practice and theory deploy a subjectivity less invested in mastery of than in collaboration with the body and a spiritual practice involving the decentering of the subject before a deeper and less accessible but far more potent source of identity, the breath.[11]

It is, then, possible that Irigaray's valorization of gender difference in breathing and by extension in prayer is neither as abstracted from phenomenological experience nor as absolute and essentialist as it may at first seem. Especially important may be her point that erotic experience involves a spiritually valuable recognition of the limit or border at which self meets other and a refusal to appropriate that difference back into the same. Certainly, too, the erotic model for human-divine interaction that Irigaray prefers has both a long pedigree in many religious traditions and a continued and valuable capacity to disturb or unsettle their more reified and dogmatic formulations (though it may coincide with and even fund repressive institutionalizations of these in other ways as well). Indeed, Irigaray's later remarks on tantric male-female practices point in the direction of a possible expansion of her own philosophical work on difference, gender, and community in ways that go well beyond the reflections she offers in *Between East and West*.

Pushed a step further, this understanding might even suggest that there may well be, at least in potential, a feminine *mode* of prayer, a prayer with a special relationship to the word, to breath, and to silence and a special recognition of the limit of difference between orders of being rather than an insistence on a univocal and absolute logocentrism. While there is, to my knowledge, little or no empirical evidence that men and women pray differently, there is a great deal of evidence in many traditions that an intense prayer life is thought to be optimally conceived in the feminine voice. From the Song of Songs to the Tao Te Ching and from the *bhakti* devotions of Hinduism to the practice of the rosary in Catholicism and the visualizations of Sherab Chamma in Bon-Buddhism, the feminine is the preferred locus, so to speak, of devotional expressions of religious life, and we are often abjured by saints and sages of many traditions to become feminine in our interior response to the Divine. It may be as much in this sense as in the sense of her modesty, humility, and obedience that Mary is held to be the model for the Christian life of prayer.

Suspending judgment, then, for a moment on the problems raised by Irigaray's views and suggestions on gender, breath, and prayer — though without entirely forgoing the philosophical and theological critique for which her position cries out[12] — we can at the least entertain the suggestion that an understanding of the relationship between speech and breath, of the potential for cultivation of breathing, and of the role of gender in that cultivation might illuminate both the theory and practice of prayer in Western traditions.

Irigaray touches here upon other problems, too, the problems of individual versus communal prayer, of the relationship between the personal breath and spirit and the breath and spirit of a community, and, as is often the case, between what can be construed as personal authenticity, what as citational practice, and what as public ritual. Traditional yogic breath practices, at least as currently taught and practiced, tend to lie on the side of individual experience, of the personal, internal breath, and of spiritual work situated in domestic or at least nonecclesiastical spaces: on the mat or in the lecture hall. Nonetheless, as Irigaray points out, these are not necessarily their only contexts or their only homes. The use of chant and song to support yoga already tends toward the collective, and the shared breath of guru-disciple and maternal and erotic experience can, in her view, extend and refine the interpersonal and eventually the communal dimensions of religious discourse.

There are also, moreover, broader theological implications in Irigaray's opening to Eastern theory and practice of pranayama as well, some of them with a direct bearing on issues discussed elsewhere in this volume, including especially the issue of technique raised above. One such implication, to give only a single example, sheds possible light upon a problem raised by B. Keith Putt with reference to Jean-Louis Chrétien's work on the phenomenology of prayer. Putt raises the question of what happens when a person intends to pray but lacks "the requisite technical and semiotic knowledge" to do so, that is, when a person does not know *how* to pray.[13] As I have remarked above, this condition of insufficient attention to the *how* is perhaps generic to the discourse of prayer in the West, where technique in matters of spirituality has, in general, a very bad name, and where it is seen often as a way of preempting or forcing grace, the very hallmark of an inauthenticity in the religious life that is anathema to Christian piety.

In dealing with this inability to pray, Putt cites and discusses at length the remarkable statement in Paul's letter to the Romans that forms the epigraph for this essay. Speaking of just this situation of cluelessness with respect to the *how* or technology of prayer and using the metaphor of crying aloud with pain in childbirth, Paul testifies that the Spirit itself steps in at this point: "In the same way the Spirit also helps our weakness; for we do not know how to pray as we should, but the Spirit himself intercedes for us with groanings too deep for words" (Rom. 8:26, NASV). Putt notes that in his extensive work on the phenomenology of prayer, Chrétien interprets this text along Augustinian lines to mean that the Spirit in some manner supplies for us the missing speech that enables us to pray, primarily by giving divinity a human embodiment and speaking capacity so as to act on our behalf. God prays to [him]self and lets us join in the prayer. Evoking the Latin root for spirit, *spiritus*, breath, Chrétien refers to this form of praying as a "respiration," a "conspiration," a "breathing (*spirare*) together (*con*)." We inhale the Spirit's vocable prayer so as to exhale it again as an offering to God.

Though he is equally taken with the passage from Romans, Putt takes issue with Chrétien's interpretation. In his view, Chrétien maintains too much the role of rational language in the Spirit's intervention, thus foreclosing the recognition of the very point at issue: the lack, the falling short, the wound at this phenomenological level of a speaking voice inadequate to do the work of prayer. It is precisely this lack, Putt argues, that creates the problem in the first place, and the problem is not addressed merely by the substitution of the words of another. The restored prayer of those who do not know how to pray is, for Putt, not God invoking (him)self through the human voice, however adequately, but God invoking a full recognition of the abyss of impossibility from which we all pray. This abyss is marked, for Putt, by a profound silence, the silence that takes us, in a sense, beyond phenomenology. It is a silence, he argues, that:

would not be the product of a hyperousiological dynamic, as in negative theology, or the result of an ineffability ensuing from some saturated phenomenon of divine presence. Instead, it might be something more akin to an almost *khôra*-like experience of a passion for the Impossible that remains *en abîme*, that simply cannot rise to the level of reason and language. (Putt, "Too Deep," 148)

"Unlike Christ the Son," Putt continues, "who also prays to the Father on behalf of his disciples but always linguistically through prayers that are textualized and iterable, the Spirit prays without language by uttering 'groanings too deep for words'" (Ibid., 150).

There is, however, perhaps a *via media* between Chrétien and Putt here. For if we literalize Chrétien's metaphor of the breath a little, shape it a bit, and give it some attention and cultivation in terms suggested by Irigaray—although without necessarily sublating it entirely into speech—we have a form of prayer that is neither entirely captive to the logos of rational discourse, with its dangerous potential for reification, nor entirely lost in the abyss of failed discursivity, with its dangerous potential for entropy. It is a form of prayer at once communicative, intentional, embodied, and well within the human realm of phenomenology yet grounded in silence, in expectation, and in openness to the coming of the other. At the most simple and most phenomenal level, the breath of the Spirit (which is, at some level, a tautology) does exactly what Paul says it does: it continues on its own to uphold and support us at our weakest, even without our conscious volition. As fully "spirited" breath, moreover, which entails even at the physiological level both complete inhalation and complete exhalation, it naturally creates the silence into which another voice may move.

Without wanting to press this point too far, I might also add that it is perhaps no accident that Paul casts this prayer of the cosmic breath within in decidedly feminine, maternal terms: the "groaning" in question is like that of a woman giving birth, a process that also involves both activity and passivity and that gives rise to the new breath of the infant, which supplements and expands the breath of the community. It is impossible, as Irigaray points out, for one person to breath for another, with the partial exception of the mother breathing for the fetus in the womb. But it is very possible, as she has also no doubt come to see, for one person to augment another's breathing first by giving birth to that other and then by tuning, so to speak, the respirations together until both lengthen and deepen into greater amplitude and, yogis would argue, deeper peace. This augmentation is both natural and spiritual; it is a perhaps somewhat esoteric practice of the Eastern masters with their disciples, to be sure, but it is also the daily practice of mothers, and not only of mothers breathing for the fetus in the womb, as Irigaray notes, but also, I would point out, of mothers (and fathers, aunts, uncles, etc.) holding babies on their breasts

As I have noted, Irigaray links this augmentation of the breath as the basis of spiritual life specifically to the Annunciation and to Mary's conception and nurturing of Jesus.[14] Irigaray's Marian theology is a topic too complex to embark on here, but this matrix for her reflections, together with her own attempt in *Between East and West* to link Eastern spiritual techniques and philosophical thought, indicates the profound implications for Western religious discourse involved in the study of pranayama. These implications are especially rich when it comes to the subject of prayer. Indeed, in many musical settings of Mary's great prayer, the Magnificat, speech and sound are deeply supported by silence and the cultivation of breath, and these settings offer one example of prayer grounded in the body and open to the other in something of the way for which both Eastern wisdom and the Western critique of logocentrism call. This is one reason, perhaps, why this Marian prayer has appeal to many beyond the boundaries of Christian orthodoxy. In any case, it is certainly by moving beyond these bounds and perhaps even beyond the bounds of philosophy "proper" to explore the cultivation of the breath in pranayama that Irigaray has begun to reanimate not only the terms of her own Western discourse but those of a very different religious, philosophical, and spiritual perspective as well.

It is important to remember, however, that though Irigaray's perspective is dependent on some experience of yoga practice and on some exposure to Hindu and Buddhist religious traditions both in practice and in theory, it is also deeply and continuously informed by her own immersion in and creative tension with Continental philosophy. The critique of logocentrism in the work of postmodern philosophers such as Jacques Lacan, Jacques Derrida, Julia Kristeva, and Irigaray herself not only deconstructs the metaphysics of presence at a philosophical level but opens up a space for other ways of knowing and thinking, ways that often entail a change of genre, orientation, and even bodily experience as well as a change of mind. The new interest in the greater sophistication of Eastern techniques and practices with respect to these modalities to which *Between East and West* testifies is also a vital factor in their recovery, but to approach them or the philosophical assumptions and religious traditions in which they are often embedded without the salutary corrosive of a honed deconstructive awareness risks leading only to new instantiations of dogmatic and authoritarian discourse. With these problems the traditions of Eastern spirituality are as fraught as any others, though perhaps at a subtler level. Philosophy, and in particular Continental philosophy, is in this respect as necessary to the understanding of spiritual modalities as breath, and we are as indebted to the practitioners of philosophical critique — Irigaray among them — as to teachers of the physical, psychological, and mental exercises of yoga and meditation in articulating any approach to their conjunction.

8

Heidegger and the Prospect of a Phenomenology of Prayer

BENJAMIN CROWE

An attempt to contribute to a "phenomenology of prayer" ought to begin with the recognition that the word "phenomenology" means many different things to many different people. Moreover, it must be recognized that none of these usages has any obvious claim to being the normative one. Given these inescapable facts, it is therefore incumbent on one who would make such a contribution to define just what it is that he or she might mean by "phenomenology."

At the beginning of the last century, Martin Heidegger presented the world with his own views on the nature and tasks of phenomenology. Following the lead of Wilhelm Dilthey, Heidegger conceived of phenomenology as a *hermeneutical* enterprise. It is in this sense that I use the term "phenomenology" in the present essay. Hermeneutical phenomenology, at least in Heidegger's rendition, is premised on two basic claims: (1) life, even at the most immediate level, is always already meaningful; and (2) history is to be understood not primarily as a record of "facts" but as rich depository of meaningful expressions of life. Heidegger expresses both of these claims quite clearly. The first idea emerges in a lecture course from 1919: "Life as such is *not* irrational (which has nothing whatever to do with 'rationalism'!)" (G56/57 219/187). Making the same point later on, he writes that "Life is not a chaotic confusion of dark torrents, not a mute principle of power, not a limitless, all-consuming disorder, rather *it is what it is only as a concrete meaningful shape*" (G58 148). Life encounters us as

119

having been interpreted in discourse and in practice rather than as raw sense-data or an assemblage of meaningless objects. Or, as he puts it in *Being and Time*, objects have practical significance for life, they are "ready-to-hand." The second claim is also made during the winter semester 1919–1920: "The authentic *organon of the understanding of life is history*, not as historical science or as a collection of curiosities, but rather as life that has been lived, [history] as it accompanies [life] in actual living" (G58 256).

The primary aim of this essay is to present a hermeneutics of prayer. The more proximal goal, itself motivated by this larger purpose, is to clarify in more detail the nature of hermeneutic phenomenology as it applies to the phenomena of religious life. Accordingly, the discussion proceeds in two parts. The first part is largely expository and is aimed at clarifying the sense of hermeneutic phenomenology through a close reading of Heidegger's lecture course for the winter semester 1920–1921. The second part is a contribution to the hermeneutics of prayer in the form of an interpretation of the New Testament that follows the guidelines gleaned from a reading of Heidegger's essays and lectures.

1. Principles of the Hermeneutics of Religious Life

Heidegger's own approach to hermeneutics is greatly indebted to the work of Wilhelm Dilthey. This is something that Heidegger himself explicitly acknowledges on many occasions, showering rare praise on Dilthey and attempting to defend his work against superficial critiques. The most well-known of these professions of allegiance comes from *Being and Time* itself: "The researches of Dilthey were, for their part, pioneering work; but today's generation has not as yet made them its own. In the following analysis the issue is solely one of furthering their adoption" (SZ 377/429). Heidegger devoted a significant portion of his summer semester 1920 lecture course to Dilthey (G59) and gave a lecture at Kassel detailing his assessment of Dilthey's contributions to modern German thought.

If we examine both Dilthey and Heidegger closely, it becomes clear that religion was by no means a peripheral issue in the development of hermeneutical phenomenology. Hence there is a certain appropriateness in applying a hermeneutical approach to the study of prayer. Both Dilthey and Heidegger frequently attest to their conviction that religion is a vital expression of the pretheoretical meaningfulness of life. Dilthey, for example, identifies "moral-religious truth" with "our life as personal experience," a sphere that is recalcitrant to both metaphysical and naturalistic explanations (GS 1 384–5/218). Dilthey uses terms such as "personal experience," "lived experience," and the like as ways of designating the immediate reality of human life from which the more rarefied discourse of the sciences takes its departure. His conviction is that this immediate level of experience cannot be adequately described using the categories of traditional metaphysics or of the natural sciences. Instead, religion and literature are able to capture its meaning much more accurately. Heidegger, too, regards religious life as a decisive exemplification of what he calls "factical life-experience" (see G58 61; G60 82, etc.). Both Dilthey and Heidegger also hold that religious life, particularly *Christian* religious life, harbors a unique "feeling for life" that has often been covered over or distorted by subsequent work in both theology and philosophy. To put it another way, both Dilthey and Heidegger consistently maintain that documents of the Christian religion contain a rare and rich understanding of the immediacy of life.

Given these views, it is no surprise that both Dilthey and Heidegger devoted their hermeneutical efforts to understanding religious life. In what follows, I briefly describe Dilthey's approach to the hermeneutics of religious life. The primary focus, however, is on Heidegger, whose work represents a continuation and critical adaptation of some of Dilthey's basic ideas. In Dilthey's view, religion is to be understood under the rubric of "objective spirit." That is, religion is a "purposive system" of beliefs, practices, and traditions that makes both self-understanding and mutual understanding possible for individuals (GS7 151/173, 153/175, 166/187). "Objective spirit" is Dilthey's term for the manifest forms that inner life takes on a grander scale. He is careful to distinguish his usage from Hegel's; for Hegel, "objective spirit" refers to a stage in the development of moral culture (GS7 148–149/170–171). For Dilthey, on the other hand, "objective spirit" describes the shared contexts of meaning that enable both self-understanding and mutual understanding between individuals to take place. The forms of "objective spirit" include "education, economic life, the law, political activity, religion, sociability, art, philosophy, and science" (GS7 166/187). "Individuals, as carriers and representatives of the commonalities interwoven in them, can appreciate and grasp the historical genesis of these commonalities. Individuals can understand history because they themselves are historical beings" (GS7 151/173).

Because history is viewed as a repository of "objective spirit" and of other "expressions" of pretheoretical life, Dilthey holds that "History is not something separated from life or remote from the present" (GS7 147/169). In accord with these ideas, Dilthey maintains that the only way to understand religious phenomena properly is to trace them back to the "inwardness of psychic life" (GS5 372). In practice, this means delving into the developmental process in which the various forms of religious expression, for example, myth, doctrine, prayer, come to be formed and articulated (GS5 372).

While Heidegger's own approach to the hermeneutics of religious life bears many affinities with Dilthey's work, there are also important differences. The most valuable source for Heidegger's views on the hermeneutics of religion is his winter semester 1920–1921 lecture course, appropriately entitled "Introduction to the Phenomenology of Religion." In this course, Heidegger presents his own hermeneutical approach as a challenge to the usual approaches to the "science" of religion (G60 28). For this reason, Heidegger's ideas constitute a useful point of departure not only for getting clear about what the hermeneutics of religion is but also for actually contributing to it in an analysis of the central religious phenomenon of prayer.

Much of Heidegger's discussion in this lecture course is occupied with articulating the flaws of alternative approaches. One key feature of these approaches is the imposition of an alien "classificatory order" (*Ordnung*) upon the phenomena (G60 129–130). Different kinds of classificatory order have been proposed, and Heidegger considers several of them. One involves the attempt to "insert" the matter under consideration into historical, developmental contexts and then to go on to investigate the motives of this development (G60 130).[1] Other schemata might be based on what passes for "common sense" (G60 134). Heidegger does not explain what he means by these kind of classificatory schemes, but he probably has in mind the tendency to read religious concepts like other concepts that have arisen in a completely different context. Thus claims such as "God saved my soul" are *obviously* causal claims, and petitionary prayers are *obviously* like any other kind of request.

Another approach might be to classify phenomena in terms of "supratemporal problems" (G60 171), a kind of theological *Problemsge-schichte*.[2] Here, the interpretation of religion would involve tracing out various responses to "problems" such as the existence of God, the problem of evil, predestination and election, and so on. Finally, there might be an "axiologizing" approach, which employs some independent hierarchy of values to interpret religious phenomena (G60 256).[3] What all of these approaches share is a tendency to conceal the "context of sense" that belongs to religion (G60 172). Or, as Heidegger puts it in another place: "Regional ordering schemata, or transcendental ideas, not only do not suffice, but actually block the problematic" (G60 258).

While Dilthey is not named explicitly, there is another aspect of the common approach to the "science" of religion that Heidegger is quite critical of and which seems to have played an important role in Dilthey's actual investigations of religious figures.[4] In reflecting on how to go about understanding the "situation" of Paul's epistle to the Galatians, Heidegger explicitly refuses the historicist epistemological problem of "empathy" and the crucial category of "personality" (G60 88). The task of a genuine "articulation" of the phenomena involved in such a subject matter requires that one disregard psychological schemata (G60 121). For example, the "knowing" that Paul discusses in 1 Thessalonians and the related concept of "spirit" are completely falsified if one takes contemporary psychology as a starting point (G60 123). This "knowing" is an integral part of the life of a Christian, a life of "service" and "waiting." "Knowing" does not "swing free" of this context (G60 123).[5] That is, this "knowing" is not a matter of indifferent, objective cognition of neutral facts; to the contrary, it is a special kind of self-knowledge, a way of identifying oneself with a particular history or ministry. In a final remark, which surely aims at the kind of interpretation associated with Dilthey, Heidegger states unequivocally that "The *explication* of the *proclamation* does not have the purpose of producing a contributing page to some *picture of a personality as a particular type*" (G60 138; emphasis in original).

Heidegger's principal worry about the sorts of approaches outlined above is that they fail to do real justice to their subject matter, in this case religious life. After all, a cardinal principle of hermeneutics is that one should try to avoid doing unnecessary violence to the text under consideration. But how is it that justice can be done? The key concept for Heidegger at this stage in his career is "life," or "factical life-experience." For Heidegger, concepts such as "mind," "spirit," "consciousness," and the like must give way before a more nuanced appreciation between the interpenetrating context of meaning, individual, social, and environmental, that comprises the full richness of life (G60 11–14). The project for the philosophy of religion then becomes one of appreciating the sense of religious words and actions within this context rather than reducing their meaning to some kind of explanatory ground or inserting them within some alien schema.

In both the winter semester 1920–1921 and the summer semester of 1921, Heidegger is concerned with *Christianity*, with the meaning of several very specific instances of Christian language. The claim is that we must understand the things that Paul or Augustine say within the context of an "anxious worry" (*Bekümmerung*) about salvation and life (G60 69). Heidegger employs a number of different terms for this context, but they all essentially point to the same idea: the "enactment-historical situation" (G60 88), a "factical life-environment" (G60 128), a "structural context" (G60 129), a totality of relations in which linguistic content is embedded (G60 136), and a "context of enactment" (G60 138). These expressions are all more or less interchangeable ways of emphasizing the claim that religious language can be adequately understood only when it is viewed in relation to its practical context in actual life. The context in which religious words and deeds make sense is not that of giving a theory, demonstrating propositions, or explaining the way things are. Instead, to use Heidegger's language, the context is the "how" of a certain kind of life.

How do we approach this context in order to understand religious meaning? Heidegger variously terms his basic approach "phenomenological" or "enactment-historical" (G60 173). We begin with a particular, definite religiosity (G60 124). Hence we do not take it for granted that there is some universal something called "religion" or even that there is such a thing called "Christianity." The context that opens up the sense of Paul's words is not that of Augustine nor of Luther, nor of anyone else besides Paul. The task, then, is one of "explication" of the sense from out of this context (G60 129). Our job is not simply descriptive, but one of "extraction" (*Herausnahme*) (G60 129). Our job is the hermeneutical task of making the meaning explicit through the "fundamental enactment of a preconception." This is not achieved through the imposition of a classificatory order but in the hermeneutical back-and-forth between our preconception and the subject matter. Instead of uncritically utilizing our assumptions, we push ourselves out into the difficulties faced by trying to understand the sense (G60 129). What is required is not the pretended objectivity of "common sense" but radical transparency regarding one's own assumptions (G60 131).

Heidegger's studies of Paul and Augustine provide a number of illustrations of this kind of approach. In looking at *Galatians*, we must have an eye to Paul's situation, which is one of "struggle" and has nothing to do with theoretical contexts (G60 72).[6] The seeming self-evidence of our usual readings of Paul's texts needs to be called into question (G60 79). Beginning with the context of struggle and of "proclamation," we must try to explicate the meaning of what Paul says (G60 87). In general, the "what" of these letters can be grasped in an accurate way only if one pays attention to the "how" of the community (G60 145). The real content, or meaning, lies embedded in a "factical life-experience" that has "come to language" in the exchange between Paul and the Thessalonians, not in the "polish and detachment of theory" but rather in the "turnings and aberrations of factical life in its travail" (G60 145). With respect to Augustine and his discussions of *tentatio* in Book X of the *Confessions*, Heidegger argues that we cannot understand this as an objective "theory" about human life but must see it within the overall structure of the presentation of these ideas, that is, as a *confessio* (G60 212).

What, then, can one say about the principles of a hermeneutics of religion? There are five main lessons to be drawn here, which are not to be taken as independent directives but as expressions of an overall strategy for doing philosophy: (1) one ought to renounce the urge for generality, instead contenting oneself with the task of understanding a particular instance of religious sense, which itself might be more ambitious than it looks; (2) one ought to eschew uncritical constructions, particular those involving theory and common sense, but instead let one's presuppositions be challenged by the subject matter; (3) the subject matter of philosophy of religion is not "doctrine" nor is it the psychology of believers but is the *sense* or *meaning* of what religious people say; (4) this meaning must be contextualized, viewed in terms of its "situation" in life—the things that religious people say are expressions of a particular *way of life*; (5) the task, then, is to "explicate" this sense in a way that does justice to its context, a task that ultimately amounts to finding the meaning of religion in *life*.

2. Contributions Toward a Hermeneutics of Prayer

Now that some much-needed clarity regarding the nature of hermeneutical phenomenology has been achieved, the task is to offer a contribution to our understanding of prayer that follows the principles set forth above. I begin my exposition with a brief synopsis of Heidegger's reading of the basic meaning of primitive Christian life-experience. I find this interpretation to be not only substantially correct but also illuminating with respect to the phenomenology of prayer. Hence I aim to fulfill the hermeneutical requirement that one make one's guiding preconceptions about a subject matter as explicit as possible.

On Heidegger's view, the "life-world" of the first Christians is structured by the uncanny uncertainty of being existentially suspended between the intrusion of the "proclamation" of the Cross and the incalculable arrival of the Parousia. Heidegger understands the core of the "proclamation" to be the announcement that Jesus of Nazareth, a man apparently cursed by God, has in fact been exalted by God to be the agent of universal salvation.[7] The meaning of Christian life can be most clearly discerned in the community's response to this proclamation: a "turning *toward* God and *away* from idols" (G60 95; emphasis in original). Indeed, the proclamation cannot be fully understood apart from its connection to this response, which Heidegger also describes as "running the course of one's life before God [*Wandeln vor Gott*] and waiting upon him in service [*Erharren*]," and as the "achievement of a living, effective connection with God" (G60 95). It is precisely this new way of life, defined as a connection with God, which is the indispensable condition for gaining a proper understanding of prayer. It is also crucial to recognize that part of the meaning of Christian life is *eschatological expectation*. The proclamation of the Crucified is also the proclamation of the Coming One (G60 97–98). Hence, rather than allowing his flock to indulge in worldly curiosity about the date and time of the Parousia, Paul admonishes them to be "wakeful" and "sober" (G60 105). Again, the accent is not on getting hold of the right theory about the world or the proper view of history, but on one's own personal living link with God (G60 112).[8]

One aspect of this wakeful Christian life that Heidegger leaves out of his own discussion is *prayer*. This is somewhat puzzling, given that prayer is obviously a practice that is historically definitive for the life-experience of Christian faith. Prayer is an integral component of the web of practices and beliefs that constitutes the unique meaning of Christian life. Hence my aim in what follows is to correct this lacuna in Heidegger's exposition while attempting to remain true to his principles. How, then, must I proceed? First, I take as my material for this interpretation a specific religious "expression." Furthermore, I relinquish any claim to make pronouncements about the "essence" of prayer as something over and above the meaningful content of this particularly expression. Third, if history is truly the "organon for understanding life," then my focus will be on interpreting what has been *written* about prayer. Following these guidelines, then, I take prayer in the early Christian community as my theme, relying on this community's own self-expressions in the New Testament.

Before carrying out this project, however, a few cautionary remarks are in order. First, what follows is not intended as a definitive theological account of the biblical concept of prayer.[9] Indeed, I am not offering a piece of biblical theology at all. Second, I will not examine in any detail many of the philological and exegetical issues involved in understanding what the New Testament says about prayer. For example, I will not explore the different kinds of prayer that are discussed, nor will I examine the absence of the Greek *"proseuchomai"* and its cognates from the "Johannine" writings.

The first thing that must be established is the claim that prayer is indeed an expression of the meaning of Christian life as it was lived in the first century of the Common Era. Fortunately, even the most cursory glance at the New Testament shows that it was indeed a crucial part of what it meant to be a Christian. For example, prayer is a central and recurring element in Luke's portrayal of Jesus. Luke depicts Jesus either praying or teaching about prayer at least twelve times. Indeed, all of the so-called "Synoptic" Gospels have Jesus praying either before or immediately after important moments in his ministry (e.g., Matt. 14:23; Mark 1:35; Luke 3:21). It is no surprise, then, that Luke also describes the centrality of prayer to the post-Easter community (e.g., Acts 1:14, 6:4, 9:40, 12:12ff., 16:25). Similarly, Paul and the other epistle writers are continually exhorting their readers to prayer, asking for their prayers, and offering prayers of their own. "I urge that supplications, prayers, intercessions, and thanksgivings be made for everyone" (1 Tim. 2:8). "Devote yourselves to prayer, keeping alert in it in thanksgiving" (Col. 4:2). The members of the early community regarded themselves as living a *new* life, albeit one that was yet to be completely fulfilled. More often than not, their prayers reflect their longing for this fulfillment. They also, however, reflect the attitude of mutual love and service that defined their ethos.

As I have already pointed out, Heidegger identifies *eschatology* as the central factor in early Christian life.[10] Eschatology, on Heidegger's reading, is not so much a matter of one's particular theoretical commitments regarding the meaning of history but rather is the context within which one leads a certain form of life. As such, it forms the deep background against which we can best make sense of what it means to *pray*. This is revealed, for example, by the scene in the Garden of Gethsemane. The eschatological meaning of prayer as it appears in this passage emerges most clearly if it is juxtaposed with an earlier scene in which Jesus delivers his eschatological message:

> But about that day or hour no one knows, neither the angels in heaven, nor the Son, but only the Father. Beware, keep alert; for you do not know when the time will come. It is like a man going on a journey, when he leaves home and puts his slaves in charge, each with his work, and commands the doorkeeper to be on the watch. Therefore, keep awake—for you do not know when the master of the house will come, in the evening, or at midnight, or at cockcrow, or at dawn, or else he may find you asleep when he comes suddenly. And what I say to you I say to you all: keep awake. (Mark 13:32–37)

Holding this passage in mind, turn now to two passages from the story about the night in the Garden:

> [1] He came and found them sleeping; and he said to Peter, "Simon, are you asleep? Could you not keep awake one hour? Keep awake and pray that you may not come into the time of trial; the spirit indeed is willing, but the flesh is weak" (Mark 14:37ff.).
> [2] He came to them a third time and said to them, "Are you still sleeping and taking your rest? Enough! The hour has come; the Son of Man is betrayed into the hands of sinners." (Mark 14:41)

This story, of course, precedes the arrest, trial, and death of Jesus. Here the disciples find themselves poised on the frontier of the new age, of the decisive revelation of God. This is clear from the saying about the "Son of Man" in Mark 14:41. Taken together with the earlier eschatological discourse, we can see that *watchful prayer* is an essential response to the message of the imminent kingdom of God. Praying in a spirit of "watchfulness" means praying with one's eyes peeled and ears opened for the fulfillment of the new creation. It expresses a life that already has one foot in God's future, so to speak. Those who are caught off guard, absorbed in worldly affairs, experience the arrival of this future as destruction and judgment. For those who are prepared, whose lives are lives of wakeful prayer, it is salvation. For Paul, too, prayer (indeed, *constant* prayer) is the appropriate attitude to take for one who expects the dawn of a new age. See, for example, the frequently referenced lines "Rejoice always, *pray without ceasing*, give thanks in all circumstances, for this is the will of God in Christ Jesus for you" (1 Thess. 5:16f.). Similarly, Paul admonishes the Romans to "Rejoice in hope, be patient in suffering, persevere in prayer" (Rom. 12:12).

What does all this tell us about what prayer *means*? Clearly, it is a practice that is integral to the "serving" and "waiting" that constitute the sense of Christian life. The primitive church regarded itself as the messianic community, the community of those who had been called out of the world to a new life of earnest prayer, mutual love, and eschatological anticipation. Unceasing prayer is taken as a definitive expression of this new life. It is an activity that, together with liturgical rites, charitable actions, and the proclamation of the Gospel, makes Christian life what it is. Divorced from this overall context, prayer takes on the character of magical formulae. Like enthusiastic eschatological expectation, a prayer that is not part of a *life of prayer* involves no personal commitment. At best it is a way to fit in with a particular group and at worst it is sheer presumption. The Christian denunciation of practices such as divination, magic, and fortune-telling is founded on the idea that these activities are rooted in a worldly *curiosity* about the divine secrets. It is as if one were trying to reduce the incalculable future of the kingdom of God to something that can be "managed." Having done so, one can go on crying "Peace and security!"

If prayer is not to degenerate in this way, then it must be seen as part of a total life, a life that is a response to the proclamation of the coming Kingdom of God. Such a life is often called a life "in the Spirit." Hence it is not surprising to find admonitions to "pray in the Holy Spirit" (Jude 1:20), to "Pray in the Spirit at all times in every prayer and supplication" (Eph. 6:18). This life "in the Spirit" is central to the meaning of the eschatological way of life that itself makes prayer intelligible to us. But what does "in the Spirit" mean, especially when it is said of prayer?

The gift of the Spirit is regarded as yet another sign that a new age has begun and the old one is passing away. Jesus had promised his followers that they would be "baptized with the Holy Spirit" and would "receive power when the Holy Spirit has come upon [them]" (Acts 1:5, 8). Praying "in the Spirit," then, means recognizing prayer itself as a *gift*, as a part of the radically altered existential situation of those who have received the gift of the Spirit. Following the return from the Babylonian exile, the consensus among large groups of the Jewish population was that the Spirit of God was no longer available as it had been during the period of classical prophecy. One of the hopes for the messianic age was that this Spirit would be "poured out on all flesh." The gift of the Spirit regenerates broken lives, gives courage to live for the future of God, and, most important for the present discussion, bestows a new intimacy with the divine. But of what sort is this gift? Paul puts it this way:

> For all who are led by the Spirit of God are children of God. For you did not receive a spirit of slavery to fall back into fear, but you have received a spirit of adoption. When we cry, "Abba! Father!", it is that very spirit bearing witness with our spirit that we are children of God, and if children, then heirs, heirs of God and joint heirs with Christ. (Rom. 8:14–17)

Prayer is the expression of a new life, a life of "adoption" or "filiation." Indeed, "expression" is a more appropriate term here than "obligation." While it is certainly true that the early Christians were admonished to "pray without ceasing" and to be "watchful," it is equally clear that prayer expresses an attitude of joy and thanksgiving on behalf of people who had been liberated from sin and death. Indeed, Paul is careful to add "rejoice" to his exhortations to constant prayer (see Rom. 12:12; Phil. 4:4–7; Col. 4:2ff.; 1 Thess. 5:16f.). The sense of the new age, of which the early Christians viewed themselves as citizens, is that sinners have been granted the ability to share in Christ's intimacy with God. This intimacy was expressed in Jesus' life not only by his preaching and healing but above all by his *prayers*. Jesus often prayed in solitary places at times of the day when he was sure to be alone and undisturbed. Even his teaching about prayer reflects this spirit of intimacy. For example, he admonishes his listeners not to "heap up empty phrases like the Gentiles do" (Matt. 6:7). Ancient people often approached their gods as they did their rulers and felt compelled to observe all the proper protocols. Jesus, however, dismisses these practices as useless and harmful for "children" addressing their "Father" in a spirit of liberated intimacy.

Employing Heidegger's hermeneutical principles has thus given us a definite picture of the meaning that prayer had in the life of the primitive Christian community. Prayer is part of a whole pattern of life, a pattern that is best understood as a joyful response to the gift of freedom and new intimacy with God. We would, however, be letting ourselves off easy were we simply to rest with this sort of "objective" description of the meaning of prayer in a particular community. This is not to say, of course, that it is easy to stick "to the things themselves," as phenomenologists like to say. But there is an element of Heidegger's hermeneutics that I have so far left undiscussed. Unlike the "objective-historical" mode of analysis that he rejects, "Phenomenological understanding . . . is determined from the enactment of the one who is engaging in reflection" (G60 82). Or, as he puts it later, "One must only be directly and absolutely interested *in* the explication and *about* it, and *must* be so authentically" (G60 129; emphasis in original).

These remarks indicate that Heidegger belongs among those philosophers, such as Pascal, Kierkegaard, and Rosenzweig, for whom philosophy of religion is not like botany or toxicology. That is, it is not a matter of establishing the "facts" about religion so that one can file them away. The philosophical search for religious meaning puts the searcher herself into question, opening up the possibility that religious meaning is more than an interesting historical aside but is a real challenge to our own self-understanding. Dilthey formulates this hermeneutical principle thus: "History is not something separated from life or remote from the present." In a lecture on Dilthey from 1924, Heidegger makes this point more dramatically: "We are history, i.e., our own past. Our future is lived from out of the past. We carry the past with us" (S 174).

This means that a hermeneutics of prayer must in the end also be a *call to prayer*. Hermeneutics illumines the life-context and basic attitudes that belong to a community not simply so that our historical curiosity might be satisfied but also so that the past might become meaningful for *our future*. The hermeneutical insight is that this cannot be accomplished by making pronouncements about the ahistorical "essence" or "nature" of a practice like prayer or by insisting on the use of "classificatory orders." Instead, by reading a concept or a practice in order to determine its meaning for life, hermeneutics makes it possible for this concept or practice to become meaningful again for *our* life. Prayer, like any religious concept, really makes sense only as a *practice*—its meaning dawns on us in the work of living it out.

The hermeneutics of prayer that I have offered here makes a number of claims on our present and on our future. First, prayer ought to be an expression of a Christian's alienation from the world of sin and death, an alienation that is ultimately grounded in the expectation of the redemption of this same world. Prayer is a practice that both expresses a new life and reconnects one with it. Second, prayer, even petitionary prayer, ought to be a joyous response to an experienced liberation from slavery of all kinds, the expression of a new intimacy with the divine. To "pray without ceasing" is to live from out of a future that places the patterns and practices of the past into question. Prayer expresses the new orientation of a life that has been set free. As an expression of such a life, prayer is not a burden or a "duty" but a grateful expression of a new creation. In the end, however, the meaning of prayer is something that must not merely be talked about but must be lived anew in each case. Apart from the actual practice of prayer in the context of a new life in the Spirit, "prayer" is a meaningless word.

Abbreviations

Works by Dilthey

GS1 *Gesammelte Schriften*, vol. 1: *Einleitung in die Geisteswissenschaften*. Stuttgart: B. G. Teubner, 1937. English translation: Rudolf A. Makkreel and Frithjof Rodi, eds. Wilhelm Dilthey: *Selected Works*, vol. 1: *Introduction to the Human Sciences*. Princeton, N.J.: Princeton University Press, 1989.

GS2 *Gesammelte Schriften*, vol. 2: *Weltanschauung und Analyse des Menschen seit Renaissance und Reformation*. Edited by Georg Misch. Stuttgart: B. G. Teubner, 1957.

GS5 *Gesammelte Schriften*, vol. 5: *Die Geistige Welt: Einleitung in die Philosophie des Lebens*, Erste Hälfte: Abhandlungen zur Grundlegung der Geisteswissenschaften. Edited by Georg Misch. Stuttgart: B. G. Teubner, 1957.

GS7 *Gesammelte Schriften*, vol. 7: *Der Aufbau der Geschichtlichen Welt in den Geisteswissenschaften*. Edited by Bernhard Groethuysen. Stuttgart: B. G. Teubner, 1958. English translation: Rudolf A. Makkreel and Frithjof Rodi, eds. *Wilhelm Dilthey: Selected Works*, vol. 3: *The Formation of the Historical World in the Human Sciences*. Princeton, N.J.: Princeton University Press, 2002.

GS8 *Gesammelte Schriften*, vol. 8: *Weltanschauungslehre: Abhandlungen zur Philosophie der Philosophie*. Edited by Bernhard Groethuysen. Stuttgart: B. G. Teubner, 1960.

Works by Heidegger

G56/57 *Gesamtausgabe*, vol. 56/57: *Zur Bestimmung der Philosophie*. Edited by Bernd Heimbüchel. Frankfurt am Main: Vittorio Klostermann, 1987. English translation: Ted Sadler. *Towards the Definition of Philosophy*. London: Athlone Press, 2000.

G58 *Gesamtausgabe*, vol. 58: *Grundprobleme der Phänomenologie* (1919–1920). Edited by Hans-Helmuth Gander. Frankfurt am Main: Vittorio Klostermann, 1993.

G59 *Gesamtausgabe*, vol. 59: *Phänomenologie der Anschauung und des Ausdrucks: Theorie der philosophischen Begriffsbildung*. Edited by Claudius Strube. Frankfurt am Main: Vittorio Klostermann, 1993.

G60 *Gesamtausgabe*, vol. 60: *Phänomenologie des religiösen Lebens*. Edited by Matthias Jung, Thomas Regehly, and Claudius Strube. Frankfurt am Main: Vittorio Klostermann, 1995.

S *Supplements: From the Earliest Essays to* Being and Time *and Beyond*. Edited by John Van Buren. Albany, N.Y.: SUNY Press, 2002.

SZ *Gesamtausgabe*, vol. 2: *Sein und Zeit*. Edited by Friedrich-Wilhelm von Herrmann. Frankfurt am Main: Vittorio Klostermann, 1977. English translation: John Macquarrie and Edward Robinson. *Being and Time*. New York: Harper and Row, 1962.

9

Edith Stein
Prayer and Interiority

TERRENCE C. WRIGHT

In her autobiography, Edith Stein tells us that at the age of fifteen she "deliberately and consciously" gave up praying.[1] Perhaps the most significant experience between this decision and her return to the practice of prayer with her conversion to Catholicism at the age of thirty was her contact with Edmund Husserl and his theory of phenomenology. In fact it may be the case, as Jude Dougherty has observed,[2] that her religious conversion was made possible by her philosophical conversion to phenomenology. Husserl, himself a convert to Christianity, understood prayer in terms of the inward turn of his transcendental phenomenology. In her major work, *Finite and Eternal Being*, Stein develops a theory of interiority that is influenced by Husserlian phenomenology but also by mysticism and medieval philosophy. This essay explores the relationship between Stein's understanding of prayer and her thinking on interiority.

In a letter to Arnold Metzger in 1919, Husserl reveals the relationship between his own conversion to Christianity and the development of his phenomenology. He writes:

> the decisive influences, which lead me from mathematics to phenomenology as my vocation, may lie in overpowering religious experiences and complete transformations. Indeed the powerful effect of the New Testament on a 23-year-old gave rise to an impetus to discover the way to God and to a true life through a rigorous philosophical inquiry.[3]

In her account of her conversations with him, Adelgundis Jagersch-
mid reveals that Husserl often considered the relationship between
religion and phenomenology. In one conversation, Husserl maintained that "my philosophy, phenomenology, is intended to be nothing but a path, a method, in order to show precisely those who have
moved away from Christianity and from the Christian churches the
path back to God."⁴ Such religious claims can be surprising for those
familiar with only Husserl's published works or even the posthumously published philosophical works. References to God and religion rarely occur in Husserl's philosophical writings, and when they
do occur, they are often relegated to footnotes.⁵

In *Ideas I*, when Husserl does speak of God, it is to say that a "divine" being:

> would obviously transcend not merely the world but "absolute"
> [i.e., human] consciousness. It would therefore be an *"absolute"*
> *in a sense totally different from that in which consciousness is* an abso-
> lute, just as it would be *something transcendent in a sense totally*
> *different* from that in which the world is transcendent.⁶

For this reason, he concludes that the phenomenological reduction
would have to be extended to God, and consequently the Divine
would have to be excluded from the field of phenomenological analysis. But this phenomenological reduction does not demand the exclusion of the relationship of consciousness to the Divine. In a letter to
Dilthey, Husserl claims that the task of the phenomenology of religion "would be to examine the consciousness that is constitutive of
religion in a suitable manner."⁷ He adds that a "phenomenological
theory of religion requires, or rather, *is* for the most part . . . a return
to *inner life.*"⁸ Included in this inner life, for Husserl, would be the
activity of prayer.

Since all consciousness is intentional for Husserl, prayer must be
understood as a mode of intentionality. In his analysis of Husserlian
philosophical theology, James Hart cites this line from one of Husserl's unpublished manuscripts: "In real genuine prayer, the praying
I is not directed outwardly but inwardly."⁹ Hart argues that the reason for this is that for Husserl, "authentic prayer breaks the bondage
of the natural attitude by reason of its apperception of the divine's
transcendence of and immanence to all significations."¹⁰ If prayer is
essentially a form of apperception, then it is ultimately an empty intentionality directed not to the world but inwardly to consciousness's
awareness of the divine. I will argue that Stein develops a similar

understanding of prayer influenced by her phenomenology of the human interior life.

In her essay "The Prayer of the Church," written in 1936, Stein argues that the life of the Church begins in liturgical prayer when Christ first enacts the Eucharistic prayer at the last supper.[11] For it is here that Christ moves beyond the Jewish Passover rite of offering a prayer of thanks to God for the bread and wine and identifies them as his body and blood in the prayer of consecration. Stein also distinguishes between Christ's liturgical or public prayer and the solitary prayer in which it is rooted. She cites the instances of solitary prayer that precede the most important events in Christ's public ministry and observes that the whole of the public ministry itself is preceded by forty days and forty nights of prayer.[12]

For this reason Stein wants to give priority to solitary prayer in the life of the individual believer. Using the example of Teresa of Avila, Stein maintains that it is "silent dialogue with their Lord" that allows individuals to understand the will of God and what He is calling them to do: "We need hours for listening silently and allowing the Word of God to act on us until it moves us to bear fruit in an offering of praise and an offering of action."[13] Stein, however, does not want to set up an opposition between inner "subjective" prayer and liturgical "objective" prayer, and so she maintains that both are authentic prayers of the Church. But she does give a priority to inner prayer, because any liturgical prayer that is not grounded in solitary prayer runs the risk of degenerating into "a rigid and lifeless lip service."[14]

This commitment to the interiority of prayer is also reflected in Stein's own prayer life. Letters and biographical accounts reveal a women who spent long hours in solitary prayer. And she was strongly attracted to forms of spirituality that required hours of intensely focused contemplation and meditation. In a letter from 1928 she says: "The only essential is that one finds, first of all, a quiet corner in which one can communicate with God as though there were nothing else, and that must be done daily."[15] While the primary purpose of such isolated contemplation is to encounter God and in this encounter discern His will, it is significant to note that for Stein an important point of this discernment is to carry the will of God into the world. According to Stein, in prayer we come to understand our own abilities and our obligation to act as God's instrument. For example, this is how she understood her own intellectual abilities: "We are to see them [our abilities] as something used, not by us, but by God in us."[16]

So, like Husserl, Stein understands prayer as essentially an act of interiority directed to the relationship between human consciousness and God. To understand her idea of prayer better, then, it is necessary to understand her theory of interiority, which she develops in *Finite and Eternal Being*. This work was completed in 1937 while she was a member of the Carmelites of Cologne. Stein understood this work to be an "inquiry into the meaning of being" and a "comparative elucidation of Thomistic and phenomenological thought."[17] While it draws much from Scholastic thought, Stein's approach remains decidedly phenomenological, particularly in her description of interior experience.

Stein follows Aristotle in speaking of the soul as the form of the body. She recognizes the importance of understanding human beings as embodied souls and the role the body plays in intentionality. And while her language often seems to accept a traditional body/soul dualism, the description of the experience of the lived body we find here cautions us against dismissing Stein as offering a metaphysics of binary oppositions. Still, when she turns to the experience of interiority, she argues for the ability of human beings to suspend the body's outward intention of the world and turn the intentional gaze inward. For Stein, "The dark ground from which all human spiritual life arises—the soul—attains in the ego-life to the bright daylight of consciousness (without, however, becoming transparent)."[18] So while she accepts Husserl's inward turn to consciousness, she rejects his idea that this consciousness is transparent to itself.

Stein understands the soul as the center of the body-soul-spirit totality:

> As sentient soul it abides in the body, in all its members and parts, receiving impulses and influences from it and working upon it formatively and with a view to its preservation. As spiritual soul it rises above itself, gaining insight into a world that lies beyond its own self—a world of things, persons, and events—communicating with this world and receiving its influences.[19]

She borrows from Teresa of Avila the image of the soul as an "interior castle." Stein likes this image because it allows her to speak about the soul using the necessary language of metaphors to describe the activities of the soul:

The soul as the interior castle . . . is not point-like as is the *pure ego*, but "spatial." It is a space, a "castle" with many mansions in which the I is able to move freely, now going outward beyond itself, now withdrawing into its own inwardness. And this space is not "empty," even though it can and must receive and harbor a fullness in order to become capable of unfolding its own individual life.[20]

For Stein this image of space is relevant because it captures both the sense that the soul can be understood as capable of motion between the interior and the exterior and that through experience the soul acquires fullness. Further, this metaphor of space is helpful when considering self-knowledge as a form of illumination. For Stein, in gaining knowledge of one's self, one dispels the darkness about one's essential nature on both a personal and a universal level. Some of this knowledge is simply given in the natural process of gaining self-awareness. But other aspects of this knowledge must be pursued through free cognitive activity. Finally, for Stein the understanding of the soul as a sort of "space" allows her to speak about the surface and the depths of the soul. In returning to the castle image, she maintains: "The 'I' inhabits this castle, and it may choose to reside in one of the outer chambers, or it may retire into that nearer and innermost abode."[21] For Stein, prayer is one of the interior cognitive activities of the soul that makes possible its self-knowledge and fulfillment.

Indeed, for Stein, how we inhabit "the castle" of the soul says a lot about the type of person we are: "That ego which apprehends, observes, and works upon its own self as if this self were a purely external thing evidently does not have its seat in the interior of the castle. It almost seems as if this ego has left the castle in order to be able to look at it from the outside."[22]

Such persons would fail to realize their true selves and actualize their highest intellectual and spiritual powers. In an example, Stein contrasts two men who intellectually grasp the contents of a certain event, in this case the assassination of Archduke Ferdinand in 1914. One person may hear the news, think no more about it, and continue to plan his summer vacation. Such a person would remain superficial in this situation because he would fail to employ his intellect, his imagination, and so on in recognizing the consequences of the act. But the other person hears the news and is shaken to the core: "In his case the news has struck deeply at his inner life, and he understands the external events from the point of view of his own interiority. And because his full intellectual power is alive in his understanding, his mind penetrates into the context and into the 'consequences' of the external event."[23]

So for Stein interiority does not close off the world but allows the world to penetrate us deeply. External events that remain purely external are never understood in their full meaning. Hence the person who remains on the surface not only fails to understand the self but also fails to understand the world.

It is necessary to cultivate this interiority to reach the truth about the world and about ourselves. But Stein recognizes that this not easy to do. Most of us do not lead such "collected" lives, and even on those occasions when we are drawn to the depths of interiority, we do not remain there for long. Stein observes:

> Although the ego is on some occasions shaken and drawn toward the depth of the soul by "great events" and then attempts to correlate its behavior with the significance of these events, it returns to the surface sooner or later. And that which approaches the soul from without is indeed often of such a nature that it can without too much difficulty be effectively "dealt with" and disposed of from a superficial or, at any rate, from a not very deeply anchored standpoint.[24]

In *The Science of the Cross*, a spiritual study of St. John of the Cross that she was working on at the time of her death, Stein makes a similar observation:

> There are very few souls who live *in* their inmost self and *out of* their inmost region; and still fewer who constantly live *from* and *out of* their deepest interior. According to their nature — that is, their *fallen* nature — these persons keep themselves in the *outer rooms* of the *castle* which is their soul. What approaches them from the outside draws them to the outside. It is necessary that God call and draw them insistently so as to move them to "enter into themselves."[25]

For Stein, the failure to be deeply anchored and to live out of one's deepest interior results in a failure of the person to gain a true possession of him or herself. The lack of such possession obscures the individual's ability to understand the meaning of events in life. Gaining such possession, according to Stein, makes individuals open to the demands of these events and puts them in the best possible position to evaluate them. This possession can be aided through the study of philosophy and the cultivation of faith: "Reason and faith are both appeals of the soul, calling it 'to enter into its own self' and to mold human life from the innermost center."[26] And it is clear that Stein is not advocating a nonrational mysticism when she maintains that "a conscious life of the soul in the depths of its interiority is, of course, possible only after the awakening of reason."[27]

In the preface to *Finite and Eternal Being*, Stein states that she was "deeply impressed" with Martin Heidegger's *Being and Time*.[28] And, though she is very critical of Heidegger in an appendix to her work,[29] his influence is evident in her discussion of superficiality. When reading it, one is reminded of Heidegger's analysis of inauthentic *Dasein*. Like Heidegger, Stein understands the movement beyond superficiality to be instigated by a type of "call." But Stein offers a very different account of the source and the essence of this call.

What is the nature of this call for the soul to enter into its own self? For Stein, it is a call to the intellect, to the power of the understanding and the power of reflection. It is also an appeal to freedom, because it is a call that elicits a response. But it is not for Stein, as it is for Heidegger, the self calling itself to be itself. Rather, it is a response to a power beyond the self, a power strong enough to call one away from the surface of the external world, a power who is supernatural and divine. It is here that interiority and prayer are intimately related. Prayer, for Stein, is an activity that places us at the center of ourselves and simultaneously in relation to God. Without prayer, one cannot hear and heed the call to be oneself. Without prayer, one remains on the surface, in the realm of what Heidegger would call the fallen and the inauthentic.

Just as Husserl (at the end of the *Cartesian Meditations*) appeals to Augustine's claim that "Truth dwells in the inner man,"[30] so Stein too draws from Augustine to support her own appeal to interiority: "If thou seekest an exalted place, a sacred place, then offer God this inner life as a temple. 'For the temple of God is holy, and thou art this temple.' Wilt thou pray in the temple? Then pray within thine own self. But before thou doest, thou shouldst be a temple of God, for in this temple he listens to the one who prays."[31]

So at the center of interior of the castle we find a temple of God. It is here, for Stein, that one can hear the call of God and respond to this call. And this response is, in its first manifestation, prayer. But we must consider prayer only a first manifestation if we are to understand Stein's theory of interiority. As we have said, the purpose of the inward journey for Stein is not to escape the world but to rightly understand it, and in so doing to understand the meaning of one's life in light of one's relationship to God. The point of the interiority of prayer is not to remain in the interior but to return to the external world. God's call, experienced in the act of prayer, is, for Stein, ultimately a call for the individual to act in the world.

In conclusion, as Stein came to understand herself as an instrument of God, she developed an understanding of prayer as an encounter with His call. Her experience of prayer lead her to conclude that this call can best be heard in what the poet would call, "the deep heart's core."

10

"Too Deep for Words"
The Conspiracy of a Divine "Soliloquy"

B. KEITH PUTT

Those who interpret deconstruction as another species of nihilism believe that Jacques Derrida preys—specifically, that he preys upon texts like some hermeneutical savage, some rough beast slouching toward the arid desert of relativism, dragging behind him the Holy, the Beautiful, and the Good, in order to drop them rudely into the abyss of epistemological meaninglessness and ontological simulacra.[1] Such interpreters of Derrida would certainly never assume that he would have any sensitivity for religion, or theology, or piety; consequently, they would most definitely never hear "Derrida preys" as "Derrida prays." Yet such a nihilistic misinterpretation of deconstruction egregiously misreads Derrida's texts. Throughout his works, he continually reiterates religious and theological topics, such as God, the gift, forgiveness, the messianic, negative theology, and faith. While claiming to pass rightly for an atheist, he testifies to a personal religious sensibility *sans religion* and admits to working with a theological thesaurus that supplies multiple synonyms for the word "God." Moreover, Derrida confesses a faith *au fond*, a fundamental trust that, although operating *sans voir, sans avoir, et sans revelation*, nonetheless affirms the enigmatic promise of a grace and a justice to come.[2] Given these recurrent themes, and given that Derrida has already shown a serious inclination toward transmuting *e*'s into *a*'s— such as *différence* into *différance*—it should come as no surprise that he claims to pray, "p-r-*a*-y," claiming that his life has been one of constant prayers.[3]

Derrida interprets prayer as essentially apostrophic, a "turning [*strephein*] away [*apo*]" toward the other in order to address the other as other, whether the "other" is God or another individual. He agrees with Aristotle's theory that prayer is a rhetorical or poetic employment of sentences that being neither true nor false, should not be prosecuted as offering logical arguments or making empirical claims. Prayer uniquely exemplifies, therefore, a performative use of language. It instantiates a language game, the rules of which do not include predication or any truth-functional propositionalism, at least with reference to an *adequatio intellectus et rei*. Instead, prayer manifests the illocutionary forces of vocation, invocation, provocation, and convocation. Prayer calls (*vocare*) to the other, calls the other to come in (*in-vocare*), to be present in some way, and calls forth (*pro-vocare*) the other in order to arouse or entice the other to respond. Consequently, prayer is "asking, supplicating, searching out" the other; one might say that it aims at calling the other into the gathering of relationship (*con-vocare*).[4]

Yet Derrida interprets the vocative dynamic of prayer as always a second word, as an address that responds to a prior call. In other words, prayer, like all discourse, depends upon a primordial promise, the arche-trace of the Other's having addressed the "I" who speaks. Even before opening my mouth, language has already been spoken to me and a certain linguistic faith has been established. Before "I" am a subject calling to the Other, "I" am the object of the Other's call. For Derrida, then, prayer not only concludes with "amen" but begins with it as well. "Amen" signifies the "yes," the "*oui, oui,*" the "so be it" that responds affirmatively to the trace of the primordial promise. This "amen" always finds expression within the environment of faith and truth, the faith that contextualizes prayer, attestation, confession, and testimony—any expression of trust and believability—and the truth that gives the horizons within which every statement, even the lie, must take place.[5] John Caputo associates Derrida's "yes," his "*oui, oui,*" explicitly with theology, prayer, and even with one of the "names" of God. He claims that "the best way to think of *oui, oui* is to think of a great sweeping *amen!* to the world and to language and beyond that, to think the *oui, oui* of deconstruction in reference to *Yah-weh*'s *Ja*, to the divine *oui, oui* which lets things be."[6] Indeed, for Caputo, to pray "is to open one's mouth and say 'yes.'"[7] In using my voice to say the "amen" in prayer or confession, I thereby commit myself to a relationship of trust, promising implicitly to speak the truth.

But if prayer has no purchase with truth and falsity, then how can one say that prayer as discourse predicates a fideistic context of promise, commitment, and truth? Caputo and Derrida salvage the interaction between prayer and truth by moving from Aristotle to Augustine and defining truth pragmatically instead of constatively. In other words, the truth of prayer is not truth as empirically correspondent but truth as act and deed or, in Augustine's words, as *"facere veritatem,"* the "doing of the truth."[8] Such a rendering of prayer and truth undermines the arrogance of narcissism since it insists that prayer does not result from the autonomous self who, as subject, exercises power over the direct object of the address. Instead, in a certain Levinasian sense, prayer, for Derrida, establishes the humility of response, since the one who prays does so initially in the accusative case, as the object of a prior summons. As Caputo intimates, my prayer responds to the divine "yes" (*Ja*) previously spoken by Yahweh; consequently, every prayer translates a *"me voici,"* a "here I am" in response to God's (or any other's) summons.

Although Derrida considers prayer to be a dative expression of truth, promise, and fidelity without reducing it to the cognitive dimension of predication, he does recognize that prayer is correlated quite often with another form of expression that does carry the predicative element, that is, with the encomium or the hymnic. The hymnic, or discourse as praise, implicitly or explicitly predicates particular traits of the Other, specifically the Other as God. One does not praise what one does not consider praiseworthy; consequently, praise always predicates, always attributes to God characteristics worthy to be praised. Praise determines who God is, in that it responds to God's power, mercy, and holiness in a spirit of gratitude and commitment. Derrida does admit that in negative theology, prayer and praise are related intimately, that in prayer, God is described, for example, as Trinity. Such need not be the case, however. He insists that prayer can be understood as more of a "pure" vocative, as implying "nothing other than the supplicating address to the other, perhaps beyond all supplication and giving" (and, one might add, beyond assigning any qualities to the addressed Other).[9]

Interestingly enough, Caputo seems to attenuate the distinction that Derrida makes between prayer and praise when he writes that the second of the two things that "Saint Jacques" says about prayer in the essay "How to Avoid Speaking: Denials" is that "prayer contains another element, of encomium or praise, which not only speaks *to* God, but *of* God, so that prayer preserves a relationship with a predicative content, a constative."[10] As stated above, Derrida does admit that prayer and praise often accompany each other; however, in that essay he insists on a definite cleavage between the two. That cleavage finds even stronger expression in his response to Regina Schwartz in *Questioning God*, where he moves past the "supplicating" intent of prayer to the position of a pure noninstrumentalizing of prayer, prayer as simple address, or one might say, prayer as expressing the noneconomy of gift.[11]

Prayer as gift references the possibility that the call to the Other remains unanswered, that no response returns, or that there "is" no Other to respond. Concerning this eventuality, Caputo emphasizes the Derridean complication of the language of prayer. Prayer as a form of discourse cannot escape the play of *différance* and *khôra*, the differing, deferring, and desertlike spacing that disallows any absolute closure to referentiality or signification.[12] Prayers remain open to iterability and recontextualization just as do all semiotic expressions. As Derrida indicates, prayers can be written and quoted and, as texts, sent to others other than God.[13] But iteration always questions destination. When one calls to God or to any other, one is never assured that the call will go through, that the *envois* will be delivered to the proper addressee. Like all language, prayer has a structural *destinerrence* to it that leaves open the undecidability of the "to whom." To whom does one call? Who is the object of the apostrophe? How does one know whether to expect a response or not? Caputo would claim, in his best Augustinian voice, that just as one does not always know what one loves when loving God, one also does not know to whom one prays when addressing God.[14] Although admitting that negative theologians sought to ensure the destination of their prayers through the addition of hymnic theological determinations, Caputo insists that the name of God remains "safe" and secret in that it never serves as a transcendental signified guaranteeing that prayers "to heaven rise."[15] Our prayers, therefore, may fall on deaf ears or on no ears or may simply echo across the empty chasms of the abyss.

Derrida confirms that the potential *destinerrence* of any prayer questions whether praying may genuinely be construed in each instance as a speech act having genuine performative capability. He suspects that prayer may not always be a *facere veritatem* since, in its "purely" apostrophic expression, prayer depends solely on the possible response of the Other, the Other's response as an event, as an *événement* that cannot be preprogrammed within any horizon of expectation.[16] In this environment of the undecidability of the event, the one who prays awaits the interruptive "happening" of the Other's response, tries to remain open to the incoming of the Other, the *l'invention de l'autre* or the *l'invention de tout autre*. So Derrida contends that "the happening of the other, if it is an authentic happening, an unpredictable happening, should just defeat performativity—and constativity even more."[17] The one who prays wields no perlocutionary power over the future event of response. Consequently, instead of "doing the truth" through praying, the one who prays awaits the occurrence of truth, cultivates a spirit of hospitality in order to welcome the truth that comes through the deed of the Other.

Yet if prayer does rely on the coming event of the Other's reply, then, for Derrida, prayer addresses the significant issue of the messianic. Derrida's prayer adds to the *"oui, oui"* ("amen") of primary affirmation the *"viens, viens"* (come, come) of messianic expectation, which awaits the coming of gift, or of justice, or of faith, or even of the Messiah.[18] He refuses to separate these two components, since any discourse about the future—the future as *l'avenir*, as the "to (*a*) come (*venir*)"—necessitates both the iterability of signs and the *"confirmation* of the originary *yes."* In other words, there may be no "to-come without some sort of messianic memory and promise, of a messianicity older than all religion . . . [and] of an *elementary promise"* (emphasis added).[19] The messianic prayer says amen to and yearns for a "kingdom to come." It joins St. John the Revelator in requesting that the Messiah come and that he come quickly (Revelation 22:17–21). Caputo emphasizes this intimate Derridean connection among prayer, promise, and the messianic when he insists that to pray is "to open one's mouth and say 'come.' Let the Other come. Let something Other, something In-coming, come."[20] For Derrida, the incoming of the Other as the aleatoric irruption of the unexpected goes under the name of the "Impossible," the Impossible as that which cannot be domesticated and foreseen, as that which betrays genuine difference and alterity.[21] Yet, as Caputo indicates, the Impossible functions as a religious and theological category, as a cipher for God who is "the chance for something absolutely new, for a new birth, for the expectation, the hope, the hope against hope in a transforming future."[22] Consequently, one could infer that prayer as an address to God is, indeed, a response to and a passion for the Impossible, a call to the Wholly Other who promises to come, to break into existence in unimagined ways, to disrupt the *status quo* of the present through a future that comes like a thief in the night. As a result, one might say that prayer begins *by* the Impossible, with a provocation *from* the Impossible, and is directed *to* the Impossible.

But what if prayer itself were impossible, at least impossible as a linguistic phenomenon? How would prayer relate to iterability, *différance*, the apostrophe, the Impossible, and the messianic if it could never be brought to language? And how would that linguistic impossibility correlate with a performative impossibility? In other words, what if prayer could not be performed not only because the addressee remains passive before the response of the in-coming Other, as Derrida contends, or because prayer might reach the purified state of the *unio mystico* in which silence manifests the intimacy of encounter, as Caputo theorizes,[23] but because the individual simply does not know *how* to pray, does not possess the requisite technical and semiotic knowledge? Or, to confound the problematic of prayer even more, what if the impossibility *of* prayer actually provoked the Impossible *to* pray? That is, what if God as the Impossible "prayed" an impossible prayer? The Apostle Paul provokes such enigmatic questions in his epistle to the church at Rome when he writes, "In the same way the Spirit also helps our weakness; for we do not know how to pray as we should, but the Spirit himself intercedes for us with groanings too deep for words" (Rom. 8:26, NASV).

How should one understand this amazing verse? Paul insists that the individual reaches a point where she or he no longer knows how to pray, how to speak to God, and that precisely at that point (in some variant of Nietzsche's *Geniestreich*), God actually takes over the responsibility of praying, of speaking to Godself! Furthermore, he contends that when the divine Spirit engages in such substitutionary praying, the Spirit does so without language, articulating the inarticulate through groans and sighs that have no discursive dynamic.

Jean-Louis Chrétien, in his attempt to develop a phenomenology of prayer, cites Paul's elusive and astonishing verse, but he diminishes the full impact of its nondiscursive nature by relying on Augustine's reading of the text as a *clamare facientum*, a "making one cry." Chrétien claims that prayer always dispossesses the self of egocentrism by reminding the one praying of his or her dependence upon the God who is addressed.[24] The self-manifestation inherent in all praying reveals to the individual that she or he does not know how to pray, that she or he must keep praying in order to learn that prayer comes only as a gift from God.[25] So, in agreement with Augustine, Chrétien interprets the Pauline text as claiming that the Spirit's "praying" provokes us to pray. In some manner, the Spirit supplies the indispensable knowledge and language that enable us to address God. He refers to this Spirit-empowered praying as a form of respiration, of our inhaling the Spirit's prayer so that we might exhale it again as an offering to God. The result is a certain divine/human "conspiracy," a "breathing (*spirare*) together (*con*)" that symbolizes the intimacy of relationship.[26] Ultimately, the gift of this conspiracy might well lead to what Chrétien considers to be the "perfect prayer": "the prayer that would go from God to God, in a voice, and therefore in a human body, the prayer by which God would invoke himself."[27]

Of course, Chrétien gravitates toward Augustine's reading because he wishes to maintain his phenomenological approach to prayer. Without the voice and without the possibility of recitation that linguistic prayer offers, one could not do a phenomenology of prayer. Yet that "without" might well be the most significant implication of the Pauline passage—that the impossibility of human prayer leads to the nonphenomenological "phenomenon" of divine prayer. If so, the "perfect prayer," then, would not be God's invoking Godself through the human voice, but God's invoking Godself precisely as a response to the silence of human impossibility. This silence would not be the product of a hyperousiological dynamic, as in negative theology, or the result of an ineffability ensuing from some saturated phenomenon of divine presence. Instead, it might be something more akin to an almost *khôra*-like experience of a passion for the Impossible that remains *en abîme*, that simply cannot rise to the level of reason and language.

Surprisingly, the extended literary context of Romans 8:26 connects the issue of divine substitutionary praying with Derrida's and Caputo's perspectives on human praying. Paul claims that the Spirit does not pray on our behalf just over any issue but specifically over the issue of the messianic. He confesses that the same Spirit who resurrected Christ as an "eschatological preenactment" of the messianic kingdom "to come" now enlivens believers and gives them a spirit of adoption as sons and daughters of God.[28] Of course, this filiation as children of God does not inoculate believers against the existential infections of anxiety, uncertainty, and suffering. Indeed, Paul honestly attests that the Spirit of adoption arouses a longing and a passion for what has yet to come, for the "in-vention" (coming in) of the hoped-for redemption; it establishes a spiritual "ad-venture" (coming to) of an awaiting and openness for the impossible kingdom that comes in ways beyond anything that can be thought or imagined.

Paul calls the messianic passion for the Impossible a "groaning" for what is to come and compares the groaning to the pains of childbirth. He analogizes creation and humanity as pregnant with the im/possibility of what God has promised, as experiencing the contractions that will lead to the birth of salvation (Rom. 8:22–23),[29] but like all births, one accompanied by suffering and complaint. During this time of eschatological gestation, Paul declares that we make our way with a certain blindness, unable to see the full presence of the gift of liberation and unable to hold in our grip, to prehend and comprehend what God has promised (Rom. 8:24–25).[30] So we live this time of expectation with hope and with faith in a context *sans voir et sans avoir*—without seeing exactly what awaits us and without holding on to the security of our own presuppositions.

In the darkness of anticipation, we persevere by holding on to a messianic hope that "threads a ray of fire in the black web of immanence."[31] We lament over the present suffering by holding tenuously but tenaciously to our hope in the "glory that is to be revealed to us" (Rom. 8:18). The groanings that erupt from creation and from our own longing hearts eventually require the supplementation of the Spirit's prayers. We seek to voice these groanings, to address them to God and receive divine solace, but cannot, for we do not know how to address God as we should (*katho dei*). Paul implies that we should pray; that it is necessary for us to pray; yet he concedes that we lack the required knowledge and skill, which is somewhat inexplicable, given that Jesus has already taught his followers how to pray. Jesus instructs us in the Model Prayer (Luke 11:2–4) to address God as Father, even as the Spirit allows us to cry "Abba! Father!" (Rom. 8:15), and he explicitly educates us to pray messianically by voicing the petition "Your kingdom come." Yet notwithstanding Jesus' rather clear instructions, Paul insists that we finally do not know how to pray for the coming kingdom. As a result, with reference to praying for the Impossible to come, we not only live in the context of *sans voir et sans avoir* but also *sans savoir* (without knowledge). This *sans savoir* might well lead one to say "*Je ne c'est pas. Il faut prier*"—I do not know. It is necessary to pray. Derrida reminds us, however, that "*il faut*" means not only "it is necessary" but also "it lacks" or "it is wanting."[32] So "*Il faut prier*" means "I *must* pray; I *cannot* pray; it is *impossible* for me to pray."

So at the point of our lack, of our inability to pray as we should, and in the midst of our suffering and sighing for redemption, the Spirit intercedes and, *mirabile dictu*, prays for us, on our behalf, in our stead, as our advocate and substitute. Considering Paul's Trinitarian theology, one can effectively interpret the Spirit's intercessory praying as God's addressing God, that is, as a divine "soliloquy." One must place "soliloquy" in scare quotes, however, since in the relational calculus that grounds the Trinitarian logic, the unity of Father, Son, and Spirit should not be understood in the sense of "self-sameness" but as an intimate integrity of divine alterity, that is, in the sense of a unity-in-difference. Consequently, the Spirit does not pray centripetally by addressing the Spirit's "self" but centrifugally by addressing the Father (and/or the Son). Still, the Spirit as God addresses the Father (and/or the Son) as God and, therefore, in something of a perichoretic manner, prays as a divine "soliloquist."

Unlike Christ the Son, who also prays to the Father on behalf of his disciples but always linguistically through prayers that are textualized and iterable, the Spirit prays without language by uttering "groanings too deep for words" (*stenagmois alalētois*).[33] *Alalētois*—too deep for words—literally means "that which cannot be uttered," "the inexpressible," or "what cannot be said." The divine Spirit conspires with our spirits, breathes with us the same air of anticipation and anxiety, in order to relate to us so intimately as to be able to utter our unutterable groanings and to join us (and creation) in longing for the Messiah who is to come. Indeed, one can say that the Spirit, too, has a passion for the Impossible and expresses this passion not in Chrétien's sense of using the human voice to incarnate the divine voice but in lieu of the impossibility of human expression. The Spirit addresses the Father and articulates the inarticulate eschatological desire for the coming kingdom and laments over the sufferings that mark the messianic *contretemps* and *milieu*.

Comprehending the Spirit's prayerful "soliloquy" as an eschatological lamentation intentionally references Paul Ricoeur's interpretation of the biblical significance of what he terms "prayers of lament." Ricoeur contends that prayer is "the most primitive and original act of language that gives form to religious experience,"[34] a sentiment shared by Chrétien, who also insists that prayer "is the sole human act that opens the religious dimension and never ceases to underwrite, to support, and to suffer this opening."[35] For both, prayer distinguishes itself as a direct address to God and as, in some manner, a "wounded word." For Ricoeur, the "wounded" nature of prayer finds a "scandalous character [in] the prayer of lamentation," since he holds that lament carries with it both a sense of complaint and a sense of accusation.[36] He insists that such prayers attempt to bring to language deep feelings of distress, abandonment, and suffering that could possibly remain "only cries, tears, and sighs."[37] Prayers of lamentation, however, have the potential to reverse paradoxically into expressions of praise, that is, to move from address to predication by implying that in spite of circumstances, God remains a God of grace, promise, and hope.[38] Kevin Hart concurs generally with Ricoeur's position and claims that "the experience of God is always an experience of the saying of God: disturbance and irruption, to be sure, but also the possibility of a response to abandonment and vulnerability."[39] Hart also situates the issue within the context of the messianic—the "divided present" of an experience with a God who responds with an "already but not yet."

Given Ricoeur and Hart's perspectives, one might well interpret the divine "soliloquy" as an example of a prayer of lamentation, albeit one that remains below the level of language where the Spirit utters inarticulate expressions of complaint and accusation while awaiting the messianic revelation of redemption. In the Spirit's inarticulate prayers, we encounter the absurd as that which cannot be spoken or heard; we encounter the *a*-logical as that which cannot be gathered together by *logos*; we encounter *oratio* without *ratio* as that which remains beyond conceptuality. The ineffability of the Spirit's prayers means that there is no oral phenomenon, no linguistic *phainesthai* for our consciousness to intend, and no *logos* to ground a discernable meaning or content to the prayers. Thus we find it impossible to engage in a phenomenology of the divine "soliloquy" and must believe in the Spirit's intercession *sans voir, sans avoir, sans savoir, et sans phénoménologie*.[40]

Likewise, the nonsemiotic character of the divine "soliloquy" means that the Spirit's prayers escape both *différance* and iterability. As neither spoken nor written, these nonphenomenological prayers join justice, the gift, faith, and the messianic as also nondeconstructible. Through the *hermeneusis* of faith, we trust that the Spirit knows whom the Spirit addresses and that the Spirit's prayers reach their destination. That divine destination does not close the human adventure of undecidability and messianic longing but suggests that God accompanies us on this adventure as the transfiguring and transfigured "God Who May Be Otherwise" when the kingdom comes.[41]

Could there be a more evocative example of Derrida's nonperformative *événement* of prayer?

Since the conspiracy of the divine "soliloquy" disallows any phenomenology of the Spirit's prayers, one should recognize that it also escapes the restrictions placed on the intentionality of soliloquy by Husserl's phenomenological distinction between indication as an external signification and expression as an internal intimation of conscious meaning. For Husserl, soliloquy functions as the purest form of expression, devoid of any hint of indication, because in the "solitary mental life" of self-reflexive intentionality, the *noesis* and the *noema* remain present within the very structures of consciousness. The ideal *vouloir dire*, that "spirit" (*Geist*) of intentionality, and the ideal object intended by that spirit bracket empirical reality with its alterity and difference. Interestingly enough, Husserl contends that such pure expression reveals a certain nonlinguisticality, in that it has no need for "real" words. Instead, it can actually do without the medium of external linguistic signification. Only imaginary, nonexistent words fully present to the individual compose this internal monologue.[42] Were one to comprehend the divine "soliloquy" of the Spirit's praying from this Husserlian perspective, one would reduce divine prayer to an act of God *in se* with no redemptive referentiality toward creation and humanity.

But Paul clearly states that the Spirit's prayer "helps our weakness," functions *pro nobis*, and thereby betrays a definite indicative force by uttering the unutterable in order to reference the passion and suffering of the other, the other who is not God. This empirical dynamic ensues from the agapic motivation of the Spirit's groanings that inexpressibly communicate the redemptive promise that the coming God will work all things for good (Rom. 8:28).[43] This promise repeats the divine "yes" to creation and humanity. As the promise and the "yes" act protologically as quasi-transcendentals for all discourse and for the messianic, so, too, they serve eschatologically as the end—not the closure—of the divine intent to establish a kingdom of grace and of justice. The Spirit's praying, therefore, functions messianically as another aspect of salvation as a gift of God and not of human performance.

The Spirit's prayer, then, formally indicates the iterability of the "*oui, oui,*" but as the *oui sans mot*, as the *oui* that comes not as word, or *logos*, but as the divine "amen" too deep for words that "begins" and "ends" God's prayers for the world. Caputo notes that Derrida uses the phrase "*oui sans mot*" in a postscript to *Ulysse gramophone:*

Deux mots pour Joyce, a postscript inexplicably omitted from the English translation. In this text, Derrida explicitly associates the "yes" with the "amen" of prayer and insists that there is the potential for a nonlinguistic "*oui*," a *oui* without word. Caputo explains that "*oui* is not so much a word as a silent companion to words, a quasi-word which provides words with their element and force."[44] Elsewhere, he emphasizes the interrelation of silence and prayer, especially as this interrelation is given expression in mysticism and negative theology and specifically as it relates to the messianic yearning. He calls mystical silence "one of our most beautiful forms of *prayer*, of praying and weeping for the coming of the *tout autre*, for something that eye hath not seen nor ear heard, something beyond."[45]

Of course, with reference to the context of the divine "soliloquy," the *oui sans mot* should not be understood primarily as a "silent companion to words," since the Apostle Paul's assertion that the Spirit's prayer is nonlinguistic does not imply that it is mute. Instead, the Spirit's prayer of divine intercession, divine lament, divine yearning, and divine affirmation manifests an agapic aphasia, a gracious praying, not in silence but otherwise than in language. It is the "otherwise" of the "yes" of *le dire* and not *le dit* in Levinas's terminology, the saying that affirms otherness without delineating explicit content.[46] So in the salvifically performative "*oui, oui*" of *Ya*-weh as Spirit, we cannot know the locutionary force of the divine "soliloquy" but we can trust in its illocutionary force as promise and affirmation and we can respond to its perlocutionary force by repeating the "*oui, oui*" through our prayers of gratitude and through the sacrifice of praise that comes from obedience. As the Spirit dons the tallith, raises its corners over us like the wings of a dove, and blesses us through those unheard and unspoken prayers, we can address God in prayer, respond to God's apostrophe of grace, by crying, "*Me voici! Viens, Viens! Oui, Oui!*"[47]

11

Plus de Secret
The Paradox of Prayer

BRIAN TREANOR

> I am making this confession not only before you with a
> secret exaltation and fear and with a secret grief touched
> by hope, but also in the ears of believing sons of men,
> sharers in my joy, conjoined with me in mortality, my fel-
> low citizens and pilgrims, some who have gone before,
> some who follow after, and some who are my companions
> in this life.
>
> — Augustine, *Confessions*, X

St. Augustine begins his *Confessions* with a prayer, a prayer that questions how and why we pray: "How shall I call upon my God, my God
and Lord?"[1] Much has been said about the epistemological issues
raised by prayer, which questions what can be known of God, and
of the implications of confessing to an omniscient God who knows of
our guilt and our remorse before the confession is given voice.[2] However, in addition to these individual questions of knowledge, guilt,
expiation, and forgiveness, Augustine also questions the collective
significance of his confession-*cum*-prayer and asks, near the end of
the *Confessions:* "Why then should I be concerned for human readers
to hear my confessions?"[3] These two concerns—how we pray and
how our prayers affect others—frame the narrative of the *Confessions*
and raise the question of how our prayers, which address God, are
related to our relationships with other persons.

How and why are we to pray? Where is the other in my prayers? In other words, what is the relationship between my piety and my social or ethical obligations? Ready answers to these questions are complicated by conflicting messages in biblical accounts of prayer that alternately characterize prayer as private and social. While one biblical voice affirms that prayer and other acts of piety are essentially communal or public, there is another voice that insists that prayer is most authentically conducted as a private relation between supplicant and God. This contrast raises the question: Is prayer essentially private or essentially intersubjective? Is public prayer inevitably artificial and affected? If so, is it inauthentic? Is private prayer selfish? If so, is it justifiable? Is it ethical? Or does the religious necessarily transcend the ethical?[4]

In what follows, I want to question the meaning of these two voices, one calling us to private, even secretive, prayer, and the other calling us to gather with others, reminding us that our prayers are always concerned with and located in the context of a community. After a consideration of key biblical passages that appear to counsel either solitary or communal prayer, we appear to be left with two opposing, exclusive positions. This opposition forces us to consider whether we must choose between these two ways of prayer or whether there is, perhaps, some way to reconcile the apparent contradiction of public and private piety. I claim that such reconciliation is not only possible but is also necessary in order to gain an understanding of authentic prayer. The hermeneutic recovery of such an authentic prayer is made via a detour through Derrida and Levinas, who suggest we should think of prayer in terms of love. Building on these thinkers, I propose that we can reconcile the conflicting biblical accounts of private and public prayer by returning to biblical accounts of love, which allow us to see that what appears to be a contradiction is really the same phenomenon manifesting itself in two different ways.

Public Prayer

Numerous biblical accounts of piety affirm the communal nature of religious life.[5] For example, we are instructed, "Pray like this: Our Father who art in heaven, hallowed be thy name" (Matt. 6:9). The fact that the Lord's Prayer, the prayer offered as a model for all prayers, is addressed not to "Father," or "the Father," or "my Father," but to "*Our* Father" is significant. In addressing a father common to all humanity, I am tacitly reminded of my kinship with all people, who, like me, are created *Imago Dei*. In addition to reminding us that other persons are our brothers and sisters, "Our Father" is a prayer spoken in the first-person plural rather than the first-person singular, implying that prayer is something done in community.

The communal nature of religious life is reemphasized when the disciples are told, in the course of discussing fault, rectification, and forgiveness, "where two or three are gathered in my name, there I am in the midst of them" (Matt. 18:20). Paul, in his first letter to the Corinthians, makes a similar point when he tells them that in a body, "if one member suffers, all suffer together; if one member is honored, all rejoice together." In order to remove any doubt that the community of believers is such a unified "body," he tells them, "you are the body of Christ and individually members of it" (1 Cor. 12:27).[6] Hence certain biblical passages seem to indicate that community is an essential part of religious life. In addition, however, several philosophical accounts affirm the intersubjective aspect of prayer and religious life and consequently support this reading.

St. Augustine speaks at length of the importance of public piety.[7] In recounting various stories that inspired his own conversion, Augustine makes special note of the rhetorician Victorinus, who would often confide to a friend, "Did you know I am already a Christian?" However, the reply was always, "I shall not believe that or count you among Christians, unless I see you in the Church of Christ."[8] When, after time, Victorinus was ready actually to convert, he was given the option of making the profession of faith privately so as to avoid public censure and scandal. However, his opinion of the relationship between faith and external manifestations of faith—such as attending church and insuring that his public conduct and speech reflected his faith—had changed (or at least become more nuanced). "He preferred to make profession of his salvation before the holy congregation" rather than be "guilty of a grave crime" by being ashamed of his faith.[9] Augustine clearly equates one kind of private piety with a lack of conviction or lingering shame regarding what one purports to believe.[10]

In addition to Augustine, several philosophers of intersubjectivity—for example, Buber, Marcel, and Levinas—speak of the communal aspects of piety.[11] For example, Levinas claims that an individual or private relationship with God would lead to an unconscionable abandonment of other persons.[12] This is why he is adamantly opposed to such relationships, which would allow one to focus on one's own individual salvation as if it could be bracketed off from the salvation of one's fellows:

> The texts of Ezekiel take aim at the impossibility of private righteousness; of the righteousness of the righteous who save their own selves, who think of their own selves and their own salvation. The existence of evil people by their side attests, in fact, to the defect in their righteousness. They are responsible for the evil that remains. . . . Saints, monks and intellectuals in their ivory tower are the righteous subject to punishment.[13]

This reading stresses, as Levinas's philosophy also does, our responsibility for others; however, Levinas makes the case for communal piety even stronger by claiming that individual piety is not only irresponsible, it is impossible.

Levinas maintains that the "relationship between men" and the "idea of God" are both "nonsynthesizeables," things outside of the totality of things that we can know.[14] As such, "the problem of transcendence and of God and the problem of subjectivity irreducible to essence, irreducible to essential immanence, go together."[15] In fact, he claims that the connection between these two relationships is stronger than mere kinship. The face of the other person is the only mode of access we have to God, the only relationship possible with the divine:

> "Going towards God" is not to be understood here in the classical ontological sense of a return to, or reunification with, God as the Beginning or End of temporal existence. "Going towards God" is meaningless unless seen in terms of my primary going towards the other person. I can only go towards God by being ethically concerned by and for the other person.[16]

Hence it is not possible to have an individual relationship with God. The religious is, in this sense, dependent on the ethical. "The existence of God is not a question of an individual soul uttering logical syllogisms. It cannot be proved. The existence of God, the *Sein Gottes*, is sacred history itself, the sacredness of man's relation to man through which God may pass."[17] God passes through history in the face-to-face relation, or, stated in another way, the other person stands in the trace of God.

In his treatment of the face and the trace, Levinas so clearly has Exodus 33 in mind that it bears repeating. When Moses asks God to reveal his "glory" and his "ways," God grants this request, making all his goodness pass before Moses and proclaiming his name. However, God will not let Moses see his face:

> "You cannot see my face; for man shall not see me and live."
> And the Lord said, "Behold, there is a place by me where you
> shall stand upon the rock, and while my glory passes by I will
> put you in a cleft in the rock, and I will cover you with my hand
> until I have passed by; then I will take away my hand, and you
> shall see my back; but my face shall not be seen." (Exod.
> 33:20–23)

Moses cannot see the face of God but he can see God's back, his wake, and the trace of his passage. We encounter God only as trace and we encounter that trace in the face of the other person.

If we encounter God only as trace, and this trace is revealed only in the face of the other person, the religious does not transcend the ethical. Rather, *pace* Kierkegaard, the ethical *is* the religious. "Ethics is not the corollary of the vision of God, it is that very vision."[18] There are no individual, numinous encounters with the divine; it is the presence of others—both *autrui* and third—which allows a relationship with God. "The sentence in which God comes to be involved in words is not 'I believe in God.' . . . It is the 'here I am,' *said to the neighbor.*"[19] God becomes involved in the world not through any individual encounter or revelation but through human service—and not service directed at God but service to the human other. Under this strict ethical demand, "here I am" ceases to be the response of an individual before God, and becomes my response to the faces of other persons.[20] Levinas ties the question of discourse with God to the question of responsibility and, in doing so, inscribes righteousness, piety, and prayer within the field of ethics.

Both the biblical and philosophical accounts that emphasize the communal nature of prayer appear to make a strong case. Communal prayers remind us of our kinship with other people by reminding us that God is *our* Father. In addition, public prayers express willingness to identify oneself with the faith, the community, and the prayer itself. In so doing, public prayers testify to the conviction behind the piety. Finally, public piety combats the self-absorbed, ethically suspect obsession with one's own salvation at the expense of others. However, if one biblical voice reminds us of our communal obligations, there is a second voice that counsels another approach.

Private Prayer

While it seems clear, on the one hand, that prayer is an essentially communal and therefore public act, there are other biblical exhortations that warn of the dangers of public piety.[21] This second voice advises us to reject marriage (1 Cor. 7:25–31), family (Matt. 10:35–37), and the world itself (Mark 10:17–22; Luke 12:22–34), calling us to a life of private piety focused on the individual relationship to God.

The question of how to pray is given clear expression and a strongly individual emphasis in the Gospel of Matthew, which warns us, "beware of practicing your piety before men" (Matt. 6:1). Why? Given that Matthew's own Gospel account reminds us that God is present when we are gathered together in his name and that God is *our* Father, it seems to make sense that piety is something very public, perhaps even necessarily so. However, we are admonished as follows:

> And when you pray, you must not be like the hypocrites; for they love to stand and pray in the synagogues and at the street corners, that they may be seen by men. Truly I say to you, they have their reward. But when you pray, go into your room and shut the door and pray to your Father who is in secret; and your Father who sees in secret will reward you. (Matt. 6:5–6)[22]

This passage, which seems more direct and clear than some of those calling us to public piety, gives explicit reasons for urging us to private prayer: public prayer is rewarded by elevation in the eyes of men, while private prayer is rewarded by elevation in the eyes of God. In order to emphasize the point, this passage is framed by two others that respectively exhort us to fast in secret (Matt. 6:16–18)[23] and to give alms in secret (Matt. 6:2–4). These three passages go beyond, I think, guidelines for how to pray. They actually distinguish "authentic" prayer from "inauthentic" prayer.[24]

Although we would all agree that piety adopted for social expediency is inauthentic, it raises difficult questions. How are we to identify inauthentic piety? Judging others on this count would be well neigh impossible and, moreover, would demonstrate significant hubris and hypocrisy ("Let he who is without sin cast the first stone" [John 8:7]). Should we be at all concerned with the piety of others, either false or true? Kierkegaard, in stark contrast with Levinas, insists that, "You do not carry the responsibility for your wife, nor for other men, nor by any comparative standard with other men, but only as an individual."[25] Of course this is because, for Kierkegaard, faith operates beyond the sphere of ethics; the individual relationship to God is one that *transcends* the boundaries of the ethical.[26]

In a great many cases we have neither the duty, nor the authority, nor the ability to judge whether the piety of others is authentic. Therefore the question of identifying false piety is one that is ultimately self-referential. How are we to identify such behavior *in ourselves*? Kierkegaard is well aware of the difficulties here, noting that faith is a "task for a whole lifetime."[27] Everything Kant says about the difficulty of teasing out our motivations applies with equal force in the realm of prayer. Kant points out that our motivations, never fully transparent, are almost hopelessly opaque when an action is both in accord with duty and in accord with our inclinations.[28] If an action is in accord with both duty and inclination, it is difficult, perhaps impossible, to determine if it was done "for the sake of" duty. In a similar sense, if my piety is public, can I ever be absolutely sure that my piety was motivated by a desire to please God and not, at least in part, by the desire to please others or please myself? One way around this problem is simply to eliminate public prayer in favor of private prayer. This is not to say that if I pray in private or in secret, the motivation of my piety is necessarily pure. However, private prayer does do away with one possible kind of corruption: that of the ostentatious or superficial piety all too frequently associated with public display.[29] The motivation of public prayer and hence the authenticity of public prayer is always an open question.

Why do I genuflect, kneel, fast, or pray? Can one really focus on piety when others are present? The answer is not as simple as attempting to pray in public as if others are not present. Can one pray without recognition of others who, even when part of the same community, pray in a manner that is perceptibly different, whether that difference lies in visual, oral/aural, or kinetic variations? These differences, innocent in themselves, distract us from prayer *even when we do not judge others or ourselves* regarding these differences. The very fact that I notice that someone else stands after the *Agnus Dei* rather than kneeling, or keeps *kashrut* in a manner more or less strict than I do, or is or is not a *haji* means that the pious activity has been interrupted, turned from the transcendent back toward the immanent. Augustine is well aware of this problem and confesses that:

> My life is full of such lapses, and my one hope is in your great mercy. When my heart becomes the receptacle of distractions

of this nature and the container for a mass of empty thoughts, then too my prayers are often interrupted and distracted; and in your sight, while I am directing the voice of my heart to your ears, frivolous thoughts somehow rush in and cut short an aspiration of the deepest importance.[30]

Given the possible corruptions of prayer undertaken in public — from relatively innocent distractions to pernicious concern with human rather than divine opinion — are we justified in abandoning the ethical or human in favor of the religious or divine? Is it necessary to do so?

In *The Gift of Death*, Derrida addresses the three "secret acts" of piety and the corresponding "rewards" described in the Gospel of Matthew and finds there a "line demarcating celestial from terrestrial economy."[31] Like any economic exchange, something is given and something is received. According to Derrida, the exhortation to pray, fast, and give alms in secret, where only the Father can see you, is made in light of a promise of remuneration and is therefore economic in nature. The Beatitudes enumerate the rewards for piety, which will be heavenly rather than earthly. Invisible (secret, individual) prayer is rewarded with invisible (secret, individual) rewards. However, the economy of secret prayer transcends the "earthly economy" and operates within an "economy of sacrifice," and the economy of sacrifice is, says Derrida, a matter of *justice*.[32]

If piety is part of an economy, even a sacrificial one, we must give in order to receive and therefore we must question how we should give and what it means to give. The Gospel of Matthew, by presenting the contradictory calls to public and private piety, calls on us to question what it means to *give for Christ*, "for" being taken here in both the sense of substitution and in the sense of donation.[33] To give for Christ means to give in place of Christ, to give to others in fraternity with Christ, as Christ gave himself for others (Matt. 20:26–28); it also means to give to Christ, to give up the things of this world in order to follow Christ (Luke 18:18–27).

However, whatever such "giving" may mean, it does not, Derrida cautions, mean a simple and reciprocal exchange of prayers for salvation.[34] We cannot "win paradise economically."[35] The motive for private prayer cannot be to insure against the corruption of a gift given to God in exchange (*re-merciement*) for salvation.[36] If private prayer protects the authenticity of motive, it does so for reasons other than maintaining the quality of a product to be bartered with God. The economy of sacrifice—the spiritual economy, the economy of the gift—is not an economy of retribution or equal exchange. Rather, the spiritual economy is one of an "absolute surplus of value, heterogeneous to outlay or investment."[37] The spiritual economy is one of gift without reserve, that is, one of love:

> If you love only those who love you and to the extent that they love you . . . then you give nothing, no love, and the reserve of your wages will be like a tax that is imposed or a debt that is repaid, like the acquittal of a debt. In order to deserve or expect an infinitely higher salary, one that goes beyond the perception of what is due, you have to give without taking into account and love those who do not love you.[38]

Prayer, then—and fasting, almsgiving, and other acts of piety—is part of a spiritual economy that is concerned with giving and, ultimately, loving. Nevertheless, while such praying/giving/loving is obviously inscribed in some sense in the intersubjective world, it is the private, secret prayer that (re)establishes the spiritual economy. In fact, Derrida ultimately claims that such a secret is more radical than a secret between the pious person and the Father; prayer, almsgiving, or fasting must be a secret from even the person who gives, a gift given "without having it known by other men, in secret, without counting on recognition, reward, or remuneration. Without even having it known to oneself."[39] The absolute secret of the prayer insures that it is beyond or outside the economy of calculation, retribution, and exchange.

Now, there are certainly objections to Derrida's extreme formulation of the gift, which in its perfect state is without a giver, without a receiver, and even without anything given.[40] However, these objections are not our focus here. Let us say that Derrida has, in his way, pointed toward a just or ethical element in prayer, even, *pace* Levinas, "private" prayer. As part of a spiritual economy, prayer, fasting, almsgiving, and other acts of piety are, according to Derrida's analysis of the gift, ultimately acts of love.

Prayer as an Act of Love

The double call to private piety and public piety results in a tension that, if we are to avoid a contradiction or breakdown in the coherence of piety, calls for a hermeneutic reading. What are we to make of these conflicting demands that make prayer impossible by claiming private prayer is unethical and public prayer is inauthentic? How can we work through the contradiction, reread it as a paradox, and recover a "second naïveté" that will make prayer possible again?[41] One way, perhaps, is via a consideration of *love*.

Why love? We noted, in considering private prayer, that Derrida inscribes private prayer within the sphere of love; however, Levinas, who disagrees with the call to private prayer, agrees with Derrida in terms of prayer and love. Levinas views prayer as an *ethical act*. That prayer is an ethical act ultimately means that prayer is, for Levinas, like Derrida, an *act of love*:

> From the start, the encounter with the Other is my responsibility for him. That is the responsibility for my neighbor, which is, no doubt, the harsh name for what we call love of one's neighbor; love without Eros, charity, love in which the ethical aspect dominates the passionate aspect, love without concupiscence."[42]

We noted that Levinas insists that righteousness and piety are essentially intersubjective. However, if piety is intersubjective, it is ethical. The ethical relationship is responsibility, but to be responsible is to love.

Approaching the question from either side—the call to private prayer or the call to public prayer—leads to the same claim: prayer is akin to love. Levinas reaches this conclusion by critiquing the unethical aspects of private piety, insisting that prayer should be concerned with the other, that it is inscribed within the field of ethics and responsibility, which are other names for love. Derrida comes to the same conclusion from the opposite direction by considering the implications of the gospel caution against public prayer. In doing so, he reads private prayer in terms of the gift, as one element in a "spiritual economy" that inscribes prayer in the field of justice, giving, and, insofar as it approaches giving without reserve, love. Prayer— considered either as a private concern or as a public responsibility—is ultimately an act of love. What, then, do the biblical accounts have to say about love of God and love of humanity?

Both the private and the public, the individual's relationship to God and her relationship to the community, are addressed in the gospel accounts of love:

> One of the scribes came up and heard them disputing with one another, and seeing that he answered them well, asked him, "Which commandment is the first of all?" Jesus answered, "The first is, 'Hear, O Israel: The Lord our God, the Lord is

one; and you shall love the Lord your God with all your heart, and with all your soul, and with all your mind, and with all your strength.' The second is this, 'You shall love your neighbor as yourself.' There is no other commandment greater than these." (Mark 12:28–32)

The paradox of human love of God and interhuman love, as well as the paradox of private and public piety, are present in the answer to the scribe's question, which asked for the first (i.e., the most important) commandment. In answer, Jesus cites two commandments—not one—forcing us to ask ourselves what the relationship between these two commandments of love is and in what way they are, *together*, the first commandment.

Read literally, the love of God and the love of neighbor are a contradiction. When "he who loves father or mother more than me is not worthy of me; and he who loves son or daughter more than me is not worthy of me" (Matt. 10:37) is coupled with "you shall love the Lord your God with all your heart, and with all your soul, and with all your might" (Deut. 6:5), it seems difficult to see how *any* earthly or mortal love is appropriate. God demands and deserves all your love given with your entire heart, soul, mind, and strength, meaning—or at least implying—that love of earthly things, including your neighbor, detracts from time, effort, and love that is more properly directed at God.[43] How, then, are we also to love our neighbor? Love God with all your heart. Love others as yourself. Pray to your Father in secret. Gather with others in God's name. The juxtaposition of these demands points us toward and calls us to authentic prayer, prayer that is both individual and communal, both secret and open, both private and public.

We would do well to question whether these two loves (of God and of our neighbors) and therefore these two spheres (the private and public) are really so neatly separable. If the love of God and love of neighbor are inextricably tied, then prayer, as an act of love, must necessarily take place in both the private and public spheres. And, indeed, this is what we are told: "Those who say, 'I love God,' and hate their brothers or sisters are liars; for those who do not love a brother or sister whom they have seen, cannot love God whom they have not seen. The commandment we have from him is this: those who love God must love their brothers and sisters also" (1 John 4:20–21).

Hence what appears to be a contradiction—two different and infinite calls to love[44]—is, when considered from another perspective, a paradox. What conceptual thinking or philosophical thematization sees as contradictory and subsequently breaks up in analysis is, and in fact always was, coherent and harmonious. These two absolute demands are somehow incomplete without each other, even though, as conflicting demands, they appear to prevent each other's completion.

If prayer is in fact an act of love, then these two passages — Jesus' answer to the scribe in the gospel account of Mark and John's discussion of God and love — indicate how we may reconcile (or mediate between) private prayer and public prayer: they are two forms of one authentic prayer, just as love of God and love of neighbor are two forms of *one* love, or two requirements of the *one* "first commandment." Hence Derrida's characteristically clever play on the words *plus de secret* is the very essence of prayer.[45] We should pray to our God in secret (*plus de secret*) and we should gather with others in God's name (*plus de secret*).

Conclusion

We began by speaking of prayer in terms of essences, asking whether prayer is essentially intersubjective or essentially private. However, it has become clear that this is the wrong question. Prayer is not "essentially" either. It is wrong to think of prayer in terms of *eidos*, at least in the sense that there is a universal, immutable, and clearly demarcated definition of "true" prayer to which we have access.[46] Thus when we say, "prayer is love," we do not mean to provide a eidetic definition — as if the meaning of "love" were unambiguous! "True" or "authentic" prayer is not static or distinct; it is indefinite, capable of multifarious manifestations, what postmodern thought would call "translatable."[47] However, while prayer — like other limit experiences — is translatable, it is not infinitely translatable. That is, while an incalculable number of things can be done prayerfully, not any thought, speech, or act is a prayer. It is because prayer is translatable, but not infinitely so, that it calls for a hermeneutic account. It is here that I distinguish myself from radical versions of deconstruction and align myself with a (still radical, I hope) hermeneutic, one that takes a middle path between certitude, dogmatism, and privileged access to the Truth, on the one hand, and complete undecidability, translatability, and relativism, on the other.

True prayer, like true love, can take many forms but it cannot take any form. Therefore it is somewhat determinable but not perfectly so. It is true that we can never exhaustively describe prayer or precisely demarcate the boundaries of authentic prayer. However, it is also true that we can accurately describe prayer and roughly demarcate the boundaries of authentic prayer. How would such a descriptive project begin? If prayer is something that must be addressed hermeneutically, what preliminary conclusions can be drawn from the preceding discussion, which attempts to interpret biblical accounts of prayer in terms of biblical accounts of love via a detour through Levinas and Derrida?

We have come to characterize prayer as having some kinship with either justice or ethics. On the surface, this might appear problematic, as the just and the ethical are notoriously difficult to circumscribe and, moreover, frequently in conflict. However, on this reading, justice and ethics are preliminary stages en route to thinking prayer in terms of love. To think of prayer in terms of gift without reserve or in terms of responsibility for the other is ultimately to describe prayer as a kind of loving. This, then, is the first conclusion to be gleaned from our consideration of prayer: prayer has a certain kinship with love. Still, one might object that identifying authentic prayer by its affiliation with love merely defers the question, substituting one indeterminate term for another. That might be the case if we were searching for the *eidos* of prayer. However, while love is resistant to the sort of eidetic definition that would allow us to *comprehend* authentic prayer, it is open to a hermeneutic account that will help us to *recognize* authentic prayer. How? While love provides neither an exhaustive account nor a precise definition of prayer, it does allow us to eliminate certain possibilities by a sort of *via negativa*.[48] Thinking prayer in terms of love may not tell us what prayer is, but it can identify some things that prayer is not.[49] In addition, the kinship between prayer and love gives us access to a rich tradition of philosophical and theological reflection on love, which can now be brought to bear on questions relating to prayer.

A second conclusion stems from the first and allows us to answer the question of private and public prayer that initiated this inquiry. Reading prayer as love, we find a solution to the potential conflict between public and private prayer in the very text that seemed to raise the specter of contradiction. Rather than advocating an exclusive, specific manner of prayer, the calls to public and private prayer caution us against excesses on either side. We are called to an ongoing examination and interpretation of our prayers in order to do justice to both our relationship to God and our relationships with each other. We might say that private and public prayer—and love of God and love of neighbor—"bleed into" each other. Therefore prayer is neither solely an individual matter between oneself and God, nor is it something merely a matter of community and tradition—authentic prayer takes place at the chiasmus where the individual and the intersubjective meet.[50]

12

Praise—Pure and Personal?
Jean-Luc Marion's Phenomenologies of Prayer

CHRISTINA M. GSCHWANDTNER

> Prayer remains without answer in a room without windows.
>
> —Emmanuel Levinas

In "Education and Prayer," Emmanuel Levinas complains that our prayer has too often become a purely isolated and individuated experience and that we have lost the social and collective dimension of prayer.[1] Prayer, he suggests, always has a liturgical and communal function. Prayer requires openness and truth and hence has ethical significance and import. Jean-Luc Marion is profoundly influenced by Levinas's philosophy. His own account of prayer bears traces of Levinas's thought and orients itself along Levinasian suggestions regarding relation to the other. Yet Marion's account of prayer lacks precisely the communal, social, and ethical dimension for which Levinas calls.

In this paper, I examine what Marion has to say about prayer and set his account of prayer in relation to his larger phenomenological project. Marion writes of prayer in two distinct fashions. On the one hand, he focuses on the function of prayer and on the kind of language it employs. On the other hand, he describes the phenomenon of prayer as a loving exchange of gazes between the praying person and God. My goal in this paper is to articulate these two accounts, to bring them together by investigating their mutual motivation, and to arrive at a critique of the phenomenologies of prayer presented by Marion.[2] I contend that Marion's analysis of prayer is ultimately a very individualistic one that does not take into account the public or communal aspect of prayer and hence stops at purely personal experience.[3] I argue that such is the case because Marion is more concerned with the pure form of prayer than any particular content or ethical dimension of prayer, paralleling his emphasis on a pure phenomenology of the given as such as opposed to more particular phenomenological concerns or ethical implications. Thus, Marion's more general phenomenology strongly influences—or maybe even jeopardizes—his phenomenologies of prayer.

Due to the care to protect God in his accounts of the language of prayer, Marion's analysis of prayer tends to dissolve into a concern about how the individual person at prayer can speak rightly about God. I show that despite Marion's strong ecclesial concerns in his more theological writings, his accounts of prayer must remain focused on the individual, because they so strongly depend upon his phenomenology. His first analysis of prayer parallels his explication of the purity of the appeal, while his second analysis is closely linked to his phenomenological account of love. On the one hand, as the claim that comes to the phenomenological recipient must be pure, radical, and undetermined, God's name must remain radically undetermined in prayer. On the other hand, as love is described phenomenologically as the crossing of two invisible gazes, prayer becomes collapsed into erotic vision by being defined in almost identical fashion. The near-solipsism of Marion's phenomenology is thus carried over into his theological depiction of prayer, forcing it to remain individualistic and personal instead of corporate and ecclesial.[4] Let us begin by examining the two accounts of prayer Marion provides.

I. Prayer as Protection of God

Marion's intent in "In the Name" is to protect the name of God[5] and to preserve it from blasphemy and idolatry.[6] In other places, he has employed the terminology of icon and idol to explicate this concern. While idolatrous language speaks of God falsely and is limited by the viewer's gaze (and is ultimately reflected back upon itself as in an invisible mirror), iconic language goes beyond the gaze of the observer and traverses an infinite distance.[7] In this particular context, Marion takes issue with Derrida's writings on "negative theology" (which Marion would prefer to call "mystical theology").[8] He engages in an analysis of Dionysius' treatises *Mystical Theology* and *On the Divine Names* and finds in them three movements: one of predication or affirmation, one of denial or negation, and a superior or third way, which he describes as a way of "eminence" or "un-naming."[9] Derrida, so Marion argues, only recognizes the first two ways and therefore remains stuck in predicative language about God (or at least accuses negative theology of such).

Marion wishes to explicate this third way, which he contends Derrida misses.[10] He speaks of it as a path of prayer or praise, a movement that goes beyond both affirmation and negation in a higher discourse of praise that no longer seeks to say anything determinative about God. It is a way that plays outside of the duality of affirmation/negation, synthesis/separation, true/false and thus transgresses the values of truth which are exercised by logic and metaphysics. In so doing, it shows the insufficiency of the first two ways.[11] Marion sees the three ways inscribed in a hierarchy: negation is superior to affirmation (and more appropriate than it), the way of eminence or praise is superior to both (and more appropriate than either). Negation rejects the affirmative names given to God and shows them to be insufficient or even false. To deny specific names for God is a first step away from idolatry. Yet even apophaticism is too limited. Beyond speaking of God negatively, saying what "God is not," we must move toward praise, which no longer allows any predication of God, either positive or negative. In praise, all names for God are denied and disqualified. The point is neither "naming" nor "not naming" (both remain ultimately idolatrous) but "un-naming" (which is iconic). The very pertinence of all predication is hence eliminated.[12] Similarly to his "radical" phenomenology that explicates the purity of the "claim as such" and not any particular determinate claims, Marion seeks to move beyond concrete manifestations or specifications of God to a "pure" naming that is no longer predicative. I pursue this parallel in more detail later.

Prayer, then, transgresses the metaphysical function of language.[13] The point of praise is no longer to say but to listen: to be said, recognized, and "loved by goodness."[14] Marion concludes that we must ultimately be silent about God in order to protect God from our idolatrous namings.[15] The theologian must practice deconstruction.[16] This silence itself, however, has to be both deserved and qualified. It is not an ignoring of God or a "silencing" of theology, but an appropriate silence: one of awe in which the focus moves from me talking about God to God addressing me. It is not so much that Marion is interested in the effect of this speech or silence upon human beings; but his reversal of emphasis designates the important impossibility of speaking about God. God cannot be named; there cannot be any conceptual possession of God; God's name and essence must be protected.[17] Again, this move may be said to parallel his more general phenomenological reversal, in which I no longer control the phenomenon, but the phenomenon comes to me as its passive recipient. Prayer thus is dissolved in pure (and mute) praise.

Furthermore, instead of speaking adequately of God, in this kind of prayer the movement is inverted, and the one who is praising becomes named by God whom one seeks to praise. The person praying no longer speaks but gives him- or herself to the one whom the prayer "unsays." According to Marion, this constitutes a pragmatic function of language, not a predicative one.[18] He links the movement of prayer with that of naming and ultimately of baptism.[19] Prayer, then, does not consist in making the one invoked come down but in "raising us toward God in a sustained attention."[20] Marion concludes that "the Name does not have as its function to inscribe God in the theoretical horizon of our predication but to inscribe us, according to a radically new pragmatics, in the horizon itself of God: which is accomplished exactly by baptism, where, far from our attributing to God a name intelligible to us, we enter into his unpronounceable name, in order to receive by surplus our name."[21] Mystical theology thus does not find a name for God but helps us receive our name from such prayer. Prayer becomes an openness to the divine naming that envisages me and reduces me to awe and bedazzlement.[22] Relation is here ultimately impossible, because the distance is so great.

Reflection on the phenomenon of prayer in this article is therefore dissolved in a reconsideration of the possibility of revelation.[23] Prayer, for Marion, although it begins with the praying subject, very quickly becomes an explication of God's activity. Prayer is not about what we do or say or who we become but first about what we should not say and secondly about what God does for us. The human subject is both paralyzed in its address and becomes completely passive as it merely marks the response to the divine other who is the primary and sole actor. This phenomenology of prayer, then, becomes solely a way of acknowledging our impotence to speak of God and the highest articulation of what happens in the pure phenomenological encounter. Indeed, that is the actual point of Marion's article. It is primarily an explication of the impossibility of speaking about God or saying anything adequate about the divine. Prayer merely serves as a name for the awe inspired by the unnameable and as a way of claiming that such awe is no longer predicative.[24] Although Marion's treatment of prayer, then, remains cursory here, I think it well represents his views on prayer in which he consistently describes the "right" human attitude before God as an experience of excessive bedazzlement to which awe and silence can be the only appropriate responses. This kind of prayer, then, is not meant to be practiced in community or to transform an individual or a group of people, but rather provides a safeguard to protect prayer from any form of adulteration, to turn it into pure praise. It speaks more about the excessively saturated phenomenon of R/revelation than about that of prayer.

II. Prayer as a Crossing of Gazes

Marion's other account of prayer in *La croisée du visible* is set in the context of an exploration of aesthetics (in particular, an analysis of painting). Marion considers a phenomenology of the image, broadly conceived. He analyzes the status of the image in contemporary society and its impact on how persons perceive themselves. Ultimately, so he concludes, we become defined and imprisoned by the image that we must convey to our visually obsessed media culture.[25] He thus proposes to liberate us from the tyranny of the image by an analysis of the religious icon. In this context, his explication of the icon is far more explicitly linked to Byzantine theology and iconography, to the point of quoting both treatises defending the use of icons and using phrases from the Byzantine liturgy.[26] The icon does not function here as a defense of a certain speech about God or a protection of God from such speech (nor is it explicitly opposed to the idol or worked out in conceptual terms). Rather, the icon is read as a "kenosis of the image" and an alternative to the detrimental effect of the image upon people.[27]

Marion examines the use of the icon for prayer in light of the "crossing of gazes" within it.[28] The icon, Marion contends, is a particular doctrine of visibility of the image and of the use of this visibility.[29] Before the icon, I both see and am seen. Yet, unlike the image which is completely exposed to visibility, the icon does not ultimately give itself to be seen but to be venerated. An icon is painted as a window to another reality and hence must be traversed in response to the gaze that transits across it and imposes itself upon the person praying. The two gazes cross and expose themselves to each other.

The icon is kenotic because God humbles God-self to appearing in an image or a figure, thus showing not only the face of Christ but a trace of God.

The icon therefore provides a transition from the invisible to the visible and makes the invisible visible.[30] This transition is possible only in prayer and cannot be accomplished by any other attitude. Marion describes this movement of prayer:

> The icon can only be contemplated with honor by the gaze, which venerates it as a stigmata of the invisible. Prayer alone can thus go back from the visible to the invisible (according to the type), even as the spectator can only compare the visible to the invisible (according to the mimesis). The holy things for the holy: prayer alone traverses the icon because it alone knows the function of the type.[31]

The inverse perspective of the icon attempts to draw our gaze into it toward the invisible. The icon imitates inner-Trinitarian life: the transferal of glory that takes place between Father and Son. It performs the same movement of holiness and glory, directing it to an other than itself. The icon is a sign, a figure of the distance of the invisible. In the icon, I always see an invisible gaze that envisages me.[32] To pray is to open oneself to a gaze coming from elsewhere but located in the medium of the icon that refers to the other to whom one prays. The icon thus becomes an instrument of communion between the one praying and God and allows for an encounter between them.[33] Marion concludes, "the icon defines itself thus as the gaze of a prototype who demands the veneration of my own gaze to remount, by traversing this type, toward him. The icon has one stake: the crossing of gazes, thus, strictly defined, love."[34]

Prayer is therefore the balanced tension between two invisible gazes that cross each other and weigh upon each other. Prayer allows God to become incarnate and simultaneously allows humans to ascend toward the divine: "In the icon, the visible and the invisible enflame each other with a fire which no longer destroys, but illuminates the divine face of humans."[35] This phenomenological description of what happens in the experience of prayer is far more balanced than the analysis of prayerful language in the account explored above. Marion takes great pains to speak of God's vulnerability and self-giving in love to the believer or the one praying.[36] Yet on the one hand, the emphasis is still predominantly upon God, who is the primary actor in this relationship. On the other hand, this depiction is even more clearly a strictly individual one. The depiction of two gazes that cross each other, hold each other in balance as they weigh upon each other, not only closely corresponds to Marion's description of the erotic relationship but also cannot possibly be accomplished by more than the two gazes involved. Such prayer always borders on the solipsistic: the praying person is alone with God and invisible to the world. Such prayer cannot happen within community, and in effect it serves to shut out the fellowship of others, since it exists in splendid isolation—a soul intoxicated with its individual mystical experience of divine love.

III. Prayer as a Corporate Phenomenon

Such accounts of prayer, it seems to me, ultimately fail to take account of the ecclesial and corporate dimensions of prayer. Prayer—at its best—transforms and affects our living within the world, not merely the subjective mental or emotional state of the individual at prayer. Prayer has an ethical dimension: it binds believers together with others and shapes them into a people commissioned to transform their world. In prayer, people cease to be isolated individuals and participate in each other. They become one in their prayer and instantiate something new. In liturgical/ecclesial prayer, the world is transformed in some way to resemble more closely the holy community it is supposed to become.

In Christian prayer, this transformation is specifically eucharistic.[37] On the one hand, that transformation is eschatological: the Church's transformation into the body of Christ is ongoing and never fully accomplished. On the other hand, the liturgical prayers of the community are centered around the performance of the Eucharist. The body of Christ is the bread that is broken within the body of Christ that is the Church. The hope of the future is instantiated in the prayer of the liturgy, in which that "not yet" is in fact already present in some fashion. It can only be "here," however, can only happen, if the people do not remain a group of isolated individuals praying but become together a new body, the body of Christ. Much more than a predicative or pragmatic function in regard to God, prayer has a performative function in regard to the world and of people within it: first and foremost the worshipping people of the community gathered in that particular time and space and second the world that they carry to God in their prayer and that they reenter as they leave. Being thus transformed by their prayer, this new people works actively within the world in order to transform it also into its eschatological reality, to make it become that which it shall be. Such prayer is public in at least two ways. First, it is practiced together visibly by the involvement of one's whole body and the liturgical actions of such corporate prayer. Second, it actively seeks to transform the world and its public sphere into a place of justice and peace.

Marion himself has pointed to some aspects of the transformative nature of the Eucharist and the Church as the body of Christ. In *Prolegomena to Charity*, Marion explores the notions of presence and absence in light of the accounts of the ascension.[38] He finds an important link between presence and blessing. Only in the disciples' blessing of God can God become present and be recognized. The gift of God's presence is given when it is received as gift and blessed in that reception. In recognizing the gift and blessing it within the temple, the disciples are transformed into Christ and become themselves a paschal gift of presence. They imitate Christ's gift, repeat his sacrifice, and become "actors of presence." Marion links the body of Christ that has ascended into heaven to the body of the Eucharist and to the disciples constituting Christ's body as the Church. This gift of presence can be assimilated when it is recognized as such in prayer and blessing.

Blessing, Marion insists, also relates to mission. The disciples have to perform the mission of Christ and thus become actors of Christ as they act in love/charity. He argues that the community is newly constituted by the resurrection and supposed to perform the body by its becoming or "playing" Christ as in a *commedia dell'arte*. Marion even points to the eschatological nature of this liturgical action:

> Presence: not to find oneself in the presence of Christ, but to become present to him (to declare oneself present, available) in order to receive from him the present (the gift) of the Spirit who makes us, here and now (in the present), bless him like he blesses the Father—until and in order that he return. The highest presence of Christ lies in the Spirit's action of making us, with him and in him, bless the Father.[39]

Yet, despite his recognition of the significance of Eucharist and mission, this depiction still remains an individualistic one. It is the individual believer who is inscribed into the divine life of the Triune God and is patterned upon Christ. Marion claims that in the liturgy all our senses are brought together and directed to God. But he describes this sensual experience as a "spectacle," something that the believer observes the celebrant perform. It is the celebrant who acts in the person of Christ and takes on his role. Christ is touched, seen, eaten, heard, breathed in Scripture and Eucharistic body but, according to Marion, these actions do not affect the body but only the gaze. The attitude of my gaze before the liturgy parallels my attitude before the crossing of the visible by the invisible (in prayer).[40] Liturgy, for Marion, guides us to the "decision" of "accepting to pray," which "signifies allowing the other to observe my gaze."[41]

The "participant" in the liturgy is merely passive, an adoring observer of what the priest performs in the place of Christ. Only the priest acts *in persona Christi* and performs the work of Christ.[42] The audience is quite literally an "audience" without active participation in the liturgy. Any appropriation of this sacrifice happens only in an individual attitude of prayer before what is essentially performed by another for me and in my place. A coming together of this audience into one body active for justice and peace, transforming this present world into the one promised, is finally impossible. Believers may bless God, may take pains not to speak God's name inadequately or idolatrously, but neither they nor the world to which they return are transformed.

IV. Pure Personal Prayer and Its Phenomenology

Why does Marion's account remain so individualistic even when it is ecclesial? Why is prayer only personal and not corporate? It appears that much of this exclusive emphasis is due to the intimate tie of certain aspects of Marion's theological writings to his larger phenomenological project.[43] Marion's analyses of prayer closely parallel and even determine, on the one hand, his insistence on the purity of the phenomenological appeal and, on the other hand, his phenomenological depiction of love. Marion's description of prayer must necessarily remain limited, I suggest, because it is governed by his phenomenological presuppositions, which exclude an emphasis on ethics (or at least define it as marginal) and emphasize form as such (purity and radicality) over particularized content. In conclusion, I briefly explore three aspects of this assertion: first, the emphasis on purity; second, the marginalization of ethics; and third, the definition of love.

First, Marion's extreme emphasis on purity and the individual in prayer is linked to his desire to formulate a radical phenomenology that presses experience to its purest form and would constitute a new "first philosophy." Surely it is not accidental that his section on prayer is found in the final chapter of his work *In Excess*, which concludes his phenomenological trilogy and begins with a chapter justifying the need to push phenomenology to its utmost extreme and articulate its purest form. His project as a whole seeks to carry phenomenology to (and beyond) its most radical boundaries. Thus, he explores phenomena at the very margins of phenomenality: phenomena that are saturated and excessive. Phenomenology can be a new "first" (or rather, "last" and "final") philosophy if it becomes pure, radical, and undetermined.

Marion is interested in the very structure of phenomenality, in finding the one ultimate and final principle, in stripping phenomenology radically of any determined appeals. Everything finds a place in Marion's project: Derrida's *différance*, Ricoeur's hermeneutics, Levinas's other, Henry's flesh/life, and Heidegger's Being. Marion sees his project as the final step in phenomenology, as the third and decidedly last reduction.[44] He ranks his project alongside those of Descartes and Husserl, as their final culmination and perfection. In order to complete phenomenology, he seeks a new "first philosophy" and articulates the supreme or ultimate principle of all phenomenology. His phenomenology is radically reduced to the point where it becomes the "philosophy par excellence." His phenomena are given in pure and total appearance and with absolute certainty. No other principle can come after this final one, and no phenomenology can be more pure or more radical.[45] Everything in Marion's phenomenology is thus directed at purity, excess, and brilliance. When speaking of God, language must become doubly pure, doubly saturated, and doubly excessive.[46] A consideration of prayer similarly always lapses into an analysis of pure praise, of absolute awe before the dazzling divine.

Second (but closely connected to the first), Marion deliberately deemphasizes Levinas's insistence on the ethical dimension of the face of the other, in favor of a general phenomenological description of the other, a pure claim that calls me as such and whose origin must be determined only by the response. Throughout his work, Marion seeks to dislocate what he perceives as Levinas's exclusive emphasis on ethics.[47] He often lists Levinas as one example of a specific call/appeal in phenomenology, together with such thinkers as Heidegger and Henry. For example, he sees Levinas as attempting to overcome the Heideggerian claim of Being by making the call proceed instead from the face of the neighbor.[48]

Marion regularly posits these different appeals as equivalent examples of determined claims, while he himself wishes to examine the anonymous and undetermined call, the *pure* claim, the appeal *as such*. Being, God, the Other, autoaffection, or life are all mere "figures of difference" that are already named in the form of a response.[49] The various "names" of the appeal (Being, Father, Other) limit it phenomenologically, while Marion is interested in the unlimited, in what goes beyond all such limits.[50] He seeks to separate responsibility from ethics by insisting that "I am responsible, *not just ethically*, but even for allowing the face of the other to appear."[51] Levinas's emphasis on ethics is stifling, too narrow and too specific. Thus, Marion seeks to expand it into more general analyses of wider application. He finds that "responsibility cannot be limited to only one instance (that of the Other) but must also apply to others."[52]

Marion repeatedly seeks to get beyond an exclusive emphasis on ethics. When analyzing the pure phenomenon according to donation (or givenness), he remarks, as an aside, that not only was he able to describe this phenomenality without any need to invoke transcendence, but "not even ethics was necessary."[53] Ethics often becomes relegated to a mere side issue. The icon, for Marion, replaces the face: "It is not only the Other of ethics (Levinas), but more radically the icon which imposes its appeal."[54] Clearly, Marion sees it as one of the goals of his project to get beyond Levinas's emphasis on ethics and to situate it within a larger and more radical project. It makes sense, then, that ethical considerations also play little or no role in Marion's reflections on prayer.

It is due to this marginalization of ethics and overvaluing of the purity of the claim ("as such") that Marion is unable to consider the ethical and concretely transformative aspect of ecclesial and communal prayer. As he insists on the purity of the phenomenological appeal, Marion is concerned with preserving the purity of God's name, not with explicating ethical dimensions of prayer. Marion is more interested in what prayer cannot say than in what it can or should say. The phenomenon of revelation (which, as we have seen, is the true concern of the chapter in which his account of prayer is found) is the most excessive and radical phenomenon which pushes phenomenology to its utmost extreme and boundary. It is not accidental, then, that Marion's analysis of the language of prayer in this context would coincide with requests regarding the language of phenomenology.

Yet it is the second account of prayer in its parallel to a phenomenological depiction of (erotic) love that shows even more clearly why prayer for Marion has to remain an intensely personal, if not solipsistic, exercise. The "devoted" to whom the phenomenon is given is an individual dative who is not essentially connected to any others.[55] The recipient of the phenomenon receives his or her subjectivity from any instance of saturated phenomenality, be that a historical event, a painting, or even an experience of one's own flesh. It is not necessary in Marion's phenomenology that a human (or divine) Other claim me, but in fact the appeal has to be anonymous and is identified only by a decision of the recipient who gives him- or herself over to the given.[56] The situation of love—or more generally, of intersubjectivity—is only one particular case of such individuation of the subject as the dative of a more general phenomenality. The devoted is hence primarily solitary: the experience of a saturated phenomenon comes to an individual, not to a group of people. In Marion's first account of prayer, it is precisely the kind of language expressing an experience of the saturated phenomenon of second degree, that of revelation (or God). It is, therefore, by definition an individual who has to identify it as such a phenomenal experience.

Marion's account of love[57] does not alleviate this experience of isolation and individuality. Rather, it exacerbates the inability of communication and interaction. According to Marion, love is best defined as a crossing of two invisible gazes that invisibly weigh upon each other and expose each other to the other's gaze without intending to control or even view the other. Love is a kind of loss of consciousness that gives itself to another in reciprocal vulnerability. He depicts this crossing of gazes as follows:

> Whence comes what we will from now on consider the phenomenological determination of love: two definitively invisible gazes (intentionality and the injunction) cross one another, and thus together trace a cross *that is invisible to every gaze other than theirs alone*. Each of the two gazes renounces seeing visibly the other gaze—the object alone can be seen, the eye's corpse—in order to expose its own invisible intention to the invisible impact of the other intention. Two gazes, definitively invisible, cross and, in this crossing, renounce their invisibility. They consent to let themselves be seen without seeing and invert the original disposition of every (de)nominative gaze—to see without being seen. To love would thus be defined as seeing the definitively invisible aim of my gaze nonetheless exposed by the aim of another invisible gaze; the two gazes, invisible forever, expose themselves to

each other in the crossing of their reciprocal aims. Loving no longer consists trivially in seeing or in being seen, nor in desiring or inciting desire, but in experiencing the crossing of gazes within, first, the crossing of aims.[58]

Such exposure and crossing must always remain invisible not only to the lovers themselves but especially to the outside world. Nobody sees this crossing. Everybody but the two lovers remains oblivious to the erotic gaze. Such love cannot be communicated, much less shared. Marion repeatedly argues that an experience of love is superior to the ethical relationship and a better account of intersubjectivity than that provided by Levinas. Love, although it perhaps does not exclude ethics, goes beyond it and renders it irrelevant by comparison. An account of personal love, then, is superior to one that would be corporate or have more ethical implications. Even this explicitly phenomenological treatment of love, Marion concludes on a theological note:

> Freed from intentionality, love in the end would be defined, still within the field of phenomenology, as the act of a gaze that renders itself back to another gaze in a common unsubstitutability. To render oneself back to a gaze means, for another gaze, to return there, as to a place for a rendez-vous, but above all to render oneself there in an unconditional surrender: to render oneself to the unsubstitutable other, as to a summons to my own unsubstitutability—no other than me will be able to play the other that the other requires, no other gaze than my own must respond to the ecstasy of this particular other exposed in his gaze. But to render oneself other, to surrender this gaze to the gaze of the other who crosses me, requires faith.[59]

As we have seen above, Marion uses terminology and description for his second account of the relation between God and the person at prayer that is exactly parallel (if not identical) to this definition of love. Both love and prayer are analyzed phenomenologically as a "crossing of gazes." Both expose two gazes to each other in vulnerability and ecstasy. Both are invisible and incommunicable to all others. The prayerful crossing of the two gazes across the icon is ultimately an erotic one and hence invisible (and irrelevant) to all others. Prayer is an intensely personal experience of love, not one that could be communicated. In neither account of prayer that Marion provides does prayer have any ethical implications. Or, if there are such implications, they are ultimately not relevant to the experience of prayer itself. Prayer is not something done in fellowship nor is it done for the sake of transformation, justice, or peace.

In conclusion, one should point out that prayer is not the primary concern in any of Marion's texts. Maybe if Marion was to write a theological reflection focused specifically on the topic of prayer, his treatment would look very different. Yet it is clear that in order to arrive at a more corporate or ethically conscious account of prayer, Marion would have to separate it far more obviously from his phenomenological analysis. In the passages we have examined, that is not the case. All statements he makes about prayer, even when they are marginal comments, serve to emphasize its personal nature and quickly dissolve into an account of pure praise. For Marion, at least as far as we can determine from the texts available, prayer may be participation in God but not participation in each other. While it serves to establish fellowship with God across an infinite distance that is never erased, the distance toward other human beings is not crossed.[60] Marion's present phenomenologies of prayer posits prayer as praise: as pure and as personal as possible.

PART **III**

Defining Prayer's Intentionality

13

The Saving or Sanitizing of Prayer
The Problem of the Sans *in Derrida'ↄ Account of Prayer*

MARK GEDNEY

In his book, *The Prayerↄ anↄ Tearↄ of Jacqueↄ Derriↄa*, John Caputo proposes the following hypothesis:

> What if theology were to confess itself no longer able to save the name of God? What if, beyond the economy of sacrifice, it were to give up the name of God to translatability without return? What if it were to pray without (*ↄanↄ*) knowing where to direct its prayers, without its sense of destinal assurance, without trusting that its prayers up to heaven rise? What if it were to have faith without faith, *foi ↄanↄ foi* (maybe even *foi à ↄang froiↄ*), the *ↄanↄ* serving to save faith from dogmatism, to believe without quite knowing in what it believed, so that it had to ask, "what do I love when I love my God?"[1]

This project or hypothesis is based on a series of moves made by Derrida over the past few years on the possibility of a religion without religion, faith without *faith* (as in the *Faith*, the *Creↄo*, or *ↄer Glaube*), a messianism without a Messiah, or a praying without (*ↄanↄ*) direction or addressee. Though each of these possibilities will get some attention in this essay, I shall focus on Derrida's (and Caputo's) claim that this directionless praying, which does not possess recognizable limits concerning its addressee (if one even exists), is the essential element of all praying—even the essential element of the religious life itself. In particular, while recognizing the valuable insights to be found in Derrida's rudderless and wayward prayers,[2] I shall argue that we should hesitate before according such prayers pride of place. For such a move may lead us to a blindness toward or even an exclusion of some fruitful extensions or variations of our understanding of prayer and thus to a impoverished understanding of determinate religion and of human finitude.

The key to these blind spots or exclusions lies in the difficulty of properly determining the nature of this absolute praying, insofar as it is understood as the essential element of all praying, that is, as a sort of transcendental condition for the possibility of true prayer. It is a question that has been broached in one way or another by a number of thinkers, including both Caputo and Derrida. It concerns the transformation of this minimal condition, this quasi-transcendental principle (as Derrida calls it),[3] into a concrete and particular (singular) praying/prayer or determinate religion—even if it is *only* a praying or a religion without religion or a praying or religion in the desert.[4] This problem is raised by Derrida and Caputo in terms of the following hermeneutical question: Is this disenfranchised character of prayer a transhistorical condition or is it a just a unique example or expression of prayer? This question raises an even more important one: If we take this quasi-transcendental condition to be an historical, singular event—as, I think, Caputo does[5]—then how are we to understand its relation to historical, determinate, and particular praying? In what follows, I argue that it is in large part the transforming of this transcendental condition into a determinate possibility (a historical event) that allows for the double exclusion or blindness noted above.

The first exclusion: Might not such a position tempt one to believe that Derrida is truly ready for canonization? On this view, a person who prays the prayers of his or her community—the prayers of petition or confession, say—would feel a bit left out or second class. Such a person would be regarded as too proud or perhaps not quite fearful enough. In other words, such persons, who seem to be praying in a more determinate fashion, would be lacking a certain sangfroid. In contrast, a sort of fearlessness is more clearly evidenced in Derrida's blind prayers, which, lacking any direction, seem to reach out bravely into the unknown. Following Kierkegaard, Derrida points to the relation between uncertainty (what is *secret*) and absolute, unconditioned passion for the other—even the absolute Other.[6] Caputo points to this connection in his commentary on Derrida's *Passions:* "It is only when the 'come!' calls for something it cannot know or foresee that the come really has passion."[7] Here passion is pushed to its "highest pitch," in a sense similar to Kierkegaard's understanding of the incalculable passion of faith.

A second exclusion: Does not this privileging leave other human endeavors somewhat further from grace? Would not such a prayer be directed to a God "who has nothing to do with knowing and unknowing?" It seems as if this slight possible genuflection in Derrida's direction risks losing sight of the necessary openness produced in any prayer whatsoever. As Chrétien notes, even to petition God is "to recognize in the act itself that one is not the origin of every good and gift and to recognize in the act itself Him whom we address for who He is."[8] Equally, this privileging of the wounded aspect of our relationship to the other, insofar as it may absorb other aspects of prayer, may leave out fruitful analogies with other modes of being human. It would represent a sort of jealousy that would have the paradoxical effect of limiting difference, tempting us to withhold redemption from other human dramas.

This foreclosing, as a temptation to absolute exemplification, also manifests itself in the ambivalent term used by Derrida, "messianicity" (*messianicité*), a term that is meant to capture this wounded character of prayer as a form of radical temporality. As a condition of our praying as finite human subjects, Derrida speaks of a looking forward to or expectation of an absolute justice and peace, which is inaugurated (invented) by a Messiah who, however, can never come. As Derrida points out, if one takes this messianic promise as sort of transcendental condition (or even as a quasi-transcendental condition) for the possibility of any true praying at all, then it is structurally impossible for such a messianic prayer to be answered without the destruction of prayer itself. In such a world all things would be known, all things would be present. This follows if we maintain something like the Kantian transcendental model. It would seem that such a structural messianicity would make it impossible for any particular religion or religious expression or evocation to bring us within or toward such a horizon (especially if it is not even a horizon). If we say that this condition was experienced or that such an experience provided for a singular determinate religion, this would seem to implicate one in a paralogism of the Kantian sort; namely, the substituting of a structural condition for a singular event that it structures.

James K. A. Smith has taken up this question of Derrida's "Kantianism" in his essay, "Re-Kanting Postmodernism?: Derrida's Religion within the Limits of Reason Alone." Smith notes a number of ways in which Derrida explicitly takes upon himself the mantle of the Enlightenment, generally, and Kant, specifically, in articulating the hope for a "universal religion":

> For Derrida, like Kant, such a religion is ultimately a matter of ethics or justice, such that the "religion" which Derrida discloses is remarkably similar to Kant's "moral religion," including the tie that binds it to democracy. Further, this plays itself out within a framework which understands the relationship between faith and knowledge in a manner we might describe as "hyper-Kantian," faulting even Kant for failing to radically think religion within the limits of reason alone — for not being enlightened enough.[9]

We can see the seeds of Smith's ultimate conclusions in this passage. Smith's basic concern is with Derrida's apparent desire for a universal religion that distinguishes itself from all particular or dogmatic faith. We can also see here the foundation for his critique, namely, Derrida's "hyper-Kantianism," that is, his support of reason over faith. Though my investigations here reflect similar concerns about Derrida's notion of universal religion, I think that Smith's critique, insofar as it is based on the faith/reason question, misses the radical character of Derrida's critique of dogmatic religion and of Kant. A brief look at how Derrida describes his relationship to particular religions and his hope for a universal religion, especially as it relates to Kant and Christianity, will help us to see the extent to which Derrida does follow in the footsteps of the Enlightenment and Kant while at the same time showing how his project differs sharply from Kant and the old faith/reason distinction, and this will better prepare us for a closer examination of the question of prayer.

One of the major beliefs that Derrida shares with the Enlightenment critique of particular religions is his concern for the violence that springs up from dogmatic convictions. Whether it be the "secret pathologies" of which Kant was so suspicious or the "enthusiasm" bred by sacred rites that concerns Jan Patocka, Derrida, too, worries about the inhospitality and even violence that lead to wars of religion and death. Following Kant and Patocka, however, he sees possibilities for universalizing the Christian account that would strip faith of the need for unique dogmatic revelation:

> Christian themes may be drawn together around the idea of the *gift* as the gift of death, the limitless gift of a particular sort of

death: infinite love (the Good as the goodness which is infinitely self-forgetting), sin and salvation, and repentance and sacrifice. What is brought about by and links all of these significations, in an internal and necessary manner, is a logic, which at its heart (and this is why we can still, up to a certain point, call it a "logic") does not require *a revelatory event or the revelation of an event.* This logic does not need to think about a particular revelatory event but only of the possibility of such an event. This is a major difference, which allows one to participate in such a discussion without referring to a dogmatic, institutional religion. It also allows one to propose a genealogy, which reflects on the possibility and essence of religion without being an article of faith.[10]

We can see here that Smith seems to be right in his genealogy that links Derrida's hope for a religion without religion to certain fundamental Enlightenment dreams and aspirations, but before turning directly to how these relate to the specific question of prayer, we need to examine more closely Smith's claim that this move by Derrida should also be seen as a kind of "hyper-Kantianism" that favors reason over faith.[11] This critique, for which one finds a good deal of evidence in *Faith and Knowledge*, goes too far, in my view, and risks missing the radical character of Derrida's critique of Kant and even of Patocka.

The radicalization of Kant by Derrida is not in the direction of reason or some sort of rationality, even if one were to call it a "deconstructive" rationality. Rather, the move that must be made if we are to protect the world from the violence of enthusiasm is toward a more radical passivity—a passivity that is rooted in an encounter with the other (even the Wholly Other) that breeds no violent inclinations (or martyrs) while still engendering strict moral obligation to the other:

> There is no face-to-face or exchanging of glances [*de regard échangé*] between God and me, between the other and myself. God looks at me [*me regarde*], but I do not see him; though it is from this look that looks upon me that my responsibility begins. Thus, in effect, there comes to be or is discovered the "this regards me" [*ça me regarde*], which causes me to say: "This is my concern, my business, my responsibility," though not in the Kantian sense of an autonomy over that which I do in complete liberty from a law that I give myself. Rather this claim of re-

sponsibility operates within the heteronomy of the "this regards me" even where I see and know nothing and where I lack initiative; where I lack the initiative over that which commands me to make decisions, which, nevertheless, are my own and which I alone must accept.[12]

It is precisely the desire to avoid the pitfalls of the classical distinctions cited here that provokes Derrida to redefine the fundamental nature of the condition that would make a universal religion without specific dogma possible. The paradoxical character of this condition is precisely, however, that which makes it equally an uncondition, that is, as we noted above, it is only quasi-transcendental.

Calling it "quasi-transcendental" is meant to warn us to keep a "safe distance" from the abyss that marks the danger of either seeking after such transcendental illusions or from becoming mired in dogmatic religions or faiths.[13] Despite Derrida's and Caputo's clear warnings, one sees signs or traces of such a conflation. This futural horizon may in some sense "come." One may be in a position to speak about the *messianic* as a sort of real horizon or possibility about which something, even if it is rather negative, can be said and said truly. Here, for example, is a verdict rendered recently by Derrida about this advent of the other: It will be "the end of the end of history, everything will begin again without a useless shroud."[14] Here (though in an admittedly difficult passage in a very difficult book), Derrida dreams a rather determinate, if radical, dream of a life without the constraints of a grasping subject who is always trying to peek under the veil of being, trying to speculate about his or her ultimate future in order to see what is really going on, or even one who tries to take a look under the shroud covering his or her own death in order to gain control or mastery over it. Such a de-centered and dissolved subject would no longer seek to possess and preserve his or her property, what is *proper* (the holy or the pure), or even that most proper of property, his or her own life. Here in this desert, in this deserted space, one might find a pure religion, a kind of real resurrection in the here and now that has nothing to do with surviving death but rather concerns a sur-viving of our grasping subjectivity.[15] Would not this hope resemble Kant's dream of a religion (the invisible church) within the limits of *reason* (or ultimate passion) alone?

Are we truly to say that this religion of the philosophers is the aim or end of religion? Can we claim this even if we are here speaking of a religion without religion, which is an opening, a desert in which a thousand blossoms may bloom? It is not clear how this ankhôrite or desertlike religion, with its prayers that always appear lost, could truly be the proper destination or end of prayer (or, as Caputo suggests in *Prayers and Tears*, a praying suitable for the *fin de siècle*). As Derrida himself insists in *Faith and Knowledge*, religion has (at least) two roots; namely, the belief or faith in the absolute Other to come, and a sense of the holy, the pure in our midst.[16] Even if we accept some aspects of the story that lays significant blame for religious carnage and violence on an idolization or fetishizing of our lands, temples, and rites (an idolizing that attempts to keep pure and holy things that were/are never truly or absolutely such), we need to recognize this desire for holiness. We need to recognize the presence of the divine in our midst as equally religious, as another aspect of our finitude.

Certainly, praying for one's daily bread implicates the finite character of our desires and moves us out of our own sense of rights and propriety. We pray that our daily bread comes, please (I pray you — *Je vous prie*)! In this way, uncertainty is opened up in our sense of self and our sense of mastery that puts into question the very thing for which we ask and makes possible the coming of something else. Yet this absolute end, which is not a determinate end and which may aim at a final *Verdict* — with a capital "V" — which disrupts our conceptions of what is pure or holy does not simply destroy, it seems to me, the small and not so small determinate verdicts that come to us from the other. I think that we do better to insist that the ultimate or final *Verdict* is better understood as a transcendental condition (no matter how quasi-transcendental). In doing so, we shall be less likely to find in our stumbling, all-too-human petitions, confessions, and praise something to be replaced by a pure/simple desertlike faith. And one hopes that we shall be encouraged to reflect more deeply and seriously on how these two verdicts are related.

It seems to me that we cannot avoid speaking of the essentially mediated and hermeneutical character of our existence. The other that purely (merely?) *confronts* us as a given is not yet a gift, precisely because its status as aneconomic, something outside my area of control, is not yet brought out. It is precisely prayer that enacts this by testifying to the belief that what confronts me is not my own doing, not under my control. It is in the wounded word of prayer that the giftedness of the given is testified to in the faith of the believer. This enactment is precisely the performative noted by both Derrida and Caputo.[17] Such performing, however, is always limited in its translat-

ing and transfiguring by the given situations of everyday life, something that seems to be lost at times in our rush to pronounce that
deconstruction is "faith itself"[18] and also, therefore, nondeconstructible.[19] The performing of prayer is grounded in some conception of God or the Other. As Graham Ward points out, Job's and
Augustine's questioning of God preceded from particular views
about the Divine, even as their questioning transfigures and opens
up spaces for new encounters with this Other.[20] The risk of omnidi-
rectionality and omnipositivity, the "amen!" that is reduced to an all-
encompassing, "Yes! Yes!" (*Oui, Oui*), risks a lack of engagement.[21]
Such a fear of engagement may be endemic to a culture currently
shaped in many ways by the "death of God," but any movement that
can be called "religious"—even if it is a religion without religion—
must perform something determinate.

As Caputo himself reminds us (though I think not quite forcefully
enough): "So Derrida's empty, desert-like messianic is determinately
situated at the end of this century and is turned toward an 'absolute
surprise' and the possibility of the impossible that *does* after all—what
would not?—reflect certain determinate circumstances even as it
conceives itself as a 'radicalization . . . in the tradition of a certain
Marxism.'"[22] It seems we need to see the wounded aspect of prayer
in the light of a dynamic interaction that occurs between *that which*
received the wound and the direction of healing implicit in the idea
of the wound itself. As Ricœur notes in his essay on the limits of phenomenology in the sphere of religion: "Religion is like language itself,
which is itself only realized in languages. . . . This monumental fact
condemns phenomenology to pass along the humble roads of a hermeneutic and more precisely through a hermeneutic that is textual or
scriptural."[23]

As a limited example of this hermeneutic, I would like to conclude
with an examination of a famous encounter with God by a Hebrew
prophet. The idea of the prophet has been used by some recent theologians and philosophers of religion as an important example of a religiosity that runs counter to the theological and liturgical
pretensions of determinate religion. The story is told that the prophets of old are best understood as deconstructive voices who challenged the dogmatic pretensions of the local people, denounced the
local people's ritual practices and observances, and proclaimed an ultimate and unknowable messianic future that is always to come.
While we certainly see evidence of this in the outcry of an Amos or
Isaiah for example, we must also consider that prophet proclaimed

by the Deuteronomist to be unsurpassed insofar as he saw God "face-to-face" (however metaphorically we may take this) in his tremendous majesty and mystery *and* gave the determinate Law, which formed a people. I will conclude, therefore, with an examination of one of Moses' most important encounters with God, as recounted in the third chapter of the book of Exodus.[24]

A religion without religion would take this story as centered (or decentered) around God's apparent rejection of Moses' desire for a name for God, a master name that would seal the deal with both the Israelites and the Egyptians: "And God said to Moses, 'I am who I am (I shall be who I shall be).' And He said, 'You shall say this to the children of Israel: '*I am* has sent me to you'" (Exod. 3:14). On this account, Moses is then sent off with his tail between his legs and told to free the captives! On the one hand, I have argued that we should embrace this account insofar as it points to a problematic sense of our subjectivity and our desire for such master names. We *should* be concerned by how we use and understand such names, for the possession of such master name would seem to make further prayer and action unnecessary. If you had such a name, you would need nothing else — nothing more would or could be said. We would have the absolutely holy and pure in our possession and thus would have the satisfaction of all our desires.

On the other hand, we need to recognize that we are starting in the middle of the story. God did in fact give Moses a name, and the event did in fact take place on holy ground, even if it was in the land of Midian. Moses was given a perfectly good name: He was before the God of Abraham, Isaac, and Jacob. What is more, he was confronted by a voice, the sort of voice that demands that slaves be freed. Now certainly this is not the Great Judgment, the final Verdict, and, in many ways, as Caputo points out so nicely: Thanks be to God![25] Nevertheless, it is a verdict of sorts, insofar as it sets out a determinate ground for action — even religious action. It founds yet again the people of Israel — another chapter in this long story. The verdict would not be a pure/mere revelation of God's secret nature but would, rather, speak to the alliance or covenant enacted between Moses and God. If we understand this encounter in this way, it can also be seen as a covenant that may be brought about between each one of us and the other (even, as in this case, the *absolute Other*, God), insofar as this alliance, no matter how fragile, is made possible and maintained by the very space realized in praying and listening. It is made possible for us by our rereading of and thus testifying to the story that leads up to Moses and that continues up to the present.

It is clear, I think, that we need to be more careful, ask more questions, and be more open to the silences and aporia that encircle this quasi-transcendental account of a pure "yes, yes" to an absolute (non)coming. We need to allow these questions and concerns to hover before us in order that they might alert us to possible occlusions of the other that such a desire for a religion without religion might engender toward the everyday comings and goings of our lives and to a potential disgust with the temporary holy places in which we find rest. Certainly, we are called to be aware of this ideal or quasi-prayer, this absolute prayer that would give or pledge everything over to the other as if in one go—a prayer that would give to this unknown *you* "everything, time and death, the food out of my mouth, without return."[26] However, in practice such an unperformable or quasi-performable performative might invoke a sort of self-hatred. Though there is a long-standing tradition in some theologies that edges toward such absolute mistrust, any theology must account for the fact that we enact (and must as finite creatures so enact—this dis-solving, this dis-positioning of the self within the dual demand of the religious life that keeps an eye on the future without disdaining the gifts of the present. Such a religious life can truly say "Well come!" in thanksgiving over the coming of a simple loaf of bread, over the miracle of the Exodus from Egypt or the emancipation from slavery in any time. On this view, we are called in each situation, each day, to say "Amen" to the daily tasks and gifts of life. This *amen* is not a simple "let it be" to an impossible advent but a thankful, fearful *amen* to the duties and gifts uniquely laid before each one of us. Thus Moses said to the God of Abraham, Isaac, and Jacob regarding the specific task of freeing the Israelites, Yes! *Amen*—that is, if perhaps Moses spoke French, *"Qu'il soit ainsi!"*—let it be so!

14

How (Not) to Find God in All Things

Derrida, Levinas, and St. Ignatius of Loyola on Learning How to Pray for the Impossible

MICHAEL F. ANDREWS

Introduction

> Anyone who tries to describe the ineffable Light in language is truly a liar . . . not because he hates the truth, but because of the inadequacy of his description.[1]
>
> —St. Gregory of Nyssa

What is meant by the phenomenology of prayer? Following Levinas, I shall argue in this paper that prayer, like ethics, "reverses" Husserl's model of intentionality. Prayer *disprivileges* the role of cognition in every act of genuine transcendence. On account of this radical reversal, I shall further argue that the face of God, whose only condition of possibility is that it never appear in phenomenal givenness, *founds* prayer in the same way that the face of the other founds ethics. Like ethics, prayer originates from outside every horizon of expectation. It describes how the transcendent and ineffable presence of God becomes manifest or appears within a frame or a horizon of reference. It delineates how immanence and transcendence emerge as two distinct attitudes bound by a single, intentional, constitutive act of consciousness. The question must thus be raised: How can an experience of absolute transcendence be constituted by human consciousness without violating the very principle of givenness that makes the field of transcendental experience and its universal structures possible in the first place?

In what sense can it be said that human subjectivity constitutes God as the wholly other (*tout autre*) within the sphere of ownness? Or, to put it more plainly: To what, or to Whom, do I pray when I pray to my God? Is prayer efficacious or merely self-indulgent? Is the God to Whom I lift up my soul merely a deified, analogical extension of my own ego, constituted from within a solipsistic sphere of conscious activity? Or is prayer essentially dialogical in nature, directed always toward a personal yet infinite horizon of nonthematic givenness? In light of the awareness that unfolds within consciousness's experience *of* prayer, how might the phenomenology of prayer be conceived in terms of an originary act of transcendental constitution?

The phenomenology of prayer must take into account the economy of violence that underlies every act of prayer *qua* act of consciousness. Hence what is rendered "holy" by prayer is the infinite *as such*, that is, a certain kind of givenness (*donation*) in presence of that which can be realized without any condition or restriction (*réserve*). To pray means always to pray to God, to pray with the passion of the infinite, to pray for the possibility of givenness *without condition*, to pray for the impossible. Prayer is a condition of possibility that seeks the impossible, namely, it seeks to free presence from every condition or precondition for receiving what gives itself *as* it gives itself within the horizon of any given totality. The phenomenology of prayer thus aspires to undo the very conditions that make prayer possible. It seeks to liberate prayer from every restriction placed upon it as a condition of its own possibility. Prayer undertakes an impossible intention—it seeks God in order to rid us of God.[2]

One final word by way of introduction: The task of this paper is neither to make a postmodernist of Loyola nor a Jesuit of Derrida. Rather, we shall investigate how the phenomenology of prayer keeps a safe distance from every *determinable* faith. We shall accomplish this goal by addressing several tensions that exist between (1) Derrida's phenomenological analysis of the gift; (2) Ignatius of Loyola's mandate to seek God in all things; and (3) Levinas's pure prayer of pure givenness.

Part One: Prayer as Phenomenon

> Leave the senses and the workings of the intellect, and all
> that the senses and the intellect can perceive, and all that
> is not and that is; and through unknowing reach out, so

far as this is possible, towards oneness with Him who is
beyond all being and knowledge.[3]

— St. Dionysius the Areopagite

Attempts by Jacques Derrida, Emmanuel Levinas, and other postmodern thinkers to reexamine the discoveries of Husserlian transcendental consciousness in light of a "theological turn" have left talk
of the phenomenology of prayer in various levels of disarray. Contention often leads to greater insight, however, and at least one significant result of current philosophical debate is a turning back to the
cultural and intellectual soil of an older and fruitful dialogue. For example, late in the nineteenth century, such influential thinkers as
Franz Brentano, William James, Carl Stumpf, and Rudolf Otto each
independently undertook the task of investigating acts of religious
consciousness.[4] In the spirit of these early methodological concerns,
Husserl himself articulated, in *Ideen zu einer reinen Phänomenologie und
phänomenologischen Philosophie I* (1913), that an important feature of
phenomenology concerns the way in which every act of human consciousness (including religious experience) is experienced by the
human subject, or ego.[5] Nevertheless, despite protests from many of
Husserl's colleagues, the realist empirical ego discovered by Husserl
in *Ideas I* became transformed several years afterwards into the cen-
terpiece of a full-blown transcendental phenomenology.[6]

For Husserl, of course, the experience of prayer is fulfilled neither
"inside" nor "outside" the cogito, such distinctions being nothing
more than products constituted by the snare of philosophical naïveté.
In phenomenological terms, the ego experiences in prayer a thematization of conscious activity, an articulated and structured "sphere of
being" (*ein Seinssphäre*), an intuiting of the very structure of subjectivity.[7] What constitutes the phenomenology of prayer, then, cannot
be a mere monadological distinction between constituting ego-sub-
jects. Rather, prayer manifests the essential conditionality by which
the objectivity of divine presence is given to human consciousness as
an autonomous For-itself.

What, phenomenologically speaking, is prayer? *Pregare*, "to pray,"
derives from the Latin *precare*, which means to beg or to entreat. In
an etymological sense, "to pray" signifies more than mere supplication; it means to give (*donner*), to for(e)-give, to forgive a debt, to
forgive debts freely and without reservation.[8] *Pregare* thus infers the
beseeching of request as well as the giving of pardon, it implies giving
away without condition of receiving, giving graciously: *ti pregho* . . .

grazia. For Jacques Derrida, the givenness of prayer manifests an analogous structure to the givenness of the gift. Similar to prayer, the gift evinces a condition of possibility, it makes possible the impossibility of absolute forgiveness. It gives without exchange, without expenditure; once given, it demands no recollection, and so causes its own forgetfulness as a condition of its own appearance. Prayer is a gift that deprives itself of the very condition of possibility around which it is organized; it denies its own manifest givenness. Otherwise, if the gift were noted as "gift," then the very givenness of its phenomenality would undo the conditions that make the phenomenal nonappearance of the gift possible in the first place.

The phenomenology of prayer is identical to the phenomenology of the gift, structurally speaking. "To pray" means to pray for the gift of prayer, to pray for the gift of all gifts, the gift of the *gift-itself,* which is the gift of its phenomenal nonappearance. As a gift, prayer is inscribed by pure generosity from the giver of the gift, the Giver of all gifts. Every pure prayer thus prays for acceptance without condition, without limit, without obligation, without need. Christianly speaking, prayer grounds the condition of every (impossible) possibility. It believes that the dead shall be raised and seeks the unconditional forgiveness of debt as the mark of an impossible economy. When we talk about the phenomenology of prayer, then, what we are really talking about are the conditions of possibility of a gift—a future—that has not yet arrived, a Kingdom always to come.

Prayer manifests desire, a desire for the impossible, for the future, for an impossible future in which prayers and justice flow like running streams. Prayer seeks the desire *to* pray, the desire to pray *for the desire to pray.* St. Ignatius of Loyola's exhortation in the *Constitutions of the Society of Jesus,* namely, "to seek God in all things," reflects, in this particular sense, his own desire to pray for a future filled with prayers and desire.[9] Throughout the *Constitutions* and *The Spiritual Exercises,* St. Ignatius of Loyola in effect prays such a (Derridean) prayer. He recommends repeatedly that the retreatant (or exercitant) making the *Spiritual Exercises* pray for the desire to pray whenever one's prayer becomes dry, static, desolate. Apparently, Basque Jesuits and North African deconstructionists share a striking compatibility in their conviction that authentic prayer is constituted by desolation, the desert, *khôra,* by a desire *without* desire. Such prayerful desire is a prayer whose only desire is the desire *to desire more desire.* Ignatius called this desire for "more" the *magis,* which is really another way of praying for the impossible. For Ignatius, prayer seeks to give that which lies beyond my grasp of ever receiving it; in a word, the impossible: *ad maiorem dei gloriam*. Prayer seeks to find that which must essentially remain concealed as the very condition of its being given.

And that is why Derrida, too, finally confesses that every authentic prayer is ultimately a prayer of impossibility, a prayer of the gift. Inscribed by the impossible, prayer *constitutes* the future by seeking the Kingdom amongst mustard seeds and lost sheep. Prayer says to the mountain, "Move!" and the mountain *moves*; prayer seeks not my will but that the will of *an Other* be done. Such prayer is an impossible prayer, a prayer of impossibility and madness, a prayer for the gift that forgives all debts and loses itself as the (impossible) condition of ever finding itself.

When we listen attentively (that is, with the "ears of faith") to the confessions of Jacques Derrida, we might begin to grasp that the word "God" is neither the object nor the subject of prayer but, rather, a condition of every possibility. "God," after all, is not merely a word but a proper name. Nevertheless, the word "God" names that which in virtue of itself *can never be named*, that which is never manifestly present, that which can never "be seen" or "show up" within the sphere of phenomenal givenness.[10] Derrida' discovery that prayer operates "in the blind," so to speak, means that prayer violates the very condition of possibility that Husserl believed is absolutely essential for the apprehension of knowledge *as such*. The phenomenology of prayer thus appears to transgress Husserl's law of phenomenal givenness, in that *what* is constituted—the manifestation of God's nonappearance—must finally be constituted in the sphere of ownness via appresentation. Such is the impossible faith of transcendental phenomenology. But whereas Derrida confesses a certain constitutive blindness in every act of faith, Husserl rejects such an impossibility out of hand. Yet if we look closely at the phenomenology of prayer, might we not discover just a trace of blindness in Husserl's own prayer for pure, transcendental givenness?

Does this mean that prayer can never *know* God but only *believe*? Is phenomenology a kind of prayer, a prayer not only of the impossible but a prayer of absence and abstinence? Could "faith alone" be the new rallying cry for phenomenologists who like to give (and receive) gifts? What—or Who—dwells in the heart (*sacré coeur*) of prayer?

Je ne sais pas; il faut croire.

Part Two: A Most Postmodern Prayer

> Entering the darkness that surpasses understanding, we shall find ourselves brought, not just to brevity of speech, but to perfect silence and unknowing. Emptied of all knowledge, man is joined . . . with the One who is altogether unknowable; and in knowing nothing, he knows in a manner that surpasses understanding.[11]
>
> —St. Dionysius the Areopagite

Attempting to go "beyond" Derrida's confessions, Levinas seeks the name of a more originary phenomenology. What Levinas wants to do is to "reverse" Husserl's model of intentionality in order to *dis*-privilege the role of cognition in every act of genuine transcendence. On account of this radical reversal, Levinas argues that the face—any face, every face (even, one must assume, the face of God)—is a phenomenon that can be grasped only tentatively, poorly, impoverishedly or, as St. Paul says, in a mirror darkly. The face founds ethics in the same way that prayer originates as an address from outside the horizon of every expectation. This Levinasian "radicalization" of phenomenology nevertheless remains faithful to phenomenology's original endeavor. This new heuristic of the phenomenology of prayer warrants rigorous investigation. It attempts to describe how prayer *qua* transcendence must appear outside every given frame or horizon of reference.

In what sense can it be said that the (w)Holy Other is constituted as *wholly other* within the sphere of ownness? This question, posed by Levinas in *Totality and Infinity*, stands in proximity in a number of ways to critical questions raised by St. Ignatius of Loyola in the sixteenth century as well as concerns being raised in contemporary discussions by Jean-Luc Marion: Can God appear on God's own terms, that is, as God desires to give Godself, and *still be encountered* within the limitations of human subjectivity? The implication of such an (impossible) encounter with the (w)Holy Other means that divine givenness must be grasped cognitively by the constituting ego outside the very conditions that make objectivity possible in the first place.

Let us take a moment, next, to explore the phenomenology of prayer from a somewhat unorthodox *pre*modern source. Ignatius of Loyola, the founder of the Society of Jesus (the Jesuit Order of Catholic priests and brothers), asserts that the goal of the *Spiritual Exercises* is to assist retreatants to "have God always before one's eyes." Inigo Lopez de Loyola was born in the small Basque village of Azpetia in 1491 amidst tremendous social and political instability.[12] Shortly after winning personal fame on the battlefield, a cannonball shattered his right leg and severely crippled his left side. At the age of thirty, Inigo's brash career as a soldier was over. He was laid on a litter and carried across many miles of rough terrain in order to die honorably at his family home. After many months of surgery and re-cuperation, however, Ignatius was surprisingly restored to health. Once fully recovered, Ignatius left his old life behind and walked in pilgrimage to Barcelona, stopping for a few days at a nearby Bene-dictine monastery for prayer and penance. It was while he was here, seeking prayer and mortification in a small cave high above the vil-lage of Manserrat, that Ignatius underwent a profound religious con-version that later formed the basis of the *Spiritual Exercises*.[13]

Ignatius underwent a series of intense mystical experiences and subsequently described such phenomena in terms of a dialogical model. For him, prayer constitutes a movement of human interiority that seeks to "find God in all things," beginning with the created order. Hence, while Ignatius says of prayer that God alone is its au-thor, he also describes prayer as a kind of "address" or manifestation of God's unique self-communication in time and history. In the *Exer-cises* prayer thus poses a particularly thorny problem. On the one hand, prayer is dialogical: it is constituted in a coconstitutive rela-tionship between God and creature based on various levels of anal-ogy, mutuality, and reciprocity. On the other hand, however, the first thing that prayer requires is an epistemological asymmetry that rec-ognizes the absolute *dis*unity between God and creature. Along with the character of response, prayer is a condition of possibility that seeks to express and communicate that which by nature is inaccessi-ble, mysterious, hidden.

Within the *Exercises*, Ignatius describes many different ways by which a retreatant can dispose himself or herself in order to actively discern the movement that, "in its first instance entailed turning to God in a new and more profound way."[14] Yet if prayer constitutes the condition of possibility of the appearing of a "nonappearance," then, in terms of the givenness of pure transcendence, the goal of the *Exercises* might best be described *not* in terms of a traditional meta-physics of presence. In the light of apophatic theology, the *Exercises* effectively describe what deconstructionists might today recount as learning "how (*not*) to find God in all things." What Ignatius sought is an understanding of the experience of prayer that is at one and the same time both inescapable and inexpressible. For St. Ignatius of Loyola, prayer provides the transcendental ground upon which everything that is grasped by human consciousness is brought to loving and careful concern. Consequently, Christian prayer frames the questions we ask and the answers we seek; it constitutes the condition of possibility of genuine human transcendence.

In effect, the *Exercises* do not constitute a text at all, but four autonomous texts bound together.[15] The first text of the *Exercises* functions as a "text" only in a most limited, technical sense. It consists of marks and signifiers, that is, the actual words written by the author and intended to be read by a reader:

> Our reading habits, our very concept of literature, make every text appear today as if it were the simple communication of an author (in the present instance this Spanish saint who founded the Society of Jesus in the sixteenth century) and of a reader (in the present instance, ourselves): Ignatius Loyola wrote a book, this book was published, and today we are reading it. This outline, suspect for any book (since we can never definitively demonstrate *who* is the author and *who* is the reader), is assuredly false with regard to the *Exercises*.[16]

Roland Barthes is correct in his assessment of the authorial intentions of the *Spiritual Exercises*. Ignatius of Loyola neither addressed this text to nor intended it to be read by the individual exercitant undergoing the *Exercises*. Rather, this first text within the text was intended by Ignatius to be directed toward the exercitant's director, that is, the person assigned to assist the retreatant to interpret those mental, psychological, and even physical events that transpire during the course of the four weeks of fasting and prayer. The second text intended by Ignatius is the semantic text that the director addresses to the exercitant. In fact, the exercitant, while making the *Exercises*, is instructed neither to prepare nor anticipate the *Exercises* at any time during the making of the thirty-day retreat. (In fact, the retreatant is charged not to read the *Exercises* during the course of the thirty-day retreat unless explicitly instructed by one's spiritual director.)

Consequently, Ignatius intended the *Exercises* to be read only by the retreatant's spiritual director in order to guide him or her (that is, the director) in helping the retreatant learn how better to discern what is happening in the interiority of one's own life. The text of the *Exercises* does not offer a step-by-step account of how to proceed in the spiritual life. Rather, the *Exercises* is a collection of texts from which the retreatant's director may jump from one exercise to another, thereby encouraging the exercitant actively to encounter God via prayer as an indeterminate field of signifiers.

The third text within the *Exercises* is an active text written by the exercitant, composed of prayers, meditations, colloquia, gestures, penances, offerings of thanksgiving, and so on, and directed toward God. Such a text of interiority reflects the ensuing intimate conversation addressed between the exercitant and the Divinity. Finally, the fourth text is that of the Divinity's response, by which the exercitant receives interiorly the graces most desired (such as gratitude and generosity). This is one aspect of what Ignatius of Loyola means by contemplative prayer. Since the ongoing conversation between the exercitant and the Divinity is infinite by its very nature, one goal of the *Exercises* is to assist the retreatant to seek God (e.g., infinity) in all things.

Hence the structure of prayer described in the *Exercises* parallels to a significant extent Derrida's formal description of the structure of the impossible. If the Infinite constitutes real infinity, then the retreatant must learn to seek God *by not finding God*. If God is found, then we must conclude that one has not found *God* (who is unfindable) but simply an idol of merely determinable meaning pretending to be God. Speaking in terms of the interplay between these four texts within the *Exercises*, Roland Barthes comments that, "as can be seen, the multiple text of the *Exercises* is a structure, i.e., an intelligent form: a structure of meanings."[17]

The *Spiritual Exercises* constitutes a text intended to be not *read* but *encountered*. In effect, *one never finishes making the Exercises*. The various texts that comprise the *Exercises* do not promulgate a text in the traditional sense at all, but the lived experience of the retreatant. Such lived experience originates, as every experience must, in language and memory. The interior structure of the *Exercises*, therefore, constitutes a radical manifestation of absence or, at the least, what is not merely present to the senses:

> The drama [of the *Exercises*] is that of interlocution; on the one hand, the exercitant is like a subject speaking in ignorance of the end of the sentence upon which he has embarked; he lives the inadequacy of the spoken chain. . . . [H]e is cut off from the perfection of language, which is assertive closure; and on the other hand, the very basis of all speech, interlocution is not given him, he must conquer it, invent the language in which he

must address the Divinity and prepare his possible response: the exercitant must accept the enormous and yet uncertain task of a constructor of language, of a logo-technician.[18]

The signification of prayer in the *Spiritual Exercises* does not imply that Ignatius Loyola was a deconstructionist, a closet Derridean at heart. The *Exercises*, after all, do have a center, an original presence, an *arché*, namely, the life of Christ. And it is this centered structurability concerning the life of Christ which is constantly being repeated and reproduced by the retreatant. In much the same way that the use of images by the retreatant is meant to imply an original pattern to be imitated (viz., the life of Christ), so also the words of the *Exercises* as a text are meant to refer back to the *Logos* described in the opening line of the Gospel of St. John. Ignatius of Loyola was not lost in the khôral desert in precisely the same way deconstruction claims to be lost. Nevertheless, the closest proximity by which Christian prayer can attend this *khôra* is the dark night of divine nonpresence. Described as "prayer" by the Spanish and German mystics of the fifteenth and sixteenth centuries (the author of the *Spiritual Exercises* preeminent among them), such a nonphenomenal experience of a (non)presence corresponds significantly to what Derrida describes in terms of the phenomenology of the gift.

Part Three: Prayer beyond Prayer

> The brethren asked Abba Agaton: "Amongst all our different activities, father, which is the virtue that requires the greatest effort?" He answered: "Forgive me, but I think there is no labour greater than praying to God. For every time a man wants to pray, his enemies the demons try to prevent him; for they know that nothing obstructs them so much as prayer to God. In everything else that a man undertakes, if he perseveres, he will attain rest. But in order to pray a man must struggle to his last breath."[19]
>
> — The Sayings of the Desert Fathers

Since Christian prayer confesses what it does not know (*esse absconditum*) and believes what it does not see (*credo visibilium omnium et invisibilium*), prayer may be defined as the experience of a nonpresence. Such a "nonpresence," however, must either be something or nothing. If prayer is the experience of something, then nonpresence *is* and can be manifest to consciousness either thematically or nonthematically. But if prayer is the experience of nothing, then nonpresence is merely nothing and therefore not experienceable; prayer cannot experience a "nonpresence" that is nothing. This distinction, I submit, is vital to understanding the play of presence that lies at the heart of phenomenological givenness: *Lord, I believe; help my unbelief.*

In this context, prayer is the attempt to name that which lies beyond all naming, it seeks to experience God as a nonexperience, that is, an (im)possible manifestation of divine nonphenomenality. According to Derrida, Emmanuel Levinas's prayer offers such a prayer of nonphenomenality. Such an impossible prayer can best be described in phenomenological terms as a "postmetaphysical" prayer similar, to a large extent, to what Jean-Luc Marion means by the "liberation of presence." The prayer of every prayer, the pure prayer for which every prayer *prays*, is a rigorous reduction to *transcendence*, to pure givenness, to purity itself. For Levinas, "to pray" means to seek for givenness without condition, to seek "more" than can ever possibly be *given*; hence, to seek what St. Ignatius called the *magis*.

What we have so far seen in our comparison between Levinas and Loyola is the emergence of a phenomenon quite similar to what Marion describes in terms of a third reduction. Marion seeks a phenomenon that is not constituted by the ego but that in fact constitutes the ego, makes a claim upon it, and calls the ego to infinite responsibility. According to Marion, only the nonphenomenality of a pure prayer can appear in the sense of a nonappearing.[20] But in what sense can it be said that God—the (w)Holy Other, the Other *qua* other, the other as *tout autre*—appears beyond phenomenality? Is it possible to hear or respond to a "call" from outside every conceivable totality?

For Levinas, prayer exposes a structure of expectation within every horizon of foreseeability. But a "prayer" prays for that which is not yet seen; hence, Levinas's prayer for "pure" givenness is a condition of possibility that breaks up every totality but that itself is never fully exposed as being part *of* that totality. We shall designate prayer, then, as a "structure of expectation," that is, a *quasi*-transcendental, a condition of possibility that makes something possible and at the same time undoes it. For Levinas, the face of the child, that is, the face of justice, the face beyond the face, functions as such a quasi-transcendental. Like prayer, the face is a condition of possibility of expectation that lies outside every horizon of expectation, without which there is neither transcendence nor expectation but only immanence. As a structure of possibility, prayer allows the unexpected to be engaged and encountered *as such*. Inscribed outside the measured horizons of predictability, prayer functions as a quasi-transcendental. The face of the Other resembles God, Derrida reminds us, so much so that, like the Other, "the face of God disappears forever in showing itself."[21] Prayer seeks the inauguration of something completely new and totally unexpected yet it possesses no clear idea what it will be, where it comes from, or where it will lead: *Thy* will be done.

A pure prayer is a supplication for deliverance; it begs for givenness from every conceptualization and grounds *the experience* of infinite positivity. Every claim by which prayer glimpses the impossible betrays the fact that it does not yet grasp the implications of what it has discovered. In this sense, prayer shares a certain affinity with Descartes's assertion in his third meditation that the idea of infinity, like prayer, *is visited upon us*.[22] Similarly, prayer shares a certain affinity with apophatic theology. Classically formulated, Christian prayer constitutes a fall into darkness, a groping, an incongruity and unrecognizability of what is impossible to be seen.

We have arrived at a crossroads in our discussion. On the one hand, the phenomenology of prayer makes possible an experience of the (w)Holy Other. It constitutes a trace between self and Other, between what is similar to (yet different from) that which constitutes. On the other hand, the positive infinity of *l'infini* is so wholly and absolutely other (*tout autre*) that neither Derrida nor Descartes (nor Levinas nor Loyola, for that matter) would be able to catch *even a glimpse* of it, since it leaves no trace. What the phenomenology of prayer grasps is a God who is so utterly transcending that even (especially) God denies the possibility of ever being conceived.[23] But does such pure givenness leave nothing of itself behind, not even a trace? Might the nongrasping of a nontrace *itself* be a sign of something, of something whose only desire is to play hide and seek in the pure givenness of concealment?[24] Could a nontrace be grasped as an essential *difference*, as a sign of a different heuristic structure? "It is at this level that the thought of Emmanuel Levinas can make us tremble," Derrida warns. "At the heart of the desert, in the growing wasteland, this thought, which fundamentally no longer seeks to be a thought of Being and phenomenality, makes us dream of an inconceivable process of dismantling and dispossession."[25] It is in the heart of the desert, in the heart of silence, that the prophets learn to pray. St. Isaac the Syrian notes, "Speech is the organ of this present world. Silence is the mystery of the world to come."[26]

In the end, Levinas's postmetaphysical prayer remains a nomadic prayer of wondering and wandering, a prayer filled with absence, radical silence, fear and trembling. Every postmodern prayer is *ultimately* still a prayer. Even the most pure prayer of absolute givenness ultimately seeks to erase its own marks, wipe away its own effects, annihilate every trace of itself from every prayer. What is left behind is nothing: silence, which is itself a sign. A sign of what? A sign of confession. For Derrida, every postmodern prayer secretly confesses an epiphany of absolute purity and pure, unblemished innocence. Phenomenologically speaking, Christian prayer embraces a postmodern structure, it manifests the infinite that troubles consciousness. Authentic prayer seeks to pray without words, without discourse, without *why*. As the Russian religious philosopher Vasilii Rozanov comments, "There is no life without prayer. Without prayer there is only madness and horror. The soul of [Christian] Orthodoxy consists in the gift of prayer."[27]

Conclusion

> The true knowledge and the true vision of what we seek consist precisely in this—in not seeing: for what we seek transcends all knowledge, and is everywhere cut off from us by the darkness of incomprehensibility.[28]
>
> —St. Gregory of Nyssa

The phenomenology of prayer involves radical freedom and an individual's capacity to forge one's own authentic identity out of the tumultuous events of daily living. For Derrida and Ignatius of Loyola, prayer is somehow always *pregnant*. In phenomenological terms, this means that prayer is concerned with what is always yet to come, with that which absolutely and with no clear evidence of success prods ahead without ever quite arriving. In an etymological sense, prayer is a condition of possibility that constitutes meaning; it disseminates, shares, contextualizes, *structures*. What is the significance of the phenomenology of prayer? For one thing, prayer desires to step outside its own horizonality. What makes prayer both possible and impossible at the same time is that prayer seeks presence outside the structure of Being.

For Ignatius of Loyola, the impossibility of prayer constitutes a radical movement of interiority in a preeminently *theological* sense, that is, movement toward metanoia, to what is *new*, toward inner transformation. Prayer essentially displaces sameness and makes difference possible. It deconstructs language and discourse. It exposes the structurability of every archstructure and unconceals every metaphysics of presence.

Every prayer thus betrays some kind of horizonality, some sort of structure in its phenomenal givenness. Nevertheless, the impossibility to pray outside a horizon of disclosure confirms for Derrida that Husserl was right all along. Prayer needs a horizon—especially in terms of what Ignatius of Loyola designated as the *magis*—as a condition of possibility of every act of phenomenal givenness. Consequently, Derrida confesses that even postmetaphysical prayer cannot use the simple strategy of negative theology, namely, of saying that we have an experience of an infinite alterity but we just do not have the language to say it. Levinas deprives prayer of that recourse because he argues that infinity—unlike the mystic's infinity—is delivered up to me in language, that is, in the "Welcome!," the *"Bonjour!,"* the *"Amen!"* of solicitation. As Ignatius of Loyola witnessed in the *Spiritual Exercises*, God's silence may be a *sign* of what we seek.

15

Prayer and Incarnation:
A Homiletical Reflection

LISSA MCCULLOUGH

In the opening chapters of *Confessions*, the question Augustine broaches before all others is whether we must first beg for help from God to know who God is, or must first know who God is in order to beg for help. Is prayer, then, essentially "begging," and is "begging" the surest avenue to the divine? Or is begging simply the final resort left to us when all other presumed resources have revealed their finitude and exhaustibility, exposing the naked truth of crucifixion? Is God precisely the crucified one who is there when nothing — absolutely nothing — else is, unveiled in the emptiness of the purest poverty or, in Simone Weil's language, in the *void*?

The void arises in us when we run out of what Weil calls our "earthly bread"; that is, the daily bread of incentives that serve as our sources of vital energy. She articulates this in her meditation on the Lord's Prayer: "Money, ambition, consideration, decorations, celebrity, power, our loved ones, everything that puts into us the capacity for action is like bread. If any one of these attachments penetrates deeply enough into us to reach the vital roots of our carnal existence, its loss may break us and even cause our death."[1]

In contact with the void, we despair of earthly bread, we despair of the world, we despair of ourselves, and we release our despair into prayer in order that it be transfigured into miraculous hope, or a "heavenly bread" actually available on earth; for to pray is to petition for ultimate hope — or to rejoice in its attainment.

The void is radically simplifying. It aggregates all matters of relative concern, of profit and loss in their myriad forms, to concentrate our attention on the one ultimate concern: the question whether there is *ultimate* hope, a hope beyond relative hopes, a heavenly bread to eat here on earth in the midst of suffering and void. That concentrated petitionary attention is prayer. But precisely as ultimate petition, prayer opens wide for the one who prays a dual abyss: an ultimate manner of hoping and an equally ultimate manner of despairing. In the midst of the ongoing incarnational venture that is this world, the one who truly prays from the void realizes that every action, every thought, every petition is a movement toward damnation or salvation: one will find ultimate hope or one will not. Relative hope, in any case, has turned to despair.

The deepest mystery lies precisely here: What *is* ultimate hope that it has the power to dispel despair? It cannot be simply "more of the same"—more of what eventuated in our despair: the earthly bread that runs out. Ultimate hope does not offer us a *reason* to hope, an object for our hope. Rather, it is hope itself sui generis. In asking, What is hope? then, despite the literal form of the question, our sights should be trained on a *how* rather than a *what*. For hope—ultimate hope—is not bound up with a *what*. It is a *how* regardless of *what*. So our question comes to be configured: How does one hope without a *what*? How does one petition for ultimate hope without covertly asking for or seizing on "more of the same"—more of the earthly bread that issues in despair?

Even his capacity to pray is a gift perfectly mystifying to Augustine. Where does it come from, he wonders? And why does it draw him so relentlessly to request a seeming impossibility, an absurdity: to wit, begging God, the creator of heaven and earth, to *come into him*? Or as he puts it, "How shall I call upon my God for aid, when the call I make is for my Lord and my God to come into myself? What place is there in me to which my God can come, what place that can receive the God who made heaven and earth?"[2] Augustine discerns that his longing for God is induced by God's prevenient presence in him, and yet that presence only induces an unslakable thirst for the fullness of God, which can never be *in him* but in which he must instead find a way to be, through the grace of God.

Augustine deduces that the ultimate fulfillment he longs for requires an otherworldly becoming: a conversion from God as relatively present (in temporal things) but absolutely lacking, to God as relatively lacking but absolutely present (beyond the temporal world). Hence his repeated counsel of patience in this life: Endure this life with the patience of the pilgrim. Suffer it with the patience of the chrysalis. Keep patient vigil in this life for the world to come. The eternal city is *not yet* for as long as time is with us, but our "time" will come when time is no more.

In radical contrast to Augustine's premodern, otherworldly paradigm, modern Continental Christian thinkers such as Søren Kierkegaard and Simone Weil revolutionize the task of faith, and of prayer accordingly, as they propose a fully dialectical and resolutely this-worldly paradigm. Creation and incarnation, as Kierkegaard and Weil view these theological acts, are movements of coming into time, and this coming into time is God's way of becoming—and of becoming, in some sense, more than merely absolute. The God who creates time and comes into time is not merely absolutely present in and to all things aboriginally but is relatively present as absolute Word made relative in the flesh. In creation and incarnation, then, the infinite *invests* itself in time, in finitude. The absolute continues to be absolute *qua* the will that wills the relative, the temporal.

If this is so, our task or calling in life is not to "suffer" the temporal in patience, waiting it out in our quest for the eternal at the end of time, but to inhabit it and love it as the manifest and living will of God in the flesh. We must not only be prepared for the grace that carries us into eternity, or death, but we must be prepared for the grace that delivers us—in a heartbeat—back into our very flesh, into the task of life, regaining the finite in faith, such that the "city of God" or "kingdom of God" is actively incarnate in us, here and now, in the very midst of the "city of man." This is the radically dialectical task that Kierkegaard describes as bringing eternity to bear within time. Our existential task is not to live disincarnationally toward God but to live into the world incarnationally in faith. Prayer is our means to effect this incarnational task. We are called to exist in prayer, even bodily so, such that all our actions are fueled *on earth* by "heavenly bread," or faith.

Kierkegaard's knight of faith is our primary model for how to invest infinite hope in the finite without fixing an object for our hope—so that we hope incarnationally but do so purely, without a *what*.[3] Faith, as Kierkegaard portrays it, is an infinite resiliency of finite spirit (the concretely existing individual) in response to the providential unfurling of the will of God, regardless of determinate outcome—an unconditional readiness of faith that conquers despair. The knight of infinite resignation, by comparison, achieves a radical detachment from any specific outcome, but this knight lacks the infinite resiliency of faith because instead of being attached to an outcome, he or she is attached to resignation, and as Weil comments, "We must not even become attached to detachment" (*WG* 146). Faith attains a perfect freedom vis-à-vis the incarnational will of God, in that faith is not only prepared to give up every outcome in the incarnational venture but is prepared to receive it back in grace—that is, to *live it forward* in concrete existence—just as flexibly.

In a similar vein, Weil writes that when we pray, "Thy kingdom come," we express an unconditional invitation to the Holy Spirit to enter and transform all things, ourselves included. Hence we hope on the basis of an open desire directed toward the future but we do not specify "the kingdom," or the content of the desire. We hope entirely openly, holding our desire responsive to the incarnational will. After this upsurging of desire toward the possible, the unforeseeable, we once again ask for that which is when we pray, "Thy will be done." This is, Weil writes, to petition for the infallible conformity of everything that happens in time with the will of God (*WG* 145). The purpose of this petition is not to ensure that everything happens in conformity with the will of God, for by definition, Weil insists, everything that happens without exception manifests this conformity; reality as such is the providence of God. Rather, this petition effects *in us* a discipline of our desire in response to the crucifying afflictions of reality. Prayer is the spiritual exercise through which we learn to make any accomplished fact, despite ourselves, an actual object of desire:

> After having, in our first petition ["Our Father who art in heaven"], torn our desire away from time in order to fix it upon eternity, thereby transforming it, we return to this desire which has itself become in some measure eternal, in order to apply it to time. Whereupon our desire pierces through time to find eternity behind it. That is what comes about when we know how to make every accomplished fact, whatever it may be, an object of desire. (*WG* 145)

To "pierce through time to find eternity behind it" is to recognize and honor time as a creation and incarnation of eternity, as God's way of becoming other than merely eternal, more than merely absolute. Weil makes clear that this transfiguration of our perspective on the temporal is something quite different from resignation, and "acceptance" is too weak a word for it. Our petition is not merely to excel at resignation or accept what happens in time without resistance, for such passive-reactive responses are only forms of tolerance or patience vis-à-vis the temporal. To be sure, patience and resignation are indispensable for coping with our *resistance* to the destining of incarnational will, but truly to *love* that will is to embody it in our flesh by living it forward — not in resignation, not in patience, but in expectant hope, in faith.

This addresses once again the problem of how to hope without a *what*: we can be converted to unconditional hope only by unconditional love for the incarnational divine will. Our calling is to *love* the actual form of reality, to love reality as providential from the "lost" perspective of an eternal *epoché* beyond reality. This dialectical *epoché* enables us to be *in* the world but not *of* the world. Hence in prayer we petition for the grace to convert our bodily attitude to an active and voluntary embrace of the world as divine creation and incarnation; we petition to love the will of God as it becomes manifest in and as reality, in all that really and actually takes place, Weil posits, including all evil: "We have to desire that everything that has happened should have happened, and nothing else. We have to do so, not because what has happened is good in our eyes, but because God has permitted it, and because the obedience of the course of events to God is in itself an absolute good" (*WG* 145).

While relative good lies within the ready grasp of our understanding, absolute good does not. How can we love it — this absolute good — a good that incomprehensibly includes in itself every real evil, every actual horror? For Weil this absolute good is the *mysterium tremendum* that lies beyond all distinction between "good" and "evil" as we apply these judgments according to our arbitrary and quite possibly "evil" criteria.

As absolute good manifests itself beyond good and evil, so it transcends us, lying beyond or outside the limits of our desire. Only sacred petition — or spiritual "begging" — can transport us beyond our relative judgments of good and evil to apprehend an absolute good that is comprehensive of both yet free of both and can reconcile us to the incarnational will of God as that will is actually unfurled providentially in events. Every event, Weil insists, however negative or evil, if it actually happens, reveals the will of God. For the divine will to incarnation is no less a will to crucifixion. Ours is to embrace the revelation of that will quite apart from our desires and judgments, conforming our desire to an actual incarnational providence, which is a crucifying providence.

What kind of "conformity" is this? Is it a manner of conforming that eliminates freedom? No, Weil insists, to the contrary: this is purely a work of love, and love is the one thing that is always free; precisely this distinguishes genuine love from attachment. Attachment is a conditional love and, because conditional, restricted, unfree. Pure love, by contrast, is inherently a freedom to love under any conditions, however degraded and horrific those conditions may be, and that love is the light in the darkness that the darkness does not overcome (John 1:5). Hence the conformity of our desire to the incarnational will of providence, as this is effected by prayer, is not a servitude but a liberation, inasmuch as it fulfills in us a movement—a transfiguration, really—from conditional to unconditional love. Unconditional love is a freedom to say "yes" to any destiny that is unveiled. It is a perfect freedom to say "yes" absolutely to whatever eventuates in time.

Such a realization of freedom calls for a higher discipline of the will, a discipline of the kind that Nietzsche's prophet Zarathustra expounds. We must know the limits of our will precisely in order to transcend it—as we are called to do again and again in the perennial newness of becoming in the world.[4] Zarathustra's is not a teaching of *self*-aggrandizement, but a teaching of selfless cosmic aggrandizement that leaves the attachments and constraints of selfhood behind, shedding it like a too-tight skin. "Behold," life confides to Zarathustra, "I am *that which must always overcome itself*" (*Z* 115).

The will to power attested by Zarathustra is thus a willing appropriation of embodied destiny, come what may. It is inherently a selfless will, as each newly acquired identity is the next paradigmatic limit that must be overcome, sacrificed unto death in the name of new life and new birth. It is a protean will to becoming, liberated vis-à-vis every particular and specific identity, a detached will that wills only new creation, new manifestations of incarnation, spontaneous new forms of beauty: "When power becomes gracious and descends into the visible—such descent I call beauty" (*Z* 118). To this end, the gift-giving virtue is ever spending itself outward, boldly greeting new incarnations, new awakenings, which entail the death and "going under" of the present for the sake of the destining future. The only real failure, Zarathustra warns, is to begrudge giving oneself over as a place of new creation and new life here and now, wholly invested in perfecting and redeeming the gift of the earth where we are. "I love those," Zarathustra teaches, "who do not first seek behind the stars for a reason to go under and be a sacrifice, but who sacrifice themselves for the earth" (*Z* 15). Why does the Christian nihilistic-ally search for fulfillment outside or beyond the earth, in a transcendent "heaven," rather than in the earth and its destiny? "I teach men: no longer to bury one's head in the sand of heavenly things" (*Z* 32). Zarathustra's prophecy would redeem the earth as divine; for what heaven is greater than the earth, when one loves the earth rightly?

To venture forward in the flesh, in the task of becoming, in faith and creative expectation—this is our "spiritual" calling. Prayer exercises us in how to live sacrificially, day in and day out, through joys and tribulations, with an abiding hope in the world and an incarnational faith, but without specifying a *what* or definite object for our hope. It exercises us in how to hope in the void, when the flesh that incarnation posits is a crucifying flesh—a body more of death than life. Without fixing our desire on any object—not even detachment or resignation—but keeping a channel open to the gracious, creative, incarnational, and crucifying will at work providentially in the world and us, we are called to embody love practically in the flesh as our one real and realizable freedom.

In this spirit, then, when Augustine asks: "What place is there in me to which my God can come, what place that can receive the God who made heaven and earth?" we moderns have the option to respond—even after the death of God—in a fully dialectical Kierkegaardian or Weilian spirit: our flesh, our embodied lives are that place, and ours is not to judge the place inadequate or unworthy but only to "beg" for the grace that makes it suffice in any concretely manifest moment as a place in which love might take root and increase in the very midst of a crucified world. Our ultimate hope is our conviction that no set of conditions, no degree of void, no agony of crucifixion can block or prevent love's incarnation in us, if we pray purely enough to embody it in our flesh and our actions.

God's own movement is incarnational; we know this because there is a world. As long as there is a world, the world gives us our task. An Augustinian *conatus* toward the transcendent would seem to dishonor the sacrificial gift of the world—that world that is produced out of a divine *conatus* toward creation and incarnation. Ours is not to decline this gift—not to despise the world!—but to love the world rightly instead of wrongly, so that in the midst of suffering and death, it is heaven, not hell. Ours is not to despise the *conatus essendi*, but to redeem its incarnational core—its divine core—through which the divine will asserts, Let there be flesh, let there be life. Therefore ought we let our spiritual energies, our prayers, every bit of them, the best of them, be directed not toward the transcendent disincarnationally, but into the world, toward the body and the earth, giving rise to a fully incarnate saintliness or holiness. The world teaches us the crucifying depths of difference — abyssal difference that is the ultimate challenge to love. The world is that place the providential will has given us to fulfill the rending travails and joys of communion, for the world is God's way of saying *après vous* — calling us to *our* divine task.

Our task is to love; not to despise anything, but to redeem everything. And yet, when we truly open ourselves to the ecstasies and agonies of the world, we can rarely respond with an unequivocal "no" or unequivocal "yes." Our "no" always betrays a "yes," and our "yes" betrays a "no." Prayer is the agon of our "yes" and our "no" — the confluence of ultimate hope (salvation) and ultimate judgment (damnation) — as these coincide in our living flesh. To suffer this rending ambivalence is to be alive indeed. It is to submit to the blessing-curse of incarnation-crucifixion. In response to the travails of this blessing-curse, prayer is our final and ultimate recourse. It empowers our reconciliation with the incarnational will of God, which is the yes-saying of the incarnate body to its destiny. So finally we must pray with our bodies, with our flesh, when we pray our way forward, sometimes in fear and trembling, sometimes in ecstasy — not away from the earth toward a transcendent God, as Augustine prays, but toward the earth and the body in a movement of spirit fully into flesh, fully into the crucifying world, where we are bequeathed the supreme task of existence. Every suffering teaches love. Love redeems the sacrifice.

16

The Infinite Supplicant
On a Limit and a Prayer

MARK CAUCHI

Preserve my soul; for I am holy.

—Psalms 86:2[1]

As if prayer (*precāri*) were not in a precarious (*precārius*) enough position, teetering at the limit between myself and the Other, prayer also has two further difficulties. The first of these two additional difficulties is that prayer is often alleged to be uttered, vocally or silently, by a *finite* self to an *infinite* Other, especially that other named God. This is a difficulty, because if I am properly finite—and what is the proper if not the absolutely finite, the indivisible?—can anything I do ever get beyond myself to reach another? This is a question that recent Continental thought, concerned as it is with the finitude of the subject and the transcendence of the Other (for instance, in Levinas, Derrida, and Marion), has not yet adequately addressed. For no matter how powerful an infinite Other would be, would it actually ever be able to hear the words of a finite supplicant, to receive the bread from a finite mouth, as it would have to for Levinas? If I am finite, how would bread get from me to you? Would it not be stopped at my limit, as if by a guard at a refugee camp who lets no one out? And if my finite limit actually is a finite limit, so that *whatever* is encompassed within this limit *would have to be* finite, would not the infinite, too, if it is to avoid being confined, be stopped by my limit, like a foreigner turned away by an inhospitable immigration officer?

But if the Other *did* happen to hear or taste what came from my mouth, what would that tell us about the relations of the finite and the infinite within prayer? What would prayer tell us about these designations we have been using—too comfortably, I want to suggest—of the *finite* and the *infinite*?

Beyond this difficulty, there is still, and perhaps worse, another. For prayer is not simply the sending of words from me unto the infinite Other and thus across the precarious limit between us. More terrible still is that prayer has the dignity or indignity of being, somewhere within it, a petition. Whatever other things prayer does, at bottom, and what distinguishes it from praise and confession, with which it no doubt bears close relations, structurally and in practice, is that prayer is the sending of a *request* or *question* to the Other and thus the *seeking* of an answer, the *asking* of the Other to respond to me, to be *responsible*. Without disputing that prayer certainly involves a questioning of myself, to pray is also, nevertheless, to question the Other. But that is not all. For, as we shall see, if the question to the Other is truly a question, so that the Other does not remain safe and unquestioned by it, then the question must *call the Other into question*. The question I pose to the Other must, in a sense, depose the Other, challenging his or her sovereignty. If this is not the case when one speaks to the Other, I want to suggest, then one may be praising or confessing, but one is surely not praying. Prayer must question the Other, call the Other into question, even if this other is God, lest it be something other than prayer.

Prayer thus opens up a different set of questions from the ethical questions Continental thought has been asking in recent years. For rather than the Other calling into question the self or subject, prayer seems to reverse the trajectory: the subject in prayer questions and calls into question the Other. One might be tempted—too easily, I think—to view prayer as I have configured it here as the most inexcusable act of hubris. What nerve to question God! For by what right, by what authority, would we do so? This, too, is an important question and one to which we must respond. But if asked too quickly, it will pass over two very important and interconnected moments: First, it will evade the fact that we do call God into question, as we shall see. Second, that calling God into question is itself not without fear and trembling.

The Othering Prayer of Abraham

In the second-ever prayer performed within the Abrahamic traditions—what is sometimes called Abraham's "intercession" on behalf of Sodom and Gomorrah and which the Qur'ān describes as Abraham's "pleading" (11:74)—we witness both of the moments just described above. In the well-known episode, once God/the three strangers have told Abraham that he and Sarah will bear a child, the Lord suggests to Abraham, after a most peculiar "private" deliberation,[2] that he will destroy Sodom and Gomorrah (Gen. 18:20–21). The text then tells us, with cinematic direction, that "the men turned from there, and went toward Sodom; but Abraham still stood before the Lord" (or "The Lord remained standing before Abraham").[3] Following this narration, Abraham "draws near" and begins his fearful attempt to talk God out of destroying the righteous with the wicked.

One imagines the men walking away, with Abraham standing still, deeply troubled, shocked even, in a silent meditation to which we are not privy (unlike God's, just previously), and then taking steps toward God, slowly but determinately, full of reverence but also fear. It is perhaps due to this fear that when Abraham launches his interrogation, he is careful to acknowledge that it is in honor of God's supreme righteousness that he questions him: "Far be it from thee to do such a thing, to slay the righteous with the wicked, so that the righteous fare as the wicked! Far be that from thee! Shall not the Judge of the all the earth do right?" (Gen. 18:25). It is with this appreciation for the righteousness of God and for the awkwardness and, frankly, the danger of his situation that Abraham continues fearfully to cross-examine the "Judge of all the earth." He says twice, "Oh let not the Lord be angry, and I will speak" (18:30, 32), and also twice, "Behold, I have taken upon myself to speak to the Lord, I who am but dust and ashes" (18:27, 31). Abraham is fully aware, with all the fear and trembling this entails, that he is crossing a line, transgressing a limit, that he is trespassing on another's property, and that there is the frightful risk that he will be prosecuted.

Let us consider this transgression in more detail. Following Sinai, the Israelites will develop a legal system delineating the clean and the unclean, the holy and the unholy, with any *improper* transgressions of the line and limit between them resulting in contamination and punishment. Granting that in the biblical narrative Abraham is prior to Sinai, would we, just as a thought experiment, be justified in viewing Abraham's trespass as a prefiguration of contamination? Does

God's contact with Abraham's "dust and ashes" profane God's transcendence, disrespecting God's supreme holiness and so making Abraham justly punishable?[4] As Abraham himself might say, "far be it." If anything, in this episode, the dusty and ashen Abraham is helping God to be God, helping him to be more himself, to be holy as he should be holy.

Many commentators have attempted to deny this central theme of the story,[5] but there is enough evidence to believe that even though in the end God does destroy Sodom and Gomorrah, God's sense of justice has been altered (made other) by Abraham's protests. Note that at the beginning of the episode, God says to Abraham that he will visit the cities to determine whether they are "greatly" and "gravely" sinful (Gen. 18:20–21), from which Abraham correctly infers that if the cities are greatly sinful, God will destroy them in total (18:23). During the time that Abraham and God have their famous conversation, two of the three angels go to investigate the sinfulness of Sodom, whereupon Lot, as did Abraham, receives them with customary hospitality (although, note, with less hospitality than Abraham—he does not offer them as elaborate a meal as did Abraham). Literally every one else in the city ("all the people to the last man" [19:4]), however, wants to sodomize the visitors. Lot tries to protect his guests—again demonstrating a sense of hospitality—however, he does so, horribly, by offering his own virgin daughters (which the guests prevent) (19:7–8), thus once again demonstrating less judicial acuity than Abraham.[6] Lot is not exactly righteous but (at least in his ancient context) is not absolutely wicked either. So he has not completely forgotten the ways of the Lord.

Meanwhile, Sodom's situation does not look promising. Had God made his final adjudication prior to Abraham's interrogation, based on what we are presented with in this scene, it seems likely that the less-than-wicked Lot would have been destroyed with the thoroughly wicked Sodom. As it is, however, "when God destroyed the cities of the valley," the text tells us, "God remembered Abraham, and sent Lot out of the midst of the overthrow" (Gen. 19:29). As John E. Hartley writes, with a conclusion that is rarely reached by commentators, "God showed mercy to Lot on the basis of Abraham's faithfulness and his intercession for Sodom. Abraham, therefore, was the reason for Lot's deliverance."[7] It is Abraham's voice echoing in God's conscience that saves Lot. But in a way, Abraham's voice saves God too: for we have to ask, what kind of God would God be if he had killed Lot and his family?

We must be careful, then, in interpreting the Bible when it asks in the voice of God (as often is the case) such questions as found in Second Isaiah: "Who has directed the Spirit of the Lord, or as his counselor has instructed him? Whom did he consult for his enlightenment, and who taught him the path of justice?" (Isa. 40:13–14). We cannot simply answer "no one," for the Hebrew Bible recognizes in a remarkable moment that God would be less Godly if it were not for the prayers of Abraham. In this case, human prayer sustains and enriches God's divinity, his transcendent otherness. I shall analyze this process in more depth below. But note that this episode is not the only such example in the Bible. We can, for instance, point to Moses's two intercessions, the first when Moses asks God to remember his covenant and "repent," which God does (Exod. 32: 7–14), and the second when Moses says "pray thee" to God, saying to him, "be great as thou has promised" (Num. 14: 10–25). We can point also to the book of Amos, where in two different instances it is said that "The Lord repented" after the prayers, "O Lord God, forgive, I beseech thee" (Amos 7:2–6). And then, of course, there is Job, who, as the Rabbis long ago noted, makes the same protest against God as did Abraham: "It is all one; therefore I say, he destroys both the blameless and the wicked" (Job 9:22).[8] There are so many examples that they cease to be exceptional.

How is this possible? How is it that the supplicant can somehow, through his or her prayer, enable God to be holy as he should be holy? What would the nature of each, the human and God, and their relationship in prayer have to be in order for this divinizing of God to come to pass? How are we to understand the limits between the human and the divine, self and wholly Other, within biblical prayer? The hypothesis I want to put forward is that there must be a sense in which, within prayer, within the sending of words from my mouth unto God (a-ðieu), and thus across their limits, one *is* holy as God is holy; the limit has already been trespassed.

Holy Prayer

Are we getting above ourselves? Is this trespass the sin of pride, as opposed to what Luther meant by a bold sin? Is this arrogance? On the contrary: pray thee, listen.

In Augustine's "Exposition of Psalm 85,"[9] the second verse of which is sometimes translated, "Preserve my soul, for I am holy" (*bāsīd*),[10] Augustine (with feigned worry) acknowledges that he does not know "if anyone has the right to say, *I am holy*," except Jesus.[11] He writes, "If I meant 'holy' in the sense of making others holy and standing in no need of anyone to sanctify me, I should be arrogant to claim it, and a liar" (EP 224). Before we read Augustine as dismissing what I have claimed to be the case in Abraham, we must read on, for Augustine continues: "but if it means 'holy' in the sense of 'made holy,' as Scripture uses the phrase, *Be holy, because I am holy*," then "[t]his is not the pride of a conceited person, but the confession of one who is not ungrateful" (EP 224). If one has been *made* holy by the grace of Jesus, Augustine reasons, then it would be ungrateful *not* to understand oneself as holy. But the verse we quoted justifies the request "Preserve my soul" with the reason "for I am holy"; the speaker seems to be holy already. Despite the seeming givenness of this speaker's holiness, however, Augustine points out that she or he still needs the assistance, the preserving act of God; holiness, at least in the case of the human supplicant, is not self-subsistent. And so Augustine concludes that in the Psalm, "This holy person is not proud," since it is evident that "he hopes in the Lord," that is, that his holiness is somehow conditioned upon his prayer to God (EP 225).[12]

The aporia here is palpable. For, if it is *because* I am holy (as God is holy) that I can pray for God's assistance, as the Psalm suggests, then two seemingly contradictory things would appear to follow. First, I cannot pray *unless* I am holy. Second, my holiness is clearly not self-subsistent, and thus I must pray *in order* to be holy. On the one hand, then, if I am not already holy, I cannot pray, I cannot ask God questions. This indeed is what God indicates in Ezekiel when, after listing the profanities of Israel, he says, "shall I be inquired of by you, O house of Israel? As I live, says the Lord God, I will not be inquired by you" (Ezek. 20:31). As unholy, one lacks the credibility to pray; one cannot approach the holy. Therefore, it is only because I am holy that I am entitled to pray to God, that I may ask questions. But on the other hand, *in order* to be holy, *in order* to enter into the holiness of the covenant, I *must* pray and ask. Here, on this side of the aporia, it is by means of prayer that I become holy, that I may be praised as holy.

We need to examine this latter side of the aporia more closely. While I have said, expanding upon Augustine, that in order to be holy I must pray and ask, it is important also, since I have spent some time here discussing the Hebrew Bible, and since Augustine himself does, to acknowledge that in the Torah there is no law to pray. When in Leviticus the priestly authors distil the Law into what is called the

Holiness Code (Lev. 17–26) by repeatedly invoking God's command, "You shall be holy; for I the Lord your God am holy" (11:44; 19:2; 20:7, 26; 21:6, 7, 8; and its negations, 22:2, 15, 32), and then proceed for the rest of the Book to recast the Law in terms of holiness (*kāš*, "holy," appears in sixteen of twenty divine speeches), they never once say that one shall pray.[13] What the Holiness Code does prescribe are (1) ritual practices, which always involve the participation of a priest and which usually cost something, and (2) an ethical code, the most famous maxims of which are "love your neighbor as yourself" (Lev. 19:18) and "love the stranger [*ger*] as yourself" (Lev. 19:34).

Nevertheless, as Samuel E. Balentine has helpfully shown, because rituals and offerings were often quite costly and usually depended on one's access to a priest, prayer was increasingly accepted among the ancient Hebrews as one of the ways that the poor and the dislocated—and, we can add, increasingly after the destruction of the first Temple (587 B.C.E.), everyone else—could convene with God and so be holy as God is holy without the hierarchical intervention of the priests.[14] Indeed, once the synagogue, the place of assembly for prayer (*synagōgē*, Greek, "assembly"), replaced the Temple as the dominant site of worship, the priest had no more than a ceremonial authority over the layperson. Even in the account of the Temple's inauguration during Solomon's dedication, which is essentially a prayer about prayer spoken before an assembly (a *synagōgē*, we might say), we witness the hierarchical notion of holiness being called into question. According to Solomon, all a supplicant has to do, no matter where he or she is, is face toward the Holy of Holies and pray, and God, whom Solomon also asks to face toward the Holy of Holies, will listen and forgive (1 Kings 8:28–30).

Despite the central position of the Holy of Holies here between the supplicant and God, it is less a literal site of contact and presence than it is the site or sign of their nonpresent meeting, what Levinas might call, in the language of the Bible, their face-to-face, which is not reducible to the presence of one face to another. Here holiness is not reducible to divine presence, to literal contact with the divine. Remarkably, Solomon's prayer for the Temple results in the depresencing and detemporalizing of holiness. It was this that Solomon recognized when, during the dedication, incredible after his monumental feat of construction, he asked the question, "will God indeed dwell on the earth? Behold, heaven and the highest heaven cannot contain thee; how much less this house which I have built!" (1 Kings 8:27).

At its very founding, then, the foundation of the Temple is deconstructed by prayer to produce a synagogue,[15] calling into question the allegedly untouchable authority of the priest, his Temple and, more importantly, their inaccessible God. In principle, prayer allows every one to be holy as God is holy, fulfilling God's promise to make Israel "a kingdom of priests and a holy nation" (Exod. 19:6).[16]

Like the Other

As should now be evident, the relation between the supplicant and God cannot be structured according to the great chain of holiness often presupposed by the priests.[17] In prayer, one does not pass across an ever-holier quantitative series of limits until one reaches a holy of holies in which the divine Presence, separated from most people, is present to the privileged. Instead, like the ethical maxims of the Holiness Code with which prayer is in parallel—for they too sidestep the priests' great chain of being—prayer presupposes a relationship where one is *like* another. Be holy, *as* God is holy. Love your neighbor/stranger *as* yourself. Both of these maxims attempt to establish a relationship, a likeness, between the subject and its other (in the former case, God; in the latter, the neighbor/stranger).

This relationship of likeness, it is critical to observe, is not reducible to a logic of quantity or hierarchy. Whereas in priestly ritual the distance and proximity of the Holy *is* a quantitative distance and proximity, the likeness of prayer and ethics is not a quantitative likeness and therefore (as we will see) not reducible to sameness either. Recalling Solomon's dedication, Levinas remarks in a reading of Rabbi Hayyim Volozhiner's book, *Nefesh ha'Hayyim* (The Soul of Life), that "When the Talmudic scholars . . . recommend turning one's heart towards the Holy of Holies when praying, they do not just mean turning in a certain direction but are indicating an act of identification or an intention to identify: one must become the sanctuary itself, the place of all holiness, and responsible for all holiness."[18] Levinas here distinguishes between a literalist interpretation of turning toward the Temple, which would be governed by an ontotheology of presence, versus what he calls an act of identification with holiness. To pray, according to Levinas, *is* to be holy *like* God.

But Levinas is also clear in this piece that this likeness is not what he would elsewhere identify as an ontology of sameness. For Levinas himself observes that this likeness also establishes a difference: while this relationship is "not a pure distinction," it is, he says, "certainly not a pure and simple identification" either (BV 158). Praying produces less an A = A than it does an A = B, a likeness between two irreducibles (similar to what Levinas would call in his more philosophical work the "separation" within the face-to-face). Likewise, in neither of our two maxims is one commanded to occupy only a single position: the texts do not say "be God" or "love yourself."[19] In fact, in the former, one must be oneself *and* be like God; and, in the latter, one must love the neighbor as if he or she were both him- or herself *and* like oneself (which, conversely, also means that one is like him or her). Both presuppose a dual stance.

This likeness of the subject to both God and the neighbor/ stranger, and thus the duality of each of these members, is arguably one of the most fundamental and orienting conceptions of both the Hebrew and Christian Bibles. It is most evident in the canonical statement of it in Genesis 1:26, "Then God said, 'Let us make man in our image [*tselem*], after our likeness [*demuth*],'" a phraseology that the priestly authors repeat, although invert, to describe Adam's procreation of Seth at Genesis 5:3: "he became the father of a son in his own likeness [*demuth*], after his image [*tselem*]." If the claim that man is in the likeness of God did not merit the attribution of an equality between the two, then one must at least acknowledge that the text understands the relationship of one human to another in the very image and likeness of the relationship between the human and God, which results in the same thing: one human is like another in much the same way in which the human is like God.

In the second narrative of creation, the J narrative, man is not originally created in the image and likeness of God but is formed out of the earth and God's breath, so that, just like every other animal, it is called a "living creature" (Gen. 2:7; 2:19).[20] The human becomes unlike animals only when, consistent with the P narrative, it said to become like (*damah*) God, namely, after the transgression, the trespass of the limit that would have separated the human and God but that now gives humans knowledge (*yd'*) like God.[21] And we must not be dissuaded by Second Isaiah's question: "To whom then will you liken God?" (Isa. 40:18, 25; 46:5). For in each of the three instances in which Second Isaiah poses this question, the only response he entertains—so as to dismiss it—is natural objects such as idols and the starry heavens: "To whom then will you liken God, or what likeness compare with him? The idol! a workman casts it, and a goldsmith overlays it with gold, and casts for it silver chains" (Isa. 40:18–19). Isaiah's point here, as in the other passages, is that the idol is not comparable with God. The text does not entitle us to deduce, however, that there is nothing like or comparable with God.

This likeness of the human and the divine is exploited in Matthew (22:37–40), whose style, as Gundry has observed, is typically to pair heaven and earth.[22] This pairing and likeness is clearly evident when Jesus commands, first, that one must love God with all one's heart — the very way the Hebrew and Christian Bibles repeatedly say one should pray — and, second, that one should love the neighbor as oneself. Note that the second command is prefaced by the phrase "*like* the first." (This "like" by which Mathew binds the two laws together is *homoioún* [similar, like], which is the same word the Septuagint and most of the Christian Bible uses to translate *demuth* [likeness].) Loving the neighbor like oneself is, according to Matthew's Jesus, *like* loving God, which Leviticus told us makes us holy like God is holy. As in the Hebrew Bible, the relation between humans is like the relation between the human and God. Thus Matthew's Jesus commands, again like Leviticus, "You . . . must be perfect, as your heavenly Father is perfect" (Matt. 5:48). This command, however, is Jesus' summary of the more general attitude one must have in order to be, like him, a son of God (Matt. 5:45) and which, more concretely, requires one to love and pray for one's enemies (Matt. 5:44). To love and pray for one's enemies is Jesus' radical interpretation of the Holiness Code's radical command to love — not only the neighbor but the stranger. To love and pray for the enemy is, therefore, to be perfect like God, to whom one sends one's prayers for the enemy. It is not surprising, then, that Jesus will bring these likenesses together in his famous prayer. He says "forgive us our trespasses, *as* we forgive those who trespass against us" (Matt. 6:12).[23] Jesus here directly links the act of praying (forgive us our trespasses) with ethics (as we forgive those who trespass against us). There is therefore something about giving forgiveness and asking God for forgiveness (giving God a question) that is fundamentally similar, even if they are not the same. This likeness exists, no doubt, because according to Jesus, giving love or forgiveness to one's neighbor/enemy/stranger is being *like* God: "A new commandment I give to you, that you love one another; even *as* I have loved you" (John 13:34).[24] Loving the neighbor/enemy like yourself here becomes like loving the neighbor like God has loved you: the performance of love is like the grace of

God. To forgive and love another is thus to be *like* God, which itself is *like* praying for forgiveness.

It would be terribly wrong, I think, if one read this genealogy of likeness as suggesting that likeness means identity—to be *like* God would mean that one *is* God, and this grid of likenesses would somehow render all the *relata* within it the same. It is absolutely essential, in fact, in order for this likeness to operate, that each of these members be radically different, indeed wholly other (and so, paradoxically, capitalizing one of the "others" to differentiate between them is no longer possible). If I were the same as God or the neighbor, I could not love or pray to either, nor could there be any grace of the other. In order for me to be *like* the other, I cannot *be* the other. On the contrary, in order to be like the other, I must be other than the other, we must be irreducible to each other. Being irreducible, however, does not make us unlike each other; rather, irreducible to each other, we are each, like the other, the other's other. We must be like each other in order to be irreducible to each other, in order for there to be otherness.

The Infinite Supplicant

It would seem that given this structure of likeness, one must be *like* God in order to pray *to* God. I must already be on the other side of my limit if I am to address, to give a question to, another. Conversely, if I am contained absolutely (in a strict sense) within my limit, within the borders of my property, then neither I nor the other will ever be able to free me, will ever allow me to speak across my limits to another. Any act of address, especially prayer, would thus presuppose that one has already crossed one's limit to the other side (the side of the other) and thus is already *like* the other. Prayer thus presupposes that there be an archtrespass, perhaps an original sin.

But note, on the other hand, that having already crossed the limit does not preclude or prevent actually stepping and speaking across the limit—the actual *event* of prayer.[25] As I said, following Augustine, one must pray in order to be holy. In order to become *like* God, one *must* take a step. But this means, to emphasize a moment Derrida usually deemphasizes, that my prayer, my question to the other, must be *given to* and so arrive *at* God for the first time. The prayer, the question, cannot come simply *from* the other.[26] For if my prayer is literally already there, so that God knows it already before I speak, as s/he would in the most literal and banal of sense of omniscience, then it is not a real prayer, for God has not really been *given a question*.[27] If God preknows the question, it is not a question, and there is no prayer. Precisely because it is *a question* that prayer gives to the other and that the other receives *as a question*, prayer must be understood to *call the other into question*.

It is perhaps here that we can test the mettle of the true prayer. According to this test, a false prayer would be one to which God could respond as if automatically, on the basis of a literal and quantitative omniscience and omnipotence. For example, please make or do not let X happen. True prayers, on the contrary—such as why do I or You do X (e.g., destroy the righteous with the wicked)?—would be those for which God's omnipotence and omniscience are of no help and to which God would be forced to respond with new thoughts and actions, singularly and without certainty, perhaps out of nothing. Perhaps, then, what makes God the other par excellence and, therefore, the one to whom we most usually pray is his or her kenotic openness and readiness to being called into question (a borderlessness that has at the same time a certain limitedness). The only adequate response, then, to such an openness is for the supplicant actually to take the step of giving a question unto God.

This dual structure of prayer, where one is already beyond one's limit but still yet to cross it (always already *and* still to come), is precisely the one that Augustine uncovers in the famous opening of his *Confessions* and which is consistent with his reading of Psalm 85. After beginning his confession in the standard manner of an address to God—with a praise, in this case quoted from the Psalms (47:2 and 146:5)—Augustine immediately adds, almost out of place, that "Man, a little piece of your creation, desires to praise you [God], a human being 'bearing his mortality with him' [2 Cor. 4:10], carrying with him the witness of his sin and the witness that you 'resist the proud' [1 Pet. 5:5]."[28] Much like Abraham at Sodom, Augustine is drawing attention to the ostensible discrepancy between the human and God, pointing out what many would call (but which Augustine is just about to call into question) the finitude of the human being: that we are created by God as but a piece, and that we are mortal, sinful, and proud.

But Augustine then adds, "*Nevertheless* [*et tamen*], to praise you is the desire of man, a little piece of your creation" (emphasis added). Why "nevertheless"? What is so remarkable, so nearly incongruent, that it is *despite* its alleged finitude that the human desires to praise God? What is remarkable, for Augustine, is simply that a finite being could have the desire to praise an infinite God. For is it not peculiar that the finite somehow finds within itself the resources to pray to the infinite? Would not the very finitude of the supplicant prevent it from praying to God?

> How shall I call upon my God, my God and Lord? Surely when I call on him, I am calling on him *to come* into me. But what place is there in me where my God can enter into me? . . . Lord my God, is there any room in me which can contain you? . . . Without you, whatever exists would not exist. Then can what exists contain you? I also have being. So why do I request you to come to me when, *unless you were [already] within me*, I would have no being at all?[29]

How could I, as limited, receive God? Given this situation, it would seem impossible that a finite being could even pray to God. And yet the very fact that I pray demonstrates that God is in me. For, if God were not in me, I would not exist, let alone pray. In order to pray to God *to come*, therefore, I must *already* have God within me, which surely raises questions about my alleged finitude. For again, it would seem impossible that the finite proper could "contain" (Augustine's word) anything other than the finite. Indeed, this is what Augustine so brilliantly confesses to having such a hard time thinking through. For by praying to God I acknowledge my limits, but I also demonstrate, whether I acknowledge it or not, that I am beyond simple or absolute limitation; I am both within my limits and beyond them, trespassing on the property of the other. Thus Augustine not only sees that in order for God to come to me, God must be here already, he also sees that, in order for my prayer to be sent to God, I must already have had knowledge of God and hence have already crossed the limit between us: "who calls upon you when he does not know you? For an ignorant person might call upon someone else instead of the right one. But surely you may be called upon in prayer [in order] that you may be known."[30] Hence both God and the human may cross the limit that differentiates them and so, for each other, be *to come*, only if each has already crossed the limit. It would not be enough, then, to stress only, in a Derridean manner, that prayer is for what is to come, for it can only be to come if it is also and therefore undecidably always already.

Thus prayer is precarious, for in two steps it both (1) *must* take a step across a limit; and (2) *cannot* take a step, for there is no longer a limit. In step one it is essential, since I take a step, that I not simply be without limit. With no limit, no difference between us, *I* cannot give *you* anything. With no limit between us, we are the same; there is nothing else toward which I can step. It is necessary for this first step that I be limited. But it is important that we do not understand this limitation as finitude proper, for that limit which is absolutely finite can never be stepped across, not by me toward God nor by God toward me. Hence if the supplicant were truly finite, she or he could never pray, and God could not respond. Indeed, there can be nothing precarious, nothing aporetic, within the finite realm.[31] In the second (non)step, however, both the supplicant and the prayer are beyond their own limits. The supplicant is irreducible to any finite "here and now." But we must be careful, with this second step, that we do not simply assume that prayer or the supplicant is absolutely without limitation, like some kind of Hegelian spurious infinite. The supplicant is more precarious, more supple, than that; it must be irreducible to any limit without simply being absolutely unlimited.

This description of the supplicant—as both within and beyond its limit—gives the supplicant the structure that some in the Abrahamic traditions have attributed to God; namely, a certain infinitude, but an infinitude that cannot be spuriously reduced to a quantitative Greek *apeiron*.[32] As such, to call the supplicant infinite is not to ascribe a literal and quantitative omnipotence or omniscience to the supplicant in which the supplicant could literally do or know everything. Such a situation would preclude the need for prayer, as Augustine argued. Not even God, thankfully, could satisfy such requirements, as we have seen. God transcends the very literality, the ontotheology of presence and quantity, that would think him/her in such terms.

But that transcendence does not preclude God from a certain limitedness, as Anselm saw so well. When Anselm argued in the *Monologion* that God is irreducible to the law of noncontradiction, which limits space and time (and thus is unthinkable in terms of quantity and presence), he recognized that God, therefore, cannot be outside of these limits (such would be a metaphysics of presence). To think God otherwise than finite, Anselm concludes (with incredible rigor) that we must speak of God not *"in"* these finite limits, as he says, which would finitize God, but *"with"* them, which means that s/he is not without them.[33] By thinking God as irreducible to finitude (as infinite), we are forced in the same thought to think God as limited, but with a limitation that is clearly not that of finitude proper. Whereas a finite limit can do nothing other than confine or exclude, the limits that demarcate God, that differentiate him/her from us, do neither: God is not absent from us (even if s/he is not *in* us, as Augustine showed) and we are not prevented from going unto God (as, for instance, in prayer).

The infinite limit is porous, which, insofar as it still acts as a limit, makes it aporetic. As I said, there is no aporia for the finite. Thus God is both beyond and within limits, and *as such* is infinite. And it is this very infinitude of God which makes us *like* God. For, again, God could only pass beyond his/her limits and come unto us, as we ask in prayer, if the limit between us, if we ourselves, were not absolutely finite. If God is to be infinite, if we are to have an other beyond our limit to whom we pray, we cannot be finite. It is thus in God's very nature for us to be infinite. That we pray to an infinite God demands, then, that we, like God, be infinite. Indeed, infinitude *is* this relation of one-being-*like*-another, one infinite like another infinite. If there is to be even one infinite, there must be at least two. In order for me to pray to an infinite God, to confess my limitations, I, like God, must be infinite.

17

Proslogion

PHILIP GOODCHILD

Chapter One

I was reading St. Anselm:

> Up now, slight man! Flee, for a little while, thy occupations;
> hide thyself, for a time, from thy disturbing thoughts. Cast
> aside, now, thy burdensome cares, and put away thy toilsome
> business. Yield room for some little time to God; and rest for a
> little time in him. Enter the inner chamber of thy mind; shut out
> all thoughts save that of God, and such as can aid thee in seek-
> ing him; close thy door and seek him. Speak now, my whole
> heart! Speak now to God, saying, I seek thy face; thy face,
> Lord, will I seek. And come thou now, O Lord my God, teach
> my heart where and how it may seek thee, where and how it
> may find thee.[1]

And I began to wonder: What do I love, when I love thee, O my
God? And I thought: I love that than which nothing that matters
more will be conceived. For indeed this is my love: that there is nothing that matters more than that which I love.

Then into my loneliest loneliness there crept a demon, who asked:
"Is your love not mistaken? Do you not love that which does not
matter?"

My mind began to waver. Do I love that which matters? Or do I
take that which I love to be that which matters? Do I pray to God?

Or do I take as my God the one to whom I pray? In truth, who is the God for whom I long?

My mind began to tremble. Have I not just asked to name the holiest of names? Have I not begun to think the most perilous of thoughts? And, if I cannot name and thus call upon God, do I not expose my soul to mortal danger?

My mind began to falter. Who can speak of that than which nothing that matters more will be conceived? Who can declare the holiest of names, but God alone? Do I not betray God when I pray to God? Then I prayed: Let this be my offering: let me sacrifice my prayer. I pray to God to rid me of God. Let my beloved be unknown. I pray to God to rid me of prayer. For, since I love that than which nothing that matters more will be conceived, I do not love my sacrifice and I do not love my prayer. I will no longer seek thee, O my God. Let me walk into damnation, for I can do no other; God may save me if God wills. For I love that than which nothing that matters more will be conceived.

At once there resounded within me an angelic voice, repeating the prayer of St. Anselm: "Teach me to seek thee, and reveal thyself to me, when I seek thee, for I cannot seek thee, except thou teach me, nor find thee, except thou reveal thyself. Let me seek thee in longing, let me long for thee in seeking; let me find thee in love, and love thee in finding."[2]

Chapter Two

Three times more the demon came unto me to persuade me that my love was mistaken, and each time I welcomed his voice as that of a friend. The demon came unto me a first time and asked: "Is there no such being as that than which nothing that matters more will be conceived? For the Bohemian has said, 'Nothing really matters. Anyone can see, nothing really matters to me.'"[3]

And I wondered in my heart at the Bohemian. What a curious paradox he is. For perhaps the Bohemian is playing the fool, and the import of his words does not matter; he is merely singing a refrain. No one pays the least attention to his meaning. Or perhaps the Bohemian is serious, and the import of his words demands my attention. He means what he says and he speaks of that which matters. He demands that I bear witness to the import of his proposal: that nothing really matters to him. He asks that I become complicit in his disavowal of the matter. Indeed, he prays that I show respect to the matter by disavowing my witness of the matter, as though it did not matter to me. He shows me the matter in order that I will not speak of the matter. "No, nothing really matters to him," he prays me to affirm. Indeed, he asks me to repeat his disavowal, as though the matter that he has shown me does not matter to me.

And so I bore witness to his suffering by repeating his refrain, "Nothing really matters. Anyone can see, nothing really matters to me."

And hence, in my very disavowal, I declared to the demon that there is that which matters. For I can think of the matter as existing merely in the understanding or existing in reality. And that which matters matters more if it exists in reality than if it exists in the understanding alone. Hence when I think of that which matters more than anything that will be conceived, I must think of it as existing in reality. Now, is thinking of it existing in reality sufficient to make it really exist? In general, one would think not. For it would appear that I can think of anything as existing without it necessarily existing in reality. But I am not thinking in general nor am I thinking of anything. For anything is that which does not matter; it is any thing, it does not matter which. But when I think of that which matters, I must think of it seriously. And I cannot think seriously about that which exists in the understanding alone. For that which exists in the understanding alone can be any thing; it does not matter which. Hence I am constrained to think of that which matters as existing. This constraint is that which matters; it is the mattering of that which matters; it is the matter of understanding. Hence it may be possible that I can merely speak the words, and they may mean nothing to me. But if I understand their meaning at all, then that meaning matters.[4]

The demon replied: "What is the matter? It is a matter of understanding. The Bohemian, when he says that nothing really matters, understands, and hence he is in despair. In despair, he wishes to be rid of the matter. He wishes that it did not matter, for he understands only too well that it does. Yet the matter is his despair and, in despair, in wishing to be rid of the matter, he brings the matter upon himself. Thus the matter is merely himself."

And I began to wonder: Is it a matter of the understanding only? If the Bohemian could understand that he brings the matter upon himself, could he, in wishing to be rid of the matter, liberate himself through his own understanding?

Then the angelic voice spoke: "If, in despair, he once brought the matter upon himself, he does so no longer, for in despair, he cannot be rid of himself or the matter of his despair."

And then I understood. He longs for a time when nothing will matter, when he will be free of himself and his despair. Yet it is not within his power to make the matter not matter. It will no longer matter to him when he is freed from himself, when, in death, he is separated from matter. Yet so long as he endures, then it matters, for his every act or word is an act of despair in that he acts and speaks in order to be rid of himself. Moreover, he is in despair because he is going to die. He will no longer be himself. And in despair, he longs to be himself. It matters that he be himself. And despairing of being himself, he wishes to be free of himself, so that it will no longer matter. What matters in despair, therefore, is that he be himself, he who, despairing of being himself, wishes to be free of himself, so that he can be himself. So that at last rid of himself, he can be he who does not matter.[5]

What a curious paradox the Bohemian is! He is not himself at all. At one and the same time, he longs to be himself and be free of himself. At one and the same time, he longs to have the matter and escape from the matter. The paradox is the matter that constrains his understanding. But the Bohemian is not alone. I bear witness to him. And in bearing witness to him, I speak of that which matters that exists in reality and not in his understanding alone. And since the matter exists in reality, it does not exist in my understanding alone. And since I love that than which nothing that matters more will be conceived, I love that which exists in reality and not in the understanding alone. Hence, like the Bohemian, I do not possess that which matters. I love that which cannot be merely understood. And in hope, I wish to be free of myself, my own understanding, so that I may be myself, my love. I, too, am a curious paradox. I long for that which exists in reality and I long to be myself. Both longings are one and the same, and in repeating them, I bear witness to that which matters more than anything that will be conceived.

And I understood that it is not a matter of understanding alone. For the despair of the Bohemian matters in reality. For once he is dead and he understands no more, the matter of his words still demands a witness. It demands that I repeat his refrain, "Nothing really matters. Anyone can see, nothing really matters to me." And either I merely speak the words, and no one pays the least attention to their meaning, or else I am serious, and the import of these words demands that even after his death, I continue to bear witness to the matter of his despair. What matters is that he matters; even after death, he cannot rid himself of the matter. For his understanding will have existed in reality.

And I understood that the reality of understanding matters more than the understanding of reality. For while thinking alone does not matter, in reality, thinking is never alone. The reality of my understanding is that I always have my angels and demons. My demons tell me that that which I think does not matter. In their very disavowal, they draw my attention to that which matters. They show me that thinking has a necessary relation to existence; they show me the existence of my own thinking.[6] My angels understand that which I cannot understand. They conceive of that which matters more than anything that I can conceive. When my attention is drawn to that which matters, my angels speak to me of that which matters more. They show the necessary relation between thinking and paradox. For that which is most worthy of thought, that which is most thought-provoking, that which draws my attention, is that which I cannot understand. The supreme paradox of all thought is that it attempts to discover something that thought cannot think.[7]

And I understood that that which constrains thought yet can never be thought is that than which nothing that matters more will be conceived.

Chapter Three

The demon came unto me a second time and asked: "Does God matter? Does the lover love God for nothing? The lover loves God because God illuminates the matter. The lover longs to possess the beloved. The lover seeks the use of divine power, divine blessing, divine grace, divine understanding—in relation to which God is a mere occasion. Truly, the lover loves God for the sake of the divine essence. It is the essence that the lover loves, not God, who does not matter. Indeed, the lover longs to be God, to possess the divine power. And God seems to matter only insofar as devotion is the mode of access to divine power. For the Cynic has said, 'The value, or worth of a man, is as of all other things, his price; that is to say, so much as would be given for the use of his power.'"[8]

And I began to wonder at the Cynic. For if God is that than which nothing that matters more will be conceived, then it would seem that one cannot love any matter more than God. How, then, can the Cynic deny that God matters? Yet perhaps the Cynic understands this only too well. For if one loves that than which nothing that matters more will be conceived, then what matters most for one's love is how well one can conceive. For how can one love that of which one cannot conceive? One's power of conception is the condition for one's love of God. Then, in order to love God, one must first of all improve one's power of conception. What matters most in loving God is improving one's power of conceiving of God. Hence that than which nothing that matters more will be conceived is simply the improvement of one's power of conceiving; and this, by definition, is God.

And I understood the superior power of understanding held by the Cynic; and I understood that in order to improve my understanding I would have to love and understand the Cynic; and I understood that the Cynic would stand in place of my God, for I did not have the power to understand anything that the Cynic could not understand.

Then the angelic voice spoke: "It is one thing to understand the importance of the power of conceiving. It is another thing to improve the understanding in reality."

And I began to wonder again at the Cynic. It is one thing to be a master of the powers of understanding. It is another thing to exercise those powers. And I understood that because the Cynic is a master of the powers of the understanding, there is an aspect of the understanding that the Cynic does not understand: that the understanding is unable to conceive the matter. This absolute distance between the understanding and the matter defines both the power and the impotence of the understanding. For the understanding has a necessary relation to both existence and paradox. If the understanding denies this relation, then it may have a perfect relation to itself, a relation of unimpeded power. Yet in denying this relation, the Cynic understands nothing, least of all the impotence of the unimpeded power of the understanding. Because the Cynic understands everything, he understands nothing, because he does not understand the matter.

And I began to wonder at that than which nothing that matters more will be conceived, for it seemed to resemble the thought of the Cynic. For this conception is at once that which is conceived and that which measures the power of any conception. At one and the same time, it proposes a conception and invokes a power of the understanding. Since it is the conception that measures the power of any other, it posits itself as the supreme conception, as that than which nothing that matters more will be conceived. For in relation to any conception, it posits itself as more, since it is that than which nothing that matters more will be conceived. Indeed, it is a specific power of shaping the understanding. It posits the conception of the most, since in relation to anything that will be conceived, it posits itself as more. It posits the conception of hierarchy, since in relation to anything that will be conceived, it posits them as existing on a single, quantifiable scale, in relation to which "more" can always be measured. It posits the conception of purity of heart and mind, since one tries to love and understand that than which nothing that matters more will be conceived. It posits the conception of its own existence, since it matters more to exist in reality than to exist in the understanding alone. It posits the conception of enclosure within a single understanding, since it claims to measure anything that will be conceived. It excludes anything that matters more than it from its own understanding, as it is that than which nothing that matters more will be conceived.

What a curious paradox God is! God is not Godself at all. If I think of God as that than which nothing that matters more will be conceived, then God no longer seems to matter. For to matter more is a comparative term; it exists in the understanding that is able to compare. Yet it matters more to exist in reality than to exist in the understanding alone. Hence that which matters in reality matters because of its own singular existence; it matters irrespective of any comparisons, since comparisons occur in the understanding alone and not in reality. Hence God is not that than which nothing that matters more will be conceived.

And I understood that anything that matters more than the understanding is a singular existence. And I understood that if God is treated as an object of understanding or as an eternal essence, then God is not Godself. And I understood that if God is treated as a singular existence, then one cannot enclose God within the understanding. And I understood that one cannot think about God, cannot love God, cannot pray to God.

Then the angelic voice spoke: "It is not you who needs to pray to God; it is God who prays to you."

And I began to wonder: Where do I encounter that than which nothing that matters more will be conceived?

Then once more I heard the refrain of the Bohemian: "Nothing really matters. Anyone can see, nothing really matters to me."

And I understood that the despair of the Bohemian mattered more than anything that I could conceive. And I understood that the despair of the Bohemian was a singular existence that will never be encompassed within my understanding. And I understood that the despair of the Bohemian indicated that which matters; indeed, it indicates that than which nothing that matters more will be conceived.

And I began to think that what matters in understanding is not that one understands but what one tries to understand. I began to understand that thought does not exist in isolation in the inner chamber of one's mind, where it possesses an imaginary mastery over all it surveys, for such a thought does not matter. Thought that matters, that demands serious thought, is thought that is addressed from outside. Thought that matters responds to that which matters. And I understood that that than which nothing that matters more will be conceived is that which can never be understood yet most needs to be understood. Thinking involves dialogue and address. Thinking is an event between singular existences; it is a performance within a social occasion.

Chapter Four

The demon came unto me a third time and asked: "Does singular existence matter? For if singular existence is that which will never be conceived, then it has no essence of its own. What, then, is it that matters about singular existence? It cannot be any property or power of its own, for if it is that which will never be conceived, then it has no essence. Instead, the property of mattering must be given it from without. For the Empiricist has said, 'Relations are external to their terms.'"[9]

And I began to wonder at the Empiricist. Do I love that which matters? Or do I give the property of mattering to that which I love? For if I love that which matters, then the property of mattering is possessed by what I love. Hence what I love would be subject to an understanding of its properties; the property of mattering would be separable from its singular existence. I would love what matters because I understand it, and my understanding would attribute the property of mattering to what I love.

Yet if I give the property of mattering to that which I love, then the power to give matter is my own. It belongs to my understanding. But that which matters in reality matters more than that which matters in my understanding alone. Hence I do not have the power to make matters truly matter. So that which matters is external to any singular existence, just as the power to give matter is external to my understanding. That which matters is an event between singular existences; that which gives matter is a performance within a social occasion.

The demon replied: "What is the matter? Does the performance matter? The essence of the performance does not matter, for the performance has no essence. The singular existence of the performance does not matter, for the performance does not possess the property of mattering."

And I began to wonder how to perform thinking in a relation between singular existences in such a way that gives matter to that which matters. For even if the performance has no essence, one can still perform a repetition of the Event which is that than which nothing that gives more matter will be conceived. Then the performance has no singular existence, for it is merely a repetition of the Event. Yet even if the performance has no singular existence, its repetition of giving matter to that which matters will always give a different matter to a singular existence.

Then the angelic voice spoke up within me once more: "It matters less to learn the truth than it does to give the property of mattering."

And I began to wonder: How can I learn to think the truth? How can I learn to think about what matters more? How can I learn to give matter to that which matters?

And then I understood. If I were to learn the truth and possess the condition for understanding what matters, then what would matter most would be my eternal understanding. The singular existence that I encounter matters only insofar as it functions as the occasion for my learning the truth. If the eternal truth is that than which nothing that matters more will be conceived, then the singular existence matters only insofar as it participates in the eternal truth and repeats its essence.

If, by contrast, the singular existence were to have decisive significance, then learning the truth would matter more than understanding the truth. Nothing that matters more will be conceived than the moment when the condition for understanding is given.

And I began to wonder at the moment. For if the moment were to have decisive significance, it would be at once that than which nothing that matters more will be conceived and that which gives the condition for understanding what matters. At one and the same time, it would matter and it would measure what matters. Like the Cynic, it would bear witness to itself. It would posit itself as the supreme moment, as that than which nothing that matters more will be conceived. It would posit the enclosure of anything that matters within a single moment, since it claims to give matter to that which matters. It would take away any other power of giving that which matters, since it alone gives matter to that which matters.

What a curious paradox the moment is! The moment has no singular existence at all. If I think of the moment as that which gives matter, then it no longer seems to make anything else matter. If I give the moment decisive significance, then it takes significance away from all else that matters. The moment is simply a repetition of an eternal understanding, lacking its own singular existence. Taken by itself, it is a mere abstraction. It only has a singular existence as a temporal and social performance between singular existences.[10]

Then once more I began to wonder: How can I learn to think the truth? How can I learn to think about what matters more? How can I learn to give matter to that which matters?

And then I understood that if my learning were to be a temporal process, then that which has decisive significance is not the moment, which is merely an instantaneous section through the change; nor is it the change itself, for change itself is subject to change, and my learning may turn away from that than which nothing that matters more will be conceived.

Then the angelic voice within spoke up once more: "What has decisive significance is the potential future: it is both that than which nothing that matters more will be conceived and that which gives matter to that which matters."

And then I understood that the property of mattering and the power to give matter are not possessions to be owned. Matter can only be borrowed or lent. And I understood that matter is a matter of credit. All matter is mediated by a potential future. When one takes a singular existence as mattering, one trusts that it will matter; one lends it the property of mattering. Matter is an investment; and if that which one has taken as mattering no longer seems to matter, then one loses one's investment. If, by contrast, that which one takes as mattering comes to matter more, then one's trust has been rewarded. Thus the power to make things matter is based on trust.

And I understood that one has only to lend credit and act as if the matter will matter, and, by some miracle, it will matter. For the matter has become a bearer of credit. The matter becomes capable of making an effective demand. And to make an effective demand is to lend the property of mattering to that which one takes as mattering.

And I understood that one cannot understand but only love that which matters. For that which matters addresses one; its power of mattering lies outside the understanding. Moreover, one's response to that which matters is not given by that which matters. For if the response were given by that which matters, it would belong to that which matters, and one would respond to that which matters for a reason, through understanding. Yet if the power of mattering is to lie outside the understanding, then one can respond to that which matters only as one's own spontaneous action, that is, out of love for that which matters.

Then once more I heard the refrain of the Bohemian: "Nothing really matters. Anyone can see, nothing really matters to me."

And I understood that my witness could make all the difference to the despair of the Bohemian. For the despair of the Bohemian indicates that than which nothing that matters more will be conceived. But the despair does not indicate itself. Instead, the despair indicates both the witness that it demands and the hope that one day the Bohemian will matter. Then what the witness gives to the despair of the Bohemian is not merely a response to its demand but a repetition of the hope that one day the Bohemian will matter. And one has only to lend credit and act as if the Bohemian will matter, and, by some miracle, the Bohemian does matter. For the Bohemian has become a bearer of credit. The Bohemian becomes capable of making an effective demand. And to make an effective demand is to lend the property of mattering to that which one takes as mattering.

Chapter Five

The angelic voice spoke a final time: "Whom do you pray to when you pray to your God? You pray to the One who will love that than which nothing that matters more will be conceived. For indeed this is your prayer: that you may borrow an understanding that loves that which matters."

And I began to wonder. Do my angel and my demon have a better love for that which matters than I? For my demon draws my attention away from that which does not matter. And my angel draws my understanding toward the love of that which matters.

Let me give them the credit of having a better understanding of that which matters than I. Let me give them the credit of having a better understanding of how the quality of mattering is given. Let me give them the credit of understanding how I may learn more fully what matters in life. Then, to improve my understanding, I must learn to understand how they understand. I must give them the credit of supposing that their understanding is true. I must pray to receive their understanding.

And I understood that true thinking is concerned with three things. First, true thinking is concerned with something outside itself, with that which matters. For that which matters can never be encompassed within the understanding. That which matters stimulates thought, imposing itself upon thought as a problem. And true thought, turning outside itself, exhibits charity.

Second, true thinking is concerned with something within itself, with paradox. For true thinking is not itself; it has not yet become what it will have been. True thinking is a temporal movement of learning, striving to become what it will have been. The truth is neither buried deep within it nor is it given entirely from outside it, for truth is not a property that thinking may possess but is that which thinking strives to become. In learning, true thinking strives forward in hope to become what it will have been.

Third, true thinking is concerned with the understanding of others. It rests on the faith that there are others who have a deeper understanding of what matters. Since it does not possess their understanding, it can relate to their understanding only in faith, giving them credit. Since it does not possess their understanding, it cannot determine which others have a deeper understanding of what matters. This it may learn when it actually senses what matters. This is not blind faith but a visionary faith, directing attention to One who will love that than which nothing that matters more will be conceived.

And I understood that this true thinking, directed toward the outside, toward a potential future, toward a higher understanding, characterized by charity, by hope, and by faith, is prayer.

Notes

Introduction

1. For a sampling of prayers from various faiths, see George Appleton, ed., *The Oxford Book of Prayer* (Oxford: Oxford University Press, 1985).

1. Prayer as the Posture of the Decentered Self
Merold Westphal

1. See his commentary on Mary's "Magnificat," in *Luther's Works*, vol. 21, ed. Jaroslav Pelikan (St. Louis, Mo.: Concordia, 1956), 309–12.

2. From the Gloria of the Mass: "We give you thanks for your great glory."

3. Evelyn Underhill, *Worship* (New York: Harper and Row, 1936), 5.

4. Gabriel Marcel, *Creative Fidelity*, trans. Robert Rosthal (New York: Fordham University Press, 2002), 48–49.

5. Maurice Merleau-Ponty, *Phenomenology of Perception*, trans. Colin Smith (London: Routledge & Kegan Paul, 1962), xiv–xv (latter emphasis added).

6. Carlo Carretto, *The God Who Comes*, trans. Rose Mary Hancock (Maryknoll, N.Y.: Orbis Books, 1974), 179.

7. In addition to the transcendental and hermeneutical dimensions, one might also describe this essay as an exercise in experimental phenomenology, since each of the three prayers I examine is one that anyone could try to learn to pray.

8. Unless otherwise noted, biblical citations are from the New Revised Standard Version (New York: Oxford University Press, 1991).

9. "LORD," with small caps, signifies the Tetragrammaton YHWH, once rendered as Jehovah but now usually as Yahweh.

10. Emmanuel Levinas, *Otherwise Than Being, or, Beyond Essence*, trans. Alphonso Lingis (Dordrecht: Kluwer Academic, 1991), 11, 15; see also 43, 105, 112, 114, 118, 123, and 138.

11. See Rom. 1:1, Gal. 1:10, Phil. 1:1, Titus 1:1, James 1:1, 2 Peter 1:1, Jude 1:1, and Rev. 1:1.

12. Søren Kierkegaard, *The Journals of Kierkegaard*, ed. Alexander Dru (New York: Harper & Row, 1958–1959), 44–45 (emphasis in original).

13. Emmanuel Levinas, *Totality and Infinity*, trans. Alphonso Lingis (Pittsburgh: Duquesne University Press, 1969), 66; cf. 38, 51, 77, 193, and 198.

14. See Paul Ricoeur, *Oneself as Another*, trans. Kathleen Blamey (Chicago: University of Chicago Press, 1992).

15. It is in these terms that Descartes delineates *res cogitans* in his Second Meditation.

16. See Levinas, "Beyond Intentionality," in *Philosophy in France Today*, ed. Alan Montefiore (New York: Cambridge University Press, 1983).

17. Levinas, *Totality and Infinity*, 23.

18. Johannes Tauler, *Sermons*, trans. Maria Shrady (Mahwah, N.J.: Paulist Press, 1985), 38.

19. See Martin Heidegger, *Poetry, Language, Thought*, trans. Albert Hofstadter (New York: Harper & Row, 1971), 207; and Heidegger, *On the Way to Language*, trans. Peter D. Hertz (New York: Harper & Row, 1971), 108 (emphasis in original).

20. See Jacques Derrida, "How to Avoid Speaking: Denials," in *Derrida and Negative Theology*, ed. Harold Coward and Toby Foshay (Albany, N.Y.: SUNY Press, 1992), 108–12.

21. These texts are found in *Pseudo-Dionysius: The Complete Works*, trans. Colm Luibheid (Mahwah, N.J.: Paulist Press, 1987).

22. Augustine, *Confessions*, III, 6.

23. Ibid., X, 27; cf. VII, 7, "For that light was within and I was out of doors."

24. Ibid., VIII, 3.

25. Jean-Louis Chrétien, "The Wounded Word: The Phenomenology of Prayer," in Dominique Janicaud et al., *Phenomenology and the "Theological Turn": The French Debate* (New York: Fordham University Press, 2000), 149, 154.

26. Thomas Merton, *New Seeds of Contemplation* (New York: New Directions, 1961), 21 (emphasis in original).

27. Gabriel Marcel, *Creative Fidelity*, trans. Robert Rosthal (New York: Fordham University Press, 2002), 88.

28. Ibid., 40.

29. Ibid., 40–44.

30. Rom. 8:28. The textual witnesses are not in agreement here. I cite the version followed by The Revised English Bible (emphasis added).

31. And quite possibly elsewhere.

32. Given the intertextual intertwining of Mary's prayer with those of Samuel, Job, David, and Jesus, it should be obvious that there is nothing gendered about this analysis. It asks of women only what it asks many times over of men. But what, it may be asked, if kenosis is good for men but not for women in an all-too-patriarchal society? Sarah Coakley responds to precisely this question in "Kenōsis and Subversion: On the Repression of 'Vulnerability' in Christian Feminist Writing," in *Swallowing a Fishbone? Feminist Theologians Debate Christianity* (London: SPCK, 1996), 82; reprinted in *Powers and Submissions: Spirituality, Philosophy and Gender* (Oxford: Blackwell, 2002). Her aim is "to show how wordless prayer can enable one, paradoxically, to hold vulnerability and personal empowerment *together*" (1996, 84), and she asks "whether 'vulnerability' *need* be seen as 'female' weakness rather than a (special sort of) 'human' strength" (1996, 101). "The presumption is that women *need* 'power'—but of what sort? How are they to avoid aping the 'masculinism' they criticize?" (1996, 106). In answer to her own question, she points to "the defenceless prayer of silent waiting on God" on the ground that "the 'paradox of power and vulnerability' is I believe uniquely focused in this act of silent waiting on the divine in prayer. This is because we can only be properly 'empowered' here if we cease to set the agenda, if we 'make space' for God to be God" (1996, 107). It is from Sarah that I have learned to think of decentering in terms of who sets the agenda.

33. Levinas, *Totality and Infinity*, 118, 134.

34. Chrétien, "Wounded Word," 160–61 (emphasis in original).

35. The hymn by George W. Robinson is sometimes known by its opening line, "Loved with everlasting love," and sometimes by its refrain "I am His, and He is Mine."

36. Tauler, *Sermons*, 89.

37. For this question and its meaning, see *Who Comes after the Subject?* ed. Eduardo Cadava, Peter Connor, and Jean-Luc Nancy (New York: Routledge, 1991).

38. Jean-Luc Marion, *Being Given: Toward a Phenomenology of Givenness*, trans. Jeffrey L. Kosky (Stanford, Calif.: Stanford University Press, 2002) book V.

39. Henri J. Nouwen, *Reaching Out: The Three Movements of the Spiritual Life* (Garden City, N.Y.: Doubleday, 1975), 89.

2. Who Prays? Levinas on Irremissible Responsibility
Jill Robbins

1. Jacques Derrida's phrase is from "Violence and Metaphysics" [1963] in *Writing and Difference*, trans. Alan Bass (Chicago: University of Chicago Press, 1978), 147.

2. Roman Jakobson, "Linguistics and Poetics," in *Language in Literature* (Cambridge, Mass.: Harvard University Press, 1987), 67–68.

3. Maurice Blanchot, *The Writing of the Disaster*, trans. Ann Smock (Lincoln: University of Nebraska Press, 1986), 15; Blanchot, *L'écriture du désastre* (Paris: Gallimard, 1980). See also Blanchot, "Who?" trans. Eduardo Cadava, in *Who Comes after the Subject?* ed. Eduardo Cadava, Peter Connor, and Jean-Luc Nancy (London: Routledge, 1991); Blanchot, *"Qui?"* in *Cahiers Confrontations* 20 (Winter 1989).

4. See the discussion of Levinas's later work by Fabio Ciaramelli, *Transcendence et éthique* (Brussels: Ousia, 1989).

5. Delivered at a conference and published with the discussion that followed it in 1969, before being reprinted in *Beyond the Verse*, Emmanuel Levinas, "The Names of God after Some Talmudic Texts" is a "confessional" text that significantly overlaps with and prolongs the philosophical issues raised in "Enigma and Phenomenon" and "The Trace of the Other." In this text, prayer is introduced precisely in the context of the exchange between the philosophical and the nonphilosophical. Emmanuel Levinas, *L'analyse du langage théologique: Le nom de Dieu*, ed. Enrico Castelli (Paris: Aubier, 1969); Levinas, *Débats sur le langage théologique*, ed. Enrico Castelli (Paris: Aubier, 1969).

6. See also Levinas's Preface to the French translation of Rabbi Hayyim de Volozhyn, *L'âme de la vie. Nefesh Hahayyim*, trans. with an intro. by Benjamin Gross (Paris: Verdier, 1986).

7. Gross, Introduction to *L'âme de la vie*, xxii.

8. Ibid., xxxvii.

9. The proceedings of "Assises du Judaïsme français" (14–15 June 1964) can be found in *Bulletin intérieur du Consistoire Central des Israélites de France* (ronéotypé).

10. Allan Nadler, *The Faith of the Mithnagdim: Rabbinic Responses to Hasidic Rapture* (Baltimore, Md.: Johns Hopkins University Press, 1997).

11. See Jill Robbins, *Altered Reading: Levinas and Literature* (Chicago: University of Chicago Press, 1999), 112; and Robbins, "Strange Fire," in *Addressing Levinas: Phenomenology and the Judaic Tradition*, ed. Eric Nelson and Kent Still (Evanston, Ill.: Northwestern University Press, 2005).

12. Rabbi Hayim Halevy Donin, *To Pray as a Jew: A Guide to the Prayer Book and the Synagogue Service* (New York: Basic Books, 1980), 14–15.

13. I am grateful to Claire Nouvet for helping me develop these ideas in discussion.

14. Michael Berger has drawn my attention to the way in which Levinas's attribution of the interpretation to Rashi is problematic. First, in most critical editions, the words "Rashi says" are in brackets. Moreover, this is only one of several interpretations of the passage that Rashi cites, and he does not necessarily single out or endorse the particular interpretation to which Levinas refers.

15. All translations from *Berakoth* are by Maurice Simon (London: Soncino Press, 1958).

16. See the discussion in Evelyn Garfiel, *Service of the Heart* (Hollywood, Calif.: Wilshire, 1958); and Donin, *To Pray As a Jew*, 33.

17. Emil Fackenheim, *Encounters Between Judaism and Modern Philosophy* (New York: Schocken, 1980), 48–49.

18. Thanks to Michael Berger for discussing the rabbinic material with me.

19. Gross, *L'âme de la vie*, 97–98, gives R. Hayyim's reference as *Sanhedrin* 6,5. See *The Mishnah*, trans. Herbert Danby (London: Oxford University Press, 1933), Fourth Division, *Nezikin* ("Damages").

20. Levinas, *Débats sur le langage théologique*, 65. The word "anchoretism" (*anachorèse*) occurs significantly in "Enigma and Phenomenon" (CPP 71).

21. In the discussion following the delivery of his paper, "The Names of God," Levinas specifies: "In what does this anchoretism of the irrepresentable consist? It commands me. The problem of 'what prayer means' is already posed beginning from this commandment. This absence is the movement toward the other." Levinas, *Débats sur le langage théologique*, 56, 65. See also footnote 10 in "'In the Image of God' according to Rabbi Hayim of Volozin" on the prayer dimension of all discourse.

22. Gerson Cohen, "The Blessing of Assimilation in Jewish History," Commencement Address, Hebrew Teachers College, 1966.

23. Franz Rosenzweig, *On Jewish Learning*, ed. N. N. Glatzer (New York: Schocken, 1965), 29.

24. Voici que les batisseurs d'un monde meilleur—mais qui, au nom de la Rasion en viennent à ignorer le Jugement—enferment et emmurent nos fils comme les briques vivantes de'Egypte biblique dont parle le Talmud.

25. See Adriaan Peperzak's discussion of *Totality and Infinity*'s Preface in Peperzak, *To the Other* (West Lafayette, Ind.: Purdue University Press, 1993).

26. *Yashar Shemot* 138b–148a, retold by Louis Ginzberg, *The Legends of the Jews*, vol. 2, trans. Henrietta Szold (Philadelphia, Pa.: Jewish Publication Society, 1980), 299.

27. Et voici que dans ces blocs uniformes, qui devraient préfigurer une humanité égale, se manifeste—étrange germination dans une matière aussi homogène—la Différence, sous laquelle remue, obstinée et difficile, la liberté.

3. Becoming What We Pray: Passion's Gentler Resolutions
Edward F. Mooney

1. George L Pattison, *A Short Introduction to the Philosophy of Religion* (London: SCM , 2001), 142.

2. Henry Bugbee, *The Inward Morning: Philosophical Explorations in Journal Form* (Athens: University of Georgia Press, 1958; reissued 1999). Given

his close ties to Heidegger, Marcel, Thoreau, and Emerson, Bugbee counts as a neglected original "American Continentalist."

3. Bugbee, *Inward Morning*, 225–26 (emphasis in original).

4. See David N. McNeil, "Human Discourse, Eros, and Madness in Plato's Republic," *Review of Metaphysics*, 55, 2 (2001), 235–68.

5. In a related paper, I trace the tension between the setting of prayer and the setting of academic discourse or philosophical argument. See Edward F. Mooney, "Words that Silence as they Build: Against a Boundlessly Loquacious Mind," in *International Kierkegaard Commentary: Kierkegaard's Eighteen Upbuilding Discourses*, ed. Robert L. Perkins (Macon, Ga.: Mercer University Press, 2003).

6. W. E. Hocking takes the soul to be "the self taken in terms of its profoundest passion"; Hocking, "Lectures on Religion," unpublished, 1941. Hocking was Husserl's first American student and taught at Harvard for several decades. He is best known for *The Meaning of God in Human Experience* (New Haven, Conn.: Yale University Press, 1912).

7. Derrida's attestations, "I have lived in prayer" and "I have never stopped [praying] all my life," come from *Circumfession*, in Geoffrey Bennington and Jacques Derrida, *Jacques Derrida* (Chicago: University of Chicago Press, 1993), and are quoted in John D. Caputo, *The Prayers and Tears of Jacques Derrida*, 292.

8. As an instance of the conjoint emergence of group and personal identity, consider the papers collected in the present volume. They attest publicly to the emergence of a "Continental philosophy of religion," a trend whose identity is in the making. Yet the detail of these papers was forged in relatively solitary, prayerlike labor. Nevertheless, the prospect of a group-defining conference spurred on these solitary efforts through which writers shaped their writerly identity. Each serves as facilitating another to its other in the consolidation of mutually forged identity.

9. Søren Kierkegaard, *Sickness unto Death*, trans. Alastair Hannay (London: Penguin, 1989), 70.

10. Ludwig Wittgenstein, *Culture and Value*, trans. Peter Winch (Chicago: University of Chicago Press, 1984) 56 C. Wittgenstein struggled with the view that sets wisdom and faith at odds. His attraction to Kierkegaard, I suspect, was based on a need to find a way to combine faithful passion with reason's critical wit—a combination Kierkegaard seems to have achieved.

11. On the other hand, we have Plato's non-Stoic Socrates of *Phaedrus*. See McNeil, "Human Discourse, Eros, and Madness."

12. On false passion, see Rick Anthony Furtak, *Wisdom in Love: Kierkegaard and the Ancient Quest for Emotional Integrity* (Notre Dame, Ind.: University of Notre Dame, 2005).

13. See the discussion of *thumos*, or "spiritedness," as the essential attribute of the soldier class in the *Republic*.

14. Paul Tillich, *The Dynamics of Faith* (New York: Harper and Row, 1957).

15. Bertrand Russell, *Autobiography*, (London: Routledge, 2000), 9.

16. For a discussion of the essential place of these low-key passions in language use, see Arthur Cody, "Words, You, and Me," *Inquiry* (September 2002), 277–94.

17. See, e.g., Donald Davidson, *Subjective, Intersubjective, Objective* (Oxford: Oxford University Press, 2001), and the critique in Cody, "Words, You, and Me."

18. Melville's *Moby-Dick* can be read as a meditation on the variability of passion in all its transformations. The sea that tempers, constitutes, or destroys all she holds, delivers up Ishmael to tell his tale, and remains beyond the time of his telling. The tale concludes: "Now small fowls flew screaming over the yet yawning gulf, . . . and the great shroud of the sea rolled on as it did five thousand years ago." Is this eternal and eternally turbulent "shroud of the sea" a kind of Derridean desert *khôra*?

19. Russell, *Autobiography*, 9.

20. Søren Kierkegaard, *Concluding Unscientific Postscript*, vol. 1, trans. Howard V. and Edna H. Hong (Princeton, N.J.: Princeton University Press, 1992), 237, translation altered. The passage is discussed in George Pattison, *"Poor Paris!": Kierkegaard's Critique of the Spectacular City*, Kierkegaard Studies Monograph Series (Berlin: de Gruyter, 1999), 97. I adopt Pattison's translation, which renders the Danish *Stemning* as "feeling," rather than Hong's "mood."

21. For a detailed analytic topography, see Robert Roberts, *Emotions* (Cambridge, UK: Cambridge University Press, 2003). See also his discussion of character, passion, emotion, and concern in Roberts, "Existence, Emotion, and Virtue: Classical Themes in Kierkegaard," in *Cambridge Companion to Kierkegaard*, ed. Alastair Hannay and Gordon D. Marino (Cambridge, UK: Cambridge University Press, 1998).

22. See Philip Fisher, *The Vehement Passions* (Princeton, N.J.: Princeton University Press, 2002), 36. I owe much to this remarkable study. Serenity is more a mood than a passion, but I set this subtlety aside. See Roberts, *Emotions*, for a trustworthy map of this varied terrain.

23. See Furtak, *Wisdom in Love*.

24. Our attachments—cognitive, relational, and passional—are constitutive of identity. To be cognitively truthful is to comport oneself properly in the region of claims about events, reasons, and causes. To be relationally truthful is to comport oneself properly in the region of interpersonal exchange. To be passionally truthful is to comport oneself properly in the region of significance. These regions surely interpenetrate.

25. See Annette Baier, *A Progress of Sentiments: A Study of Hume's Treatise* (Cambridge, Mass.: Harvard University Press, 1991).

26. Emily Dickenson writes several revealing love letters to someone who remains utterly unknown.

27. Critics can take petitionary prayer as craven supplication and prayers of praise or gratitude as flatteries, bribes, or payoffs. Prayer then

becomes a gambit in a self-interested bargaining transaction. Yet prayer can also be read as nonselfish celebration of the open sky, deep gratitude for a musical talent bequeathed, or a plea for possibility, even infinite possibility in deep distress, or for consolation in times of grief. In these cases it is surely not selfish in the sense of putting one's own interest above that of others. In fact, in its appeal to a more-than-human source, when that appeal is not strategic or demanding but properly humble, prayer undoes selfishness, arrogance, and pride; it acknowledges a power sufficient to disarm a grasping, aggrandizing self and presents itself disarmed.

28. One might defend a fully warranted claim with passion against those who would deny it; but the passion at issue here is required when a person in relative solitude must hold to a conviction he or she finds objectively uncertain.

29. This is, of course, an adaptation of Kierkegaard's (or Climacus's) *Concluding Unscientific Postscript* definition of faith as "an objective uncertainty held . . . with the most passionate inwardness" (203).

30. Apart from the three major instances of prayer discussed below (Bugbee, *Inward Morning*, 89, 229, and 225), other references to prayer in Bugbee, *Inward Morning* occur on 70, 143, and 214.

31. See Bugbee, *Inward Morning*, 139; and my "A Lyric Philosophy of Place: Henry Bugbee's *The Inward Morning*" *Soundings* (Fall 1999), 519–39, reprinted in Edward F. Mooney, ed., *Wilderness and the Heart: Henry Bugbee's Philosophy of Presence, Place, and Memory* (Athens: University of Georgia Press, 1999).

32. The James remark that the truths of his philosophy are to be justified *ambulando* is quoted in James Conant, "The James/Royce Dispute," in *The Cambridge Companion to William James*, ed. Ruth Anna Putnam (Cambridge, UK: Cambridge University Press, 1997), 205–06.

33. Bugbee, *Inward Morning*, 86.

34. Ibid., 86. The idea of fishing and catching *nothing* must somehow parallel the uncertain castings of prayer, as well as the "no-thingness" of the Divine.

35. Ibid., 229.

36. Ibid., 225.

37. I borrow here from Jack Caputo, *The Prayers and Tears of Jacques Derrida*, xvii–xxvi, who, with Derrida, has revived the language of impossibility as central to accounts of faith. This echoes Kierkegaard's language of "paradox" and "the absurd."

38. See n. 31 above.

4. Prayer as Kenosis
James R. Mensch

1. According to Girard, the process involves "positive feedback." He writes: "the individual who first acts as a model will experience an increase

in his own appropriative urge when he finds himself thwarted by his imitator. And reciprocally. Each becomes the imitator of his own imitator and the model of his own model. Each tries to push aside the obstacle that the other places in his path. Violence is generated by this process; or rather violence is the process itself when two or more partners try to prevent one another from appropriating the object they all desire through physical or other means." René Girard, "Mimesis and Violence: Perspectives in Cultural Criticism," in *The Girard Reader*, ed. James Williams (New York: Crossroad Publishing Company 1996), 9, originally published in *Berkshire Review* 14 (1979):9–19. Because of this feedback, the violence can get out of control.

2. This is the problem Derrida raises at the end of *Gift of Death*. Christianity, because of its promise of a heavenly reward, does not really escape being an economic transaction. In Derrida's words: "All those [who sacrifice] are promised a remuneration . . . a good salary. . . . It is thus that the real heavenly treasure is constituted, on the basis of the salary or price paid for sacrifice or renunciation on earth." Jacques Derrida, *The Gift of Death*, trans. David Wills (Chicago: University of Chicago Press, 1995), 99. The belief here is that "God . . . will pay back your salary, and on an infinitely greater scale" (112). This holds even though Christians deny that their object is a heavenly reword. Such a denial is simply a concealment of the underlying economy. Derrida thus concludes: "Christian justice denies itself and so conserves itself in what seems to exceed it; it remains what it ceases to be, a cruel economy, a commerce, a contract involving debt and credit, sacrifice and vengeance" (113–14). For Derrida, then, Christianity is inherently incapable of escaping the violence of earthly economy. This paper's emphasis on kenosis is a partial attempt to counter his position. It does not, however, bring up the question of the heavenly reward.

3. It is Zeus's wife, in disguise, who persuades Semele to ask Zeus to show himself as he is in return for her favors. Trapped by his promise, Zeus does so.

4. Charlton T. Lewis and Charles Short, eds. *A Latin Dictionary* (London: Oxford University Press, 1966), 1610.

5. Sophocles, "Oedipus at Colonus," lines 36ff, trans. Robert Fitzgerald, in *Sophocles I* (Chicago: University of Chicago Press, 1954), 81.

6. As the Bible relates their initial encounter, "God called to him out of the [burning] bush: 'Moses! Moses!' He answered, 'Here I am.' And He said, 'Do not come closer. Remove your sandals from your feet, for the place on which you stand is holy ground. . . . And Moses hid his face, for he was afraid to look at God." Exod. 3:4–6, in *The Torah, The Five Books of Moses*, 2nd ed. (Philadelphia, Pa.: Jewish Publication Society of America, 1962), 102.

7. The relation to the sacred here is justice. One incarnates God by following the law, i.e., by making it one's "life." Justice, of course, is not just

fairness in Aristotle's sense. It is also present in the admonition, constantly repeated, not to forget the widow and the orphan.

8. Søren Kierkegaard, "Philosophical Fragments," in *Philosophical Fragments and Johannes Climacus*, trans. Howard and Edna Hong (Princeton, N.J.: Princeton University Press, 1987), 30.

9. Ibid., 30.

10. To take the assertion of desertion literally, they are supposed to see God in Christ's being abandoned by God. The vision, in other words, is that of God's self-abandonment; it is one of his complete self-emptying or kenosis.

11. "JB" refers to The Jerusalem Bible (Garden City: Doubleday and Company, 1966).

12. Isaiah, whom John the Baptist quotes about making "straight the way of the Lord," writes about the Messiah, "I (God) have endowed him with my spirit" and "on him the spirit of Yahweh rests" (Isa. 42:1, 11:2, JB, 1208, 1160). The word for "spirit" is once again *ruah*.

13. With this, we can see how Paul can speak of the Incarnation as God's self-emptying and yet assert, in another epistle, "it pleased [God] that all fullness dwell in [Christ]" (Col. 1:19). The "fullness" does not contradict but rather is the result of the emptying that culminates in the Crucifixion. In Paul's eyes, the Crucifixion manifests both Christ's fullness and God's creative action. Thus Paul continues the above statement with the words, "and through him to reconcile all things to Himself making peace through the blood of the Cross." For Paul, then, the "fullness" refers to the fullness of God's love—the love that culminates in "the blood of the Cross." The self-emptying that ends on the Cross becomes, for Paul, the means for the supreme action of the Holy Spirit, which is that of reconciliation.

14. According to the Confucian *Analects*, the golden rule is: "Do not impose on others what you yourself do not desire" (15.24). Other formulations of the rule are: "This is the sum of duty: do naught to others which if done to thee would cause thee pain" (from the Hindu, *Mahabharata*); "What is hateful to you, do not do to your neighbor: that is the whole Torah, all the rest of it is commentary" (from the Jewish *Talmud*, Shabbat 31a); "Whatever is disagreeable to yourself do not do unto others" (from the Zoroastrian, *Shayast-na-Shayast* 13:29); "Hurt not others with that which pains yourself" (from the Buddhist Udana-Varga). The rule can also be formulated positively as in the Confucian precept: "Try your best to treat others as you would wish to be treated yourself, and you will find that this is the shortest way to benevolence" (Mencius VII.A.4). This mirrors the Christian precept to do unto others what you would have them do unto you. Christianity's command to love your neighbor as you love yourself can be taken as an injunction to engage in the sort of empathy that takes self and other as the same. See http://teachingvalues.com/goldenrule.html for a list of quotations on the golden rule.

15. Emmanuel Levinas, "Substitution," in *Basic Philosophical Writings*, ed. A. Peperzak, S. Critchley, and R. Bernasconi (Bloomington: Indiana University Press, 1996), 95.

16. Ibid., 90.

17. Ibid., 95.

18. This includes, according to Levinas, even the other's sins against ourselves. As he said to Philippe Nemo, "You know the sentence in Dostoyevsky: 'We are all guilty of all and for all men before all, and I more than the others.' This is not owing to such or such a guilt which is really mine . . . but because I am responsible for a total responsibility, which answers for all the others and for all in the others, even for their responsibility. . . . [In this sense] I am responsible for the persecutions I undergo." Emmanuel Levinas, *Ethics and Infinity, Conversations with Philippe Nemo*, trans. Richard Cohen (Pittsburgh, Pa.: Duquesne University Press, 1998), 98–99.

19. Girard gives the following general definition: "By a scapegoat effect I mean that strange process through which two or more people are reconciled at the expense of a third party who appears guilty or responsible for whatever ails, disturbs, or frightens the scapegoaters. They feel relieved of their tensions and they coalesce into a more harmonious group." Girard, "Mimesis and Violence," 12. This effect is particularly valuable for societies experiencing the runaway effects of mimetic violence. Here, "the sacrifice [of the scapegoat] serves to protect the entire community from *its own* violence; the elements of dissension scattered throughout the community are drawn to the person of the sacrificial victim and eliminated, at least temporarily, by its sacrifice." Girard, *Girard Reader*, 77; reprinted from *Violence and the Sacred* (Baltimore, Md.: John Hopkins University Press, 1977).

20. According to Girard, "this is what the Gospels alone tell you, that Jesus was innocent. 'We were wrong,' says the New Testament community, 'to the extent that we were involved in that [viz., the sacrifice of Jesus].'" Girard, "A Conversation with René Girard," *Girard Reader*, 274. Thus, "the text places [the collective violence] squarely on those who are responsible for it. To use the expression from the 'Curses,' it lets the violence fall upon the heads of those to whom it belongs." Girard, *Girard Reader*, 168; reprinted from *Things Hidden from the Foundation of the World* (Stanford, Calif.: Stanford University Press, 1987). In doing so, the text undermines the transference of guilt to the scapegoat that is the essential element of the notion of "sacrifice" in natural religion. This is the point behind Girard's assertion: "First of all, it is important to insist that Christ's death was not a sacrificial one. To say that Jesus dies, not as a sacrifice, but in order that there may be no more sacrifices, is to recognize in him the Word of God: 'I wish for mercy and not sacrifices.' . . . the Word of God says no to violence" (Ibid., 184).

21. Levinas, "God and Philosophy" in *Of God who Comes to Mind*, trans. Bettina Bergo (Stanford, Calif.: Stanford University Press, 1998), 68.

22. Ibid., 69.

5. The Prayers and Tears of Friedrich Nietzsche
Bruce Ellis Benson

1. *Aus meinem Leben* (written at the tender age of thirteen) was the first of Nietzsche's autobiographical reflections; *Ecce homo* was his last (completed only days before his collapse on the street).

2. Jacques Derrida characterizes Augustine's *Confessions* as "the great book of tears" in *Memoirs of the Blind: The Self-Portrait and Other Ruins*, trans. Pascale-Anne Brault and Michael Naas (Chicago: University of Chicago Press, 1993), 122.

3. While my argument is not at all that of Giles Fraser, whose central claim is that "Nietzsche is obsessed with the question of human salvation," his reading of Nietzsche as deeply religious is similar to mine. See Giles Fraser, *Redeeming Nietzsche: On the Piety of Unbelief* (London: Routledge, 2002), 2.

4. Carl Pletsch, *Young Nietzsche: Becoming a Genius* (New York: Free Press, 1991), 34.

5. Friedrich Nietzsche, *Nachgelassene Aufzeichnungen, Anfang 1852–Sommer 1858*, ed. Johann Figl, part 1, vol. 1, of *Werke: Kritische Gesamtausgabe*, ed. Giorgio Colli and Mazzino Montinari (Berlin: de Gruyter, 1995), 310. Quoted in R. J. Hollingdale, *Nietzsche: The Man and His Philosophy* (London: Ark, 1985), 19. Given this prayer, what are we to make of Nietzsche's claim that his skepticism "first appeared so early in my life, so spontaneously, so irrepressibly, so much in contradiction to my environment, age, models, origins, that I almost have the right to call it my '*a priori*'"? I take this as the later Nietzsche attempting to "reread" his earlier life in order to see it differently and thus "create" another Nietzsche (or wear a mask). I find it implausible to interpret the thirteen-year-old who prays fervently as wearing a "mask." As I will argue, this wearing of masks is also part of Nietzsche's attempt at a different sort of "prayer." See *Zur Genealogie der Moral*, vol. 5 of *Sämtliche Werke. Kritische Studienausgabe in 15 Bänden*, ed. Giorgio Colli and Mazzino Montinari (Berlin: de Gruyter, 1980), 249 (cited as KSA with volume and page numbers); *On the Genealogy of Morality*, trans. Maudemarie Clark and Alan J. Swensen (Indianapolis, Ind.: Hackett, 1998), Preface, sect. 3 (cited with essay number and section number).

6. See Fraser's discussion of Nietzsche's pietism in *Redeeming Nietzsche*, 38–44.

7. Hollingdale prefaces his citation of this prayer by saying "the intensity of [Nietzsche's] religious feeling is startling." But what else would one expect from Nietzsche than intensity, whether for matters religious or otherwise?

8. Much of Nietzsche's poetry functions as a sort of prayer (less obviously in this poem but very clearly so in the next two).

9. Quoted in Philip Grundlehner, *The Poetry of Friedrich Nietzsche* (Oxford: Oxford University Press, 1986), 15–17.

10. The connection here to Ludwig Feuerbach's *The Essence of Christianity* seems obvious, though Nietzsche had not read Feuerbach at this point.

11. *Werke*, part 1, vol. 1, 460–61; *Poetry of Friedrich Nietzsche*, 32–34.

12. *Poetry of Friedrich Nietzsche*, 25–26.

13. Lou Salomé, *Nietzsche*, trans. Siegfried Mandel (Urbana, Ill.: University of Illinois Press, 2001), 88.

14. KSA 13:265–67; Friedrich Nietzsche, *The Will to Power*, trans. Walter Kaufmann and R. J. Hollingdale (New York: Random House, 1967), sect. 1052.

15. KSA 1:30; *The Birth of Tragedy and Other Writings*, trans. Ronald Speirs (Cambridge, UK: Cambridge University Press, 1999), sect. 1.

16. Note that Nietzsche was not acquainted with Schopenhauer when he wrote *"Dem unbekannten Gott."*

17. In *Birth of Tragedy* itself there is an *implicit* connection. But in the "Attempt at a Self-Criticism," Nietzsche writes: "Indeed the whole book acknowledges only an artist's meaning (and hidden meaning) behind all that happens—a 'god,' if you will, but certainly only an utterly unscrupulous and amoral artist-god." KSA 1:17; *Birth of Tragedy*, Preface, sect. 5.

18. See Graham Parkes, *Composing the Soul: Reaches of Nietzsche's Psychology* (Chicago: University of Chicago Press, 1994), 334–46.

19. KSA 6:374; *Ecce Homo*, trans. Walter Kaufmann, in *Basic Writings of Nietzsche*, ed. Walter Kaufmann (New York: Random House, 1966), "Why I Am a Destiny," sect. 9.

20. KSA 2:15–16; *Human, All Too Human: A Book for Free Spirits*, trans. R. J. Hollingdale (Cambridge, UK: Cambridge University Press, 1986), Preface, sect. 2–3.

21. KSA 5:59; *Beyond Good and Evil*, trans. Judith Norman (Cambridge, UK: Cambridge University Press, 2002), sect. 42.

22. KSA 3:574, 577; *The Gay Science*, trans. Josefine Nauckhoff (Cambridge, UK: Cambridge University Press, 2001), sect. 344.

23. Martin Heidegger, "The Word of Nietzsche: 'God Is Dead,'" in *The Question Concerning Technology and Other Essays*, trans. William Lovitt (New York: Harper and Row, 1977), 74. Heidegger has been criticized for (naïvely) basing his charge on the posthumously published *Will to Power*. Although Heidegger's contention that this "text" (actually just a sampling of Nietzsche's notes, collected and published by Nietzsche's philosophically challenged sister) represents Nietzsche's mature thought is problematic, one cannot simply dismiss the texts that compose *Will to Power*, nor Heidegger's point.

24. KSA 4:13; *Thus Spoke Zarathustra*, trans. Walter Kaufman, in *The Portable Nietzsche*, ed. Walter Kaufman (New York: Viking, 1954), part I, "Zarathustra's Prologue," sect. 2 (cited as *Zarathustra*, with part, section title, and section number).

25. KSA 4:15; *Zarathustra* I, "Zarathustra's Prologue," sect. 3.

26. KSA 4:31; *Zarathustra* I, "Of the Three Metamorphoses."

27. KSA 3:92; *Daybreak: Thoughts on the Prejudices of Morality*, trans. R. J. Hollingdale (Cambridge, UK: Cambridge University Press, 1982), sect. 103.

28. KSA 4:189; *Zarathustra* II, "On the Stillest Hour."

29. Kathleen Higgins makes a similar claim in saying that "new festivals, new songs, new recitations are among the means we can use to bridge the chasm of nihilism that separates traditional Christian faith from a newly grounded health, which locates meaning within this life." She also sees prayer as part of Nietzsche's strategy. Yet my point diverges from Higgins in an important sense. For my question is the extent to which Nietzsche is still indebted to Christian faith (and so has not simply left it behind and merely adopted its rituals). See her *Comic Relief: Nietzsche's* Gay Science (Oxford: Oxford University Press, 2000), 35.

30. Note that this section was originally the ending to *Thus Spoke Zarathustra*. As such, its function was precisely that of an "amen" at the end of a prayer. Only later did Nietzsche append the fourth section.

31. Eternity is effectively equivalent to Life here. To love the "eternal return" is to love Life.

32. One finds this same sort of belief mingled with unbelief in the father who asks Jesus to remove an unclean spirit from his daughter: "I believe; help my unbelief" (Mark 9:24).

33. KSA 3:527; *Gay Science*, sect. 285.

34. KSA 3:527; *Gay Science*, sect. 284.

35. KSA 3:528; *Gay Science*, sect. 285.

36. KSA 4:285; *Zarathustra* II, "The Other Dancing Song," sect. 2.

37. One could even read the title of Nietzsche's second essay of his *Untimely Meditations*—"On the Use and Disadvantage of History for Life"—precisely in this sense.

38. KSA 6:63; Friedrich Nietzsche, *Twilight of the Idols*, trans. Richard Polt (Indianapolis, Ind.: Hackett, 1997), "Epigrams and Arrows," #26.

39. Heidegger argues that "will to power" functions as an ultimate metaphysical category for Nietzsche. The term "will to power" is sketchy at best, even though it is a term that appears throughout his writings. Here I will completely avoid the issue of the "will to power." As I read it, the "will to power" just *is* Life for Nietzsche. But that claim would require argumentation as well as explanation.

40. KSA 4:408; *Zarathustra* IV, "The Sign."

41. Although an earlier version of this text appears in *Zarathustra* IV, "The Magician," I quote here from Nietzsche's revised version that appears in *Dionysos-Dithyramben*. The story—particularly of this revised version—is complicated, but I will pass over those complications here. See KSA 6:398–401; *Dithyrambs of Dionysus*, trans. R. J. Hollingdale (London: Anvil, 1984), 59–65.

42. This is why the ugliest man says: "The god who saw everything, *even man*: this god had to die! Man could not *endure* that such a witness should live." KSA 4:331; *Zarathustra* IV, "The Ugliest Man."

43. KSA 4:318; *Zarathustra* IV, "The Magician," sect. 2.

44. While Nietzsche uses only the French term "*décadence*," since the English "decadence" is virtually equivalent (and certainly captures the senses in which Nietzsche uses the French term), I will simply substitute "decadence" for "*décadence*."

45. Although Nietzsche begins using the French term "*décadence*" in his published works only in 1888, it appears in all of his texts written in that year — *The Case of Wagner, Twilight of the Idols, The Anti-Christ, Ecce Homo,* and even *Nietzsche contra Wagner* (which is mainly a collection of earlier comments against Wagner).

46. *Entartung* appears in KSA 4:98; *Zarathustra* I, "On the Gift-Giving Virtue," sect. 1.

47. KSA 6:11; *The Case of Wagner*, Preface, in *Basic Writings of Nietzsche*. Given such a strong claim, it is surprising how little attention has been paid to this aspect of his thought; but see Daniel W. Conway, *Nietzsche's Dangerous Game: Philosophy in the Twilight of the Idols* (Cambridge, UK: Cambridge University Press, 1997), chap. 2.

48. KSA 6:133–34; *Twilight of the Idols*, "Raids of an Untimely Man," sect. 35.

49. KSA 6:72; *Twilight of the Idols*, "The Problem of Socrates," sect. 11.

50. KSA 6:11 *Case of Wagner*, Preface.

51. KSA 6:12 *Case of Wagner*, Preface.

52. Causality of the will is labeled by Nietzsche as one of "the four great errors"; KSA 6:90; *Twilight of the Idols*, "The Four Great Errors," sect. 3. Elsewhere, he says: "'the doer' is simply fabricated into the doing"; KSA 5:279; *On the Genealogy of Morals* I:13.

53. KSA 6:42; *Case of Wagner*, Postscript.

54. KSA 6:152; *Twilight of the Idols*, "Raids of an Untimely Man," sect. 49.

55. KSA 6:264; *Ecce Homo*, "Why I Am So Wise," sect. 1.

56. Roughly speaking, Nietzsche equates the "Evangel" with the historical Jesus and the "Crucified" with the Christ of faith.

57. Note that Nietzsche characterizes the free spirit as one that "*does not negate anymore.*" See KSA 6:152; *Twilight of the Idols*, "Raids of an Untimely Man," sect. 49.

58. KSA 6:203–07; *The Antichrist*, in *The Portable Nietzsche*, sects. 32–35. Nietzsche's depiction of the Evangel is, to put it mildly, eccentric. Although he was well aware of higher criticism and "the quest for the historical Jesus," his choice of what counts an "authentic" portrait of the historical figure Jesus (versus what is added by later tradition, particularly Paul) seems to be informed by nothing more than his own intuitive sense of the Evangel versus the Crucified.

59. KSA 6:208; *Antichrist*, sect. 36.

60. KSA 6:257; *Ecce Homo*, Preface, sect. 1.

61. KSA 6:258; *Ecce Homo*, Preface, sect. 2.

62. KSA 6:278; *Ecce Homo*, "Why I Am So Clever," sect. 1.

63. KSA 6:287; Ibid., sect. 4.

64. After defining the free spirit as one who has "a glad and trusting fatalism" that "everything redeems and affirms itself," Nietzsche goes on to say that "such a faith is the highest of all possible faiths: I have baptized it with the name of *Dionysus*." See KSA 6:152; *Twilight of the Idols*, "Raids of an Untimely Man," sect. 49.

65. KSA 3:583; *Gay Science*, sect. 347.

66. KSA 6:348; *Ecce Homo*, "Thus Spoke Zarathustra," sect. 8.

6. Attention and Responsibility: The Work of Prayer
Norman Wirzba

1. Simone Weil, *Gravity and Grace* (London: Routledge, 1963), 107.

2. "Attention consists of suspending our thought, leaving it detached, empty, and ready to be penetrated by the object." Simone Weil, *Waiting for God* (New York: Harper and Row, 1951), 111.

3. Søren Kierkegaard, *Concluding Unscientific Postscript to Philosophical Fragments*, vol. 1, ed. & trans. Howard V. Hong and Edna H. Hong (Princeton, N.J.: Princeton University Press, 1992), 201. It should be noted that in terms of the overall Kierkegaardian authorship, the work of inwardness is not complete without the life of discipleship. For a helpful discussion of the later works as they relate to the Climacus texts, see Merold Westphal, "Kierkegaard's Teleological Suspension of Religiousness B," in *Foundations of Kierkegaard's Vision of Community*, ed. George B. Connell and C. Stephen Evans (Atlantic Highlands, N.J.: Humanities Press, 1992), 110–29.

4. Thomas Merton. *Contemplative Prayer* (Garden City, N.Y.: Image Books, 1969), 23, 67.

5. For a description (one among many) of the significance of historical consciousness for self-understanding, see Pierre Manent, *The City of Man* (Princeton, N.J.: Princeton University Press, 1998). For Manent, the uniquely modern inspiration finds its fulfillment in Kant's moral philosophy. Speaking of the quintessential modern individual, Manent writes: "he can now think that he is neither a creature of God nor a part of Nature, that he is in short born of himself, the child of his own liberty" (189).

6. For further discussion on the significance of the denial of creation and its many cultural effects, see my *The Paradise of God: Renewing Religion in an Ecological Age* (New York: Oxford University Press, 2003), esp. chaps. 2 and 5. See also Nicholas Lash, who writes: "For sixteen centuries, Christian discipleship had been understood as creaturely dependence transformed into friendship: from being subjects of the king of heaven we became his kin. . . . By the end of the seventeenth century, 'believing in God' . . . had

become a matter of supposing there is, outside the world we know, a large and powerful entity called 'God.'" Lash, *The Beginning and the End of "Religion"* (Cambridge, UK: Cambridge University Press, 1996), 168–69.

7. Remembering with Aristotle (*Nicomachean Ethics*, Book II) that it is through the cultivation of specific, practical habits that moral (but also spiritual) dispositions grow and flourish.

8. If the biblical prophets are to be believed, God will not hear the prayers of the violent and dishonest: "When you stretch out your hands, I will hide my eyes from you; even though you make many prayers, I will not listen; your hands are full of blood." Authentic prayer is realized in a life of justice. And so the prophet continues: "Wash yourselves; make yourselves clean; remove the evil of your doings from before my eyes; cease to do evil, learn to do good; seek justice, rescue the oppressed, defend the orphan, plead for the widow" (Isa. 1:15–17).

9. Lash, *Beginning and the End of "Religion,"* 75–82.

10. Immanuel Kant, *Critique of Pure Reason*, trans. Norman Kemp Smith (New York: St. Martin's Press, 1929), 22–23 (Bxvii). If we turn to phenomenology—with its rallying cry "to the things themselves!"—the ubiquity of the controlling "I" remains. Speaking of the givenness of phenomena, Jean-Luc Marion observes, "transcendental or not, the phenomenological 'I' remains the beneficiary, and therefore the witness and even the judge, of the given appearance; it falls to the 'I' to measure what does and does not give itself intuitively, within what limits, according to what horizon, following what intention, essence and signification. Even if it shows itself on the basis of itself, the phenomenon can do so only by allowing itself to be lead back, and therefore reduced, to the 'I.'" Marion, "The Saturated Phenomenon," in *Philosophy Today* 40, 1 (Spring 1996), 106.

11. Both quotes are taken from Heidegger's 1923 lecture course, *Ontology—The Hermeneutics of Facticity*, trans. John van Buren (Bloomington: Indiana University Press, 1999), 65, 79 (emphasis in original).

12. Though Heidegger would complain about the technological reduction of the world to "standing reserve"—in the 1953 essay "The Question Concerning Technology," in *Basic Writings*, ed. David Farrell Krell, rev. ed. (San Francisco: Harper, 1993), 311–41—his own work represents a missed opportunity to elaborate on the practical conditions necessary for a compassionate embrace of the world. For a description of how Heidegger's early work could have been infused with a charitable impulse see my essay, "Love's Reason: From Heideggerian 'Care' to Christian 'Charity,'" in *Postmodern Philosophy and Christian Thought*, ed. Merold Westphal (Bloomington: Indiana University Press, 1999), 246–67.

13. Zygmunt Bauman, *Liquid Modernity* (Cambridge, UK: Polity, 2000), 163. See also his earlier work, *Globalization: The Human Consequences* (New York: Columbia University Press, 1998).

14. Here we should recall Henry Bugbee's subtle account of experience and understanding: "Experience is permeated with meaning by invasion. If

our experience is 'ours,' we are not the possessors of its meaning. We do not predict and control the ebb and flow of meaning in our experience. . . . Experience is our undergoing, our involvement in the world, our lending or withholding of ourselves, keyed to our responsiveness, our sensibility, our alertness or our deadness." Bugbee, *The Inward Morning: A Philosophical Exploration in Journal Form* (Athens: University of Georgia Press, 1976), 41.

15. Nicholas Lash, *Believing Three Ways in One God: A Reading of the Apostles' Creed* (Notre Dame, Ind.: University of Notre Dame Press, 1992), 104. As Lash also says, however, God's delight is lived as travail, in a world of suffering in need of forgiveness and resurrection. "God's garden, made 'in the beginning,' does not lie behind us, but ahead of us, in hope, and, in the meantime, all around us as our place of work" (124).

16. "These all look to you to give them their food in due season; when you give to them, they gather it up; when you open your hand, they are filled with good things. When you hide your face, they are dismayed; when you take away their breath, they die and return to their dust. When you send forth your spirit [breath], they are created; and you renew the face of the ground" (Ps. 104:27–30).

17. Wendell Berry, "People, Land, and Community," in *The Art of the Commonplace: The Agrarian Essays of Wendell Berry*, ed. Norman Wirzba (Washington, D.C.: Counterpoint, 2002), 187.

18. Bugbee, *Inward Morning*, 76.

19. Marion, "Saturated Phenomenon," 120.

20. Wendell Berry, *The Unsettling of America: Culture & Agriculture* (San Francisco: Sierra Club Books, 1977), 111.

7. Irigaray's *Between East and West*: Breath, Pranayama, and the Phenomenology of Prayer
Cleo McNelly Kearns

1. Luce Irigaray, *Between East and West: From Singularity to Community*, trans. Stephen Pluháček (New York: Columbia University Press, 2002), 50.

2. Aristotle, *On Interpretation*, 17 A 4–5.

3. These qualities of openness and flexibility do not pertain only to oral communication. Spelling, punctuation, page layout, and book design, for instance, are also implicated in the rhythms of breathing. What we see can catch the breath or yield a sigh of relief as sharply as what we hear.

4. Irigaray does not hesitate, for instance, to say that the body may be "deified" (62), a term that would raise serious problems for the theologian in any of the monotheisms and that may, in fact, be misleading in terms of several schools of yoga as well.

5. See Julia Kristeva, *Desire in Language*, trans. Alice A. Jardine (New York: Columbia University Press, 1980). See also the discussion of Irigaray and Kristeva in, among other places, *Feminist Theologies and French Feminisms*, ed. Maggie Kim, Susan Simonaitis, and Susan St. Ville (Chicago: Fortress Press, 1994).

6. "The role of woman as lover is in some way superior and more inclusive compared with that of the mother. She makes the breath of man pass from natural vitality or from fabricating energy to interior life" (Irigaray, 89).

7. The understanding of the *Yoga Sutra* in the anglophone world has until recently been shaped primarily by linguistics and by scholarly translation, from the work of James Woods, Harvard's leading orientalist at the turn of the twentieth century, through the collaborative version of Sri Purohit Swami and the poet W. B. Yeats, to the more up-to-date translations and critical commentaries of Barbara Stoller Miller and Georg Feuerstein. In the past few years, however, a number of practitioners have also tried their hands at renditions in English, from the learned Sri Swami Satchidananda to the fluent and accomplished Mukanda Stiles. Cf. James Houghton Woods, trans., *The Yoga-System of Patanjali: Or the Ancient Hindu Doctrine of Concentration of Mind,* Harvard Oriental Series, vol. 17 (Cambridge, Mass.: Harvard University Press, 1914); Shree Purohit Swami, *Aphorisms of Yoga by Bhagwan Shree Patanjali,* with introduction by W. B. Yeats (London: Faber and Faber, 1938); Georg Feuerstein, *Yoga: The Technology of Ecstasy* (Los Angeles: Tarcher Books, 1989); Barbara Stoler Miller, *Yoga, Disciplines of Freedom: the Yoga Sutra Attributed to Patanjali* (Berkeley: University of California Press, 1996); Swami Satchidananda, *The Yoga Sutras of Patanjali* (Yogaville, Va.: Integral Yoga Publications, 1990); B. K. S. Iyengar, *Light on the Yoga-Sutras of Patanjali* (San Francisco: Aquarian Press, 1993); Mukanda Stiles, *Yoga-Sutras of Patanjali* (New York: Samuel Weiser, 2002). Written sources, moreover, cannot entirely convey the range of meanings the breath has in the context of a yoga practice, not because these meanings are ineffable necessarily and not because they operate always as some logocentric or quasi-mystical ground from which all written expressions are but a falling off, but because they are subtle and they require a vocabulary which has not yet been fully developed in English.

8. T. S. Eliot, *After Strange Gods: A Primer of Modern Heresy* (London: Faber and Faber, 1934), 41.

9. The "ayama" part of pranayama, "control," also points toward a stance and way of moving that hovers somewhere between mastery and surrender, toward a kind of decentering of the active will vis-à-vis the breath that is at once engaged and accepting. See Richard Rosen, *The Yoga of Breath: A Step by Step Guide* (Boston: Shambhala Press, 2002), 14–15.

10. Cf. Rosen, chap. 11, "The Qualities of the Breath," 122–49.

11. I do not mean to suggest that yoga cannot provide its own form of destructive mastery and will to power, merely that its practice can provide an experiential basis for alternative views of subjectivity.

12. I would want to suggest, for instance, that at the theological level the values Irigaray so nobly wishes to defend, especially the value of recognition of the limit of the self, are in fact better served by a prayer life based

on the God-human difference and the "twoness" encoded in monotheism than on what I see as her tendency to reify gender.

13. B. Keith Putt, " 'Too Deep for Words': The Conspiracy of a Divine 'Soliloquy,' " in this volume.

14. For a fuller discussion of Irigaray's interest in Mary, see Tina Beattie, *God's Mother/Eve's Advocate: A Marian Narrative of Women's Salvation* (New York: Continuum Books, 2002).

8. Heidegger and the Prospect of a Phenomenology of Prayer
Benjamin Crowe

1. While Heidegger does not use this example, I think that Feuerbach's account of the development of religion illustrates what this might be like. Feuerbach, of course, describes the genesis and development of Christianity by means of a framework based on some assumptions about human self-knowledge. See George Eliot, trans., *The Essence of Christianity* (Amherst, N.Y.: Prometheus, 1989).

2. *Problemsgeschichte* is the name usually given to a particular neo-Kantian way of interpreting the history of philosophy. On this view, the history of philosophy records the attempts of successive thinkers to answer genuinely timeless questions of metaphysics and epistemology.

3. This approach, too, is characteristic of neo-Kantianism, which attempted to ground claims about "nonscientific" aspects of culture, such as morality or religion, on a system of a priori values. One can discern the influence of this approach in Rudolf Otto's principal work. See John W. Harvey, trans., *The Idea of the Holy* (Oxford: Oxford University Press, 1958). In this work, Otto employs the results of a descriptive analysis of religious experience to articulate the nature of "the holy" as an "*a priori* category of value."

4. Dilthey employed the quasi-romantic category of "personality" in his historical inquiries into religious figures such as Luther and Zwingli (see GS2 41, 54).

5. This attack on psychological interpretation is continued in an appendix that contains other significant methodological reflections (G60 136–37).

6. The "struggle" in question, in Galatians, is the "struggle" over the nature of Christian life as something distinct from other forms of Second Temple Judaism, particularly those which placed great emphasis on the observance of holiness codes in everyday life.

7. Heidegger uses the Lutheran formula, the "scandal of the cross," to express his conception of the content of the proclamation (G60 144).

8. The many publications of Hal Lindsay and other fundamentalist dispensationalists testify to the continuing relevance of Paul's admonitions and to the continued need properly to understand the meaning of Christian eschatology. Jürgen Moltmann, who has himself contributed to such an understanding, judges this "new apocalypticism of American fundamentalists"

as "hardly more serious than Batman fantasies." See Moltmann, *The Coming of God: Christian Eschatology*, trans. Margaret Kohl (Minneapolis, Minn.: Fortress Press, 1996), 360.

9. For an attempt as such an account, see Oscar Cullmann, *Das Gebet im Neuen Testament* (Tübingen, Ger.: J. C. B. Mohr [Paul Siebeck], 1994); English translation by John Bowden, *Prayer in the New Testament* (Minneapolis, Minn.: Fortress Press, 1995).

10. This claim is by no means peculiar to Heidegger and seems to me to be entirely correct. See, e.g., Christopher Rowland, *Christian Origins: From Messianic Movement to Christian Religion* (Minneapolis, Minn.: Augsburg, 1985), 113–16.

9. Edith Stein: Prayer and Interiority
Terrence C. Wright

1. Edith Stein, *Life in a Jewish Family 1891–1916: An Autobiography*, vol. 1 of *The Collected Works of Edith Stein*, trans. Josephine Koeppel (Washington, D.C.: ICS, 1986), 148.

2. Jude P. Doughery, "Edith Stein's Conversion: How a Jewish Philosopher Became a Catholic Saint," *Crisis* 10:11 (1992):39–43.

3. Edmund Husserl to Arnold Metzger, 4 September 1919, trans. Erazim Kohák, in *Husserl: Shorter Works*, ed. Peter McCormick and Frederick Elliston (Notre Dame, Ind.: University of Notre Dame Press, 1981), 360.

4. Adelgundis Jaegerschmid, "Conversations with Edmund Husserl, 1931–1938," trans. Marcus Brainard, *New Yearbook for Phenomenology and Phenomenological Philosophy* 1 (2001):342.

5. See, e.g., the note to sect. 51 of *Ideas I*.

6. Edmund Husserl, *Ideas Pertaining to a Pure Phenomenology and to a Phenomenological Philosophy: First Book*, trans. F. Kersten (The Hague: Martinus Nijhoff, 1983), 134.

7. Edmund Husserl to Wilhelm Dilthey, 5–6 July 1911, trans. Jeffner Allen, in *Husserl: Shorter Works*, 206.

8. Ibid., 206.

9. Edmund Husserl, E III 9, 30, quoted in James Hart, "A Précis of an Husserlian Philosophical Theology" in *Essays in Phenomenological Theology*, ed. Steven Laycock and James Hart (Albany: State University of New York Press, 1986), 148.

10. Ibid., 149.

11. Edith Stein, "The Prayer of the Church," in *The Hidden Life: Hagiographic Essays, Meditations, Spiritual Texts*, trans. Waltraut Stein, vol. 4 of *The Collected Works of Edith Stein*, ed. L. Gelber and R. Leuven (Washington, D.C.: ICS, 1992), 8.

12. Ibid., 11.

13. Ibid., 16.

14. Ibid., 17.

15. Edith Stein to Sr. Callista Kopf, 12 February 1928, trans. Josephine Koeppel, in *Self-Portrait in Letters: 1916–1942*, vol. 5 of *The Collected Works of Edith Stein*, ed. L. Gelber and R. Leuven (Washington, D.C.: ICS, 1992), 54.

16. Ibid., 54–55.

17. Edith Stein, *Finite and Eternal Being*, trans. Kurt Reinhardt, vol. 9 of *The Collected Works of Edith Stein*, ed. L. Gelber and R. Leuven (Washington, D.C.: ICS, 2002), xxviii.

18. Ibid., 430.

19. Ibid., 373.

20. Ibid., 373.

21. Ibid., 433.

22. Ibid., 433.

23. Ibid., 437.

24. Ibid., 439–40.

25. Edith Stein, *The Science of the Cross*, trans. Josephine Koeppel, vol. 6 of *The Collected Works of Edith Stein*, ed. L. Gelber and R. Leuven (Washington, D.C.: ICS Publications, 2002), 159 (emphasis in original).

26. Edith Stein, *Finite and Eternal Being*, 440.

27. Ibid., 442.

28. Ibid., xxxi.

29. See Edith Stein, *Martin Heideggers Existentialphilosophie*, in *Welt und Person*, *Edith Steins Werke 6* (Louvain: Éditions Nauwelaerts, 1962). This piece was initially written as an appendix to *Finite and Eternal Being* but was published separately. See also Antonio Calcagno, "*Die Fülle oder das Nichts?* Edith Stein and Martin Heidegger on the Question of Being," *American Catholic Philosophical Quarterly*, 74, 2 (2000).

30. Edmund Husserl, *Cartesian Meditations: An Introduction to Phenomenology*, trans. Dorian Cairns (The Hague: Martinus Nijhoff, 1977), 157.

31. St. Augustine, *In Io* 15, 25. Quoted in Stein, *Finite and Eternal Being*, 443–44.

10. "Too Deep for Words": The Conspiracy of a Divine "Soliloquy"
B. Keith Putt

1. John Caputo insists that Derrida and deconstruction have been blamed for ruining philosophy and comparative literature, for "undermining the law of gravity"(!), and for complicity in Holocaust revisionism. Caputo. *Deconstruction in a Nutshell: A Conversation with Jacques Derrida* (New York: Fordham University Press, 1997), 41. He terms the hyperbolic and unfounded criticisms of Derrida the "axiomatics of indignation" (37).

2. "The constancy of God in my life is called by other names, so that I rightly pass for an atheist"; Jacques Derrida, *Circumfession*, in Jacques Derrida and Geoffrey Bennington, *Jacques Derrida* (Chicago: University of Chicago Press, 1993), 155.

3. "I am addressing myself here to God, the only one I take as a witness, without yet knowing what these sublime words mean, and this grammar, and *to*, and *witness*, and *God*, and *take*, take God, and not only do I pray, as I have never stopped doing all my life." "If I ought to tell them that I pray, and describe how that could happen, according to what idiom and what rite, on one's knees or standing up, in front of whom or what books, for if you knew, G., my experience of prayers, you would know everything." Derrida, *Circumfession*, 56, 188.

4. "You have spent your life inviting, calling, promising, hoping sighing dreaming, convoking invoking provoking." Derrida, *Circumfession*, 314.

5. Jacques Derrida, *Monolingualism; or, the Prosthesis of Origin*, trans. Patrick Mensah (Stanford, Calif.: Stanford University Press, 1998), 20–21.

6. John D. Caputo, *The Prayers and Tears of Jacques Derrida: Religion without Religion* (Bloomington: Indiana University Press, 1997), 256 (emphasis in original).

7. Ibid., 298. Caputo also reminds Derrida's readers that this "yes" should not be construed as a master word or some species of an *Urwort*. Yet it does function as a quasi-transcendental that grounds the possibility and impossibility of language, opening and closing every word, manifesting the "primary affirmation" that founds and funds every linguistic event (256).

8. John D. Caputo, *On Religion* (New York: Routledge, 2001), 130; Caputo, *Prayers and Tears*, 297.

9. Jacques Derrida, "How to Avoid Speaking: Denials," in *Derrida and Negative Theology*, ed. Harold Coward and Toby Foshay (Albany: State University of New York, 1992), 111.

10. Caputo, *Prayers and Tears*, 38–39.

11. Jacques Derrida, "Derrida's Response to Regina M. Schwartz," in *Questioning God*, ed. John D. Caputo, Mark Dooley, and Michael J. Scanlon (Bloomington: Indiana University Press, 2001), 230–31.

12. John D. Caputo, "Richard Kearney's Enthusiasm: A Philosophical Exploration on *The God Who May Be*," *Modern Theology* 18 (January 2002), 92.

13. Derrida, "How to Avoid Speaking," 116–17.

14. Caputo, *On Religion*, 128.

15. Caputo, *Prayers and Tears*, 293.

16. Jacques Derrida, "Faith and Knowledge: The Two Sources of 'Religion' at the Limits of Reason Alone," in Jacques Derrida, *Acts of Religion*, ed. Gil Anidjar (New York: Routledge, 2002), 47.

17. Derrida, "Derrida's Response to Regina M. Schwarz," 231.

18. Derrida, "How to Avoid Speaking," 296. See also Derrida, "Faith and Knowledge," 56.

19. Derrida, "Faith and Knowledge," 83.

20. Caputo, *Prayers and Tears*, 298.

21. Ibid., 22–23.

22. Caputo, *On Religion*, 11.

23. Caputo, *Prayers and Tears*, 40–41.

24. Jean-Louis Chrétien, "The Wounded Word: Phenomenology of Prayer," in Dominique Janicaud et al., *Phenomenology and the "Theological Turn": The French Debate* (New York: Fordham University Press, 2000), 153.

25. Ibid., 157.

26. Ibid., 164.

27. Ibid., 175.

28. Calvin Schrag uses "eschatological preenactment" as a third alternative between a realized eschatology that depends too heavily upon identity and interiority and a transcendent eschatology that overemphasizes difference and exteriority. See Schrag, *God as Otherwise Than Being: Toward a Semantics of the Gift* (Evanston, Ill.: Northwestern University Press, 2002), 144.

29. "For we know that the whole creation groans and suffers the pains of childbirth together until now. And not only this, but also we ourselves, having the first fruits of the Spirit, even we ourselves groan within ourselves, waiting eagerly for *our* adoption as sons, the redemption of our body."

30. "For in hope we have been saved, but hope that is seen is not hope; for who hopes for what he *already* sees? But if we hope for what we do not see, with perseverance we wait eagerly for it."

31. Jean-François Lyotard, *The Confession of Augustine*, trans. Richard Beardsworth (Stanford, Calif.: Stanford University Press, 2000), 57.

32. Jacques Derrida, *On the Name*, ed. Thomas Dutoit, trans. David Wood, John P. Leavey, and Ian McLeod (Stanford, Calif.: Stanford University Press, 1995), 76.

33. Chrétien characterizes all prayer as related to "the deep": "he who addresses himself to God always does so *de profundis*, from the depths of his manifest distress, from the depths of his sin." Later, he intimates that the "profundity" of prayer includes not just the wounds of distress but also of joy, which raises the issue of the absurdity of grace. Chrétien, "Wounded Word," 157, 175.

34. Paul Ricoeur, "Lamentation as Prayer," in *Thinking Biblically: Exegetical and Hermeneutical Studies*, ed. André LaCocque and Paul Ricoeur, trans. David Pellauer (Chicago: University of Chicago Press, 1998), 212.

35. Chrétien, "Wounded Word," 147.

36. Ricoeur, "Lamentation as Prayer," 213.

37. Ibid., 215; see also Paul Ricoeur, *Figuring the Sacred*, ed. Mark I. Wallace, trans. David Pellauer (Minneapolis, Minn.: Fortress Press, 1995), 254.

38. Ricoeur, "Lamentation as Prayer," 231–32. Of course, Ricoeur is not alone in emphasizing the importance of lament in Hebrew theology. The Old Testament theologian Walter Brueggemann explains lament as a "bold movement and voice from Israel's side which does not blindly and docilely

accept, but means to have its dangerous say, even in the face of God." Brueggemann, "A Shape for Old Testament Theology, II: Embrace of Pain," *Catholic Biblical Quarterly* 47 (1985), 400. He calls it an alternative to the "common theology" that Israel shared with other ancient cultures. Unlike them, Israel had the courage to question God as to the legitimacy of the structures of reality, even to the point of lodging a complaint against God's apparent inactivity and often silent affirmation of radical injustice and needless suffering. But such a protest opens the future as the realm of a coming response and messianic desire for justice, healing, and comfort (ibid., 397–98).

39. Kevin Hart, "The Experience of God," in *The Religious*, ed. John D. Caputo (Oxford: Blackwell Publishers, 2002), 171.

40. Derrida claims that meaning "is the phenomenality of the phenomenon." Jacques Derrida, *Positions*, trans. Alan Bass (Chicago: University of Chicago Press, 1981), 30. Consequently, if the divine "soliloquy" manifests no discernible meaning, then no phenomenality obtains to ground a phenomenology of the Spirit's praying. Of course, one could postulate that God might engage in a divine phenomenology of the Spirit's prayer on the basis that God transcends the restrictions of human intentionality. However, were such a divine phenomenology possible, we could only know it under the conditions of human consciousness, which would necessitate some revelatory utterance that escapes the depths of the unutterable.

41. This nomenclature comes from the creative theological metaxology of Richard Kearney, who seeks a "middle way" between a purely ontotheological perspective on God and a purely eschatological one. He imagines God as mediated through Being but only as the God who is not yet who God wishes to be. The God encountered in any religious experience will be God as *Peut-Etre*, the God Who May Be in response to God's interaction with humanity. Kearney predicates this "Divine Perhaps" on a revisionist reading of the Tetragrammaton in Exodus 3:14: "'*ehyeh 'asher 'ehyeh*" as "I Will Be Who I Will Be," not as "I Am Who I Am." For Kearney, this Exodic naming "signals an inextricable communication between God and humans, a commitment to a shared history of 'becoming.' . . . God may henceforth be recognized as someone who 'becomes with' us, someone dependent on us as we are on Him. God's relation with mortals is, in other words, less one of conceptuality than of covenant." Kearney, "The God Who May Be," in *Questioning God*, ed. John D. Caputo and Michael J. Scanlon (Bloomington: Indiana University Press, 2001), 161. See also Kearney, *The God Who May Be: A Hermeneutics of Religion* (Bloomington: Indiana University Press, 2001); Kearney, *Poétique du possible: Phénoménologie herméneutique de la figuration* (Paris: Beauchesne, 1984); Kearney, "Eschatology of a Possible God," in *The Religious*, ed. John D. Caputo (Oxford: Blackwell Publishers, 2002), 175–96; and Kearney, "Desire of God," in *God, the Gift, and Postmodernism*, ed. John D. Caputo and Michael J. Scanlon (Bloomington: Indiana University Press, 1999), 112–45.

42. Husserl treats these themes in the first volume of his *Logical Investigations*. The pertinent sections are anthologized in *The Essential Husserl: Basic Writings in Transcendental Phenomenology*. ed. Donn Welton (Bloomington: Indiana University Press, 1999), 26–51. Derrida interprets Husserl's theory of expression as the intentionality of an ideal object, as an "externalizing" that remains internal to consciousness itself. Such an internal externalization does indeed come to its purest formulation in the monologue or soliloquy, which places "empirical worldly existence between brackets." This monological *epoché* does result in a semiotics of "imagined" words that neutralize real ones. See Jacques Derrida, *Speech and Phenomena: And Other Essays on Husserl's Theory of Signs*, trans. David B. Allison (Evanston, Ill.: Northwestern University Press, 1973), 32 & 43.

43. "And we know that God causes all things to work together for good to those who love God, to those who are called according to *His* purpose."

44. Caputo, *Prayers and Tears*, 255–56.

45. John D. Caputo, *More Radical Hermeneutics: On Not Knowing Who We Are* (Bloomington: Indiana University Press, 2000), 249.

46. Caputo, *Prayers and Tears*, 38.

47. The image of the tallith, or prayer shawl, derives from Derrida's reflections on the significance of that symbolic covering in Derrida, "A Silkworm of One's Own (Points of View Stitched on the Other Veil)," in *Acts of Religion*, 311–55. In this article, he explains how in the paternal blessing the father lifts his tallith over his sons in some symbolic gesture of covering them in prayer, actually "constructing" something of a fabric temple over them. In that same context, he then inquires, "what color would have been the tallith of someone who said: I am the truth and the life, I have come, they saw me not, I am coming" (328). I think that such a christological reference allows a "perichoretic" transferal of the tallith imagery to the Spirit.

11. *Plus de Secret*: The Paradox of Prayer
Brian Treanor

1. Augustine, *Confessions*, trans. Henry Chadwick (Oxford: Oxford University Press, 1991), 3.

2. See, e.g., Jacques Derrida, *Circumfession*, in Geoffrey Bennington and Jacques Derrida, *Jacques Derrida* (Chicago: University of Chicago Press, 1993); John D. Caputo, *The Prayers and Tears of Jacques Derrida: Religion without Religion* (Bloomington: Indiana University Press, 1997); and many of the contributions in *Questioning God*, eds. John D. Caputo, Mark Dooley, and Michael J. Scanlon (Bloomington: Indiana University Press, 2001).

3. Augustine, *Confessions*, 180.

4. The clearest formulation of the claim that the religious necessarily transcends the ethical is, of course, Søren Kierkegaard, *Fear and Trembling*, trans. Howard V. Hong and Edna H. Hong (Princeton, N.J.: Princeton University Press, 1983). See below, n. 26.

5. Although the following discussion will, for the most part, consider gospel passages, this is due to the limitations of space and the clear example of contrasting calls to piety present in the same gospel account (the Gospel according to Matthew) rather than due to a lack of similar passages in the Old Testament/Hebrew Scriptures. See below, n. 23.

6. In fact, this latter reference indicates one way of speaking about religious life that is both collective and individual. See below.

7. Of course, Augustine also makes numerous statements that suggest an emphasis on the private or individual relationship to God, most notably in *De Magistro*, trans. Peter King (Indianapolis, Ind.: Hackett, 1995), which tells us that other persons are merely pointers that encourage us to consult "Christ within." "Concerning universals of which we can have knowledge, we do not listen to anyone speaking and making sounds outside ourselves. . . . Our real Teacher is he who is so listened to, who is said to dwell in the inner man, namely Christ, that is, the unchangeable power and eternal wisdom of God" (95).

8. Augustine, *Confessions*, 136. The friend in question was, in fact, Simplicianus, the spiritual father of St. Ambrose. Given what follows in this paper, it should be noted that Victorinus would retort to Simplicianus' demand that he attend church by asking, "Is it walls, then, that make men Christian?" (136).

9. Ibid., 136.

10. Note that Augustine himself was at one time concerned with the opinions of others in matters of piety. See, e.g., Augustine, *Confessions*, 27–28.

11. Buber notes that spiritual life is marked by "relation," which requires others, rather than "experience," which does not. Martin Buber, *I and Thou*, trans. Ronald Gregor Smith (New York: Collier Books, 1958), 5–9. Marcel also concurs with Levinas regarding the essentially intersubjective nature of prayer. Prayer is, for Marcel, the archetypal example of "participation," a necessary element in his account of love, fidelity, hope, and transcendence. Gabriel Marcel, *Reflection and Mystery*, trans. G. S. Fraser, vol. 1 of *The Mystery of Being* (London: Harvill Press, 1951), 110–14. Prayer that focuses on me and me alone is, accordingly, inauthentic. Marcel, *Faith and Reality*, trans. René Hague, vol. 2 of *The Mystery of Being* (London: Harvill Press, 1951), 100.

12. See also Jill Robbins, "Who Prays? Levinas on Irremissible Responsibility," chap. 9 in this volume.

13. Emmanuel Levinas, "Damages Due to Fire," in *Nine Talmudic Readings*, trans. Annette Aronowicz (Bloomington: Indiana University Press, 1990), 188.

14. Emmanuel Levinas, *Ethics and Infinity: Conversations with Philippe Nemo*, trans. Richard A. Cohen (Pittsburgh, Pa.: Duquesne University Press, 1985), 77.

15. Emmanuel Levinas, *Otherwise than Being or Beyond Essence*, trans. Alphonso Lingis (Pittsburgh, Pa.: Duquesne University Press, 1998), 17.

16. Richard Kearney, *States of Mind: Dialogues with Contemporary Thinkers* (New York: New York University Press, 1995), 189.

17. Ibid., 183. In some places, Levinas seems to say that the face of the other is the detour through which we must relate to God. However, in other places he seems to indicate that God "is" the ethical relationship between human beings. See Edith Wyschogrod, *Emmanuel Levinas: The Problem of Ethical Metaphysics* (New York: Fordham University Press, 2000), 106–109.

18. Emmanuel Levinas, *Difficult Freedom*, 17.

19. Levinas, *Of God Who Comes to Mind*, trans. Bettina Bergo (Stanford, Calif.: Stanford University Press, 1998), 75; emphasis added.

20. Hilary Putnam notes that part of the paradox of *hineni*, of the "Here I am" of Abraham—to which Levinas's *me voici* always refers—is that Abraham says *hineni* to both God (Exod. 22:1) and to Isaac (Exod. 22:7); see "Levinas and Judaism" in *The Cambridge Companion to Levinas*, ed. Simon Critchley and Robert Bernasconi (Cambridge, UK: Cambridge University Press, 2002), 33–62, esp. 38. Also see n. 50 below.

21. In fact some of the calls to private piety occur alongside calls to public or communal piety in the same biblical account (e.g., the Gospel of Matthew), which would seem to support the reading offered below, that these two voices are articulating two aspects of one authentic way of praying. Certainly Matthew would be aware of the conflicting message of his Gospel account; however, this obvious contradiction could be read as calling attention to that which reconciles the contradiction, as is the case with the treatment of "love" in the Gospels of Mark and John (see below). Many thinkers point out that contradictions can in fact operate as symbols that point beyond the apparent contradiction to a higher meaning that reconciles the apparent contradiction. Kierkegaard notes that the paradox (presented by the man-god) reveals itself as a contradiction to reason, a limit against which reason shipwrecks. Maimonides asserts that contradictions can be obstacles that hide esoteric knowledge from the vulgar and reveal it to those who are initiated or prepared to receive it. Ricoeur observes that symbolic meaning is both revealed and concealed in the apparent incommensurability of the overt and covert meaning.

22. This is one of the most curious readings in the Catholic tradition, insofar as it is read each year just before Catholics receive a visible mark, the cross of ash on the forehead, that is a very public manifestation of faith (or at least of denominational affiliation) pointing to an interesting expression of the paradox of public and private piety.

23. This passage is mirrored in the Old Testament/Hebrew Scriptures. "Behold, in the day of your fast you seek only your own pleasure, and oppress all your workers. Behold, you fast only to quarrel and to fight and to hit with wicked fist. Fasting like this will not make your voice to be heard

on high. Is such the fast that I choose, a day for a man to humble himself? Is it to bow down his head like a rush, and to spread sackcloth and ashes under him? Will you call this a fast and a day acceptable to the Lord?" (Isa. 58:3–5).

24. Public prayer always runs the risk of being concerned with the public arena in which the praying is done rather than the activity of prayer itself. While examples are too numerous to list, Tolstoy provides a particularly biting description of this sort of conspicuous piety: "Pyotr Ivanovich went in bewildered [upon arriving at the funeral/wake]. . . . The one thing he knew was that on such occasions it never did any harm to cross oneself. He was not quite certain whether he ought also to bow and so he adopted a middle course: on entering the room he began to cross himself and make a slight movement resembling a bow. . . . When he felt he had overdone the crossing, he paused and began to examine the dead man." Leo Tolstoy, *The Death of Ivan Illych*, trans. Lynn Solotaroff (New York: Bantam Books, 1981), 38–39. Of course, Pyotr acknowledges that this "piety" is only the "tedious demand of propriety." Nevertheless, it has "the desired effect," in this case the demonstration (i.e., imitation) of proper regret and respect for the passing of a colleague, Ivan Illych, which in reality only concerns Pyotr insofar as it means an opening in the judiciary for his brother-in-law. Pyotr's "piety" is concerned only with the opinion of other people, not the opinion of God.

25. Søren Kierkegaard, *Purity of Heart Is to Will One Thing: Spiritual Preparation for the Office of Confession*, trans. Douglas V. Steere (New York: Harper Torchbooks, 1956), 187–88.

26. For Kierkegaard, the fact that the religious transcends the ethical is necessary, if problematic. He would not see a problem with the claim that my individual relationship with God might, in transcending the ethical, cause me to violate the ethical. "During the time before the result (of the trial on Mt. Moriah), either Abraham was a murderer every minute or we stand before a paradox that is higher than all mediations." Kierkegaard, *Fear and Trembling*, 66. However, in this paper I characterize the abandonment of the ethical for the religious as an unnecessary disjunction. As will become clear, an individual relationship with God need not abandon humans in the pursuit of God or the ethical in pursuit of the religious. While I am highly sympathetic with Kierkegaard's reading of religious questions of faith as incomprehensible in terms of ethical categories of conduct, the strong disjunction between the two is problematic, for ethical horror can be justified in terms of religious obedience. Hence I hope to articulate a way in which the religious, while incomprehensible, does not abandon the ethical in transcending it. This is because prayer, as we shall see, is articulated in terms of *love*, which, while ethical, is not *merely* ethical.

27. Kierkegaard, *Fear and Trembling*, 6.

28. See, e.g., Immanuel Kant, *Groundwork of the Metaphysic of Morals*, trans. H. J. Paton (New York: Harper Torchbooks, 1964), 64–67.

29. Although one might legitimately question the extent to which even "private" prayer is free of such motivations, insofar as if one prays in private, one presumably believes that one is heard and therefore observed either by God or by oneself (to the extent that one can be other to oneself) or both. Thus even private piety is always, to some extent, piety on display. Even the anchorite and the an-*khôra*-ite must feel they are observed in the act of prayer.

30. Augustine, *Confessions*, 213.

31. Jacques Derrida, *The Gift of Death*, trans. David Wills (Chicago: University of Chicago Press, 1992), 97 and, more generally, 96–115.

32. Ibid., 99 passim. "In this way God the Father reestablishes an economy that was interrupted by the dividing of earth and heaven" (99).

33. Which, in the context of Continental philosophy and theology, immediately evokes both Levinas—see *Otherwise than Being or Beyond Essence*, trans. Alphonso Lingis (Pittsburgh, Pa.: Duquesne University Press, 1998), 99–130—and Jean-Luc Marion—see, e.g., *Being Given: Toward a Phenomenology of Givenness*, trans. Jeffrey L. Kosky (Stanford, Calif.: Stanford University Press, 2002).

34. As Derrida notes, the Gospel account rejects simple reciprocity. While God answers our secret prayers with secret rewards, we are told to "turn the other cheek" rather than reciprocally smiting the cheek of evil in return; see Matt. 5:38–42 and Derrida, *Gift of Death*, 101–104. I would point out, however, that one might note that we are also told to judge others as we would like to be judged (Matt. 7:1–2), which does seem to imply the sort of exchange that Derrida thinks the spiritual economy transcends.

35. Derrida, *Gift of Death*, 111–12. Also see Jacques Derrida, *Counterfeit Money. I. Given Time*, trans. Peggy Kamuf (Chicago: University of Chicago Press, 1992); and Caputo, *Prayers and Tears*, 160–229, esp. 212–17, where Caputo notes that Derrida is also making a comparison between the Gospel according to Matthew and the Genesis story of Abraham.

36. Derrida, *Gift of Death*, 109.

37. Ibid., 105.

38. Ibid., 106.

39. Ibid., 106.

40. There is an ongoing debate between Derrida and Jean-Luc Marion on this topic. See, e.g., *God, the Gift, and Postmodernism*, ed. John D. Caputo and Michael J. Scanlon (Bloomington: Indiana University Press, 1999). Would it be possible to have a gift without anyone giving, without anything being given and without anyone being gifted? If prayer is, qua love, a gift without reserve, would this mean that authentic prayer would be directed to no one, about nothing and (as secret even from the person praying) from no one? This is essentially what the prayers and tears of deconstruction have to be—a sort of "praying without prayer," if I may be so bold. While deconstruction does well in establishing the private secret aspect of prayer,

it does less well in articulating the public or communal aspect because its prayers are so secret that not even the supplicant is aware of the prayer and because undecidability prevents us from stating the recipient of our prayers with any certainty. However, prayer is in one sense necessarily communal, which is why religion without religion (i.e., without community, without tradition, without specific messianism) is problematic as religion. This is why Caputo points out that undecidability does not mean that we do not choose a specific messianism; we *have* to do so. As Caputo noted at the meeting of the Society for Continental Philosophy and Theology that gave birth to this volume, real prayer takes place at a chiasmus between the so-called "pure prayer" of deconstruction and the "determinate prayer" of a religious tradition. For a parallel discussion, see my *"The God Who May Be: Quis ergo amo cum Deum meum amo?"* in *After God*, ed. John Manoussakis (New York: Fordham University Press, 2005).

41. As Ricoeur notes, the "assurance of resolution is always the covert reason for paradox: in a certain way we are always confident of the unity of what we break up as we conceive of it." Paul Ricoeur, *Freedom and Nature: The Voluntary and the Involuntary*, trans. Earzim V. Kohak (Evanston, Ill.: Northwestern University Press, 1966), 353. Regarding "second naïveté," see various of Ricoeur's works, including Ricoeur, *The Symbolism of Evil*, trans. Emerson Buchanan (Boston: Beacon Press, 1967), 352.

42. Emmanuel Levinas, *Entre Nous: On Thinking-of-the-Other*, trans. Michael B. Smith and Barbara Harshav (New York: Columbia University Press, 1998), 103.

43. See also, e.g., 1 Cor.; Mark 10:17–22; Luke 12:22–34.

44. Although, we are, in addition, called to love and *pray* for our enemies (Matt. 5:43–48). Hence a fuller account of love would address the call to "love our enemies"; however, given the limitations of space, such an account will have to wait for a future development. See also, Derrida, *Gift of Death*, 104–107.

45. As Derrida notes in *Gift of Death*, 100, *"plus de secret"* has an ambivalent pronunciation. Pronounced with the "s" of *plus*, *plus de secret* means "more secrets" or "more secrecy." However, when this "s" is silent, unpronounced, *plus de secret* means "no more secrets" or "no more secrecy."

46. That is to say, prayer is not susceptible to an "eidetic" definition in the Platonic sense of the term, perhaps not even in the broadly phenomenological use of the term. There is no universal, static, clearly definable, and comprehensible form to which prayer must conform. Hence if we attempt to employ phenomenology in the consideration of prayer—which this volume and the conference that gave rise to it do—it must be a hermeneutic phenomenology, precisely because "phenomena" (if we can still use this term) at the limit do not lend themselves to unmediated eidetic definition, but to hermeneutic reading.

47. For a lucid account of deconstruction's use of "translatability," see Caputo, *Prayers and Tears*, 54–57, 331–39.

48. In fact, thinking prayer in terms of love certainly has a positive aspect (which would attempt to discuss what prayer is) above and beyond the negative aspect (which identifies what prayer is not). However, such a positive account would necessitate a significantly more detailed and extensive treatment, which is not possible here and must await a future effort.

49. Authentic prayer is related to love and therefore to justice and ethics; and because authentic prayer is related to love, injustice, immorality, and hatred are antithetical to true prayer. Murder, rape, torture, and similar acts that most people would think of as evil would all fall into the category of actions that we could identify as "not-loving" (and consequently "not-prayerful"). Moreover, it is not merely the extreme and therefore obvious examples that we could eliminate by this *via negativa*. Acts that are not evil but are still petty or malicious, overtly selfish acts, and acts that objectify or use another person would likewise be eliminated.

50. "The word 'piety' [*eusébeia*] . . . ordinarily means the worship of God. However, it is also used to express a dutiful respect for one's parents. Moreover, in everyday speech, the word *pietas* means pity or mercy. This has come about, I think, because God commands us especially to practice mercy, declaring that it pleases Him as much as or even more than sacrifices." Augustine, *City of God*, trans. Gerald G. Walsh, Demetrius B. Zema, Grace Monahan, and Daniel J. Honan (New York: Image Books, 1958), 188.

12. Praise — Pure and Personal? Jean-Luc Marion's Phenomenologies of Prayer

Christina M. Gschwandtner

1. Emmanuel Lévinas, "Éducation et Prière," in *Difficile liberté: Essais sur le Judaïsme* (Paris: Éditions Albin Michel, 1976), 374–79; Levinas, "Education and Prayer," in *Difficult Freedom: Essays on Judaism*, trans. Seán Hand (Baltimore, Md.: Johns Hopkins University Press, 1990), 269–72. Although I do not focus on Levinas specifically in this paper, his influence on Marion and Marion's rejection of some of Levinas's emphases always remain in the background of my argument.

2. Marion articulates the topic of prayer in two distinct places and discussions, which are set into and arise also out of different contexts. On the one hand, his most prominent writing on prayer is a reflection that was originally part of the Villanova discussion on God and the gift and later became part of his work *De surcroît: Études sur les phénomènes saturés* (Paris: PUF, 2001); Marion, *In Excess: Studies of Saturated Phenomena*, trans. Robyn Horner and Vincent Berraud (New York: Fordham University Press, 2002), cited as DS and IE, respectively. Here Marion reflects upon prayer in terms of its language, insisting that its function is performative or pragmatic, not predicative. Such treatment of prayer is also prepared in his well-known theological works, Marion, *God without Being*, trans. Thomas A. Carl-

son (Chicago: University of Chicago Press, 1991), cited as GWB, and Marion, *The Idol and Distance: Five Studies*, trans. Thomas A. Carlson (New York: Fordham University Press, 2001), cited as ID. Although Marion's treatment of prayer in GWB and ID is more explicitly theological, it is in no way contradictory to the account in DS/IE. A somewhat different reflection on prayer can be found in Marion, *La croisée du visible* (Paris: Éditions de la Différence, 1986), cited as CV, and Marion, *Prolegomena to Charity*, trans. Stephen Lewis (New York: Fordham University Press, 2002), cited as PC. CV was recently translated by James K. A. Smith as *The Crossing of the Visible* (Stanford, Calif.: Stanford University Press, 2004). Although prayer is here set in an analysis of the icon—a prominent theme of GWB—this account of prayer is, in fact, to be distinguished from that presented in the more popular work. It speaks less of a kind of linguistic function of prayer in general as it depicts the phenomenon of prayer itself and its effect upon the one praying. Hence one might say that while the one account stresses how prayer affects its referent or interlocutor (God), the other focuses on what prayer does to the speaker. Yet, as we shall see, both ultimately have a greater concern with God in the interaction of prayer than they do with either humans or the world and both focus on form or purity over content and particularity.

3. I am not implying, of course, that prayer should never be personal or that it has no individual dimensions. My critique is addressed to the *exclusively* personal nature of Marion's account which seems to disregard communal and ethical implications and aspects entirely.

4. It would go beyond the bounds of this paper to explicate fully how Marion's phenomenology in general remains solipsistic. I indicate this at several places and spell it out where necessary for the argument, but obviously a far more detailed treatment would be required in order to establish this more general claim thoroughly.

5. Such a desire is one Marion shares with the Derrida of *Sauf le nom* (Paris: Galilée, 1993); Derrida, *"Sauf le nom (Postscriptum),"* in *On the Name*, ed. Thomas Dutoit (Stanford, Calif.: Stanford University Press, 1995), 35–85; and with his own work in GWB.

6. Various versions and translations of this article exist; see Jean-Luc Marion, "In the Name: How to Avoid Speaking of 'Negative Theology,'" in *God, the Gift and Postmodernism*, ed. John Caputo and Michael J. Scanlon (Bloomington: Indiana University Press, 1999), 20–53; and IE 128–62. In this paper, I have relied primarily on DS/IE.

7. He spells this out in great detail in GWB and to some extent in ID. See chaps. 1 and 2 of GWB for the terminology of idol and icon, and esp. sect. 16 in "The Discourse of Praise" (ID 190–95) for a first treatment of Dionysius' language of praise and prayer. Victor Kal provides a very nice examination of Marion's analysis of Dionysius in ID and also tries to delineate Marion's criticism of Derrida. Kal shows that Marion's later articula-

tion of praise as nonpredicative is previewed in his earlier work. He explains, for example: "According to Marion, it is impossible to predicate, say something about, God. But this does not imply, in his opinion, that we should only be silent about God. Being unable to speak is only a pause, a temporary period. Ultimately, it is quite possible to say something relating to God, even to utter a word we find 'fitting for God.' Something true can be said when it is 'made true,' namely, in performative speaking. But the 'performance,' the action that makes the speaking true, is not the speaker's accomplishment; it is a gift from the other side. Truth, concerning God, resounds in me." Even in ID, this performance is already labeled "praise," and Kal wonders whether this movement is not a kind of mysterious intimacy with God, a specifically religious experience. See Victor Kal, "Being Unable to Speak, Seen as a Period: Difference and Distance in Jean-Luc Marion," in *Flight of the Gods*, ed. Ilse N. Bulhof and Laurens ten Kate (New York: Fordham University Press, 2002), 144–65.

8. DS 156–57; IE 129–30.

9. DS 162–71; IE 134–42. The English version of the article translates this as "de-nomination."

10. In his analysis of the conference in which Marion first presented his paper, John Caputo suggests that it is not Derrida who is missing something here, but rather Marion who misunderstands the thrust of Derrida's argument. He shows that in a sense, Marion and Derrida talked "past each other" at this conference, because their concerns are so different. See John D. Caputo, "Apostles of the Impossible: On God and the Gift in Derrida and Marion," in John Caputo and Michael Scanlon, *God, the Gift, and Postmodernism* (Bloomington: Indiana University Press, 1999), 185–222.

11. DS 166; IE 138.

12. In "Between Predication and Silence," James K. A. Smith spells out and criticizes in detail Marion's analysis of the three ways and especially his articulation of the way of eminence or praise. He wonders whether praise really is as nonpredicative as Marion suggests and concludes that although praise may well be predicative on some level, not all predication leads to violence, and praise may hence be an appropriate predicative discourse. See James K. A. Smith, "Between Predication and Silence: Augustine on How (Not) to Speak of God," *Heythrop Journal* 41, 1 (2000):66–86.

13. DS 173; IE 143ff.

14. DS 178; IE 148. This is a movement very close to that of GWB. There Marion also moves from a concern to protect God from blasphemy and idolatry (in favor of an iconic naming of God) to an address of God to the believer. See, e.g., the section on the confession of faith in GWB 183–97.

15. See the parallel explication of the need for silence in GWB.

16. DS 185; IE 153.

17. DS 181–90; IE 150–53.

18. DS 168; IE 140.

19. DS 171–74; IE 142–45 (also see the end of the chapter). This is a movement to which Derrida understandably objects. My concern here, however, is to defend neither Marion's reading of Derrida nor Derrida's reading of Marion.

20. DS 174; IE 144.

21. DS 189; IE 157.

22. It is not without significance that Marion first explicitly articulates his notion of the saturated phenomenon in this context. More recently, Marion has altered his stance on the saturated phenomenon in regard to revelation by regarding it as a fifth phenomenon, doubly saturated (see note 46).

23. DS 190–95; IE 158–62.

24. It is, of course, far from clear that prayer automatically ceases to be predicative, something Marion himself recognizes. In response to Derrida, who Marion thinks makes an incoherent distinction between prayer and praise, Marion contests that praying can be accomplished without naming someone: "seeing as no prayer can pray without giving a name, without acknowledging an identity, even and especially an improper one. Not only does naming not contradict the invocation of the prayer, but without the invocation the prayer would be impossible—what would it mean, in fact, to praise without praising anyone, to ask without asking from anyone, to offer a sacrifice without offering it to anyone? An anonymous prayer would make no more sense than does the claim to attain the proper by an (im-)proper name"; IE 144; DS 173. What Marion does contest is that such naming designates a referent or predicates anything of God.

25. Marion, *La croisée du visible*, 85–98.

26. See esp. CV 122–33.

27. CV 111.

28. In other contexts, this term constitutes his preferred phenomenological definition of love. I explore this parallel later in more detail.

29. CV 106.

30. CV 108, 110, 131. In this particular passage, Marion is actually analyzing the cross as a religious "type," though he repeats the same analysis for the icon (CV 133).

31. CV 133.

32. CV 134, 135, 138, 147. This definition does indeed correspond to the one given to the icon in GWB (see GWB 17–22).

33. CV 151–52.

34. CV 153.

35. CV 154.

36. See esp. his analysis of God's becoming visible in the wounds we inflict upon Christ (CV 131, 149).

37. I focus here in particular on Christian prayer, since that is the prayer which Marion assumes and emphasizes throughout.

38. See chap. 6, "The Gift of a Presence" in PC 124–52.

39. PC 145.

40. CV 114.

41. CV 115.

42. See also his analysis of the priestly function in the Eucharist in GWB 149–58.

43. Carlson makes a very similar argument about Marion's phenomenology and theology more generally in his introduction to ID. He also is uncomfortable with the close parallels between Marion's two projects, arguing, e.g., that "the structure of Marion's phenomenological vision and the structure of his theological vision are strikingly similar, if not isomorphic . . . [this] could mean that Marion's theology and phenomenology inform one another in more subtle and complex ways than Marion himself sometimes wants to allow" (ID xxxi). What Carlson shows more generally about Marion's project, I spell out specifically here regarding the experience of prayer. See Thomas A. Carlson, "Converting the Given into the Seen: Introductory Remarks on Theological and Phenomenological Vision" (ID xi–xxxi).

44. See, e.g., Marion, *Étant donné: Essai d'une phénoménologie de la donation* (Paris: PUF, 1998), 317–24, 441; Marion, *Being Given: Toward a Phenomenology of Givenness*, trans. Jeffrey L. Kosky (Stanford, Calif.: Stanford University Press, 2002), 227–33 and 322 (cited as ED and BG, respectively).

45. DS 21–31; IE 18–26. Dominique Janicaud has particularly objected to this extreme language, esp. in his recent work, *Phénoménologie éclatée* (Paris: Éditions de l'éclat, 1998).

46. He defines the phenomenon of revelation (which, as we have seen, includes his treatment on prayer) as a "saturated phenomenon of second degree," a "paradox of paradoxa," a phenomenon that is "doubly saturated" and carries all phenomenological limits to the extreme simultaneously (while the other saturated phenomena, such as the historical event, the painting, my flesh, the face of the other, are only excessive or saturated in one particular respect).

47. Jeff Kosky has argued that Levinas's injunction that ethics is "first philosophy" does not mean that Levinas is only concerned with ethics but that for him ethics is primary and all other philosophy is based on and flows out of ethics. See Jeffrey L. Kosky, *Levinas and the Philosophy of Religion* (Bloomington: Indiana University Press, 2001).

48. Jean-Luc Marion, *Reduction and Givenness*, trans. Thomas A. Carlson (Evanston, Ill.: Northwestern University Press, 1998), 197 (cited as RG).

49. RG, 202.

50. ED 367; BG 267.

51. ED 404; BG 293; emphasis added.

52. ED 405; BG 293. He insists that "the pertinent question is not deciding if the gifted [devoted] is first responsible toward the Other (Levinas) or rather in debt to itself (Heidegger), but understanding that these two modes

of responsibility flow from its originary function of having to respond in face of the phenomenon as such, that is to say, such as it gives itself" (BG 294; ED 405).

53. ED 246; BG 175.

54. DS 143; IE 118.

55. For a more detailed explication of the "devoted" (*adonné*), see Part V of ED/BG. The brief summary within this paragraph is based on that section.

56. Marion actually goes to great length to emphasizes the essential (not merely important, but necessary) anonymity of the giver or the self-giving phenomenon. See esp. sect. 26 "To Receive One's Self from What Gives Itself" (ED 361–73; BG 262–71).

57. I have primarily relied here on his outline of such an account in chap. 4, "The Intentionality of Love," in PC 71–101. His most recent work, *Le phénomène érotique: Six méditations* (Paris: Grasset, 2003), esp. 133–68, spells out this topic in much more detail but does not differ substantially from his earlier analysis, at least in respect to our concern here.

58. PC 87; emphasis added.

59. PC 100–101.

60. An exception, of course, is an erotic relationship with a specific other human being. But that obviously is not an account of corporate prayer.

13. The Saving or Sanitizing of Prayer: The Problem of the *Sans* in Derrida's Account of Prayer
Mark Gedney

1. John Caputo, *The Prayers and Tears of Jacques Derrida: Religion without Religion* (Indianapolis: Indiana University Press, 1997), 61–62.

2. Though I argue that there are some important limitations to Derrida's account of prayer, I think one must acknowledge something fundamental or central about his emphasis on the uncertain character of all prayer. Jean-Louis Chrétien's description of prayer as "the wounded word" (*la parole blessé*) reflects some of the concerns expressed by Caputo and Derrida. Chrétien notes that the word is broken precisely in its initial orientation toward the other. This turning affects me, "opens up a fault," in that an "other has silently introduced itself into the dialogue of the self with the self and radically transformed and broken it." If this is true, then even the most determinate and theologically or liturgically astute prayers seem to share this wound, this circumcision of the heart and ears, with Derrida's wandering and conflicted tears and prayers. See Jean-Louis Chrétien, "La parole blessé," in *Phénoménologie et théologie*, ed. Jean-François Courtine (Paris: Criterion, 1992), 48; Chrétien, "The Wounded Word: Phenomenology of Prayer," in Dominique Janicaud et al., *Phenomenology and the "Theological Turn": The French Debate* (New York: Fordham University Press, 2001), 153. All English translations are my own. Citations to the appropriate English translations, if available, will be provided after the citation to the original.

3. Though I am emphasizing the typical Kantian sense of transcendental as a condition of possibility, Derrida uses the idea of a "quasi-transcendental" to highlight his contention that in this case, the condition that makes prayer possible is also equally the condition that makes prayer impossible. Though I examine a few of the implications that follow from such a paradoxical notion below, a full treatment of it is beyond the scope of this investigation.

4. The image of the desert as a harsh and empty space without obvious points of reference or shelter is used extensively by Derrida, Caputo, and others to indicate a form of religious experience without the comforts of our everyday concrete beliefs and practices.

5. See Caputo, *Prayers and Tears*, 142.

6. See Jacques Derrida, *Passions: "L'offrande oblique"* (Paris: Éditions Galilée, 1993), 64–71; Derrida, *On the Name*, ed. Thomas Dutoit, trans. David Word (Stanford, Calif.: Stanford University Press, 1995), 28–31; Derrida, *Donner la mort* (Paris: Éditions Galilée, 1999), 202–205.

7. Caputo, *Prayers and Tears*, 102. Also see Derrida, *Donner la mort*, 112ff; *Gift of Death*, 79–81.

8. Chrétien, "La parole blessé," 49; "Wounded Word," 153.

9. James Smith, "Re-Kanting Postmodernism? Derrida's Religion within the Limits of Reason Alone," *Faith and Philosophy* 17 (October 2000), 558. Smith cites Derrida's argument in *Faith and Knowledge* that Kant's equating of true Christian faith and morality really implies that true faith requires one take on the burden of the death of God—as Nietzsche later argues. Jacques Derrida, *Foi et Savoir suivi de Le Siècle et Le Pardon* (Paris: Éditions du Seuil, 1992), 22; Derrida and Gianni Vattimo, ed., *Religion* (Stanford, Calif.: Stanford University Press, 1996), 11.

10. Derrida, *Donner la mort*, 74–5; *Gift of Death*, 49.

11. See Smith, "Re-Kanting Postmodernism?" 568.

12. Derrida, *Donner la mort*, 126; *Gift of Death*, 91.

13. See Caputo, *Prayers and Tears*, 150.

14. "Attendre sans horizon, donc, mais revenu de si loin, de si bas, vif ou mort, attendre l'autre qui vient, qui vient interloquer l'ordre du savoir: ni connu ni inconnu, trop connu mais étranger de pied en cap, encore à naître. Ce sera la fin de l'histoire en ce sens. Verdict: fin de la fin de l'histoire, tout va recommencer, sans linceul dont on [ne] sache quoi faire." Hélène Cixoux and Jacques Derrida, *Voiles* (Paris: Galilée, 1998), 34; Jacques Derrida, *Acts of Religion*, ed. Gil Anidjar (New York: Routledge Press, 2002), 317–18.

15. See Geoffrey Bennington and Jacques Derrida, *Jacques Derrida* (Paris: Éditions du Seuil, 1991), 178–79; Geoffrey Bennington and Jacques Derrida, trans. Geoffrey Bennington, *Jacques Derrida* (Chicago: University of Chicago Press, 1993), 190–92.

16. Derrida, *Foi et Savoir*; 88; *Religion*, 58.

17. See Caputo, *Prayers and Tears*, 297.

18. Ibid., 195.

19. Ibid., 224.

20. Graham Ward, "Questioning God," in *Questioning God*, ed. John Caputo, Mark Dooley, and Michael Scanlon (Bloomington: Indiana University Press, 2001), 284ff. Bruce Ellis Benson, while very appreciative of Derrida's contribution to the postmodern critique of ideology, raises similar concerns using the language of incarnation to make his point. See Bruce Ellis Benson, *Graven Ideologies: Nietzsche, Derrida, and Marion on Modern Ideology* (Downers Grove, Ill.: IVP, 2002), 166–68.

21. The role of this absolute affirmative in Caputo's account of Derrida's praying is clearly central: "When Derrida speaks of his prayers and tears in *Circumfession*, he means not the determinate prayer of a determinable faith, not a particular grammatical category, but the deeply affirmative invocation, the *oui, oui*. Such a prayer would be, according to 'the strange syntax of the *sans*' . . . , a prayer without prayer, the prayer of the *sans*, in a religion without religion, a religion of the *sans*. This *sans* separates Derrida's prayers and tears from, even as it joins them to, the determinable faiths." Caputo, *Prayers and Tears*, 97. This last "joins," of course, is precisely the issue that is acknowledged by Caputo and Derrida, but which, as I have been arguing, is not sufficiently attended to in their writings.

22. Caputo, *Prayers and Tears*, 142, 68.

23. Paul Ricœur, "Expérience et langage dans le discours religieux," in *Phénoménologie et théologie*, 19; Ricœur, "Experience and Language in Religious Discourse, in Janicaud et al., *Phenomenology and the "Theological Turn*," 130.

24. For a powerful reading of this encounter that also attempts to steer a course between a straightforward ontotheological reading of this text and a radical deconstructive reading, see Richard Kearney, *The God Who May Be: A Hermeneutics of Religion* (Bloomington: Indiana University Press, 2001), esp. chap. 2, "I Am Who May Be."

25. Caputo, *Prayers and Tears*, 60.

26. Caputo, *Prayers and Tears*, 308.

14. How (Not) to Find God in All Things: Derrida, Levinas, and St. Ignatius of Loyola on Learning How to Pray for the Impossible
Michael F. Andrews

1. Many sayings by the Greek and Latin Fathers are scattered throughout this text. For a collection of these and other sayings, please refer to Kallistos Ware, *The Orthodox Way* (Crestwood, N.Y.: St. Vladimir's Orthodox Theology Seminary Press, 1979), 30.

2. "When Meister Eckhart says, 'I pray God to rid me of God,' he formulates with the most astonishing economy a double bind by which we are all bound: how to speak and not speak, how to pray and not pray, to and for the *tout autre* [which] goes (and comes) under the name of God." John

D. Caputo, *The Prayers and Tears of Jacques Derrida: Religion without Religion* (Bloomington: Indiana University Press, 1997), 4.

3. Ware, *Orthodox Way*, 30–31.

4. This period, roughly from the late nineteenth to the early twentieth centuries, was rich in discussions in both Europe and the United States describing the phenomenon of religious experiences. See, e.g., Stumpf's *Tonspychologie* (1890), James's *Principles of Psychology* (1890) and *Varieties of Religious Experience*; Otto's *The Idea of the Holy* (1917); as well as various works in psychology and philosophy by Feuerbach, Marx, Freud, Scheler, Hedwig Conrad-Martius, and Roman Ingarden.

5. The genesis of Husserl's development of this important theme in phenomenology can be traced even earlier to his classic Göttingen lecture series, *The Idea of Phenomenology* (1908; The Hague: Nijhoff, 1964), and even his *Logische Untersuchungen* (1900–1901; New York: Humanities, 1970).

6. The classic Husserlian formulation of the transcendental ego is described in the fifth of his *Cartesian Meditations*. Many of the twists and turns that led Husserl to affirm the doctrine of a transcendental phenomenology, as well as the strenuous objections from many of his closest friends and colleagues on precisely this point, are well documented. See, e.g., Spiegelberg's foundational two-volume introduction to the history of phenomenology, Herbert Spiegelberg, *The Phenomenological Movement* (The Hague: Martinus Nijhoff, 1969).

7. For a fuller description of what Husserl is up to, see Paul Ricoeur, "Transcendental Experience and Egology: Second Meditation," in *Husserl: An Analysis of His Phenomenology* (Evanston, Ill.: Northwestern University Press, 1967), 90–93.

8. In Christian scripture, Jesus tells his disciples, "When you pray, say: 'Father . . . forgive us our debts, for we ourselves forgive every one who is indebted to us'" (Luke 11:5).

9. St. Ignatius of Loyola, *The Constitutions of the Society of Jesus*, trans. George Ganss (St. Louis, Mo.: Institute of Jesuit Sources, 1970), 165.

10. Derrida himself concludes: "The expression 'proper name' is improper. . . . What the interdict is laid upon is the uttering of what functions as the proper name. And this function is consciousness itself. The proper name in the colloquial sense, in the sense of consciousness, is . . . only a designation of appurtenance and a linguistico-social classification." See Jacques Derrida, "The Violence of the Letter," in *Of Grammatology*, trans. Gayatri Spivak (Baltimore, Md.: Johns Hopkins University Press, 1976), 111–14.

11. Ware, *Orthodox Way*, 31.

12. The events of Ignatius de Loyola's life are well documented. For more information and clarification, I recommend the following three sources: Candido Dalmases, *Ignatius of Loyola: Founder of the Jesuits* (St. Louis, Mo.: Institute of Jesuit Sources, 1985); William J. O'Malley, *The*

Fifth Week (Chicago, Ill.: Loyola University Press, 1976); Ignatius Loyola, *A Pilgrim's Testament* (Rome, Italy: Gregorian University Press, 1983).

13. Much of this historical material is discussed at length in a number of biographies of Jesuit saints and martyrs. For Ignatius of Loyola's firsthand account of the events of his life, see *The Autobiography of St. Ignatius Loyola*, trans. Joseph O'Callaghan (New York: Harper and Row, 1974).

14. This understanding of "movement" is developed in detail in John W. O'Malley, *The First Jesuits* (Cambridge, Mass.: Harvard University Press, 1993). "[*The Exercises*] . . . brought with it a process of spiritual growth and an increasing recognition of God's activity in everything in the world. Concomitant with this movement and a test of its authenticity was the inner experience of consolation or, as Nadal said, 'a relish for spiritual things'" (89).

15. Roland Barthes, *Sade, Fourier, Loyola* (New York: Hill and Wang, 1976), 52ff.

16. Ibid., 41.

17. Ibid., 42.

18. Ibid., 44.

19. Ware, *Orthodox Way*, 140.

20. This is a very complex argument and I can touch on it only briefly in this essay. For more detail, see Jean-Luc Marion, *God without Being* trans. Thomas A. Carlson (Chicago: University of Chicago Press, 1991).

21. Jacques Derrida, "Violence and Metaphysics," in *Writing and Difference*, trans. Alan Bass (Chicago: University of Chicago Press, 1978), 108.

22. René Descartes, *Meditations on First Philosophy*, trans. Donald Cress (Indianapolis, Ind.: Hackett, 1993), 24–35.

23. Evagrius of Pontus comments, "God cannot be grasped by the mind. If he could be grasped, he would not be God." Ware, *Orthodox Way*, 12.

24. Derrida notes: "Doubtless this encounter of the unforeseeable itself is the only possible opening of time, the only pure future. . . . But this future, this beyond, is not another time. . . . It is present at the heart of experience. Present not as a total presence but as a trace." Jacques Derrida, "Violence and Metaphysics," in *Writing and Difference*, 95.

25. Ibid., 82.

26. Ware, *Orthodox Way*, 178.

27. Ibid., 141.

28. Ibid., 176.

15. Prayer and Incarnation: A Homiletical Reflection
Lissa McCullough

1. Simone Weil, "Concerning the Our Father," in *Waiting for God*, trans. Emma Craufurd (New York: HarperCollins, 2001), 147, cited as WG.

2. Augustine, *Confessions*, trans. R. S. Pine-Coffin (New York: Penguin, 1961), 22.

3. Søren Kierkegaard, *Fear and Trembling*, trans. Howard V. Hong and Edna Hong (Princeton, N.J.: Princeton University Press, 1983).

4. Friedrich Nietzsche, *Thus Spoke Zarathustra*, trans. Walter Kaufmann (New York: Penguin, 1988), cited as *Z*.

16. The Infinite Supplicant: On a Limit and a Prayer
Mark Cauchi

I want to thank Brayton Polka, Avron Kulak, Rui Pimenta, and Bruce Benson for their careful readings of earlier versions of this paper and for their helpful suggestions. I also want to thank Anna Isacsson for her reading and inspiring encouragement.

1. While this Bible reference is from the King James Version for reasons that will be clear later (see note 11), all other Bible references will be to the Revised Standard Version (RSV) unless otherwise stated.

2. "The Lord said, 'Shall I hide from Abraham what I am about to do, seeing that Abraham shall become a great and mighty nation, and all the nations of the earth shall bless themselves by him? No, for I have chosen him, that he may charge his children and his household after him to keep the way of the Lord by doing righteousness and justice; so that the Lord may bring to him what he has promised him'" (Gen. 18:17–19). If this passage is a soliloquy, as it is usually considered, how did it end up in the text? What extraordinary authority do the authors of the text claim for themselves by including this passage? It is surely no less bold than Abraham's own intercession. And is the very fact of its extraordinary inclusion not consistent with the fact that within it we witness a hesitant God deliberating, conversing with himself, asking questions, and answering, unsure as to what is right and just?

3. It has been suggested that this sentence was doctored by the ancient Rabbis to make Abraham wait for God, and not the other way around as it was originally written, because such a situation was deemed inappropriate for God.

4. In fact, the *Midrash Rabbah*, Genesis I, trans. Rabbi H. Freedman (London: Soncino Press, 1939), reports that the sentence, "Far be that from thee" (*hallilah lak*) (18:25), Abraham's protest against God, was interpreted by Rabbi Judan as "It is a profanation [*halalah*] for Thee, it is alien to Thy nature"; and Rabbi Aha similarly said, "*Halilah* is written twice, implying, Such action would profane [*hilal*] the Divine Name" (chap. XLIX, 9, 428).

5. For instance, E. A. Speiser, trans., *The Anchor Bible: Genesis* (New York: Doubleday), says that when Abraham looks down into the smoldering valley, he thus gets "his answer to the question he had posed the night before" (143) — i.e., that God did not find ten righteous people there. Claus Westermann, *Genesis 12–36: A Commentary*, trans. John J. Scullion (Minneapolis, Minn.: Augsburg, 1985), recognizes that the episode belongs to a post-Exilic tradition concerned with questions about the justice of God and

even about the doubtfulness of it (286–87). But he then goes on to object that this episode is not properly a prayer since it does not follow the classic prayer formula of petition and concession, and that there is, therefore, no genuine bargaining going on between God and Abraham. Westermann's explanation for this is that "Abraham, for all his questioning, is aware from the start that God will go through with his decision to punish Sodom" (291). It is not clear how Westermann knows of what Abraham was aware. But in the previous paragraph, he insightfully notes that the only way the reader can grasp the "real intent" of the passage is if the reader can ask: "'How far will Abraham go?' and 'How will God react?'" In other words, Westermann himself suggests that the reader can only understand by *not* knowing the intent of Abraham or God ahead of time. The narrative *qua* narrative is pointless if there is not built into it the possibility that God can change as a result of Abraham's intervention.

6. I am indebted to W. Lee Humphrey, *The Character of God in the Book of Genesis: A Narrative Appraisal* (Louisville, Ky.: Westminster John Knox Press, 2001), for noting this parallel and contrast between Lot and Abraham (124). This parallel in the text in fact precedes the destruction scene. From the moment that we first meet the always generous and righteous Abraham, we meet his nephew, Lot, who never seems to do anything quite right. When strife over land develops between the herdsmen of Abraham and Lot, and Abraham tries to settle the strife by allowing Lot to choose which land he wants, Lot selfishly chooses the fertile Jordan valley, home of Sodom and Gomorrah, and leaves the arid land to Abraham (Gen. 13:8–13). When, while living in Sodom, Lot is taken captive with the rest of the city by enemy armies, it is the more competent Abraham who rescues him and his property and who then refuses any reward (Gen. 14).

7. John E. Hartley, *Genesis*, New International Biblical Commentary (Peabody, Mass.: Hendrickson Publishing, 2000), 189.

8. *Midrash Rabbah* XLIX, 9. Job's protesting prayers were in the end confirmed by God, "whose wrath is kindled against" Eliphaz, Zophar, and Bildad, for they, in their unquestioning prayers, had "not spoken of me what is right, as my servant Job has" (Job 42:7). Consequently, it is Job's prayer that God accepts in the end, not theirs (42:8–9).

9. Psalm 86 in Hebrew-derived translations.

10. This is the King James Version, which is fairly close to Augustine's Old Latin version (translated in *Exposition of the Psalms* as "keep guard over my soul, for I am holy." While hāsīd more literally means "devout" or "pious," and not strictly speaking holy (*kdš*), I think the effect is the same: for as is clear in Ezekiel (20:39–44; 36:16–36), it is because Israel has not been devout, because the Israelites have disrespected the holiness of God and his name, that they have profaned themselves; in other words, the goal of devotion is holiness. This may account for the variety of translations: the RSV states, "Preserve my life, for I am godly"; The Anchor Bible says,

"Protect my life for I am devoted to you"; the New Jerusalem Bible writes, "Guard me, for I am faithful."

11. Augustine, *Exposition of the Psalms, 73–98*, trans. Maria Boulding, ed. John E. Rotelle (New York: New City Press, 2002), 223; cited hereafter as EP.

12. *Midrash Tehillim*, vol. 2, trans. William G. Braude (New Haven: Yale University Press, 1959), on Psalm 86 responds similarly to Augustine: "The Holy One, blessed be He, called Himself Holy, as it is said *For I am Holy, saith the Lord* (Jer. 3:12). But for David to call himself holy? R. Abba explained in the name of R. Alexandri: Any man who remains silent when he hears himself reviled, even though he has at hand the means to strike back, becomes a partner of the Holy One, blessed be He, who *likewise* remains silent as He hears the nations of the earth revile Him to His face. So, when David heard himself reviled, but remained silent, he could say, *Keep my soul, for I am holy.*" (69; emphasis added). We consider below this likeness that the Rabbis discern between God and the human.

13. At one point, however, the text does say that if the Israelites "confess their iniquity," God will remember his covenant (Lev. 26:40–42). But it should be kept in mind that iniquity is presented in the preceding verses as the breaking of the cultic laws.

14. Samuel E. Balentine, *Prayer in the Hebrew Bible: The Drama of Divine-Human Dialogue* (Minneapolis, Minn.: Fortress Press, 1993). See, e.g., this psalm: "Let my prayer be counted as incense before thee, and the lifting up of my hands as an evening sacrifice!" (Ps. 141:2).

15. It is perhaps worth keeping in mind that while the Temple was built c. 952 B.C.E., 1 Kings likely received its final "Deuteronomistic" redaction after the destruction of the Temple. The post-Temple theology of prayer would have already begun to affect how the holiness of the Temple was conceived and presented in narrative accounts of it.

16. On the politically egalitarian and occasionally anarchic possibilities of prayer, see Moshe Greenberg, *Biblical Prose Prayer: As a Window to the Popular Religion of Ancient Israel* (Berkeley: University of California Press, 1983), 52–57; Balentine, *Prayer in the Hebrew Bible*, 44–47.

17. On the priestly worldview as structured by a continuum of holiness, see Philip Peter Jenson, *Graded Holiness: A Key to the Priestly Conception of the World* (Sheffield, UK: Sheffield Academic Press, 1992). This distinction I am developing between the priestly ontology, on one hand, and prayer/ethics, on the other, should be taken more as shorthand for two different conceptions of holiness and relation rather than as a strict or absolute schema. For while the priests do tend to emphasize this conceptuality, it must be acknowledged that when the prophets or Jesus eventually critique the priests, it is done in the name of the ethics originally articulated by the priests. The priestly world is (always) already differed from within.

18. Emmanuel Levinas, "'In the Image of God,' According to Rabbi Hayyim Volozhiner" (1978), *Beyond the Verse: Talmudic Readings and Lectures*,

trans. Gary D. Mole (Bloomington: Indiana University Press, 1994), 159 (cited as *BV*). Levinas presents a very similar reading in the later (1985) "Judaism and Kenosis," *In the Time of the Nations*, trans. Michael B. Smith (Bloomington: Indiana University Press, 1994). One of the sections of this latter piece is on prayer.

19. See Levinas's lovely reading and translation of "love your neighbor as yourself" in which he argues against such an interpretation: "Questions and Answers," in Levinas, *Of God Who Comes to Mind*, trans. Bettina Bergo (Stanford, Calif.: Stanford University Press, 1998), 90–91.

20. Here I would agree with some of Gerhard Von Rad's analysis in, Von Rad, *Genesis: A Commentary*, rev. ed., trans. John H. Marks (Philadelphia, Pa.: Westminster Press, 1972): "God 'forms' [Adam] from the ground; the bond of life between man and earth given by creation is expressed with particular cogency by the use of the Hebrew words ʿādām [man] and ʿadāmā [earth]. . . . This man, however, formed from the earth, becomes a living creature only when inspired with the divine breath of life. . . . This divine vital power is personified, individualized, but only by its entry into the material body; and only this breath when united with the body makes man a 'living creature.' . . . [Breath] distinguishes not body and 'soul' but more realistically body and life." (77)

21. In John, Jesus recalls this passage when he is accused of making himself God: "Is it not written in your law," Jesus asks "'I said, you are gods'?" (John 10:34).

22. Robert H. Gundry, *Matthew: A Commentary on His Literary and Theological Art* (Grand Rapids, Mich.: William B. Eerdmans, 1982), 106.

23. A more literal translation of Matthew would produce "release us from our debts as we also release our debtors." Luke, however, uses "sins," which is how most of Matthew's audience would have understood "debts" anyway. "Trespass," or false step, is not far from "sin" and is in fact a suitable translation of the addendum to the prayer in Matthew (6:14–15), which essentially restates this petition. Since "trespass" resonates more with my purposes, I use it here.

24. Similarly, see Derrida's comment that *tout autre est tout autre* can be reproduced both as "every other (one) is every (bit) other" and as "every other (one) is God": "In one case God is defined as infinitely other, as wholly other, every bit other. In the other case it is declared that every other one, each of the others, is God inasmuch as he or she is, *like* God, wholly other." Jacques Derrida, *The Gift of Death*, trans. David Wills (Chicago: University of Chicago Press, 1995), 87.

25. "Perhaps nothing ever comes to pass except on the line of a transgression." See Jacques Derrida, *Aporias*, trans. Thomas Dutoit (Stanford, Calif.: Stanford University Press, 1993), 33.

26. Derrida, of course, acknowledges that the question is addressed *to* another, but ultimately he will stress that the question comes *from* the other:

"Isn't the question of the foreigner a foreigner's question? Coming from the foreigner, from abroad?" See Jacques Derrida, "Foreigner Question," in *Of Hospitality*, trans. Rachel Bowlby (Stanford, Calif.: Stanford University Press, 2000), 3.

27. In his last meditations on the question of God, Derrida had begun addressing similar issues. See, e.g., "Epoché and Faith: An Interview with Jacques Derrida," in *Derrida and Religion: Other Testaments*, ed. Yvonne Sherwood and Kevin Hart (New York: Routledge, 2005), 44: "the weakness, the powerlessness, of God is first of all the possibility of God to be affected by an event. If something *happens* to God, it implies some vulnerability in God. . . . For something to happen to God, God must be exposed, must be limited in a certain way, must be made finite in his infinity. The event must affect not only human existence but also divine existence. . . . This event remains unpredictable, as every event should be. One cannot see it coming. If God could simply predict an, as in providence, could see the passion coming, there would be no event. The event must be totally unpredictable, even to God." See, similarly, Jacques Derrida, *Rogues: Two Essays on Reason*, trans. Pascale-Anne Brault and Michael Naas (Stanford, Calif.: Stanford University Press, 2005), 156.

28. Saint Augustine, *Confessions*, trans. Henry Chadwick (New York: Oxford University Press, 1992), 3.

29. Ibid., 3–4 (emphasis added).

30. Ibid., 3.

31. I have developed this argument elsewhere. See my "Traversing the Infinite through Augustine and Derrida," in *Difference in Philosophy of Religion*, ed. Philip Goodchild (Aldershot, UK: Ashgate Publishing, 2003).

32. For both the Greek proponents and opponents of the infinite, the infinite was conceived of in quantitative terms. For proponents of the actual infinite, such as Anaximander and Milesus, it was because the infinite was absolutely big and contained absolutely everything that it was the privileged category. For opponents, such as Aristotle, it was because such an idea seemed absurd and contradictory that the infinite was relegated to potentiality, to the endless addition or division of finite quantities to or from finite quantities. The notion of infinitude that develops in and out of the Abrahamic traditions, however, consists precisely in being irreducible to quantity.

33. See sect. 22 of the *Monologion*, in Anselm of Canterbury, *The Major Works*, ed. Brian Davies and G. R. Evans (New York: Oxford University Press, 1998), 38–39.

17. Proslogion
Philip Goodchild

1. Anselm, *Proslogium*, trans. Sidney Norton Deane (Chicago: Open Court, 1903), chap. 1.

2. Anselm, *Proslogium*, chap. 2. Scott Matthews has argued that Anselm's aim in the *Proslogion* is to write a devotional prayer for his monks and patrons that would contribute to a renewal of God's image within the soul. Matthews argues further, in contrast to the otherwise excellent commentary of Gregory Schufreider, that the prayer does not lead to a vision of how God is in Godself, but remains apophatic—the image being renewed is human reason itself. The prayer never loses its opening humility of being unable to contemplate the being of God. See Scott Matthews, *Reason, Community and Religious Tradition: St. Anselm's Argument and the Friars* (Aldershot, UK: Ashgate, 2001); and Gregory Schufreider, *An Introduction to Anselm's Argument* (Philadelphia, Pa.: Temple University Press, 1978). My aim in rephrasing Anselm's definition to remove its assumptions of hierarchy and to renew in contemporary thought the following objectives of Anselm: to practice thought within the humility of apophaticism, to ground ontology in axiology—what matters is what is most real—and to renew the basis of human reason by directing attention to what matters most, thus forming human reason in the image of God, as defined below in Chapter 5. The three "temptations" are purifications of reason.

3. These words are from Freddie Mercury's song "Bohemian Rhapsody," released by the group Queen in 1975. The apparent tragedy of the story conveyed in the song, that of a murderer awaiting execution, is subverted by its ironic, camp, rock portrayal. Hence the message of the song is that nothing really matters, not even tragedy. Anyone can repeat the refrain without thinking seriously, and yet part of the popular appeal of the song is that it allows people to express otherwise inadmissible emotions of despair while at the same time affirming that these do not matter.

4. Anselm, *Proslogium*, chap. 4.

5. This discussion reflects on Søren Kierkegaard, *The Sickness unto Death*, trans. Alastair Hannay (London: Penguin, 1989).

6. This dimension of St. Anselm's ontological argument has been developed by Brayton Polka, "The Ontological Argument for Existence," in *Difference in Philosophy of Religion*, ed. Philip Goodchild (Aldershot, UK: Ashgate, 2003).

7. This is an important theme in the work of Kierkegaard's pseudonymous author, Johannes Climacus, as well as in the work of Martin Heidegger and Gilles Deleuze.

8. Thomas Hobbes, *Leviathan* (Cambridge, UK: Cambridge University Press, 1996), 93.

9. Gilles Deleuze, *Dialogues*, with Claire Parnet, trans. Hugh Tomlinson and Barbara Habberjam (London: Athlone, 1987), 55.

10. This directly contests Johannes Climacus in *Philosophical Fragments*, trans. Howard V. Hong and Edna H. Hong (Princeton, N.J.: Princeton University Press, 1985).

Contributors

Michael F. Andrews is Assistant Professor in Philosophy and Director of the Faith and the Great Ideas Program at Seattle University in Seattle, Washington.

Bruce Ellis Benson is Associate Professor of Philosophy at Wheaton College in Wheaton, Illinois.

Mark Cauchi is completing the doctoral program in Social and Political Thought at York University in Toronto, Canada.

Benjamin Crowe teaches in the Department of Philosophy at the University of Utah.

Mark Gedney is Associate Professor of Philosophy at Gordon College in Wenham, Massachusetts.

Philip Goodchild is Senior Lecturer in Religious Studies at the University of Nottingham in the United Kingdom.

Christina M. Gschwandtner is Assistant Professor of Philosophy at the University of Scranton in Scranton, Pennsylvania.

Lissa McCullough is Assistant Professor of Religion at Muhlenberg College in Allentown, Pennsylvania.

Cleo McNelly Kearns is a Fellow at the Center of Theological Inquiry in Princeton, New Jersey.

James R. Mensch is Professor of Philosophy at St. Francis Xavier University in Nova Scotia, Canada.

Edward F. Mooney is Adjunct Professor of Religion at Syracuse University in Syracuse, New York.

B. Keith Putt is Professor of Philosophy at Samford University in Birmingham, Alabama.

Jill Robbins is Professor of Religion and Comparative Literature at Emory University in Atlanta, Georgia.

Brian Treanor is Assistant Professor of Philosophy at Loyola Marymount University in Los Angeles, California.

Merold Westphal is Distinguished Professor of Philosophy at Fordham University in New York City, New York.

Norman Wirzba is Associate Professor of Philosophy at Georgetown College in Georgetown, Kentucky.

Terrence C. Wright is Associate Professor of Philosophy at St. John Vianney Theological Seminary in Denver, Colorado.

Index

Note: The editors wish to thank Andrew Garrett for compiling the index, as well as for help at crucial stages along this volume's journey. Shane Wilkins has also provided much appreciated assistance.

Church, the, 129, 135–36, 156, 174–75, 271n8
Clamare facientum, 147
Cohen, Gerson, 45
Conatus essendi, 19, 33, 36, 215

Darwin, Charles, 53
Dasein, 15, 35, 93, 140
Derrida, Jacques, 6, 20–21, 30, 52–53, 152–53, 169–70, 177, 185, 197, 205–208, 227, 250n7, 256n2, 269n40, 270n42,47, 281n2, 282n3–4, 284n10; on prayer and love, 7, 163–66; prayer as gift, 63, 145–49, 186–92, 198–99, 203–204, 253n2, 274n40; on public and private prayer, 161–63, 274n34, 275n45; roots of religion, 191
Deconstruction (deconstructionist), 142–43, 165, 170, 192, 198, 201, 266n1, 274n40
Detachment, 22, 125, 212, 215
Différance, 145, 147, 151, 177. *See also* Derrida, Jacques
Diksha, 109
Dilthey, Wilhelm, 6, 119–23, 131, 264n4
le dire, 33, 153
le dit, 33, 153

Eckhart, Meister, 8, 283n2
Economy, 5, 32–33, 65–67, 70–72, 145, 161–63, 185, 196, 198, 253n2, 274n32, 34, 283n2. *See also* Derrida, Jacques
Eidos, 165–66
Ekstasis, 79
Election, 42, 46
Eliot, T. S., 104, 111
Empathy, 56, 68–70, 254n14
Eros, 28, 30, 54, 163. *See also* Erotic
Erotic, 110, 113–14, 169, 174, 178, 180
Eschatology, 47, 127, 264n8, 268n28
Eucharist (Eucharistic), 136, 174–76

Face, the, 19, 46, 173, 177–78, 200, 205, 272n17, 280n46; face-to-face, 50, 61–62, 64–65, 157, 189, 193, 223, 225; of God, 43, 75, 158, 195, 232,

262n16, 288n12. *See also* Levinas, Emmanuel
Facere veritatem, 144–45
Fraser, Giles, 256n3

Gelassenheit, 21, 25
Geniestreich, 147
Gift, the, 14, 23–24, 29, 72, 129–30, 148, 151–52, 166, 175, 187–88, 207, 210, 274n40, 276n2, 278n7, 280n52; economy of, 145–46, 161–63, 191; phenomenology of, 198–99, 204; of the Spirit, 129–30, 152; the World as, 8, 100, 106, 214–15. *See also* Derrida, Jacques
Girard, René, 5, 63, 70, 252n1, 255n19
Grace, 23, 107, 115, 142, 187, 203, 213, 215, 222, 226–27, 268n30; and the Divine, 2, 75, 151–53, 210–12, 236; in the world, 89, 92, 96–97, 99–100

Hart, James, 135
Hart, Kevin, 151
Hartley, John E., 220
Haskalah, 45, 47
Hegel, G. W. F., 15, 18, 47, 121
Heidegger, Martin, 21, 131, 140, 257n23, 258n39, 261n12; on Christianity, 124–27; Dasein in the World, 93–93; on hermeneutical phenomenology, 119; on religious life, 121–23
Hermeneutics, 120–23, 125, 131
Hermeneutical phenomenology, 119–20
Higgins, Kathleen, 258n29
Holy Spirit, the, 3, 6, 67–68, 70, 129, 212, 254n13. *See also* Spirit, the
Hospitality, 65, 146, 188, 220
Hume, David, 53, 57
Humility, 26, 37, 42, 55, 59, 99, 114, 144, 291n2
Husserl, Edmund, 3, 152, 284n6; on intentionality, 197, 199–200; on prayer, 135, 137, 140; on religion and phenomenology, 134–35

Icon (iconic), 169, 170, 172–73, 178, 180, 276n2, 278n14

Idol (idolatry), 7, 90, 126, 169–70, 172, 191, 203, 225–26, 277n7, 278n14
Ignatius of Loyola, Saint, 8, 198, 200–208
Immanence, 32, 35, 135, 149, 157, 195, 205
Impossible, the 8, 53, 62, 147, 149, 192, 196, 198–99, 203, 206. *See also* Derrida, Jacques
Incarnation, 6, 64–66, 68, 107, 216, 254n13, 283n20. *See also* Kenosis
Intentionality, 19, 135, 137, 152, 179–80, 269n40, 270n42
Interior intimo meo, 21
Intersubjectivity, 156, 179–80
Irigaray, Luce, 262n4; on breath and gender, 109–14, 117, 263n6; on cultivation of right breathing, 107–108; on speech and breath, 105–106, 116
Isaac the Syrian, Saint, 206

Jakobson, Roman, 32–33
James, William, 60, 252n32
John of the Cross, Saint, 14, 139
Judaism, 4, 36–40, 42, 44–48, 264n6
Justice, 142, 146, 151–52, 161, 163, 166, 187–88, 205, 253n7, 261n8, 269n38, 276n49, 287n5; social justice, 4, 44–45, 48, 175–76, 181

Kal, Victor, 277–78n7
Kant, Immanuel, 93, 160, 188–90, 260n5, 261n10, 282n9
Kearney, Richard, 269n41
Kenosis, 5, 18, 22, 26, 37, 43, 64–69, 71, 172, 247n32, 253n2. *See also* Incarnation
Khôra, 116, 145, 148, 191, 198, 204, 251n18, 274n29
Kierkegaard, Søren, 13, 18, 30; on the ethical, 158–60, 273n26; on faith and passion, 52–54, 186–87, 252n37; on the incarnation 65–66, 211, 215, 272n21; on truth and subjectivity, 90–91, 131
Kirtan, 109
Kosky, Jeffery L., 280n47
Kristeva, Julia, 109, 117

Lash, Nicholas, 93, 260n6, 262n15
Law, the, 23, 65, 86, 91, 121, 193, 222–23, 253n7
Leiris, Michel, 33
Levinas, Emmanuel, 4, 7–8, 17–18, 29, 46–47, 153, 195, 205–206, 224, 248n14, 255n18; on the face, 19, 157, 177, 200, 223, 225, 272n17; prayer as ethics, 33–37, 69, 71, 158, 164, 205, 249n21; on public and private prayer, 38–45, 156–59, 168, 271n11
Luther, Martin, 14, 124, 221, 264n4

Magis, 198, 205, 208
Manent, Pierre, 260n5
Marcel, Gabriel, 14–15, 22–23, 156, 271n11
Marion, Jean-Luc, 7, 30–31, 100, 169, 177, 205, 261n10, 274n40; on ethics, 177–78; on the Eucharist and liturgy, 175–76; on love, 179–81; on prayer and language, 169–72, 276n2, 277n7, 278n12, 14; on prayer and the gaze, 168, 172–74
Mary, 4, 20–27, 103, 114, 117, 247n32
Matthews, Scott, 291n2
Me voici, 4, 17–18, 33–34, 144, 153, 272n20
Merleau-Ponty, Maurice, 15
Merton, Thomas, 22, 91
Messianiac (messianism), 6–7, 21, 129–30, 142, 146–53, 185, 187, 190, 192, 269n38, 275n40. *See also* Derrida, Jacques
Minyan, 39
Mithnagdim, 35–36, 38
Moses, 8, 43, 64–65, 67, 157–58, 193–94, 221, 253n6
Mysticism, 26, 134, 140, 153

Nietzsche, Friedrich, 147, 214–15, 282n9; on decadence, 84–85; on Dionysian faith, 74, 79–83, 85, 260n64; early faith of, 75–78; on the Evangel, 84, 86, 259n58
Nouwen, Henri, 31

Oui, oui, 6–7, 143, 146, 152–53, 192, 283n21. *See also* Derrida, Jacques

Perspectives in
Continental Philosophy Series
John D. Caputo, series editor

14. Mark C. Taylor, *Journeys to Selfhood: Hegel and Kierkegaard*. Second edition.

15. Dominique Janicaud, Jean-François Courtine, Jean-Louis Chrétien, Michel Henry, Jean-Luc Marion, and Paul Ricœur, *Phenomenology and the "Theological Turn": The French Debate*.

16. Karl Jaspers, *The Question of German Guilt*. Introduction by Joseph W. Koterski, S.J.

17. Jean-Luc Marion, *The Idol and Distance: Five Studies*. Translated with an introduction by Thomas A. Carlson.

18. Jeffrey Dudiak, *The Intrigue of Ethics: A Reading of the Idea of Discourse in the Thought of Emmanuel Levinas*.

19. Robyn Horner, *Rethinking God As Gift: Marion, Derrida, and the Limits of Phenomenology*.

20. Mark Dooley, *The Politics of Exodus: Søren Kierkegaard's Ethics of Responsibility*.

21. Merold Westphal, *Toward a Postmodern Christian Faith: Overcoming Onto-Theology*.

22. Edith Wyschogrod, Jean-Joseph Goux and Eric Boynton, eds., *The Enigma of Gift and Sacrifice*.

23. Stanislas Breton, *The Word and the Cross*. Translated with an introduction by Jacquelyn Porter.

24. Jean-Luc Marion, *Prolegomena to Charity*. Translated by Stephen E. Lewis.

25. Peter H. Spader, *Scheler's Ethical Personalism: Its Logic, Development, and Promise*.

26. Jean-Louis Chrétien, *The Unforgettable and the Unhoped For*. Translated by Jeffrey Bloechl.

27. Don Cupitt, *Is Nothing Sacred? The Non-Realist Philosophy of Religion: Selected Essays*.

28. Jean-Luc Marion, *In Excess: Studies of Saturated Phenomena*. Translated by Robyn Horner and Vincent Berraud.

29. Phillip Goodchild, *Rethinking Philosophy of Religion: Approaches from Continental Philosophy*.

30. William J. Richardson, S.J., *Heidegger: Through Phenomenology to Thought*.

31. Jeffrey Andrew Barash, *Martin Heidegger and the Problem of Historical Meaning*.

32. Jean-Louis Chrétien, *Hand to Hand: Listening to the Work of Art*. Translated by Stephen E. Lewis.

33. Jean-Louis Chrétien, *The Call and the Response*. Translated with an introduction by Anne Davenport.

34. D. C. Schindler, *Han Urs von Balthasar and the Dramatic Structure of Truth: A Philosophical Investigation*.

35. Julian Wolfreys, ed., *Thinking Difference: Critics in Conversation*.

CPSIA information can be obtained
at www.ICGtesting.com
Printed in the USA
BVHW032016210619
551685BV00001B/18/P